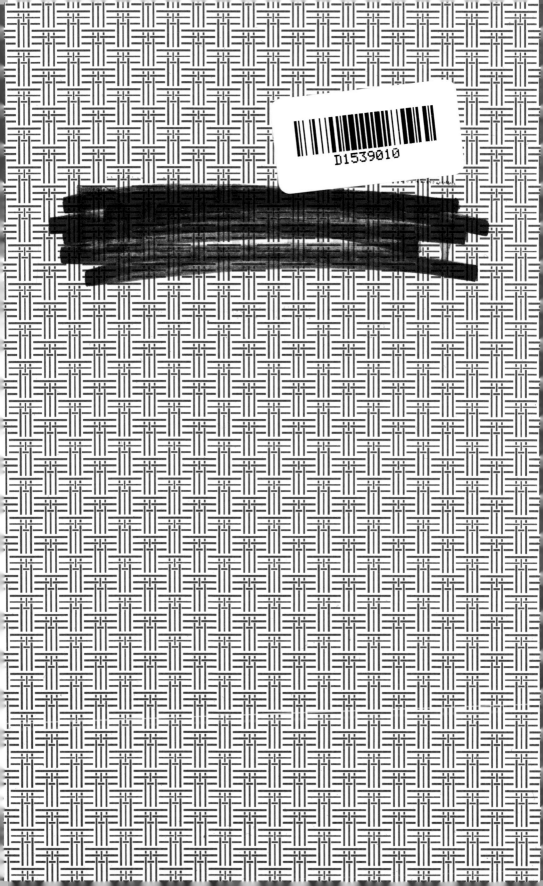

Iceberg Risk

Iceberg Risk

An Adventure in Portfolio Theory

KENT OSBAND

TEXERE

New York • London

Published in 2002 by

TEXERE LLC
55 East 52nd Street
New York, NY 10055

Tel: +1 (212) 317 5511
Fax: +1 (212) 317 5178
www.etexere.com

In the UK

TEXERE Publishing Limited
71–77 Leadenhall Street
London EC3A 3DE

Tel: +44 (0)20 7204 3644
Fax: +44 (0)20 7208 6701
www.etexere.co.uk

This publication is designed to provide accurate and authoritative information in regard to the subject matter covered. It is sold with the understanding that the publisher is not engaged in rendering legal, accounting, or other professional services. If legal advice or other expert assistance is required, the services of a competent professional person should be sought.

TEXERE books may be purchased for educational, business, or sales promotional use. For more information please write to the Special Markets Department at the TEXERE address in New York or London.

Designed and project managed by Macfarlane Production Services, Markyate, Hertfordshire, England (e-mail: macfarl@aol.com).

Library of Congress Cataloging in Publication Data has been applied for.

ISBN 1-58799-068-7

Printed in the United States of America.

This book is printed on acid-free paper.

10 9 8 7 6 5 4 3 2 1

Contents

Part II: Insights into Ignorance

Acknowledgments

Due to a combination of good deeds unrewarded and bad deeds punished, I found myself at midlife cast adrift from most of what I cared about. The only thing left to me was a fog of uncertainty, which despite my best efforts I had never managed to dispel. When life deals you a lemon, all you can do – unless you think whining is doing – is to try to make lemonade. So I plunged into the fog and there found all the treasures I had been looking for. A few of these treasures are displayed in this book. Here I want to thank some people who helped me cart them back.

Having decided to tackle options theory in earnest, I picked out the fattest tome I could find for the price and took it on an island getaway. I fully expected to fall asleep after a few pages, thereby salving my conscience without spoiling the fun. To my shock it was so clearly written and entertaining I finished it and emailed the author my thanks. He turned out to live around the corner. Thus began a friendship with Paul Wilmott. Paul taught me that finance theory needn't be stuffy and that it was OK to combine calculus with chuckles. Paul also introduced me to his editor, David Wilson.

David has been super to work with; I've enjoyed every exasperating minute. For starters, he was willing to back the idea of a math novel when even I was hesitant. Moreover, David took it on himself to teach me how to write a decent story. Now the problem is, between the mathematical/literary divide and the American/British divide, what sounded good to me didn't always sound good to him, and vice versa. Since at least one of us is stubborn we went through quite a few drafts. But every iteration got better, the characters took on lives of their own, and somewhere along the way I found the voice of my imagination. Thank you, David, and forgive me for taking so long.

I am also grateful to project manager Stuart Macfarlane and a host of people I never met for transforming my electronic scribble into a published book. Their professionalism leaves no one to blame but me for any lingering mistakes.

The story depicts conventional portfolio risk management as obsessed with appearance over substance. Three years ago when I began writing in the midst of the biggest bull market in history, such a characterization would have been considered harsh. Not now. So I owe some thanks to fate for bursting the Nasdaq bubble and revealing so much Wall Street puffery.

My biggest regret about the book involves the time it deprived me of with my children: Ian, Valerie, Alexander and new-born Eric. Fortunately, my wife Annette and my ex-wife Jan Moffat shower them with loving attention. The children also have fine grandparents, including my own parents Richard and Shirley Osband. These are the greatest blessings of my life.

Annette, thank you for reading and commenting on the math when no one else would, for arbitrating some debates with David, and for the illustrations that grace these pages. May we have many more adventures together and leave most of them unwritten.

Finally, thank you Louis Bachelier, for blazing a path forward in finance half a century before anyone was prepared to follow. Some of us who never met you still remember.

Preface: A Dialogue

You: Hmmm. Iceberg Risk: An Adventure in Portfolio Theory. Strange title. What's this book about?

Me: Portfolio analysis. The theory of risk/reward tradeoffs in bundles of financial assets.

What's that have to do with icebergs?

I use icebergs as a metaphor for big, unusual, semi-obscured risks that standard portfolio theory can't deal with.

Can't deal with, or chooses not to?

Can't. The core assumption of normality rules them out by modeling overall risk as a bell curve.

I thought a big diversified portfolio is bound to be nearly normal. Isn't that what the Central Limit Theorem is about?

The Central Limit Theorem applies only when the underlying risks are independent.

Hold on a second. Normality can handle correlated risks.

Yes, provided the risks can be decomposed into lots of small independent building blocks. But often that's not possible.

For example?

For example, you own a hundred different Nasdaq stocks and Nasdaq crashes. More generally, whenever some pervasive common factor affects a huge chunk of your portfolio and that factor's not even approximately normal.

Obviously. I thought you were going to tell me something profound.

The profound part is that standard theory misses it.

You keep saying that but I don't believe it. I just came across a whole rack of books on "Value at Risk" methodology. Doesn't that tackle icebergs?

Yes, but in an ad hoc way that doesn't mesh with standard theory.

So what? Black cat, white cat, I don't care as long as it kills mice.

Bad analogy. Good portfolio managers don't exterminate all risks. They balance them against rewards. Typical value at risk methodology either doesn't measure rewards or implies some irrational investment decisions.

How do you define "irrational"?

By a willingness to make trades that are bound to lose you money.

Name me an investor who's never been irrational.

I can't. But that's no excuse for advising it. Theory's supposed to help, not make things worse.

OK, so I take it your book tries to integrate iceberg risk within standard theory.

The first half of the book does. Only it fails.

What do you mean?

It can't help but fail. Standard finance theory assumes normality. Iceberg risks aren't normal.

If it can't help but fail, why do you bother trying?

To help clear readers' minds of illusions. They need to see that normality is abnormal.

And that takes half a book?

I wonder whether half a book's enough. Normality's an awfully entrenched prejudice in theory, even for people who reject it in practice.

Why do you think that is?

Because it's so simple. Normality allows you to calculate every possible risk/ reward tradeoff just from data on means, variances, and correlations between assets.

I wouldn't call that simple. Won't 100 assets have around 5,000 distinct correlations?

Yes, but without normality even trillions of parameters might not suffice to model the tail risks of different portfolios. Because you still might not be able to answer questions like: If the first 50 assets go down the drain, what are the odds that the other assets go down the drain too?

What if I gather additional information about the tail risk on each asset?

That's less useful than it sounds. Fat-tailed assets can make for very smooth portfolios. Conversely, nearly normal assets can generate huge tail risks.

What matters then?

I told you. Common factors that make most of your assets go down together.

And how do you propose to model those?

The only way that's tractable. Conditional normality.

You just told me that normality doesn't work.

That was unconditional normality. Conditional normality is different.

How is it different?

Think of unconditional as overall averages. Think of conditional as averages under particular market regimes, like "bull market" or "bear market".

Look, I want a straight answer. Do bell curves describe risks or don't they?

Conditional risks, yes. But the overall risk is an overlay or weighted average of different bell curves. That needn't resemble a single bell curve any more than a mountain range need resemble a single mountain.

With enough bell curves I imagine you can imitate any clump of risks.

You can imitate uniform risks too. But you would need a lot of different regimes. In practice it's more useful to segregate out a few regimes at a time.

I'm not sure I get all this.

You will if you read the first half of the book.

Pardon my asking, but how much math does it involve?

About as much or as little as you want.

How is that possible?

I've divided every chapter into two sections. The first section explains the intuition and presents a couple of illustrative charts. The second section contains the supporting math, carved up into bite-sized nuggets.

So if I'm really smart I should focus on the math.

No, if you're really smart you should focus on the intuition. Once you understand that, everything else is easy. Math's just a language for expressing things more clearly. I translate slowly in case you're interested but rusty. If you know the math already or couldn't care less, skip it.

Thanks for the confidence booster. I'll try to keep that in mind.

But I don't want to boost your confidence. I want to deflate it. Imagine discovering that the risks you've been hired to analyze and help manage are most likely bigger than you thought but harder to pin down. That the models you've been using don't work but you can't come up with a viable alternative.

Do you think that's really the norm in financial risk management?

No. I think the norm is trying to cover those truths up. So that at least you can manage the appearance of risk.

You sound cynical.

Just experienced. Besides, it is important to manage the appearance of risk. At least if you want to keep your job.

Then what's the point of deflating my confidence?

So that the second half of the book can rebuild it on sounder foundations.

How?

By modifying standard theory enough to incorporate iceberg risk.

Are the modifications simple?

As simple as they can be.

Simple enough for ordinary people to use them?

They'd probably need help with the math.

I thought you said the math wasn't essential.

It's not essential to understanding what's wrong. It is essential to getting things right.

And if I can't understand the math?

Then delegate the details to someone who does, and just stay focused on the intuition.

Fine. By the way, can you summarize your core modifications in a few words?

Sure. Partition functions.

Never heard of them.

I'm not surprised. Partition functions come from thermodynamics. And what they bring to portfolio theory isn't obvious.

So what do they bring to portfolio theory?

The ability to incorporate regime-switching and options.

How?

I give recipes in the book.

Are they complicated?

A bit. I develop them gradually, though, to help you appreciate how the parts fit together.

Can I still use the recipes if I only appreciate things halfway?

Absolutely. A computer spreadsheet can easily handle all the calculations. You can get answers nearly instantly or have someone else get them for you.

Do the answers differ a lot from the conventional answers?

That depends on what kind of information you feed in and what you ask. Garbage in, garbage out.

Suppose I just feed in the usual stuff: the risk and rewards of the various assets and their overall correlations. Will it tell me the portfolio tail risks?

No. Like I said before, it can't be done.

Nonsense. People answer those questions all the time with no more information than I have.

I didn't say they couldn't answer those questions. They just can't answer them right.

Approximate answers are OK too.

The answers won't even be approximately right. Not without some hidden assumptions.

Surely you're exaggerating.

No, I'm not. For example, suppose you have three fair, uncorrelated coins. What's the probability they all turn up tails?

One-eighth of course. One-half times one-half times one-half.

Nope. Chapter 1 gives some counterexamples.

I don't see how.

Good. That means the book will challenge your perceptions.

Even if the counterexamples are valid, why shouldn't I dismiss them as minor exceptions?

Because subsequent chapters in Part I show they're not.

But Part II shows how to deal with them.

Given the minimal extra information needed, yes.

You mean information about the conditional bell curves.

Yes, but that's still not quite enough information. We also need information on risk aversion. How willingly you would risk, say, a quarter of your wealth in return for a colossal gain.

And how do you tie those two together?

I told you: thru partition functions.

Which I told you mean nothing to me.

Alright. They're weighted sums of exponentials, where each regime contributes one exponential and the weights depend on the probabilities of the various regimes.

Interesting. What determines the exponents?

The risk-adjusted expected returns for every regime times a factor related to the risk aversion.

Why are you adjusting twice for risk?

One factor adjusts for risk within regimes. The other adjusts for risk across regimes.

How do you adjust for risk within regimes?

Subtract a multiple of the conditional variance from the conditional mean.

How big a multiple?

That depends on the risk aversion too. Forgive me if I don't tour every nook and cranny here.

Fair enough. But why doesn't the recipe just average out the various risk-adjusted returns?

That's basically what it does. Only the weights don't just depend on the odds of the various regimes. They also depend on how bad the regime is. The worse the risk-adjusted return, the more weight the regime gets.

What's the point of that?

It makes you more cautious.

I thought penalizing for variance was supposed to make you more cautious.

That too. Remember, risk aversion penalizes both for risk within a given regime and for risk across regimes.

OK, that makes sense. Any other twists I should know about?

Plenty. The most important is that that you can incorporate options and other nonlinear assets without resorting to Monte Carlo regimes.

How do you do that?

By adjusting the risk-adjusted returns in each regime for delta and gamma contributions from options.

That's neat how you've managed to boil all this down to a simple formula.

Well, it's as simple as it can be. But it isn't simple. And unlike standard mean-variance theory there's generally no closed-form solution. Still, computers can calculate numeric answers very quickly.

If your theory's right, it could revolutionize mainstream portfolio analysis.

My theory is right. But it might not change the mainstream at all.

Why not?

The mainstream seems less interested in managing risk than the appearances of risk. And my theory, by acknowledging possible changes in regime, makes risks more visible.

Surely if someone came along and carefully explained the problems with standard theory and how to fix them they would be welcomed with open arms.

I take it you haven't met Conway or Devlin.

Who?

Never mind. I wouldn't want to spoil the adventure. Welcome to *Iceberg Risk.*

PART I

Standards of Deviation

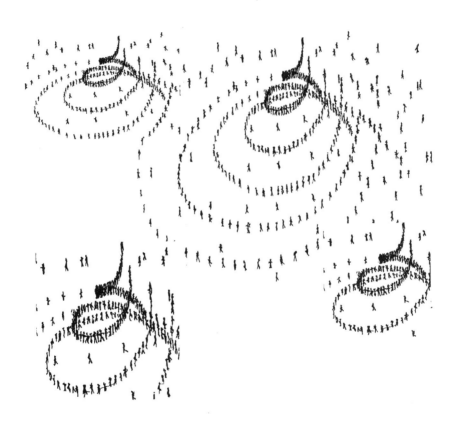

Introduction: "Missing the Iceberg for the Ice Cubes"

Tuesday April 9th 1912

Captain Smith stepped out from his cramped office in the White Star Line Building on Southampton Dock. He was fuming. He had a huge amount of paperwork to complete before tomorrow, and was in no mood for interruptions.

"This had better be important."

His clerk, who had moments ago reluctantly knocked on the Captain's door, gestured nervously toward a dubious young man sitting in the reception, smoking a foul smelling cigarette. "I'm terribly sorry, Sir. I've been trying all morning to explain to this – gentleman – that you can't be interrupted. But he insists on seeing you and won't leave until he has. He seems to think that your ship is at risk."

"My ship at risk." Captain Smith slowly repeated this last phrase. "The *Titanic*. The biggest, fastest, safest ship ever built is at risk. I have no time for such foolishness."

The clerk smiled smugly and turned to the visitor. "You see. I told you that the Captain would not be interested. Now if you would be so kind as to leave, we can get back to our work in peace."

The visitor rose to his feet. "Captain, please give me just a few moments to explain. I am not here to criticize your wonderful ship. Our agents' reports concur that the *Titanic* may indeed be the finest ship ever built. To lose such a vessel would be a tragedy. I am here to prevent precisely that."

"Your agents?" thundered the captain. "Prevent a tragedy? Are you trying to threaten me young man?"

"No, Captain, nothing of the sort." The young man thrust out his hand.

3

"Please allow me to introduce myself. My name is Jacques Bachelier and I represent a consortium of shipping insurers. We are willing to offer extremely favorable rates to the *Titanic*, provided you instigate the required scientific precautions to avoid icebergs."

"Icebergs! Come now. I have been sailing the North Atlantic for twenty years. In all that time I cannot recall one single incident of a ship hitting an iceberg. Granted, on rare occasions icebergs do stray into the shipping lanes. We understand this smallest of risks, and take the necessary steps to guard against it. The *Titanic* has six lookouts amongst its crew. If anyone sees an iceberg we will simply sail around it. Satisfied?"

"An excellent system, Captain. Provided you spot the iceberg in time. The *Titanic* by your own admission is very fast, and its great size will prevent it from making any quick maneuvers."

"The *Titanic* is also very tall Monsieur Bachelier. Our lookouts can spot potential problems from a great distance. We shall have plenty of time to take the required action."

"In the midst of fog? On a moonless night?"

"Do you take me for a simpleton? Under such conditions I can do what sailors have done for centuries: slow down. Now, if you will excuse me Monsieur I ...".

"Certainly you *can* slow down Captain. But *will* you? Do you really think the risk of icebergs is such to justify slowing down on every occasion of imperfect visibility? Slow down and the crossing takes longer. Slow down too often and you make fewer trips per year than White Star Line had anticipated. Think of the cost to your employers, Captain. You cannot eliminate every risk. We understand that perfectly. We simply want you to manage the risks scientifically."

A quick glance at his pocket watch told the Captain he was already running late. But he was intrigued. "Manage the risk scientifically? What precisely do you have in mind?"

"I propose to apply a theory developed by my brother Louis more than ten years ago. It concerns the statistics of interactions between millions of floating particles. Although individual interactions are nearly impossible to predict, most deviations wash out in the aggregate. The residue is random motion that is normally distributed, with a mean drift and variance that rise linearly with time."

Now the Captain had him. He smiled inwardly. A career spanning many years of long sea voyages brings with it one particular luxury. Time to read.

And with gambling popular amongst seamen, the Captain had undertaken some study of chance and probability. "Surely you refer to the theory of Brownian motion. Discovered, I believe, by Albert Einstein in 1905. I do not recall your brother's name in that connection."

Jacques Bachelier was at once astonished and indignant. "Let me assure you, Captain, that my brother developed this theory five years before Mr. Einstein, in a doctoral thesis during his time at the Sorbonne. His "Théorie de la Spéculation" offers magnificent insight into the random movement of securities prices. But my brother's advisors were blind. They couldn't see the value in his work and it has languished in obscurity. I mean to change that." His voice softened. "But I am most impressed with your knowledge, Captain. Impressed and delighted. You, of all people, must surely appreciate the merits of my new system for forecasting encounters with icebergs. I call it IceMetrics."

The Captain's fascination with mathematics had now firmly got the better of him. "Please step into my office and explain in more detail if you will."

Warming to his subject, Bachelier followed the Captain into the office, continuing to speak as he went. "Basically, IceMetrics estimates the mean frequencies of encounters with large and small lumps of ice in the ocean, the variances in their frequencies, and the pairwise correlations between large and small lumps. Assuming that ice lumps follow multivariate normal distributions, we can calculate the probability of encounters with icebergs."

"Would you not expect these probabilities to vary with location and season?"

"Of course. I propose to sample ice concentrations every hour in the ocean surrounding the ship, and update the mean frequency and correlation estimates using the new information. Granted, encounters with large icebergs are fairly rare. But bear in mind that an iceberg can be viewed as a highly correlated collection of much smaller lumps. So by using information on smaller lumps of ice and their correlation, we can estimate the frequency of very large lumps."

"Very clever, in theory. How accurate have your forecasts been?"

Bachelier reddened a bit and paused to light another cigarette. "In most cases very respectable. Extreme events do tend to occur significantly more frequently than theory predicts. Fortunately, colleagues at the Bureau of International Ship Insurance, or BISI, have devised a practical remedy."

The Captain raised a questioning eyebrow. "Which is?"

"They multiply the IceMetric estimates by three or a bit more."

"Why three?"

At this, Bachelier had to smile. "Really, I don't know. I suppose the BISI favored a simple system, in order not to exaggerate its own prowess, so chose to multiply by an integer. At the same time, it did not want to be accused of cutting corners on safety, so it skipped two to arrive at three."

"Not four?"

"As I explained, we insurers do not wish to avoid all risk, just to manage it. The BISI multiplies stated risks by four only for very poorly run ships. In any case, the patch seems effective. All our insurers using IceMetrics feel quite comfortable underwriting iceberg risk."

The captain was puzzled. "You call this science, Monsieur Bachelier?"

"Captain, IceMetrics lays a scientific foundation for monitoring iceberg risk. But it does not purport to give exact assessments. Rather, it is a practical tool. On the one hand, it conveys to insurers the order of magnitude of the risks they insure. On the other hand, it helps deflect ex-post criticism from regulators and shareholders should disaster strike. We call the latter the "CYD effect", for "cover your derrière", and believe me it is very effective. In this new century, no responsible manager should lack a good scientifically grounded excuse for his mistakes."

"Somehow," mused the captain, "I doubt that posterity would forgive me should I let the *Titanic* hit an iceberg, even if my excuse was firmly grounded in science."

"Captain, I can understand your skepticism. But allow me the chance to convince you. Let me and my research assistant, Fleur, join you on the voyage tomorrow. We will forecast ice concentrations hourly using the IceMetrics methodology and you can compare our predictions against the ice you actually encounter. If you are satisfied, we would ask you to recommend that White Star Line adopt IceMetrics as their risk management technique, and permit us to advertise that to other prospective customers. If you are not satisfied, then you have no further obligations. In either case, to show our appreciation, our consortium will insure the maiden voyage at our lowest rates."

"Your offer is very tempting I must admit. But I must also consider my passengers. There are a number of highly influential people on board this maiden voyage, including the Astors no less. I cannot have you taking ice samplings on deck and raising alarm."

"Captain, I fully endorse your sentiments. We have no desire to draw attention to ourselves. I assure you that my assistant and I will be discreet."

On board the ship, Jacques and Fleur set about their task with great enthusiasm. Often they perched on the very brow of the great ship to better haul in their ice collection nets. Such apparent derring-do caused quite a stir amongst the other passengers, but was soon explained away as the antics of youthful lovers and they were left in peace.

The hourly sampling proved uneventful. The only tricky part was the updating of forecasts. Originally, IceMetrics forecasts had been based on a simple rolling average of the preceding 20 samples. However, Jacques quickly noticed that ice tended to come in clusters, so that more recent observations deserved extra weight. So he introduced the so-called Exponentially Weighted Moving Average or EWMA technique, which allowed past observations to fade gradually in influence. On further study, he noticed additional wave-like tendencies in the variance. He incorporated this through a technique he called IGARCH, for Ice-Guarding Auto-Regressive Conditional Heteroskedasticity.

The captain cringed at the terms but was impressed with the results. The hourly forecasts were far more reliable than could be ascribed to blind luck. Granted, they were only four days into the voyage and the *Titanic* had not yet encountered any patches with high concentrations of ice, but Jacques assured the Captain that the results under average conditions could be extrapolated to the extremes, and even proved this mathematically using multivariate normal distributions. In none of the samples did the ratio of the actual frequencies of extreme events to the predicted values even approach the BISI-recommended cushion of three.

That evening, Quartermaster Hitchin reported to the Captain from the bridge that a heavy fog had set in. A rather old-fashioned chap, he advised the Captain to slow down for safety. Just as the Captain was about to concur, Jacques appeared with the latest IceMetrics forecast. Ice concentrations had been negligible for the past 24 hours, so both the estimated means and standard deviations were very low.

"Monsieur Bachelier," said the Captain, "it is time for a practical test. What are the current chances of striking an iceberg big enough to sink the *Titanic*?"

Jacques was thrilled. "According to my calculations, Captain, a *Titanic*-sinking iceberg currently represents a ten standard deviation event. For all practical purposes, the probability is zero."

"Then let us maintain our speed," said the captain, brushing aside Hitchin's objections. "From here on, the *Titanic* will use IceMetrics to gauge its iceberg risks. I believe this decision will be remembered as a historic moment both for us and for the science of risk."

Within a few hours, the captain's prophecy would be proved catastrophically right . . .

⸻

Let us not fret too much over poor Jacques Bachelier. His brother's scientific contributions were indeed rediscovered, and the family name won honor. Indeed, a thrilling though distorted account of Jacques' relationship with Fleur on that fateful voyage became one of the world's most popular films. Even Jacques' failure proved fruitful, for it motivated other innovations in ocean travel that greatly reduced the risk of big things that go bump in the night.

But I worry that the world has not yet grasped the broader lessons of IceMetrics. No financial radar yet penetrates the fog that shrouds the risk of big financial crashes, and distressingly few lifeboats are at hand. Moreover, while managers and regulators of big financial institutions continually monitor their vulnerability to large losses, the methodologies they rely on are distressingly similar to IceMetrics.

Consider, for example, the conventional use of means, standard deviations, and pairwise correlations between assets to predict the risks of high losses on broad asset portfolios. Technically, this is justified only when assets are multivariate normal; that is, when every possible portfolio is normally distributed. As is increasingly recognized, this condition rarely holds. Much effort is spent estimating alternative distributions that can capture the fat tails of individual assets. But hardly any effort is spent working through the implications of these distributions for overall portfolio risks. This curious omission has several causes:

- On a practical level, many value-at-risk calculations only get used the way a drunkard uses a lamppost: more for support than illumination. When justifying a risk decision that's already essentially been made, it is not worth fitting one's best analytic bulb: normal approximations will do. The Bank for International Settlements inadvertently encourages this in banking by requiring that the calculated values at risk be multiplied by a factor of three for safety. This means that a truly diligent risk manager will look for legitimate ways to report only a third of the true value at risk.
- Dropping assumptions of multivariate normality opens up a can of worms. Most alternative assumptions are either theoretically

unappealing or computationally intractable. So even where analysts concede the unrealism of multivariate normality, they may retain it for practical work. This is especially true in finance, which puts a premium on decisiveness.

- Most people blithely assume that portfolios are bound to suffer less than individual assets from high standard-deviation outliers. That's not true. Granted, according to the Central Limit Theorem, portfolios of many independent, identically distributed assets have approximately normal distributions even when the distributions of individual assets are very fat-tailed. But even a small degree of dependence can render the Central Limit Theorem inapplicable.

Let me be more specific. The single most widely used measure of financial risk is the volatility, or annualized standard deviation. It's an attractive measure because the volatility of a portfolio depends only on the volatilities of the individual assets, their weights, and their correlations. Moreover, we can always approximate the portfolio's risks by a normal distribution having the same mean and the same volatility, just as we can approximate the individual asset's risks by a normal distribution. The relevant question is: how good an approximation is this likely to be for the portfolio, compared with the approximation for the individual assets?

While this question is rarely posed explicitly, it frequently comes up implicitly. Every time the normal distribution is used for portfolio analysis even when the constituent assets are clearly non-normal, the implicit answer is "yes, the approximation is relatively good". Indeed, the implicit answer is "yes" virtually any time an analyst gauges portfolio risks simply by the mean and volatility, for with most other distributions the mean and volatility would not suffice to characterize risks.

In reality, the normal approximation tends to be reasonable for the central region of portfolio risks, where it improves with the number of assets. In the tails, the approximation is much worse. Even in large portfolios, high standard-deviation events tend to occur far more often than a normal distribution suggests. This seems especially true on the downside, which investors fear most. However, tail risks vary enormously from one scenario to another.

I will call this variable excess risk "iceberg risk" because it is mostly hidden from view but threatens major damage. It might also be called "Noah risk", after the proverbial flood that drowned the world. However, "Noah risk" conventionally refers to any extreme risk, whereas I want to focus on the tail risk in portfolios. Portfolios can and generally do have large iceberg risks even when the constituent assets have tail risks that are nearly normal or thinner than normal. Also, in the Biblical story, the world was amply warned about the flood but refused to listen. In contrast, icebergs reflect a type of risk that people look for but may not see.

Iceberg risk has helped drive a huge wedge between portfolio theory and portfolio practice. For example, theory frequently recommends massive long positions in a few assets offset by a few nearly equally massive short positions. Such portfolios brook such obviously massive iceberg risks that no practitioners will consider them, apart from a few heading for the title of "ex-". Modelers who want to keep their jobs learn to restrain this by imposing fairly tight floors and ceilings on position sizes. Things look much better that way, but privately most modelers will admit to dismay. *Ad hoc* constraints often end up driving the core result, reducing the theory to a window dressing.

In most fields of modern science, such a huge disjuncture between theory and practice would prompt a serious rethinking of theory. Quantum theory, for example, was inspired by classical physics' false prediction that a black box should burn your eyes out with X-rays. Unfortunately, finance theorists have a crutch to fall back on that most other scientists lack. That crutch comes in various fancy carrying cases but basically it amounts to saying that people are stupid. Why don't markets obey theory? People are stupid. Why don't portfolio managers accept theory's advice? People are stupid.

"People are stupid" arguments are hard to refute because, well, people are stupid. There, I've fallen into it myself. What I mean is, rather, that the charge of stupidity can itself be rather mind-numbing. Think about it. Suppose a child darts across the street to fetch his ball and gets run over. There are several good candidates for stupidity here: the child, adults who should have been monitoring, and the driver. However, it might be fairer to just call it an accident. The charge of stupidity presumes more information was readily at hand than participants may have realized.

Hence, at risk of appearing foolish, I would rather talk about ignorance and learning than stupidity. Unlike conventional finance theory, I will not assume that market risks and rewards are clear traffic lights to investors. Rather, I will allow the risks and rewards to occasionally change without giving clear warning of what they've changed to or of when and how they may change again. It follows that investors will rarely know exactly what the current risks and rewards are. Instead, investors have to make guesses based on past data and their current theories about the world.

Most readers, I suspect, will find the preceding comments totally plausible. So plausible, perhaps, that some may dismiss them as banal. Or regard them as implicit in conventional theory. Or doubt their potential for application. This book proves otherwise, at least to those willing to read it, and maybe even to those willing to skim it. But if you're a busy and impatient person like me, perhaps you're not even willing to invest that much time lacking more concrete evidence of why this approach matters. So let me give two examples.

The first concerns the abundant evidence that stock markets overreact to news about earnings. More precisely, they overreact if you assume that investors by and large understand the risk parameters of the markets they're investing in. Some economists consider this proof that investors are economically irrational, aka stupid. However, if you allow for the possibility that the risk parameters evolve (note that I'm not even requiring the risk parameters to change, but simply that investors think they might change), you can easily account for excess volatility.

The second example is personal. My flirtation with what I'll call the "theory of ignorance" began back in economics graduate school in the early 1980s, where I wrote my dissertation on the problems of motivating and evaluating economic forecasters. However, I ended up marrying the mistress I knew best – Soviet economic reform – and watched her blossom into post-Soviet reform. I was in love until some stuffed-shirt advisors stole her heart. Having seen no good deed go unpunished, I defected to Wall Street in early 1994 and immediately stumbled into my old flame, looking more radiant than ever.

You see, my new business card gave me recognized expertise in calling post-Soviet debt markets as magically as the Wizard of Oz's diploma had given Scarecrow a brain. Too bad it didn't give me Scarecrow's peace of mind. For example, within a few weeks of joining, I was asked to estimate future default risks for Bulgaria's forthcoming

Brady bonds. Despite having worked a lot on Bulgarian economic reform at the IMF and World Bank and knowing some key players, I didn't have much of a clue. I didn't know where to find clues. I didn't even know enough to know that on Wall Street, no analyst should ever say he doesn't know.

It was a rocky start. How I envied my colleagues specializing in Latin America. Compared with the post-Soviet bloc, a country like Mexico had much better data, a much more stable and experienced political regime, and a much longer relevant debt-servicing record. Based on extensive consultations with the IMF, with major investors, and with Mexican government officials, my guru colleagues confidently predicted the Mexican peso would hold to its announced exchange rate band against the US dollar. They were right too. They were right down to the date that they were proved dead wrong.

The Mexican iceberg was a revelation for me. Wow, I thought, some of these gurus are just as ignorant as me. More productively, I realized that the markets I specialized in were bound to move largely on perceptions and changes in perceptions, with only occasional wake-up calls from reality. Ever since, I have focused on better understanding the role of ignorance in financial markets, both from a theoretical and a practical perspective. Call it an odyssey in ignorance.

This book, if you let it, will launch you on that odyssey too. Part I explores the basic mathematics of iceberg risk. Its main intent is destruction: destruction of the presumption that iceberg risk is typically small. It begins with some simple examples, so simple that readers wedded to the conventional view will be tempted to dismiss them as exceptional. I urge skeptics to maintain an open mind. The examples will progressively be elaborated until the supposedly exceptional case becomes the norm and the supposedly normal case the exception.

Fortunately, in the midst of destruction a more robust modelling approach starts to emerge. It is founded on the division of a complex dependence into common and independent parts. The resulting probability distributions are known as mixed (conditional) multivariate normal. Allowing even a limited degree of mixing can make financial risk models far more plausible.

Part II of the book applies the new approach to portfolio analysis. After reviewing the strengths and weaknesses of various alternatives, I opt for a hybrid system that grafts extra "regime-switching" branches onto the rootstock of the conventional theory. While the extra switches add some math complications, they make the theory much easier to apply. The results are more satisfying as well, since they tend to avoid implausibly extreme recommendations.

However, if you think that the new approach justifies all the conventional rules of thumb, guess again. Convention has turned risk management into a lumbering elephant. The new approach says the elephant needs to dance. To put it more prosaically, funds need dynamic "risk overlays", the risk counterpart to the "currency overlays" increasingly in vogue. These overlays will vary not only with managers' reading of an ever-changing environment, but also with their attitudes to risk.

Before setting sail, let me warn you about the ride ahead. I don't present either a polished academic treatise or a comprehensive how-to guide. Instead I introduce a new way of thinking about portfolio risk. Actually, I should say "unfamiliar" rather than "new", because none of the elements is new, just the way they are put together, and even the latter may be disputed. Still, this is a daunting task, because one of the hallmarks of conventional thinking is a dismissal of criticisms as either uninteresting or impractical.

Thus, if I plunge into a formal mathematical treatment of iceberg risk, few potential readers will follow me in. If I downplay the math, the approach will look hokey. If I harp on criticisms of the status quo, I will be begged for constructive suggestions. If I focus on remedies, I will be challenged to prove there is a serious disease.

This recalls an old joke: How many preachers does it take to change a light bulb? The answer is: Just one, but the light bulb has to really want to change. Unfortunately, most financial risk analysts would bristle at the suggestion their light bulbs are burning dim. Either they have grown accustomed to working in the gloom or reject other light bulbs as offering too little improvement for the price.

I was in despair about how to proceed until I chanced into two old friends who worked in risk management for a major investment bank. As they told me about the practical problems they were encountering and the remedies they were developing, I saw that their intellectual evolution paralleled my own. Yet their adventures and lively debates were far more entertaining than my dry theory. One day it dawned on me that readers would likely feel the same. My friends kindly gave me permission to recount their experiences and to use them as a foil for theoretical reflection – provided, of course, that I camouflage their names and the business-sensitive details. So, without further ado, let me introduce you to my friends and the chance incident that first shook their faith in chance.

Let me use this one and only footnote in the book to lament its most shameful feature, namely the dearth of footnotes citing others' work. There are two main reasons for this. First, reflecting my own distance from academic finance, I am largely unfamiliar with who said what first when. Second, most of the readers I want to reach don't care. Still, I regret not giving others toiling in the same vineyard more credit for the wine. To help make amends, the book closes with suggestions for further reading. Between those readings and the books and articles they cite you can plug into a rapidly expanding field at whatever mathematical level you prefer.

1 | Odd Odds of Odds

Conway, head of risk management for Megabucks Investment Bank, shuffled again through the auditors' report. On the bright side, the auditors praised the new monitoring system he had introduced. For every asset in its portfolio, Megabucks now had up-to-date information not only on the mean and standard deviation but also on the skewness and kurtosis. Conway's team also meticulously tracked the correlations between assets. But the auditors went on to fault the team for sloppy implementation at a portfolio level. "In one particularly egregious example," wrote the auditors with thinly disguised contempt, "an analyst argued that three completely uncorrelated assets bore absolutely no risk of plunging together."

The report did not name the analyst and didn't need to. Only Devlin was reckless enough to argue openly with the auditors. Devlin was the quintessential Devil's Advocate. At first this had put Conway off, as it did most people. Over time he had come to appreciate Devlin's challenges. They kept him on his toes. And more often than not Devlin turned out to be right.

But this time Devlin has clearly gone too far. Why defend the indefensible? Conway shook his head and sighed. A few years previously, when the Asian crisis lured the two of them into risk management, Conway figured they would rise or fall together. Instead, only Conway had thrived. Devlin was too much of a perfectionist in a business that craved quick results. Indeed, Devlin only kept his job thanks to Conway's intervention. *Now they'll be gunning for him again. And maybe for anyone who harbors him. I'd better look into this.*

Conway found Devlin hunched over his desk, looking even more frazzled than usual. Peering over his shoulder, Conway watched him pull coins out of a bowl on his desk, rearrange them into groups of three, scribble furiously in his notebook, and then toss the coins back in the bowl to start all over again. After a few minutes of this spectacle, Conway spoke up. "I certainly admire your conversion to the more practical aspects of risk management, but I hardly think those coins represent much of a threat to the profit margins of Megabucks."

A startled Devlin spun around. "Oh, it's you, Conway. Ha-ha. Very funny. But I am being practical. I was just running some simulations on the options book."

"With three coins?"

"Granted, it's a bit crude. But I like to start with the basics. It sharpens my intuition."

"Imagine that. And here was I idly worrying that my old sparring partner had blown a fuse. You need to lighten up, my friend. You're beginning to remind me of the young psychiatrist in the joke."

"What joke?" asked Devlin. He smiled in spite of himself. Conway was a charmer.

"An old and a young psychiatrist worked in the same building. Every day after work the old psychiatrist would come by, bursting with energy, and propose some interesting activity: tennis, jogging, attending a concert, etc. But the young psychiatrist was exhausted and kept turning the old man down. After a few weeks, the young psychiatrist couldn't stand it any longer. 'I just don't understand how you can do it. All day long people tell me their problems. Unbelievable problems. It just wears me out. You're thirty years older and must hear the same kind of problems that I hear. And yet you're full of energy. What's your secret?' he asked. 'I don't listen,' said the old psychiatrist."

Devlin laughed, but at the same time he felt an all too familiar anxiety welling up within him. Conway cares more about having a neat system for labelling risk than about the accuracy of the labels, he thought. If it's talked and written about often enough, then Conway thinks it must be right. Mr Conventional Wisdom. Faced with a problem, Conway's first inclination – and usually his second and third – was to follow the accepted authorities.

Nevertheless, Devlin had come to respect Conway for his pragmatism. Conway did not idolize conventional wisdom; he simply considered it far more likely than not to be approximately correct. If Devlin or someone else could demonstrate otherwise, Conway would change his mind. Those qualities were the secret of Conway's success in risk management.

Devlin, on the other hand, was born to question and doubt. The more he studied stochastic financial variables, the more questions and doubts he had. And the more Devlin doubted, the more depressed and frazzled he became. At times he wished he had entered a field with more scientific certainty, say, the study of the origins of the universe.

"Eh, Devlin. Hello."

"Sorry. I was daydreaming. Come on, Conway, tell me what you really want to talk with me about." Devlin smelled trouble. Devlin had a good nose for trouble once he was in it. Too bad he rarely smelled it sooner.

"The auditors wrote you up for unreasonable valuations."

"Those bozos!" exclaimed Devlin. "I tried to set them straight but they wouldn't listen."

If that's the way you talked to them then no wonder. "Why don't you tell me what happened?"

"Do you remember the problems I was having last month in valuing the aggregate risk exposure on three different binary options? You told me to use some common sense and for once I followed your advice."

"Wonders will never cease. Now if I recall correctly, you valued the payoffs, leaving aside fixed fees, at plus or minus $10 million each, with 50-50 odds of success, and zero correlations.

"You have a good memory."

"How could I forget? The options desk was screaming to be allowed to keep them, despite a strict injunction not to risk aggregate losses of more than $20 million. Frankly, I couldn't understand the fuss. The matter seemed cut and dry."

"That's how I felt too, so I let the desk keep its positions." "You what?" cried Conway. This was far worse than he feared. Devlin had gone beyond spouting gibberish. He had acted on it. "I'm sorry, Devlin, you need help, but I've got a business to run and now some damage to limit. Go home while I sort things out and try to figure out what to do with you."

"Conway, hold your horses. Just hear me out. I'm not crazy. Not yet anyway."

"You could have fooled me. Now listen, how much simpler can a problem be? You're the one flipping coins, so you tell me: If heads and tails are equally likely, what are the odds that three tails will appear in a row?"

"That depends. If the coins are independent, then $\frac{1}{8}$. That's what most people assume."

"Of course. What else is there? If the probability of two tails is $\frac{1}{4}$ and a third uncorrelated coin has a probability $\frac{1}{2}$ of tails, the probability of three tails has to be $\frac{1}{8}$."

"That's not the only possibility. For example, suppose the coins come in two equally prevalent types, with one weighted to always come up heads and the other weighted to always come up tails. If you choose one coin randomly but then toss it three times, the odds of three tails will be $\frac{1}{2}$."

"Come on Devlin, I don't have time for this. This isn't a schoolyard experiment." Conway was determined not to get sucked into another of the great Devlin Theoretical Debates. But then a thought sprang up. "In any case, that's irrelevant. In your last example, the three tosses would be perfectly correlated. The options we're dealing with were uncorrelated. So we're back to $\frac{1}{8}$."

Devlin allowed himself a brief smile. He knew he had Conway now. "Slow down, slow down. While independent assets are never correlated, uncorrelated assets can be dependent. Granted, with only two Bernoulli assets, one definition is equivalent to the other: namely, that the probability of two tails is the square of the probability of one tail. But that is a special case. Besides, correlation applies only to pairs of assets, not larger groups."

"What about the three options we discussed? Each was pairwise uncorrelated with every other. That makes three pairs of uncorrelated assets, versus only one pair in the two asset case. Doesn't that amount to independence?"

"No, it does not. Let me give you an example." Devlin fumbled excitedly on his litter-strewn desk for the pad he had had earlier. In the process he tipped an old half-eaten sandwich off the desk and into the waste bin below. *Now was that random chance or a calculated move?* "Suppose we start by tossing three independent, unbiased coins but add the following condition: Every time an odd number of tails appears, all three outcomes are disqualified and the coins are tossed again. In that case, the only feasible orderings are HHH, TTH, THT, and HTT, each of them equally likely. You can readily check that the odds of heads and tails are equal for every coin, and that, for any given pair of coins, the probability of two tails equals $\frac{1}{4}$."

"Why doesn't the 'no odd tails in triples' restriction affect the correlation?"

"Suppose the third coin is heads. Then the first two coins must either both turn up tails or both turn up heads. Conversely, if the third coin is tails, then one of the first two coins must be heads and the other tails. Hence, the pairwise correlation is either $+1$ or -1 conditional on the outcome of the third coin, but since the third coin is equally likely to be heads or tails, the overall or unconditional correlation is zero. Yes?" Devlin looked up expectantly.

Conway felt dizzy. He glanced at his watch and hesitated. He had a management meeting in a couple of minutes. With a sigh he slumped down at Devlin's desk and began to play with the coins. After a few minutes, he looked up. "Remarkable," he said. "I wouldn't have thought this could be. How many possible unbiased, uncorrelated solutions are there?"

"Too many to count. Note that, by symmetry, 'no odd heads in triples' must also be a solution. Now suppose that at every triple toss, one of the restrictions 'no odd heads' or 'no odd tails' is randomly imposed with probabilities λ and $1 - \lambda$ respectively. No matter which restriction is imposed, we have an uncorrelated fair solution. Hence each randomization must also represent an uncorrelated fair solution, with probability $\lambda/4$ of three tails."

Conway took a deep breath. "OK, I will concede your theoretical point. But the options traders are playing with serious money, not petty coins. I still don't see why, out of all the possible solutions, you assumed the least possible tail risk for their trades. It is quite implausible. Why not be conservative and assume the most tail risk, or choose the average which corresponds to independence?"

"Theory told me I needed more information. So I went to talk with the traders. It turns out that the options applied to three companies vying to establish a new industry standard for computer networking. Four choices for a new standard were considered equally likely: the three different companies' in-house solutions, or continuation of the no-standard status quo. Each company was expected to thrive unless a rival's solution was adopted. You can check that this corresponds exactly to the 'no odd tails' scenario we discussed.

Conway's jaw dropped open and his eyes stared at the coins on Devlin's desk ...

While Conway regains his composure, let me clarify a few of the terms that he and Devlin used, for they are important building blocks for what follows. In the process I will also list a few useful formulas. This is fairly elementary stuff, so feel free to skim through it. The only material likely to be unfamiliar concerns higher-order cross-moments.

UNIVARIATE RANDOM VARIABLES

When we identify the return on an investment with a toss of a coin, we are abstracting from every feature other than risk. Mathematically, this is formalized in the notion of a stochastic or random variable X, which can take on various outcomes k from a set K. X is univariate when each outcome k is associated with a single real number x_k.

A scalar function h of a univariate random variable X is also a univariate random variable, taking the values $\{h(x_k)\}$ for the various k in K.

BERNOULLI EXAMPLES

In our coin-tossing examples, X corresponds to an individual coin and K to the outcomes heads and tails. We will generally assign the numbers 1 to heads and 0 to tails, although this can be altered without loss of generality.

Any random variable that takes outcomes of only 0 or 1 is known as Bernoulli, in honor of one of the fathers of probability theory. With Bernoulli variables other than coins, the outcome 1 is generally labeled "success" and the outcome 0 "failure".

PROBABILITY MEASURES

Every subset of K defines a possible event. An event is said to occur if and only if one of the outcomes in the associated subset occurs, so we can use the same label for both. The probability $Pr\{L\}$ of any event L denotes the limiting relative frequency or "likelihood" of L in unbiased samples, assuming that limit exists. However, this definition is not adequate, since bias is typically defined in terms of probabilities. Formally, probability is defined as a measure of the subset relative to the whole set, which measure in turn is associated with a limiting likelihood. By definition, all probabilities range between 0 and 1 with $Pr\{K\} = 1$. Probabilities are also additive in the following sense. For any countable union of mutually exclusive events (i.e., no outcome is associated with more than one of the events), its probability equals the sum of the constituent probabilities.

PROBABILITY POINT DISTRIBUTIONS

For a set K of discrete outcomes, the probability distribution is a function p associating each value x with some probability $p(x) \equiv Pr\{x\}$. From the definition of probability, each $p(x)$ must be nonnegative and the sum $\sum_{k \in K} p(x_k)$ over all k in K must equal 1. If $p(x_k) = 1$ for some x_j, then the outcome is certain and the distribution is said to be degenerate. The next simplest probability distribution pertains to a Bernoulli distribution, which is completely characterized by $p(1)$, since the only other probability $p(0)$ must equal $1 - p(1)$.

The probability $Pr\{X \leq x\}$ is called the cumulative probability at x and is generally denoted $F(x)$. Viewed as a function of X, F is nonnegative, non-decreasing, and takes a maximum value of 1. Given such a function, the point probabilities $p(x)$ can be calculated as $p(x) = F(x) - max_{y<x}F(y)$ when K is discrete.

SUPPORT OF A DISTRIBUTION

A probability distribution may attach zero weight to some outcomes in K. The subset of K that carries positive weight is called the support of the distribution. A distribution with support on n distinct outcomes is called an n-point distribution.

TAIL RISK

Tail risk refers to the probability of unusually low outcomes. It is defined in terms of a threshold T and the cumulative probability $F(T)$ that X lies in the tail. When interested in the probability $Pr\{X \geq T\}$ of unusually high outcomes, I shall speak of the upper tail risk.

MULTIVARIATE RANDOM VARIABLES

The notions of probability can be easily extended to variables taking on multivariate outcomes. Each outcome is associated with a point k in multidimensional space and the probability measure is again taken over the set K of all outcomes. For discrete outcomes, the joint probability distribution is given by a function p associating each outcome $(x_{1k}, x_{2k}, \ldots, x_{nk})$ with a nonnegative number $p(x_{1k}, x_{2k}, \ldots, x_{nk})$, such that

$$\sum_{k \in K} p(x_{1k}, x_{2k}, \ldots, x_{nk}) = 1$$

CONDITIONAL PROBABILITIES

Conditional probabilities measure the probability $Pr\{L_1|L_2\}$ of one event L_1 given that a second "conditioning" event L_2 has occurred. This is defined as the probability that both events occur divided by the probability that the conditioning event occurs:

$$Pr(L_1|L_2) \equiv \frac{Pr(L_1 \cap L_2)}{Pr(L_2)}$$

In many applications, the probability of the second event is not readily at hand but must be calculated from data on the joint distribution. For example, let X and Y be two random variables characterized by a joint probability $p(x,y)$. Then the probability distribution of Y alone can be calculated as $p_Y(Y) = \sum_{k \in K} p(x_k, y)$. Hence

$$p(x|y) = \frac{p(x,y)}{p_Y(y)} = \frac{p(x,y)}{\sum_{k \in K} p(x_k, y)}$$

Conversely, given the probability distribution of Y and the conditional probability distribution of X given Y, we can calculate the joint distribution as $p(x,y) = p(x|y)p_Y(y)$.

MIXTURES OF DISTRIBUTIONS

The preceding formula can also be interpreted as a way to concoct new probability distributions out of old ones. Namely, any weighted average $\sum_i \lambda_i p_i(X)$ of a set of probability distributions $\{p_i(X)\}$ is also a probability distribution, provided the weights $\{\lambda_i\}$ are nonnegative and sum to 1. To verify this, just associate each subscript i with a value of Y, so that $\lambda_i \equiv \lambda(y)$ and $p_i(X) \equiv p(X|y)$.

A probability distribution formed in this way is called a mixture of distributions. Note that any expectation of a mixture equals the mixture of its expectations. Mixtures are also called convex combinations (the formal name for nonnegative weighted averages summing to 1) or randomizations. The probability distribution that determines the weights for the randomization is called the mixing distribution.

INDEPENDENCE

Two random variables are perfectly dependent if one can be expressed as the deterministic function of the other. At the other extreme, two random variables are said to be independent if and only if the outcome of one has no bearing on the outcome of the other. In other words, the conditional probability $Pr\{x|y\}$ must be a function of x alone. Recalling the definition of conditional probability, this means that X and Y are independent if and only if, for all outcomes x and y,

$$p(x, y) = p_X(x) \cdot p_Y(y)$$

Hence, if X and Y are independent, their joint probability is the product of a factor that depends only on X and a factor that depends only on Y. The converse is readily shown as well. In other words, independence is mathematically equivalent to multiplicative separability of the joint probability measures.

EXPECTATIONS

The expectation E of a random variable X denotes the weighted average of the various values that X can take, with weights proportional to the probabilities. The formula for a discrete set of outcomes is:

$$E[X] = \sum_{k \in K} x_k p(x_k)$$

Expectations need not be finite. Suppose that $p(k) = \dfrac{1}{k} - \dfrac{1}{k+1} = \dfrac{1}{k(k+1)}$ for all positive integers k. This is a legitimate probability measure, as it is nonnegative and sums to 1. However, the expectation is $\dfrac{1}{1} + \dfrac{1}{2} + \dfrac{1}{3} + \dfrac{1}{4} + \ldots$, which is unbounded. When the expectation is infinite, the average from any sample – also known as the "sample mean" – remains finite, but tends to grow without bound as the sample increases in size.

EXPECTATIONS OF FUNCTIONS

Since a function h of a random variable X is also a random variable, we can calculate its expectation $E[h(X)]$ as $\sum_{k \in K} h(x_k)p(x_k)$. For example, the affine transformation $aX + b$, where a and b are constants, has the expectation $aE[X] + b$, which is the affine transformation of the expectation.

Likewise, we calculate a conditional expectation $E[X|Y]$ as $\sum_{j \in J} x_j p(x_j|Y)$. The expectation $E[X|Y]$ is in turn a function of Y so we can take its expectation with respect to the probability distribution of Y. It is readily demonstrated that $E_Y[E[X|Y]] = E[X]$. In other words, the expectation of the conditional expectation equals the unconditional expectation.

Expectations are also readily applied to mixtures of distributions. To calculate the probability of every outcome under a mixture of distributions, find the outcome's probability under each individual distribution and take the expectation over the mixture: $p_X(x) = E_Y[p(x|y)]$. Indeed, the expectation of any function over a mixture of distributions equals the mixture (more precisely, the expectation over the mixture) of the individual expectations.

BIAS AND FAIRNESS

Devlin and Conway used the word "unbiased" to indicate a coin that is equally likely to come up heads or tails. By extension, they will use the word "unbiased" to describe any Bernoulli random variable with 50% probability of success. Technically, this usage is sloppy. Bias is not a purely objective property. Rather, it refers to the difference between the supposed and actual values. If a Bernoulli variable is expected to never fail and never does so, there is nothing inherently biased about it.

In gambling and game theory, fairness is interpreted more properly as equivalence between expected returns and entrance fees. That is, after including entrance fees and conditioning on current information, a fair game's expectation should be zero. In theoretical finance, this concept of fairness is enshrined in the concept of a "martingale".

Unprepared to reject either conventional conversation or finance theory, I ask the reader to tolerate the dual usage. Fairness will mean a 50% probability of success in Bernoulli games and a zero expectation in other games.

FIRST MOMENT

For n a positive integer and X a univariate random variable, the expectation $E[X^n]$ is known as the nth moment of X. The first moment $E[X^1]$ is the mean or expected value $E[X]$ itself, and is often denoted by μ. For a Bernoulli random variable, the mean μ equals the probability of success. Indeed, every moment of a Bernoulli variable equals μ.

The mean of a weighted sum of random variables equals the weighted sum of their means. That is, if $\{a_i\}$ are constants:

$$E\left[\sum_{i=1}^{n} a_i X_i\right] = \sum_{i=1}^{n} a_i E[X_i]$$

SECOND MOMENT

The second moment $E[X^2]$ adds information about the dispersion of X around its mean, so it is often reported in the form of a so-called variance

$$Var[X] \equiv E[(X - \mu)^2] = E[X^2] - \mu^2, \text{where } \mu \equiv E[X]$$

The variance is always positive except for a degenerate distribution, where it is zero. For Bernoulli variables, the variance equals $\mu(1 - \mu)$.

The square root of the variance is known as the standard deviation $Std[X]$ and has the same units as X, which facilitates comparison. It is often denoted by σ or σ_X, which makes the variance σ^2 or σ_X^2.

Adding a constant to a random variable does not affect its variance. Multiplying a random variable by a constant multiplies the variance by the constant squared. Hence, when a and b are constants, $Var[aX + b]$ $= a^2 Var[X]$ and $Std[aX + b] = a \cdot Std[X]$.

HIGHER-ORDER MOMENTS

To highlight the marginal information value, higher-order moments of X are generally expressed in terms of the standardized transformation $\dfrac{X - E[X]}{Std[X]} \equiv \dfrac{X - \mu}{\sigma}$, which has a zero mean and unit standard deviation. The third standardized moment $E\left[\left(\dfrac{X - \mu}{\sigma}\right)^3\right]$ is called skewness.

Skewness, like all standardized odd-numbered higher moments, will be zero for distributions that are symmetric around their means. The skewness will tend to be negative if the distribution tilts toward the left of the mean, and positive if the distribution tilts toward the right of the mean.

The fourth standardized moment $E\left[\left(\dfrac{X - \mu}{\sigma}\right)^4\right]$ less three is called kurtosis. Kurtosis measures the relative fatness of the outer values or tails. The minimum kurtosis is -2, which occurs when X has a two-point distribution with equal weights. Kurtosis is close to zero for the average of a large number of independent, identically distributed random variables. Distributions with distinctly positive kurtosis are called leptokurtotic or fat-tailed.

MULTIVARIATE MOMENTS

Multivariate moments take the form $E\left[X_1^{k_1} X_2^{k_2} \ldots X_n^{k_n}\right]$ where the various exponents k_i are nonnegative integers and at least one is positive. The sum $\sum_{i=1}^{n} k_i$ of the exponents is called the order of the moment. For example, $E[X_1 X_2 X_3]$, $E[X_1^2 X_2]$, and $E[X_3^3]$ are all third-order moments. If at least two exponents are positive, multivariate moments are called cross moments. The rest are essentially univariate and are called own moments.

Cross moments arise naturally in the calculation of moments of weighted sums of random variables. Each additive term of $E\left[\left(\sum_{i=1}^{n} a_i X_i\right)^J\right]$ consists of own moments or cross moments of order J.

COVARIANCE

A second-order cross moment takes the form $E[XY]$. As with second-order own moments, measuring the variables as deviations from the mean helps to distil the marginal information. The resulting quantity is called the covariance $Cov[X, Y]$ and can be expressed in various forms. Denoting the means of X and Y by μ_X and μ_Y respectively,

$$Cov[X, Y] = E[(X - E[X])(Y - E[Y])] = E[X(Y - E[Y])]$$
$$= E[(X - E[X])Y] = E[XY] - E[X]E[Y]$$

Adding a constant to either of two random variables leaves the covariance unchanged, while multiplying either variable by a constant multiplies the covariance in the same proportion. Hence, for constants a, b, c, and d:

$$Cov[aX + b, cY + d] = ac\, Cov[X, Y]$$

The conventional shorthand for $Cov[X, Y]$ is σ_{XY}. Since $Cov[X, X]$ equals $Var[X]$, σ_{XX} is also written σ_X^2.

CORRELATION

An even more distilled variant of a second-order cross moment is the correlation, sometimes known as the partial correlation or pairwise correlation. Correlation is the covariance between standardized random variables, and can be expressed as:

$$Cor[X, Y] = E\left[\left(\frac{X - \mu_X}{\sigma_X}\right)\left(\frac{Y - \mu_Y}{\sigma_Y}\right)\right] = \frac{Cov[X, Y]}{\sigma_X \sigma_Y} = \frac{E[XY] - \mu_X \mu_Y}{\sigma_X \sigma_Y}$$

Correlation is unitless. Adding a constant to one of the variables doesn't affect it. Multiplying one of the variables by a constant multiplies it only by the sign of the constant:

$$Cor[aX + b, cY + d] = sign(ac) \cdot Cor[X, Y]$$

The conventional shorthand for $Cor[X, Y]$ is ρ_{XY}. Like covariance, correlation is symmetric in its arguments, so $\rho_{XY} = \rho_{YX}$. Note that the correlation ρ_{XX} of a variable with itself equals one.

Two variables with zero correlation are said to be uncorrelated. All independent variables are uncorrelated, but, as Devlin demonstrated, variables can be uncorrelated without being independent. To give another example, if X is distributed symmetrically around the origin and Y equals X^2, then despite their perfect dependence X and Y will be uncorrelated.

THE MAIN USE OF COVARIANCE AND CORRELATION

By far the most common use of covariance and correlation involves the calculation of the variance of a sum of random variables. The variance of the sum equals the sum of all the individual variances and the covariances between every pair of distinct random variables. The formula is readily extended to incorporate constant-weighted sums:

$$Var\left[\sum_{i=1}^{n} a_i X_i\right] = \sum_{i=1}^{n} a_i^2 \sigma_i^2 + \sum_{i=1}^{n} \sum_{\substack{j=1 \\ j \neq i}}^{n} a_i a_j \sigma_{ij}$$

where σ_i^2 and σ_{ij} denote $Var[X_i]$ and $Cov[X_i, X_j]$ respectively. Denoting $Cor[X_i, X_j]$ by ρ_{ij} and taking account of the symmetry $\rho_{ij} = \rho_{ji}$, this can be rewritten as:

$$Var\left[\sum_{i=1}^{n} a_i X_i\right] = \sum_{i=1}^{n} a_i \sigma_i^2 + 2 \sum_{i=1}^{n} \sum_{j=1}^{i-1} \rho_{ij} a_i a_j \sigma_i \sigma_j$$

CORRELATION AND THE VARIANCE OF AVERAGES

One particularly interesting weighted sum is the simple average of n variables having a common variance σ^2 and a common correlation ρ. In that case the previous formula simplifies to:

$$Var\left[\sum_{i=1}^{n} \frac{X_i}{n}\right] = \left(\frac{1}{n} + \rho \frac{n-1}{n}\right)\sigma^2 = \left(\frac{1-\rho}{n} + \rho\right)\sigma^2$$

In other words, the variance of the average equals the common individual variance times $\dfrac{1-\rho}{n} + \rho$. The latter approaches ρ as n grows large, so diversifying across positively correlated variables can reduce risks only to a limited extent.

    This same formula applies if the outcomes of the variables are identical with probability ρ and independent with probability $1 - \rho$. Thus, in at least some applications, correlation can be viewed as reflecting a mixture of independence and perfect dependence. However, correlation is a broader concept, and unlike a probability mixture it allows ρ to be negative.

LIMITS ON CORRELATION

If each variable X and Y is treated as a vector, then ρ_{XY} indicates the cosine of the angle between the two vectors. Hence the correlation is always a number between -1 and 1. A value of $+1$ is called perfect positive correlation and implies an affine relationship $Y = aX + b$ for some positive constant a. A value of -1 is called perfect negative correlation and implies an affine relationship with a negative.

    The pairwise correlations of a set of variables are also restricted by the need for internal consistency between the angles of the corresponding vectors. For example, suppose X points exactly opposite

The geometry of correlation

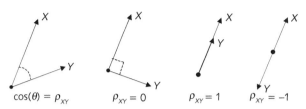

to both Y and Z, so that it's perfectly negatively correlated with either. Then Y and Z must point in the same direction and be perfectly positively correlated with each other.

These restrictions on correlation have a straightforward statistical interpretation: namely that weighted sums of random variables can never have negative variance. For example, when n variables have a common correlation, that correlation can never be less than $-\dfrac{1}{n-1}$.

CONDITIONAL COVARIANCES

The conditional covariance of X and Y conditional on a common event Z can be written as:

$$Cov[X,Y|Z] = E[XY|Z] - E[X|Z] \cdot E[Y|Z]$$

By taking the expectations of each side with respect to Z and undertaking some additional manipulation, we can establish that:

$$Cov[X,Y] = Cov_Z[E[X|Z], E[Y|Z]] + E_Z[Cov[X,Y|Z]]$$

In other words, the unconditional covariance equals the covariance of the conditional means plus the expectation of the conditional covariances. In the special case $Y = X$, the unconditional variance equals the variance of the conditional mean plus the expectation of the conditional variance:

$$Var[X] = Var_Z[E[X|Z]] + E_Z[Var[X|Z]]$$

These formulas are readily applied to mixtures by letting Z denote the mixing distribution. For example, consider the "no odd tails" and "no odd heads" scenarios that Devlin discussed. Each scenario has mean 1, variance $\frac{1}{4}$ and covariance 0. The formulas above imply that any mixture matches these moments and therefore fills all the requirements of a solution.

HIGHER-ORDER CROSS MOMENTS

As a first approximation, the average correlation among a set of standardized random variables measures the average tendency to move in (linear) synchrony. However, this average may be formed in various ways. One set of random variables may alternate between independent and identical movements. Another set of random variables may react more uniformly. Higher-order cross moments help describe the fluctuations in synchrony.

Third-order standardized cross moments are known as co-skewnesses. They take two generic forms:

$$E\left[\left(\frac{X - \mu_X}{\sigma_X}\right)\left(\frac{Y - \mu_Y}{\sigma_Y}\right)\left(\frac{Z - \mu_Z}{\sigma_Z}\right)\right]$$

and

$$E\left[\left(\frac{X - \mu_X}{\sigma_X}\right)^2\left(\frac{Y - \mu_Y}{\sigma_Y}\right)\right]$$

Fourth-order standardized cross moments are known as co-kurtoses. They take four generic forms:

$$E\left[\left(\frac{X - \mu_X}{\sigma_X}\right)\left(\frac{Y - \mu_Y}{\sigma_Y}\right)\left(\frac{Z - \mu_Z}{\sigma_Z}\right)\left(\frac{W - \mu_W}{\sigma_W}\right)\right]$$

$$E\left[\left(\frac{X - \mu_X}{\sigma_X}\right)^2\left(\frac{Y - \mu_Y}{\sigma_Y}\right)\left(\frac{Z - \mu_Z}{\sigma_Z}\right)\right]$$

$$E\left[\left(\frac{X - \mu_X}{\sigma_X}\right)^2\left(\frac{Y - \mu_Y}{\sigma_Y}\right)^2\right]$$

and

$$E\left[\left(\frac{X - \mu_X}{\sigma_X}\right)^3\left(\frac{Y - \mu_Y}{\sigma_Y}\right)\right]$$

2 | New Angles on Pascal's Triangle

After a long silence Conway spoke. "I'm sorry, Devlin. I shouldn't have jumped to conclusions. Now we need to set things straight with the auditors, so that they can amend their report."

"I don't think that's a good idea. Not yet, anyway. Most likely the auditors think our risk management system is fine save for the implementation."

"Right. That is exactly what they said. So let's get them to soften their criticisms."

"I'm afraid it won't work that way. You see Conway, this incident exposes a flaw in our system. It shows that even when we know the full probability distribution of every asset and all the covariances or pairwise correlations, we may be unable to properly value the tail risk in the portfolio. After all, we have just seen that with three uncorrelated unbiased binary assets, the risks of a simultaneous plunge can vary between 0% and 25% depending on other conditions our monitoring system does not normally record."

"What are we missing?"

"To begin with, we're missing the co-skewnesses. For example, the co-skewness between three uncorrelated, unbiased Bernoulli assets can vary between $+\frac{1}{8}$ and $-\frac{1}{8}$. The probability of three losses will then work out to $\frac{1}{8}$ less the co-skewness."

"We can handle this. Let us start recording co-skewness between trios of assets. I will draw up the new reporting specs while you revise the value-at-risk formulas for portfolios."

Devlin shrugged. "I can't do it. To provide a general formula for three non-binary assets, we would also need information on co-skewnesses that span pairs of assets. Granted, you could add that to your reporting specs. But still that wouldn't specify the full risk on quadruples of assets. For that we would also need to know the co-kurtoses, which come in four different types. With quintuples of assets, we would need to know the fifth-order cross-moments, which come in six different types. With . . ."

"Stop," pleaded Conway, throwing up his hands in resignation. "I get the point. Can we not manage with a simpler approximation? In fact, why not just stick with what we have? You have to admit that this binary option trio was an awfully peculiar case."

"Very peculiar. But peculiar cases sometimes provide fresh insights into the familiar. This one made me realize that aggregate portfolios might bear a whole lot more or less risk than our current system suggests."

Oh no. Devlin is heading off on one of his mental walkabouts. Please don't drag me along. "I take it you have no practical alternative to offer."

"How could I? I don't even know what we're dealing with. Perhaps when you combine a lot of similarly dependent assets, the outcomes gravitate toward a central tendency, like they do for independent assets. Alternatively, perhaps the deviations become more pronounced. Given the stakes, I think the question deserves a closer look. I've already begun a few thought experiments."

"More coin games?" asked Conway, nodding to the bowl on Devlin's desk.

"Yes. Or to be more formal, multivariate Bernoulli games. It's hard to escape the presumption that coins are either independent or identical, and I'm not ready to impose that restriction."

"What restrictions are you willing to impose?"

"Two big ones. The first is the Bernoulli restriction itself, that each variable has only two possible outcomes. The second is exchangeability, which means that probabilities depend only on the total number of successes and not on the particular ordering. These two assumptions provide the simplest possible base for considering dependence. They facilitate calculations and seem less likely to divert us from core issues."

Conway was far from eager to let Devlin pursue a pet project, as other staff would resent having to pick up the slack and accuse Conway of favoritism. However, it would keep Devlin out of trouble for a while and give him a chance to regain his bearings. *I might as well humor him. Help him work through his obsession.* "Sounds reasonable. Any ideas on how to play the games quickly?" he added hopefully. "I can't afford to have you arrange coins all day."

Devlin nodded. "Fortunately, I've just discovered a very neat method. It builds triangles that complement Pascal's Triangle. Do you recall Pascal's Triangle?"

"Yes, I do. It is the pyramid of numbers such that the top number equals one and every other number equals the sum of the nearest numbers to the right and left above it. The $k + 1$st entry in the $n + 1$st row works out to $\binom{n}{k}$, the number of distinct combinations of k objects that can be chosen from a set of n objects."

Pascal's Triangle

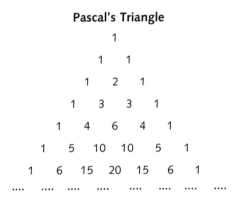

"That's right. My complementary triangles use nearly the same arrangement, except that each number equals the sum of the nearest two neighbors below it rather than above it. It turns out that every exchangeable Bernoulli game can be represented by such a triangle, where the $k + 1$st entry in the $n + 1$st row equals the probability that the first k out of n tries are successes and the rest failures. The summation condition simply indicates that if there are k successes in n tries, there must be either k or $k + 1$ successes in $n + 1$ tries."

"What else do you need beside your triangle to characterize an exchangeable Bernoulli game?"

"Nothing. The triangle contains all the relevant information. In fact, any single edge contains all the relevant information, because all the other probabilities can be calculated using the summation rule."

Conway looked puzzled, so Devlin decided to walk him through an example. He jotted down the following pyramid of numbers.

Devlin's example

Devlin explained: "The first row sets the total probability measure at one. The second row gives the failure and success probabilities per try, so this example describes an unbiased game. The third row gives the probabilities in two tries of zero successes, one success followed by one failure, or two successes, so this describes an uncorrelated game. The fourth row reveals that the game is unskewed. However, the Bernoulli variables are not independent, because if they were, every quadruple would have probability $\frac{1}{16}$. Instead, quadruples in this game are two-thirds more likely to contain even numbers of successes than odd numbers of successes."

"And you say that the summation condition allows the whole triangle to be built from one of the edges?"

"Try it yourself. If you start from the bottom row, the elements in the fourth row are given by $\frac{5}{64} + \frac{3}{64} = \frac{1}{8}$, the elements in the third row by $\frac{1}{8} + \frac{1}{8} = \frac{1}{4}$, and so on. If you start from the diagonal marking zero successes, you turn the summation into subtraction and proceed from left to right. For example, the probability of one success in five tries equals the probability of zero successes in four tries less the probability of zero successes in five tries, or $\frac{1}{8} - \frac{5}{64} = \frac{3}{64}$."

"I'm still a bit confused. If these are probabilities, why don't they sum to one?" Conway thought for a moment. "Wait. Yes, I see now. The numbers in your triangle are supposed to represent the probability of a particular permutation of successes and failures. Except for the extreme cases, several different permutations can generate the same total number of successes and failures. Because your variables are exchangeable, each of these permutations will have the same probability."

"Right again. The number of distinct permutations of k successes in n tries is just $\binom{n}{k}$, which is given by Pascal's Triangle. Hence, to calculate the total probability of k successes in n tries, simply multiply the $k + 1$st entry in the $n + 1$st row of my triangle by the corresponding entry in Pascal's Triangle."

"Let me check this on your example. In four tries, there are one distinct permutation of zero successes, six distinct permutations of two successes, and one distinct permutation of four successes. Hence the probability of an even number of successes is $\frac{5}{64}$ times $1 + 6 + 1$ or $\frac{40}{64} = \frac{5}{8}$. Similarly, there are four distinct permutations each of one success or three successes, so the probability of an odd number of successes is $\frac{3}{64}$ times $4 + 4$ or $\frac{24}{64} = \frac{3}{8}$. The probabilities do indeed sum to one as required, and evens are two-thirds more likely than odds. But what's your point?"

"So you see that four variables can be unbiased, uncorrelated, and unskewed – indeed, every trio of variables can appear independent – and yet a portfolio may still have fatter tails than it would if the four variables were fully independent. More generally, every m-member subset of n variables can be independent without implying independence at higher levels. This demonstrates clearly that, absent restrictions on the functional form, the tail risk cannot be inferred simply from information on lower-order moments."

"Not bad," said Conway, although in fact he thought it was very bad. "Are you saying that any nonnegative triangle with a one at the top, and whose neighboring row elements sum to the element above, can represent the probability measure of a multivariate Bernoulli game?"

"Yes."

"So if I just start building a triangle from the top down and keep adding rows conforming to your constraints, then I create a probability measure for a ten-, twenty-, or fifty-variable Bernoulli game?"

"Maybe. Most likely you'll make quite a few mistakes and need to correct them."

"Excuse me Devlin, but I would strongly discourage you from tossing disparaging comments my way right now. You have few enough friends as it is."

"Sorry, Conway, I didn't mean you personally. I've had those problems too. It's all too easy to insert rows that imply negative values on lower rows. The simplest example with unbiased and uncorrelated variables occurs when we try to add a row to our "no odd tails in triples" scenario. Letting q denote the probability of no failures in four tries, our triangle would have to look as follows:

Infeasible extensions

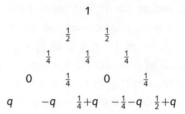

$$1$$

$$\tfrac{1}{2} \qquad \tfrac{1}{2}$$

$$\tfrac{1}{4} \qquad \tfrac{1}{4} \qquad \tfrac{1}{4}$$

$$0 \qquad \tfrac{1}{4} \qquad 0 \qquad \tfrac{1}{4}$$

$$q \qquad -q \qquad \tfrac{1}{4}+q \qquad -\tfrac{1}{4}-q \qquad \tfrac{1}{2}+q$$

"Let's try this, Conway, what value does q have to take to yield a feasible Bernoulli game?"

Conway studied the bottom row. "It can't be done. Either q or $-\tfrac{1}{4} - q$ is negative. What's going on?"

"If a set of four coins never includes a subset with one tail and two heads, the full set must contain exactly zero, three, or four tails. If the set never includes a subset with three tails, then the full set can never contain three or four tails. Hence, the only set of four coins that never contains a triple with an odd number of tails must never contain any tails at all, and cannot be unbiased."

Conway breathed a massive sigh of relief. "Great work, Devlin. You've solved the problem."

"What?"

"Your triangles show that the threat of extreme events diminishes as the number of exchangeable random variables increases. Since in most large portfolios, most suitably rescaled assets are exchangeable with many others, we can rely on standard mean-variance analysis for the bulk of our analysis, and reserve your analysis for special cases."

Devlin was distraught. Not because Conway didn't understand, but because he didn't seem to want to. "I have solved hardly anything," he moaned. "I show you a single example of risk bounds narrowing with the number of exchangeable variables and you're ready to call off the investigation."

"I am trying to be practical, unlike some of my friends. But don't let me stop you. If you come across unusual tail risks that don't diminish in large portfolios, by all means let me know."

"Then there is something else you should see."

"By all means." *I hope this is a false alarm.*

"Let's look again at games of four unbiased and uncorrelated exchangeable Bernoulli variables, but without restricting ourselves to a 'no odd tails in triples' scenario. Letting r denote the probability of no successes in triples, the full probability triangle must take the following form:

Four-variable games

$$1$$

$$\tfrac{1}{2} \qquad \tfrac{1}{2}$$

$$\tfrac{1}{4} \qquad \tfrac{1}{4} \qquad \tfrac{1}{4}$$

$$r \qquad \tfrac{1}{4}-r \qquad r \qquad \tfrac{1}{4}-r$$

$$q \qquad r-q \qquad \tfrac{1}{4}-2r+q \qquad -\tfrac{1}{4}+3r-q \qquad \tfrac{1}{2}-4r+q$$

"This triangle represents a feasible probability measure for a four-variable exchangeable Bernoulli game if and only if none of its elements is negative. From the fourth row, as we have seen, r must lie between 0 and $\tfrac{1}{4}$. On the fifth row, the second entry sets r as an upper bound for q while the last entry sets $4r-\tfrac{1}{2}$ as a lower bound for q. Hence, $4r-\tfrac{1}{2}$ must not exceed r, which implies that r must not exceed $\tfrac{1}{6}$. Similarly, the first and fourth entries imply that r must be at least $\tfrac{1}{12}$. So we confirm that the extra variable q restricts the solution range for r. However, q is free to vary provided that $\min[r, 3r - \tfrac{1}{4}] \geq q \geq \max[0, 4r - \tfrac{1}{2}]$. The minimum value of q turns out to be zero, which corresponds to the following solution:

Solution with minimum q

$$1$$

$$\tfrac{1}{2} \qquad \tfrac{1}{2}$$

$$\tfrac{1}{4} \qquad \tfrac{1}{4} \qquad \tfrac{1}{4}$$

$$\tfrac{1}{12} \qquad \tfrac{1}{6} \qquad \tfrac{1}{12} \qquad \tfrac{1}{6}$$

$$0 \qquad \tfrac{1}{12} \qquad \tfrac{1}{12} \qquad 0 \qquad \tfrac{1}{6}$$

"The maximum value of q is $\tfrac{1}{6}$, which corresponds to the mirror image of the solution above. So the extreme tail risk looks even more peculiar than before."

Conway had been listening quite attentively to Devlin's exposition, and thought he understood it. Now he was confused again. "Excuse me. In the three-variable case the extreme risks ranged from 0 to $\frac{1}{4}$. Now they range from $\frac{1}{12}$ to $\frac{1}{6}$. So why do you say they're worse?

"Because a probability of $\frac{1}{6}$ for four tails is more than twice the value given independence. In the three-variable case, the worst case was exactly twice as likely as under independence. So the tail problem is worse with four variables than with three."

Conway studied the diagram a while. "It seems to me that your conclusion about the tail risk depends on the definition of the tail. Suppose we define the tail event as 'three or more failures'. Your solution with minimum q then implies a tail probability of $0 + 4 \times \frac{1}{12} = \frac{1}{3}$, while your solution with maximum q implies a tail probability of $\frac{1}{6}$. A range of $\frac{1}{6}$ to $\frac{1}{3}$ is less severe than the range of 0 to $\frac{1}{4}$ for the three-variable case."

Devlin was very pleased that Conway was taking the time to think through his triangles. He really appreciated Conway's partnership when he could get it. So Devlin showed his gratitude in the only way that came naturally to him. "Conway, you shouldn't assume that extreme values of q, the risk of four failures, yield the extreme values for the risk of three or more failures. The latter has the formula $q + 4(r - q)$ or $4r - 3q$. Finding the extreme value amounts to solving a linear programming problem. Let's see:

- if r is $\frac{1}{8}$ or higher, then the minimum value of q is $4r - \frac{1}{2}$, so that the maximum value of $4r - 3q$ is $\frac{3}{2} - 8r$, which attains a maximum of $\frac{1}{2}$ at $r = \frac{1}{8}$.
- If r is $\frac{1}{8}$ or less, then the minimum value of q is 0, so that the maximum value of $4r - 3q$ is $4r$, which attains a maximum of $\frac{1}{2}$ at $r = \frac{1}{8}$.
- If r is $\frac{1}{8}$ or higher, then the maximum value of q is r, so that the minimum value of $4r - 3q$ is r, which attains a minimum of $\frac{1}{8}$ at $r = \frac{1}{8}$.
- If r is $\frac{1}{8}$ or less, then the maximum value of q is $3r - \frac{1}{4}$, so that the minimum value of $4r - 3q$ is $\frac{3}{4} - 5r$, which attains a minimum of $\frac{1}{8}$ at $r = \frac{1}{8}$."

Conway's head was beginning to spin. "OK, I believe you. Can you please get to the bottom line?"

"I was just about to do that. The probability of three or more failures in four exchangeable tries can be as low as $\frac{1}{8}$ or as high as $\frac{1}{2}$, corresponding to the following probability triangles:

Extreme probabilities of ≥3 losses in 4 tries

Minimum   Maximum

$$
\begin{array}{ccccccccc}
 & & & 1 & & & & 1 & \\
 & & \tfrac{1}{2} & & \tfrac{1}{2} & & \tfrac{1}{2} & & \tfrac{1}{2} \\
 & \tfrac{1}{4} & & \tfrac{1}{4} & & \tfrac{1}{4} \qquad \tfrac{1}{4} & & \tfrac{1}{4} & & \tfrac{1}{4} \\
\end{array}
$$

Minimum triangle:

	1			
	$\frac{1}{2}$		$\frac{1}{2}$	
$\frac{1}{4}$		$\frac{1}{4}$		$\frac{1}{4}$
$\frac{1}{8}$ $\frac{1}{8}$ $\frac{1}{8}$ $\frac{1}{8}$				
$\frac{1}{8}$ 0 $\frac{1}{8}$ 0 $\frac{1}{8}$				

Maximum triangle:

	1			
	$\frac{1}{2}$		$\frac{1}{2}$	
$\frac{1}{4}$		$\frac{1}{4}$		$\frac{1}{4}$
$\frac{1}{8}$ $\frac{1}{8}$ $\frac{1}{8}$ $\frac{1}{8}$				
0 $\frac{1}{8}$ 0 $\frac{1}{8}$ 0				

"That's interesting. Both extreme cases are symmetric around the mean. So neither involves any skew."

"They don't imply any dependence either until you get to the last row. Every triple is independent. So if you jump to the conclusion that all four variables are independent, your estimate $\frac{5}{16}$ of the risk of three or more failures could be $\frac{3}{16}$ too high or $\frac{3}{16}$ too low. Once again the lower moments provide little insight about the tail risk. I find that disturbing."

"So do I," conceded Conway. "I think we need to see how things play out with more variables. You said that finding the extreme tail probabilities amounts to solving a linear programming problem. I would appreciate your setting up the problem on a computer and working out some solutions. Let's meet again when you're done. In the meantime, I need to reflect on the mathematics of your triangles."

"I'll get right on it."

Conway smiled weakly at his friend. "Good". *Please let there be a simple answer.*

While we wait for Devlin's results, let's help Conway with the math.

PASCAL'S TRIANGLE

Let's begin by writing out the full formula for $\binom{n}{k}$:

$$
\binom{n}{k} \equiv \frac{n!}{k!(n-k)!} \equiv \frac{n(n-1)(n-2)\cdots 2\cdot 1}{k(k-1)\cdots 1 \cdot (n-k)(n-k-1)\cdots 1}
$$

$$
= \frac{n(n-1)\cdots(n-k+1)}{k(k-1)\cdots 1}
$$

Pascal's Triangle indicates that $\binom{n}{k} + \binom{n}{k+1} = \binom{n+1}{k+1}$ and this is readily verified:

$$\binom{n}{k} + \binom{n}{k+1} = \frac{n!}{k!(n-k)!} \cdot \frac{k+1}{k+1} + \frac{n!}{(k+1)!(n-k-1)!} \cdot \frac{n-k}{n-k}$$

$$= \frac{n! \cdot (k+1+n-k)}{(k+1)!(n-k)!} = \frac{(n+1)!}{(k+1)!(n-k)!} = \binom{n+1}{k+1}$$

DEVLIN'S TRIANGLES

Denote by $p(n,k)$ the probability that in n tries in some multivariate Bernoulli game, k successes are followed by $n-k$ failures. If the variables are exchangeable, the probability that exactly k successes occur in n tries equals $\binom{n}{k} p(n,k)$. Since the number of successes must be an integer between 0 and n inclusive, $\sum_{k=0}^{n} \binom{n}{k} p(n,k) = 1$ for all n. In other words, if we create a triangle with $p(n,k)$ as the $k+1$st entry on the $n+1$st row, then the dot product of each row of this triangle and the corresponding row of Pascal's Triangle will equal one.

To identify this triangle with one of Devlin's triangles, we simply need to verify the summation rule $p(n,k) = p(n+1,k) + p(n+1,k+1)$ for all n and k. Imagine that in $n+1$ tries, the first k yield successes and the next $n-k$ yield failures. Call this event A. Denote by B the event "A occurs and the last try is a success" and by C the event "A occurs and the last try is a failure." Clearly, if A occurs, either B or C occurs but not both, so $Pr(A) = Pr(B) + Pr(C)$. Now $Pr(A)$ and $Pr(C)$ are just $p(n,k)$ and $p(n+1,k)$ respectively. Furthermore, since tries are exchangeable, the probability of k successes followed by $n-k$ failures and one success equals the probability of $k+1$ successes followed by $n-k$ failures, so $Pr(B)$ equals $p(n+1,k+1)$. The summation rule follows directly.

We now need to show that any nonnegative Devlin's triangle represents a legitimate probability measure. Let us identify the $k+1$st entry on the $n+1$st row of Devlin's triangle with a candidate probability $\tilde{p}(n,k)$ for any particular permutation of k successes in n tries. By construction, the set $\{\tilde{p}(n,k)\}$ is nonnegative, complete, and satisfies the requirement that the probability of the union of mutually exclusive events equals the sum of the individual event probabilities.

It remains to verify that the probability $\sum_{k=0}^{n} \binom{n}{k} \tilde{p}(n, k)$ of the union of all distinct n-tuples equals one for every n. Because the top element is one, the condition is satisfied when $n = 1$. Now suppose the condition holds for some n. Applying the summation rules for Devlin's triangles and Pascal's Triangle, and defining $\binom{n}{-1}$ and $\binom{n}{+1}$ to equal zero, we can rewrite the summation as:

$$\sum_{k=0}^{n} \binom{n}{k} \tilde{p}(n, k) = \sum_{k=0}^{n} \binom{n}{k} \left[\tilde{p}(n+1, k) + \tilde{p}(n+1, k+1) \right]$$

$$= \sum_{k=0}^{n+1} \left[\binom{n}{k-1} + \binom{n}{k} \right] \tilde{p}(n+1, k) = \sum_{k=0}^{n} \binom{n+1}{k} \tilde{p}(n+1, k)$$

So the condition must hold for $n + 1$, and by induction applies throughout.

A BINOMIAL EXAMPLE

Suppose n Bernoulli variables are independent with probability μ of success. Then the probability of a given permutation of k successes and $n - k$ failures equals the product of the individual probabilities, so that $p(n, k) = \mu^k (1 - \mu)^{n-k}$. The summation rule is readily checked:

$$p(n+1, k) + p(n+1, k+1) = \mu^k (1 - \mu)^{n+1-k} + \mu^{k+1} (1 - \mu)^{n-k}$$

$$= (1 - \mu + \mu) \mu^k (1 - \mu)^{n-k} = \mu^k (1 - \mu)^{n-k} = p(n, k)$$

It follows that, given independence, there is probability $\binom{n}{k} \mu^k (1 - \mu)^{n-k}$ of achieving a total of k successes in n tries, for any integer k between 0 and n inclusive. This set of probabilities is known as a binomial distribution of order n.

TOP-DOWN SOLUTIONS TO DEVLIN'S TRIANGLES

A Devlin's triangle must have nonnegative elements satisfying various equality and inequality constraints. All constraints are linear, while tail risk is linear in the probabilities. It follows that the search for extreme solutions for tail risk boils down to a linear programming problem.

At first glance, the problem looks unwieldy for any large n-variate triangle, as the total number of variables and constraints exceeds n^2. Fortunately, major simplifications are possible. Given all the elements on one row and one element on the next, the rest of the next row can be generated using the summation rule. Each extra row allows exactly one extra degree of freedom, which we can identify with the first element $p(m,0)$.

Each predetermined element uses up one degree of freedom. The top element must be one to reflect the probability of a whole, $p(1,0)$ is predetermined if the mean is specified, and $p(2,0)$ is predetermined if the mean and correlation are specified. Hence, for an n-variate Bernoulli game with mean and correlation specified, $n-2$ variables can vary freely subject to the nonnegativity constraints. As for the inequality constraints, we need simply check that none of the $n+1$ elements on the bottom row are negative. If not, none of the higher elements will be negative either.

This "top-down" solution method has a lot of intuitive appeal. In particular, it highlights the dual impact of adding an extra row: one extra choice variable versus extra inequality constraints on the preceding row. As in any linear programming problem, optimization is straightforward once the algorithm is seeded with a feasible solution. We have already seen a feasible solution for uncorrelated games, namely the binomial solution corresponding to independence. In a later chapter, Devlin will present a feasible solution for correlated games.

MOMENT-MATCHING SOLUTIONS

A second method builds Devlin's triangles from the bottom up. Since Bernoulli variables sum to k if and only if there are exactly k successes in some order, the $n+1$st row defines the entire distribution of the sum of n variables. Furthermore, each row uniquely defines the row above it through the summation rule. To ensure feasibility, we need to check that the bottom row is nonnegative and that the probability measure of the whole (which can be viewed as its 0th-order moment) is one. In addition, the bottom row must be consistent with the common individual mean μ and common correlation ρ implied by the third row. Applying formulas derived in the previous chapter, the first and second moments on the bottom row must equal $n\mu$ and $n^2\mu^2 + [(1-\rho)n + \rho n^2]\mu(1-\mu)$ respectively.

This gives us $n+1$ choice variables, $n+1$ nonnegativity constraints and three equality constraints on moments. The constraints on the measure and the first moment are linear and easily handled. However, the constraint on the second moment is quadratic. Without further adjustment we cannot apply linear programming.

Still, the moment-matching method has some advantages over the top-down method. By eliminating the intermediate rows, it makes the problem easier to set up and less likely to suffer from rounding errors in large arrays. Also, if the optimal solution is known to contain only two positive elements, the moment-matching method will provide a simple algebraic solution.

HYBRID SOLUTIONS

A third solution method is a hybrid of the first two methods. Like the moment-matching method, it places all choice variables on the last row. Like the top-down method, it uses only linear constraints, and therefore can be solved using linear programming.

The hybrid method provides linear formulas for three elements on the last row in terms of the other $n - 2$ elements. Those formulas guarantee that the probability of the whole is one and that the first and second moments match their predetermined values. One then searches among solutions that satisfy the nonnegativity constraints.

Geometrically, the hybrid method rests on the insight that slicing diagonal edges off Devlin's triangle leaves behind sub-triangles that satisfy all the requirements of a Devlin's triangle except the unit total measure. In probability terms, this just means that if the outcomes of m out of the n Bernoulli variables are known, the remaining game is like a Bernoulli game in $n - m$ variables.

Slices off Devlin's triangle

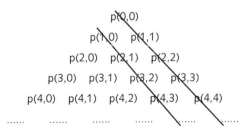

In particular, the top and bottom row elements of one of these sub-triangles satisfy a linear equation that is independent of the excised elements. The weights depend only on the size of the row and the position of the element on the row. For example, as is evident in the illustration above, $p(4,0) + 2 \cdot p(4,1) + p(4,2) = p(2,0)$ just as $p(2,0) + 2 \cdot p(2,1) + p(2,2) = p(0,0)$. More generally, for any integers $i < j < n$,

$$\sum_{k=0}^{n-j} \binom{n-j}{k} p(n, k+i) = p(j, i)$$

Hence, given a predetermined value for $p(2,0)$ and candidate values $\tilde{p}(n,k)$ for the first $n-2$ elements on the last row, we can use the preceding equation to solve for the $n-1$st element $\tilde{p}(n, n-2)$. We can then use the predetermined value for $p(1,0)$ together with the values of the first $n-1$ elements on the last row to solve the nth element $\tilde{p}(n, n-1)$. Finally we use the predetermined value one for $p(0,0)$ and the values for the first n elements on the last row to solve for the last element $\tilde{p}(n,n)$. The solution is feasible if and only if no $\tilde{p}(n,k)$ is negative.

To reduce the number of calculations and the associated risk of rounding errors, it is easier to deal with candidate values $\tilde{P}(n,k) \equiv \binom{n}{k} \tilde{p}(n,k)$ for the total probability of k successes out of n tries. In that case, the relevant formulas work out to:

$$\tilde{P}(n, n-2) = \frac{n(n-1)}{2} p(2,0) - \sum_{k=0}^{n-3} \frac{(n-k)(n-k-1)}{2} \tilde{P}(n,k)$$

$$\tilde{P}(n, n-1) = n \cdot p(1,0) - \sum_{k=0}^{n-2} (n-k) \tilde{P}(n,k)$$

$$\tilde{P}(n,n) = 1 - \sum_{k=0}^{n-1} \tilde{P}(n,k)$$

3 | Amazing Tails of Risk

A cheerfully bleary-eyed Devlin strode confidently into Conway's office the next morning carrying a bundle of printouts. As he entered he tripped on a doorstop, sending the printouts flying. Conway looked up from his newspaper. "Oh, it's you, Devlin. I wouldn't have guessed. What have you brought?"

"Amazing tails. The Loch Ness monster would be jealous." Devlin gathered up the printouts and handed one to Conway. "Here, take a look at these histograms. Each of them represents an unbiased, uncorrelated, Bernoulli game with 16 exchangeable variables. In every case the mean number of total successes is 8 and the standard deviation 2."

Unbiased, uncorrelated 16-variable Bernoulli games

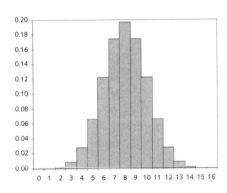 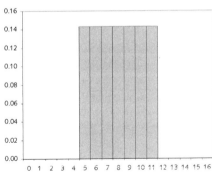

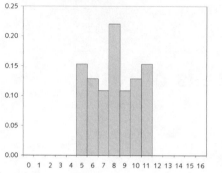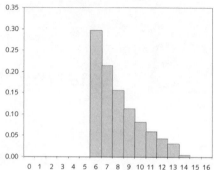

Horizontal axis indicates number of successes. Vertical axis indicates associated probability. Note that vertical scales differ across charts.

Conway scanned the charts "Interesting. The chart on the upper left is the bell I used to expect. The upper right chart is rectangular. The lower right chart looks like an exponential distribution shifted to the right. I don't know what to call the lower left chart. A cathedral? Mmm, I'm not sure how appropriate that is inside Megabucks, unless it's consecrated to Mammon. But let's move on. Are these your extreme cases?"

"The first one is. It represents the standard binomial distribution, which applies when variables are completely independent. However, the other cases are not extreme. I just chose them because they're interesting."

"So what do the extreme cases look like?"

"They vary with the definition of the tail and whether the goal is maximization or minimization. However, all of them concentrate their probability mass on just two or three points. One of those points lies at the threshold. A second point lies on the other side of the mean from the threshold, and is less than one standard deviation away from the mean if and only if the threshold is more than one standard deviation away from the mean."

"And the third point?"

"The third point, if there is one, usually adjoins the second point, as if the optimizing solution aimed to concentrate the two probability masses at an intermediate fraction. But sometimes the second and third points mark the two poles of total success or total failure."

Conway tried to picture the various shapes of extreme distributions but could not keep them straight. "I could follow this more easily if you would show me a few examples."

"I'll do you even better. Here are eight histograms that, with the help of a mirror, collectively indicate all possible extreme tail risks given 16 exchangeable Bernoulli variables and a 50% probability of success. To facilitate comparison, I have overlaid each histogram with a line graph for the binomial benchmark."

Probability distributions yielding extreme tails

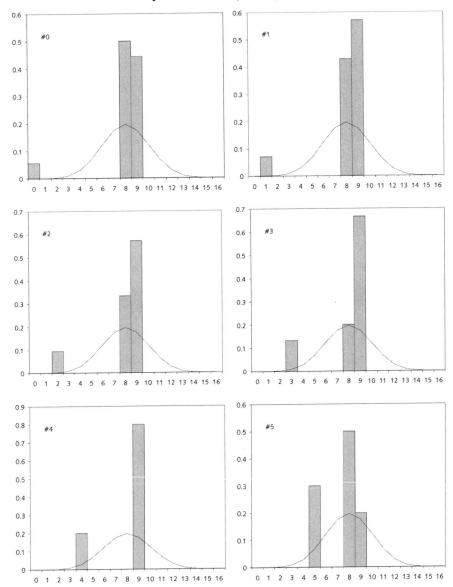

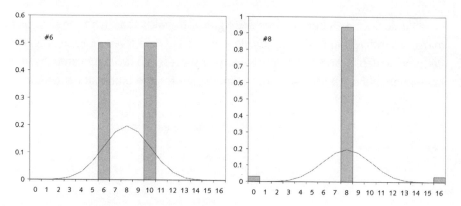

Outcomes constrained to be integers between 0 and 16 with mean 8 and standard deviation 2. Line graph represents binomial distribution.

"What is the mirror for? And why did you skip over #7 in your numbering?"

"When the probability of success is 50%, the mirror image of a feasible distribution – that is, the distribution that switches the probabilities of successes with the probabilities of failures – is also feasible. So if a distribution gives an extreme lower tail, the mirror image gives an extreme upper tail. Granted, distributions #6 and #8 are symmetric, so their mirror images are redundant. And I left out #7 because it happens to be the mirror image of #4. But here it is in case you're interested."

Mirror image distributions

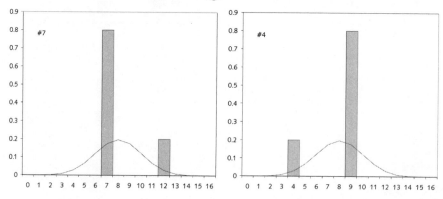

"I get it. Distribution #K indicates the maximum probability of at most K successes and its mirror image gives the maximum probability of at least $16 - K$ successes. In addition, distribution #4 indicates the maximum probability of at least 9 successes, while its mirror image indicates the maximum probability of at most 7 successes."

"Precisely. We can also read off minimum tails from these distributions. Care to give it a try?"

Conway scanned the charts again. "Let me see. Any of the first six distributions indicate that the probability of 10 or more successes can be zero, while their mirror images indicate that the probability of 6 or fewer successes can be zero. Distribution #8 indicates the minimum probability of 7 or fewer successes or of 9 or more successes. Distribution #4 indicates the minimum probability of at most 8 successes, while its mirror image indicates the minimum probability of at least 8 successes."

"Right again." Devlin handed Conway another sheet. "Here is a table I prepared summarizing the upper and lower bounds. To help compare these bounds with conventional wisdom, the table also measures the number of successes in terms of standard deviations from the mean and includes the corresponding binomial probabilities."

Probability bounds for sums of 16 unbiased, uncorrelated Bernoulli variables

Number of successes	Standard deviations from mean	Minimum probability	Maximum probability	Probability if independent
0	−4.0	0	0.056	0.00002
1	−3.5	0	0.071	0.0003
2	−3.0	0	0.095	0.002
3	−2.5	0	0.133	0.011
4	−2.0	0	0.200	0.038
5	−1.5	0	0.300	0.105
6	−1.0	0	0.500	0.227
7	−0.5	0.031	0.800	0.402
8	0	0.200	0.969	0.598

"That's a big range. Are all intermediate values feasible?"

"Yes. Any mixture of feasible distributions is feasible, because it will have the same first two moments as its components. But a mixture will have event probabilities that are intermediate to the distributions being mixed. By adjusting the weights in a mixture of distributions representing highest and lowest tail risks, we can generate any intermediate value."

"How do the risk bounds change when you increase the number of variables?"

"Remarkably little, provided we measure risk in terms of standard deviations. Let me use the label "s-tail" to describe the set of outcomes falling s or more standard deviations below the mean. For any positive s, the minimum risk of an s-tail converges to zero as the number of variables increases, while the maximum risk converges to $\dfrac{1}{s^2 + 1}$ from below."

"Why isn't it the same for negative s?"

"It is if you measure the tails properly, that is, outward for the mean. Mathematically it's easier to work with tails defined the way I did, always stretching to the left. In that case, an s-tail passes through the mean when s is negative. I call it improper because its complement is a proper tail. Obviously, no distribution can generate a zero chance of falling at or below its mean."

"I think I see. The maximum risk for an improper tail is 1 less the minimum risk for the complementary proper tail. Similarly, the minimum risk is 1 less the maximum risk for the complement. Hence the risk bounds run from $\dfrac{s^2}{s^2 + 1}$ to 1 when s is negative."

"That's nearly right. The complement of a proper upper tail doesn't include the threshold itself. So you need to adjust for that. But since improper tails don't directly interest us, we don't have to worry about this except in proofs."

Conway was pleased. *At last some good news. The fewer the complications, the better.* "How well do these asymptotic risk bounds approximate the bounds in smaller samples?"

"Fairly well. The problem is integer constraints rather than laws of large numbers. Most of the bounds in the preceding chart for 16 Bernoulli variables either reach the limits or come respectably close.

"What happens if success is more or less likely than failure?"

"Then the mean changes and the standard deviation shrinks relative to the unbiased case. That shifts the physical threshold of an s-tail. But as long as a positive s-tail includes feasible outcomes, its limiting probability bounds continue to stretch from 0 to $\dfrac{1}{s^2 + 1}$."

"Up to 4% probability of a 5 standard deviation event? Up to 1%

probability of a 10 standard deviation event? That is far beyond anything we conventionally assume."

"It sure is." Devlin laid another chart on the table. "The solid area in this chart depicts the feasible tail risks for s in the range of 2 to 10 standard deviations. The dark line depicts the tail risks assuming the variables are independent."

Feasilble tail risks for Bernoulli sums

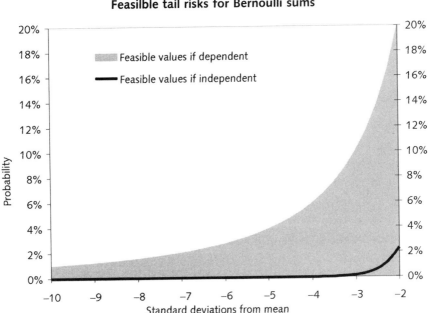

Assumes large finite number of exchangeable, uncorrelated variables.

"So this chart strongly suggests that if we use the standard mean-variance approximations, we are far more likely to overestimate tail risk than to underestimate it," commented Conway. "That does indeed tend to happen in practice. But I always wondered why."

"So did I. Granted, the values in the feasible range may not even be close to equally likely. Perhaps in practice they cluster near the bottom. But conventional analysis doesn't demonstrate that. It simply ignores the great bulk of the range."

Just then Conway's secretary spoke on the intercom. "Sorry to interrupt, Conway, but you need to get to the boardroom for the meeting of the Risk Oversight Committee."

"Thank you, Karen. I am on my way. Devlin, excuse me. Let's continue when I get back."

While Conway attends his meeting, I will confirm Devlin's claim about the feasible range for uncorrelated variables. Before we plunge in, let me offer a warning and a reassurance. Dealing with integer constraints will force some unpleasant mathematical contortions in the form of "nearly two-point" solutions. Fortunately, the analysis verifies that the integer constraints don't usually matter much, so in most cases you can ignore them.

PRELIMINARIES

Let there be n exchangeable, uncorrelated Bernoulli variables with common mean μ. As we have seen, the sum will have mean $\mu_{SUM} = n\mu$ and variance $\sigma^2_{SUM} = n\mu(1 - \mu)$. I will assume the variables are not degenerate, so that the variance is positive and strictly increasing in n.

The minimum feasible value for the sum is 0, which lies $\sqrt{\dfrac{\mu}{n(1 - \mu)}}$ standard deviations below the mean. The maximum feasible value for the sum is n, which lies $\sqrt{\dfrac{n(1 - \mu)}{\mu}}$ standard deviations above the mean. These values grow without bound with $\sqrt{n}$.

I will also adopt Devlin's shorthand notation of "s-tail" for events lying s standard deviations or more below the mean. An s-tail is proper for positive s and improper (i.e., encompasses the mean) for negative s.

TWO-POINT DISTRIBUTIONS

Consider a two-point distribution attaching probability q to a point s standard deviations below the mean, and probability $q' = 1 - q$ to a point s' standard deviations below the mean (that is, $-s'$ standard deviations above the mean). The mean and variance of standardized random variables are 0 and 1 respectively, so q, s, and s' must jointly satisfy the constraints:

$$qs + (1 - q)s' = 0$$
$$qs^2 + (1 - q)s'^2 = 1$$

This has solution:

$$s' = -\frac{1}{s}; \quad q = \frac{1}{s^2 + 1}$$

To confirm the symmetry of the solution, note that:

$$1 - q = \frac{s^2}{1 + s^2} = \frac{1}{s^{-2} + 1} = \frac{1}{s'^2 + 1} = q'$$

RISK-FREE TAILS

Whenever the two-point distribution described above applies, losses will not exceed s standard deviations. Therefore, if we can find a feasible two-point distribution for s positive but arbitrarily close to zero, we will know that the minimum proper tail risk is zero.

Let s be chosen so that $\mu_{SUM} - s\sigma_{SUM}$ equals the highest integer less than μ_{SUM}. For n sufficiently large, this can imply an arbitrarily small positive value for s, while keeping the second point $\mu_{SUM} - s'\sigma_{SUM}$ less than or equal to n. Moreover, by judiciously choosing n, we can ensure that the second point will be an integer or extremely close to an integer.

For example, suppose $\sqrt{\dfrac{1 - \mu}{\mu}}$ equals a rational fraction $\dfrac{k}{j}$, where k and j are both integers. Then if $n = i^2(j^2 + k^2)^2$ for some integer i, $\mu_{SUM} = i^2 j^2 (j^2 + k^2)$, $\sigma_{SUM} = ijk$, and $\mu_{SUM} - s'\sigma_{SUM} = i^2 j^2 (j^2 + 2k^2)$ will all be integers, while $s = 1/ijk$ will be arbitrarily tiny for i sufficiently large.

Intuitively, it is clear that the extreme values will be continuous in μ, except possibly for the end points, so the results for rational values of $\sqrt{\dfrac{1 - \mu}{\mu}}$ suffice to characterize the rest. Hence, given enough uncorrelated exchangeable Bernoulli variables, proper tail risk can be as low as zero.

RISKIEST TAILS

The previous results also provide insight about the maximum risk of an s-tail. For a large number of uncorrelated exchangeable Bernoulli variables, the least upper bound cannot be significantly less than $\frac{1}{s^2+1}$.

Could the upper bound be higher? No. Intuitively, extra variance makes it easier to add more probability mass to the tail without changing the overall mean. To economize on variance with a proper tail, add all the mass to the threshold, since that lies closest to the mean. Moreover, for a given probability mass in the tail, variance is best economized by placing the rest of the mass at a single point, if this is feasible.

NEARLY TWO-POINT SOLUTIONS FOR MINIMAL RISK

I will now demonstrate the previous points more rigorously, relying on a "nearly two-point" solution. A nearly two-point solution attaches some probability mass to a point at or near the threshold s and the rest on two points that lie next to each other.

Let $D \equiv \{D_k\}$ denote the class of two-point distributions with mean μ_{SUM} that attach positive probability to an s standard deviation shortfall and some other point $k > \mu_{SUM}$. Note that $Var[D_k]$ is increasing in k. If n is sufficiently large, $Var[D_k]$ will be less than σ^2_{SUM} for small k and greater than σ^2_{SUM} for large k, implying a unique point j for which $Var[D_j] \leq \sigma^2_{SUM} < Var[D_{j+1}]$. Some mixture of D_j and D_{j+1} will then have a mean of μ_{SUM} and a variance of σ^2_{SUM}, with no risk of more than s standard deviation loss.

NEARLY TWO-POINT SOLUTIONS FOR MAXIMAL RISK

If we measure j and $j+1$ in standard deviation terms as s' and s'' respectively, we see first that $s'' - s' = -1/\sigma_{SUM}$. Denoting the respective probabilities by q, q', and q'', the mean and variance constraints become:

$$qs + q's' + q''\left(s' - \frac{1}{\sigma_{SUM}}\right) = 0$$

$$qs^2 + q's'^2 + q''\left(s' - \frac{1}{\sigma_{SUM}}\right) = 1$$

which are distinctly messier than in the pure two-point case. Indeed, there is no general closed-form solution. Fortunately, we can appreciate the structure of the solution without it.

Defining $r \equiv \dfrac{q'}{1-q}$, $\hat{s} \equiv s' - \dfrac{1-r}{\sigma_{SUM}}$ and $\epsilon \equiv \dfrac{r(1-r)(1-q)}{\sigma^2_{SUM}}$, the mean and variance constraints can be simplified to:

$$qs + (1-q)\hat{s} = 0$$
$$qs^2 + (1-q)\hat{s}^2 = 1 - \epsilon$$

which more closely resembles the two-point case. The modification is easy to interpret statistically. The solution tries to balance the probability weight on s with weight on a second point $\hat{s}$. However, $\hat{s}$ does not correspond to an integer, so the solution puts weight on s' and s'' as a proxy. This creates some extra variance ϵ that has to be "financed" out of the overall standardized variance 1, leaving only $1 - \epsilon$ free for other uses.

Making the additional substitution $\tilde{s} = \dfrac{s}{\sqrt{1-\epsilon}}$ and $\tilde{s}' = \dfrac{\hat{s}}{\sqrt{1-\epsilon}}$, the mean and variance constraints can be further simplified to:

$$q\tilde{s} + (1-q)\tilde{s}' = 0$$
$$q\tilde{s}^2 + (1-q)\tilde{s}'^2 = 1$$

which now matches the equations for the two-point case apart from the tildes. It follows that:

$$s' = \frac{\sqrt{1-\epsilon}}{\tilde{s}} + \frac{1-r}{\sigma_{SUM}} = \frac{1-\epsilon}{s} + \frac{1-r}{\sigma_{SUM}}$$

$$q = \frac{1}{\tilde{s}^2 + 1} = \frac{1-\epsilon}{s^2 + 1 - \epsilon}$$

This is an implicit solution rather than explicit, since ϵ depends on q. Nevertheless, it is readily used to bound q. For a given q, ϵ is at least zero and attains a maximum $\dfrac{1-q}{4\sigma^2_{SUM}}$ at $r = \frac{1}{2}$. It follows that:

$$\frac{1}{s^2+1} \geq q > \frac{1-\epsilon}{s^2+1} \geq \frac{1}{s^2+1} \cdot \left(1 - \frac{1-q}{4\sigma^2_{SUM}}\right) > \frac{1}{s^2+1} \cdot \left(1 - \frac{1}{4\sigma^2_{SUM}}\right)$$

Hence, while q never exceeds $\dfrac{1}{s^2+1}$, it gets vanishingly close when n gets sufficiently large.

IMPROPER TAILS

Improper lower tails are best viewed as complements of proper upper tails. To minimize an improper lower tail, maximize the proper upper tail. Since the arguments about lower and upper tails are symmetric, the minimum probability for an improper s-tail approaches $1 - \dfrac{1}{s^2 + 1} = \dfrac{s^2}{s^2 + 1}$ when n is large. Similarly, the maximum probability for an improper s-tail approaches 1 when n is large.

CAVEATS

While integer constraints tend to bite more when n is small, that doesn't always happen. For example, we saw already that with sums of 16 uncorrelated, unbiased, exchangeable Bernoulli variables, pure two-point solutions apply for thresholds of 4, 6, 7, 9, 10, and 12, which represent ± 2, ± 1, and ± 0.5 standard deviations. In this case, the probabilities of upper or lower 2-tails, 1-tails, and 0.5-tails can attain the asymptotic upper bound despite the moderate value of n.

A second kind of problem arises when n and a proper s are sufficiently small that the second point $s' = -1/s$ of a two-point distribution would imply a negative number of successes or failures. In that case neither a pure two-point solution nor a nearly two-point solution will be feasible. I will defer further discussion until the next chapter, which incorporates nonzero correlation as well as small n.

4 | More Amazing Tails

Conway looked bedraggled when he returned from the risk meeting. He slumped into his chair. "I wish I hadn't gone," he told Devlin. "We were reviewing the capital provisions for credit risk. The regulators want us to cover 100% of the losses 99% of the time, and we were debating whether the current coverage of losses up to 3 standard deviations from the mean is too cautious or not cautious enough. They asked for any statistical insights I might offer."

"Good thing we met beforehand."

I wish we hadn't. Conway was silent a moment. "Perhaps. Anyway, based on our conversations, I told them the correct standard deviation limit could lie as low as 2 or as high as 5."

"That's 0 and 10 you mean. For uncorrelated Bernoulli variables, the lower limit is 0 and the upper limit is 9.95."

Go ahead. Spout statistics. As if that does any good. "I know that," said Conway, "but I couldn't bring myself to tell them. Just saying 5 was bad enough. Without other changes, we would have to slash risk exposures by 40%. The head of credit trading went ballistic. It took all the eloquence I could muster to change his mind."

"You changed his mind about the limits for 99% confidence? Excellent."

"No, I changed his mind about whether to demand my dismissal. I assured him that these were just theoretical possibilities, and that I would not propose any radical changes without far more reflection and back-testing."

Devlin felt badly. He hadn't meant to get Conway into trouble. "What do you suggest we do?"

Conway gazed out the window. He started thinking about what might have been and then realized it was useless. Once you've got the tiger by the tail, it's more dangerous to let go than to hold on. "More reflection."

"You want to reflect on whether to halt our investigation?" Devlin was dismayed. He had been praying this wouldn't happen. Not that he could blame Conway, really ...

"I wish that is what I meant, but it isn't. I want to know what happens to tail risk when variables are correlated. How much wider can the feasible range get?"

Devlin smiled. He still had a partner. "The range can't get much wider. Chebyshev's inequality sets an upper bound of $1/s^2$ for the probability of falling s or more standard deviations from the mean. That's the probability of both the s-tail and its mirror image upper tail taken together. For the lower or upper tail alone, the probability can't get any higher than $\dfrac{1}{s^2 + 1}$."

"So correlation leaves tail risk unaffected. Why didn't you say that in the first place, Devlin?"

"Because it's only partly true. It's true if we aggregate over all possible non-degenerate means. However, for any particular mean, nonzero correlation narrows the feasible range relative to zero correlation."

"Narrows it? That's strange. Don't the tails tend to grow as the correlation rises?"

"In absolute terms, yes. When measured in standard deviations, no. A positive correlation caps the number s of standard deviations that extreme outliers can represent. It can also force you to attach probability to both very high and very low sums. For some s, two-point and nearly two-point distributions remain feasible. There you get the full 0 to $\dfrac{1}{s^2 + 1}$ range for proper tails and $\dfrac{s^2}{s^2 + 1}$ to 1 range for improper tails. However, for s close to zero, the extreme distributions end up looking like distribution #8 in the charts I showed you for 16 variables."

"You mean the one where there's positive weight at each end as well as at the threshold?"

"That's the one. I call that kind of distribution 'tripolar'. The weight at the lower end makes the minimum risk strictly positive and forces more weight outside the tail to offset it. That crimps the lower and upper bounds. But when a two-point or nearly two-point distribution isn't feasible, tripolar is the best you can do."

"How much difference does that make?"

"That depends on other parameters. Unless the mean or correlation is high, you don't have to worry about it, at least not for the kind of tails you're likely to be interested in. For example, if you care only about shortfalls of at least two standard deviations, then tripolar distributions don't affect the feasible range unless the mean is at least 0.8. However, if the mean and correlation are both high, the lower and upper bounds tighten a lot. Have a look at this chart for a moment. It depicts the feasible tail risks when the mean and correlation are both 0.9."

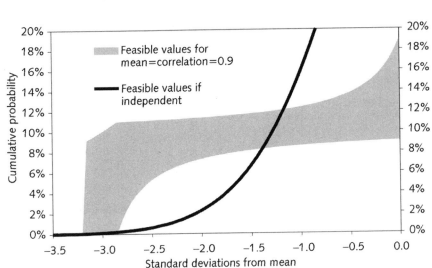

Assumes large finite number of exchangeable Bernoulli variables.

Conway studied it for a moment, and then frowned. "How on earth did you generate that, Devlin?"

"I looked at the two- or three-point distributions that represented the extreme solutions given the various feasibility constraints. I suggest we not get bogged down in the math right now but focus on the implications. What do you find most striking about this chart, apart from the odd shape of the feasible range itself?"

"The divergence between the feasible range and the estimates using the standard mean-variance methodology. For example, the odds of a 2.5-tail range from 5% to 11%, versus less than 1% if the sum were composed of independent variables."

"That's what struck me too. Except for two short intervals, the mean-variance approximation lies completely outside the feasible range."

"How common is that?"

"Not very. Both the mean and the correlation need to be high."

"Good. Not everything I thought I knew is completely wrong. But I'm still puzzled by your claim that the feasible range is narrower for any nonzero correlation than for zero correlation. If positive correlation restricts the range, shouldn't negative correlation widen it?"

"For any particular mean and feasible number of variables, it does. However, geometry caps the maximum number of variables with a common negative correlation. Otherwise the sums would have negative variance. And with a limited number of variables, the integer constraints will bite more heavily into the ranges for high standard deviation events."

Something troubled Conway. He pulled out Devlin's histograms for extreme 16-variable tails and studied them intently. After a few minutes he spoke. "These extreme distributions are awfully implausible. Or have you come up with a 16-variable illustration to rival 'no odd tails in triples'?"

Devlin grinned. "How about this explanation for distribution #4? The trading desk holds binary options on 16 computer network companies. With 80% probability, nine companies will be selected to define the new industry standard. Otherwise, four companies will be selected to define the new standard. Any combination of nine companies is equally likely, and the same is true for any combination of four companies."

"So you agree it is implausible. Moreover, just like in the 'no odd tails in triples' scenario, your underlying variables cannot be viewed as random samples from any larger exchangeable set. What happens if you exclude probability triangles that can't be extended an extra row?"

"It narrows the bounds. We've already seen that. The more rows we add to my triangles, the more we narrow the bounds at lower levels."

Conway was onto something. "Now you're talking. And does adding rows narrow the bounds a lot or only a little?"

"I can't tell you off the cuff. I would need some time to work on it."

"Then take the time. I want to know what happens to the bounds when you include only distributions that can be extended by a lot of rows. For example, what is the feasible range for the distribution of the sum of 16 variables drawn from a set of 32 exchangeable variables?"

"Why do you want to know that? At the bottom row, with variables taken 32 at a time, we'll still have the wide feasible range I've just described for tail risks. So why limit yourself to looking at only averages for equally weighted 16-variable subsets?"

"Look, Devlin, I'm not saying your results are uninteresting or useless. They show what can happen in particular cases, even when assets are exchangeable and uncorrelated. Still, I believe that extendable distributions better symbolize the generic case. For example, suppose the equity derivatives desk had held many different types of fair, uncorrelated binary options, and none of us knew of any particular event tying them together. No imminent choice of a networking standard or anything like it. How would you propose to model that?"

"I suppose we should regard the binary options as interchangeable not only with each other, but also with any other fair, uncorrelated binary options. In the limit we might even regard them as coming from an infinite collection of exchangeable Bernoulli variables."

"Good. So will you work on it?"

"I'll try. But I'll have to find some new techniques. How can I add an infinite number of rows to my triangles?"

"I'm sure you'll crack it, maestro." *At least I hope so.*

While Devlin puzzles over infinity, I will verify his claims about tail risks of sums of correlated, finitely exchangeable Bernoulli variables. I will show that two-point, nearly two-point, and tripolar distributions define the feasible range for tail risk. Then I will calculate the values that those ranges imply.

Again a warning and a reassurance. Despite my best efforts, the calculations are even messier than the preceding chapter's. Fortunately, apart from the extreme 0 to $\dfrac{1}{s^2 + 1}$ range, you don't need to remember any specific values. Read for the intuition and let the rest slide.

RELATION TO CHEBYSHEV'S INEQUALITY

Chebyshev's inequality says that the probability of positive or negative s-tails never exceeds $1/s^2$. It is simply proved. Letting z denote the outcome measured in standard deviations below the mean and $p(z)$ its probability, note that:

$$\sum_{|z|\geq s} p(z) \leq \sum_{|z|\geq s} \frac{z^2}{s^2} p(z) = \frac{1}{s^2} \sum_{|z|\geq s} z^2 p(z) \leq \frac{1}{s^2} \sum_{z=-\infty}^{\infty} z^2 p(z) = \frac{1}{s^2}$$

where the last step follows from the definition of the standard deviation. The following distribution meets the bounds exactly: $p(s) = p(-s) = \frac{1}{2s^2}$; $p(0) = 1 - \frac{1}{s^2}$. For all other distributions the inequality is strict.

A similar approach can be used to bound the risk of a single s-tail. Note that:

$$E\left[\left(z+\frac{1}{s}\right)^2\right] \geq Pr\{z \geq s\} \cdot \min_{z\geq s}\left(z+\frac{1}{s}\right)^2 = Pr\{z \geq s\} \cdot \left(s+\frac{1}{s}\right)^2$$

Since the first two moments of z are zero and one respectively, the preceding inequality can be simplified to:

$$\frac{s^2+1}{s^2} \geq Pr\{z \geq s\} \cdot \left(\frac{s^2+1}{s}\right)^2 \rightarrow Pr\{z \geq s\} \leq \frac{1}{s^2+1}$$

Hence there is no way to exceed the bounds we derived earlier for uncorrelated Bernoulli sums. Indeed the bounds may be significantly tighter, if a two-point distribution on s and $-1/s$ is not feasible or nearly feasible.

CONSTRAINED OPTIMIZATION

For a given n, the feasible range is defined by the maximum and minimum tail risks for $n+1$-point distributions of a given mean and variance. Hence one way to determine the range is to set up a constrained optimization and apply standard solution techniques. Define the lower tail by the maximum number T of successes that still qualifies as a tail event. (The T corresponds to s in the s-tail, but measured in absolute terms rather than standard deviations.) Denote by I_T an indicator variable taking the value 1 in the tail and 0 outside it, and by p_k the probability of exactly k successes. Then the probability of a tail event, which is the objective function we want to maximize or minimize, can be written as:

$$Pr\{k \leq T\} \equiv \sum_{k=0}^{T} p_k \equiv \sum_{k=0}^{n} p_k I_T(k)$$

The three equality constraints on the total probability measure, the mean and the second moment are:

$$\sum_{k=0}^{n} p_k = 1 \quad ; \quad \sum_{k=0}^{n} p_k k = \mu_{SUM} \quad ; \quad \sum_{k=0}^{n} p_k k^2 = \mu_{SUM}^2 + \sigma_{SUM}^2$$

There are also $n + 1$ nonnegativity constraints on the probabilities:

$$p_k \geq 0 \quad \text{for} \quad k = 0, 1, 2, \ldots, n$$

Next form a weighted sum, called a Lagrangean, of the objective and the constraints:

$$\Lambda = \sum_{k=0}^{n} p_k I_T(k) + \tau_0 \left(\sum_{k=0}^{n} p_k - 1 \right) + \tau_1 \left(\sum_{k=0}^{n} p_k k - \mu_{SUM} \right)$$

$$+ \tau_2 \left(\sum_{k=0}^{n} p_k k^2 - \mu_{SUM}^2 - \sigma_{SUM}^2 \right) + \sum_{k=0}^{n} \nu_k p_k$$

The various τ and ν weights are called Lagrangean multipliers. Lagrangean multipliers have the economic interpretation of shadow prices. At the optimum, they measure the "opportunity cost" or reduction in the objective function from marginally tightening the constraint.

KUHN-TUCKER CONDITIONS

According to the Kuhn–Tucker theorem, the partial derivative of the Lagrangean with respect to each choice variable must equal zero at the constrained optimum. Moreover, each multiplier ν on an inequality must satisfy the so-called "complementary slackness" condition, which has two elements. First, ν must be zero if its associated inequality is not strictly binding – that is, not met with equality. Second, the sign of a nonzero ν must penalize the Lagrangean if the associated inequality is violated.

These necessary conditions for a solution are known collectively as the Kuhn–Tucker conditions. The Kuhn–Tucker conditions for our problem are the three moment-matching constraints plus, for all integers k between 0 and n:

$$0 = \frac{\partial H}{\partial p_k} = I_T(k) + \tau_0 + \tau_1 k + \tau_2 k^2 + \nu_k$$

$$\nu_k p_k = 0 \quad \nu_k \leq 0 \quad \text{for minimization}$$

$$\nu_k p_k = 0 \quad \nu_k \geq 0 \quad \text{for maximization}$$

OPTIMAL DISTRIBUTIONS FOR MAXIMIZATION

I will now use the Kuhn–Tucker conditions to characterize the forms of optimal distributions. I begin with maximization. The necessary conditions on the multipliers that apply for every feasible k can be rewritten as:

$$-\tau_0 - \tau_1 k - \tau_2 k^2 \equiv Q(k) \begin{cases} = 1 & \text{if } p_k > 0 \text{ and } 0 \leq k \leq T \\ \geq 1 & \text{if } p_k = 0 \text{ and } 0 \leq k \leq T \\ = 0 & \text{if } p_k > 0 \text{ and } T < k \leq n \\ \geq 0 & \text{if } p_k = 0 \text{ and } T < k \leq n \end{cases}$$

Note that Q is a quadratic function confined in a certain space, and must touch the edge of that space in at least two places to generate a non-degenerate distribution. If you take out a pen and scratch paper, you can quickly satisfy yourself that there are no other ways to achieve this than the three ways I chart below. (While it is not hard to demonstrate this rigorously, the proof is too soporific to warrant inclusion here.)

Feasible shapes for Q in maximization

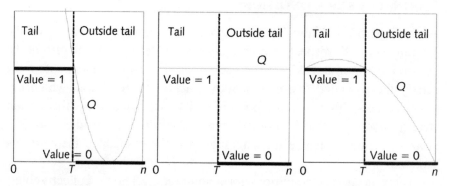

The graph on the left corresponds to a two-point or nearly two-point distribution. This will be feasible when the threshold lies well below the mean μ_{SUM}. Since Q is convex, τ_2 must be negative, so that a higher variance would allow more probability weight on T.

The graph in the middle places all the probability weight in the tail. It is feasible only if the mean exceeds T, in which case one particular feasible distribution places all its weight on T and one other point or pair of neighboring points. Since Q is flat, τ_2 must be zero, which means that marginally changing the variance can't make the tail any bigger.

The graph on the right corresponds to a tripolar distribution. This applies when T lies below the mean but close to it. Since Q is concave, a higher variance forces more probability weight out of T toward the two extremes, shrinking the tail as a whole.

OPTIMAL DISTRIBUTIONS FOR MINIMIZATION

Maximizing the lower tail probability $Pr\{k \leq T\}$ is equivalent to minimizing the probability $Pr\{k \geq T + 1\}$ of the complementary upper tail. Furthermore, an upper tail is equivalent to a lower tail with the definitions of failure and success switched. So the results for maximization apply for minimization too, subject to one small but crucial change: we should apply probability mass just inside the tail at T rather than just outside at $T + 1$. We wind up with three types of solutions:

- **T low:** attach positive probability only to T and to one higher point or two neighboring higher points. If the variance shrinks, the tail weight shrinks.
- **T near μ_{SUM}:** attach positive probability only to 0, T, and n. If the variance shrinks, the tail weight grows.
- **T high:** attach positive weight only to T and to one lower point or two neighboring points, or use any other solution with all weight in the tail. If the variance shrinks, the tail weight stays the same at 1.

INTUITIVE INTERPRETATION

Out of all distributions with a given mean, the tail risk can be maximized if one of the points is T, and minimized if one of the points is $T + 1$. If extra variance would help the objective function, then economize on the available variance by putting all non-threshold weight on a single integer point or two neighboring integer points. If extra variance would hurt the objective function, then consume as much variance as you can by splitting all non-threshold weight between the two extreme values.

MUTUAL EXCLUSIVENESS OF SOLUTION TYPES

It turns out that for any given μ, ρ, and n, exactly one distribution of a two-point, nearly two-point or tripolar type is feasible. Again I will forgo an algebraic proof in favor of a more intuitive geometric demonstration.

For every feasible sum k between 0 and n, graph the point $L_k = \langle k, k^2 \rangle$ on a plane and denote the set $\{L_k\}$ by L. Given any probability distribution $\{p_k\}$ on the sum, its first and second moment can be represented by a point $M = \left\langle \sum_{k=0}^{n} kp_k, \sum_{k=0}^{n} k^2 p_k \right\rangle = \sum_{k=0}^{n} p_k L_k.$

Hence M is a convex combination (nonnegative weighted average) of the various elements in L and must lie between them in the area known as the convex hull, which I will denote as $Conv(L)$. Geometrically, $Conv(L)$ is the smallest set containing L and all the line segments between points in $Conv(L)$.

Convex hull (feasible moment-pairs) for $n = 5$

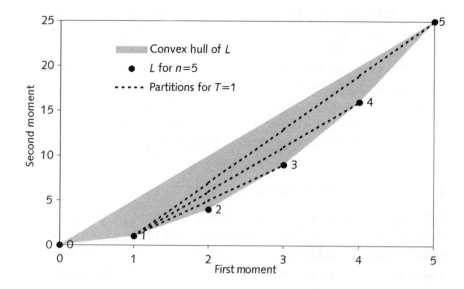

Now, for a given threshold T and for every feasible non-neighboring k, draw a dotted line between L_T and L_k. These dotted lines $L_T L_k$ divide $Conv(L)$ into $n - 2$ neighboring triangles, each with a vertex at L_T. Because L marks the graph of a convex function, each L_k lies on the boundary of $Conv(L)$, so the interiors of these triangles do not overlap. It follows that:

- A strictly two-point distribution is feasible at T and k if and only if M lies on $L_T L_k$ strictly between L_T and L_k.
- A nearly two-point distribution is feasible at T, k, and $k + 1$ if and only if M lies in the interior of the triangle $L_T L_k L_{k+1}$.
- A strictly tripolar distribution is feasible if and only if M lies in the interior of the triangle $L_0 L_n L_T$.
- If M lies on the boundary of $Conv(L)$, exactly one feasible distribution exists. It attaches positive probability to either one point k, to two neighboring points k and $k + 1$, or to the two extremes 0 and n.

To simplify the rest of the exposition, I will expand the definition of degenerate distributions to include all cases on the boundary of $Conv(L)$.

TRIPOLAR SOLUTIONS

All that's left now is to grind through some laborious calculations. If you're bored, skip to the summaries at the end of this chapter.

Let q, q_0, and q_n denote the probability weights on T, 0, and n respectively. The mean and variance constraints are:

$$Tq + nq_n = \mu_{SUM}$$

$$T^2 q + n^2 q_n = \mu_{SUM}^2 + \sigma_{SUM}^2$$

This is a linear equation in q and q_n with solution:

$$q = \frac{n\mu_{SUM} - \mu_{SUM}^2 - \sigma_{SUM}^2}{T(n - T)}; \quad q_n = \frac{\mu_{SUM}^2 + \sigma_{SUM}^2 - T\mu_{SUM}}{n(n - T)}$$

Furthermore, since $q_0 = 1 - q - q_n$,

$$q_0 = \frac{Tn + \mu_{SUM}^2 + \sigma_{SUM}^2 - (T + n)\mu_{SUM}}{Tn}$$

To express this range in standard deviation terms, we need to substitute $\mu_{SUM} - s\sigma_{SUM}$ for T and also to decompose μ_{SUM} and σ_{SUM} into more basic units. As noted previously, $\mu_{SUM} = n\mu$ and $\sigma^2_{SUM} = \tilde{p}n^2\mu(1 - \mu)$, where $\tilde{p} \equiv \dfrac{1 - \rho}{n} + \rho$. Some algebra yields:

$$q_0 = (1 - \mu) \cdot \left(\frac{\tilde{\rho}\sqrt{\mu} - s\sqrt{\tilde{\rho}(1 - \mu)}}{\sqrt{\mu} - s\sqrt{\tilde{\rho}(1 - \mu)}} \right) = 1 - \mu - \frac{(1 - \tilde{\rho})\mu(1 - \mu)}{\mu - s\sqrt{\tilde{\rho}\mu(1 - \mu)}}$$

$$q = \frac{(1 - \tilde{\rho})\sqrt{\mu(1 - \mu)}}{(\sqrt{\mu} - s\sqrt{\tilde{\rho}(1 - \mu)})(\sqrt{1 - \mu} + s\sqrt{\tilde{\rho}\mu})}$$

$$= \frac{(1 - \tilde{\rho})\sqrt{\mu(1 - \mu)}}{(1 - \tilde{\rho}s^2)\sqrt{\mu(1 - \mu)} + (2\mu - 1)\sqrt{\tilde{\rho}}}$$

$$q_n = \mu \cdot \left(\frac{\tilde{\rho}\sqrt{1 - \mu} + s\sqrt{\tilde{\rho}\mu}}{\sqrt{1 - \mu} + s\sqrt{\tilde{\rho}\mu}} \right) = \mu - \frac{(1 - \tilde{\rho})\mu(1 - \mu)}{1 - \mu + s\sqrt{\tilde{\rho}\mu(1 - \mu)}}$$

Where a tripolar solution is feasible, the probability of an s-tail will range from q_0 to $q_0 + q$.

FEASIBLE RANGE FOR TRIPOLAR SOLUTIONS

A strictly tripolar distribution will be feasible if and only if all of the implied probabilities are positive. This requires:

$$\mu_{SUM} - \frac{\sigma^2_{SUM}}{n - \mu_{SUM}} < T < \mu_{SUM} + \frac{\sigma^2_{SUM}}{\mu_{SUM}}$$

when looking for maximum tail risks. When looking for minimum tail risks, replace T by $T + 1$. In standard deviation terms, letting s replace T or $T + 1$ as appropriate, the preceding inequalities work out to

$$-\sqrt{\frac{\tilde{\rho}(1 - \mu)}{\mu}} < s < \sqrt{\frac{\tilde{\rho}\mu}{1 - \mu}}$$

When a tripolar distribution is not feasible, some feasible distribution attaches zero probability weight on one side of the threshold T. So the range above can also be called the "no-zero-tails" range. The chart below depicts the upper bound of the no-zero-tails range as a function of μ and ρ. This bound is low if either μ or ρ is low.

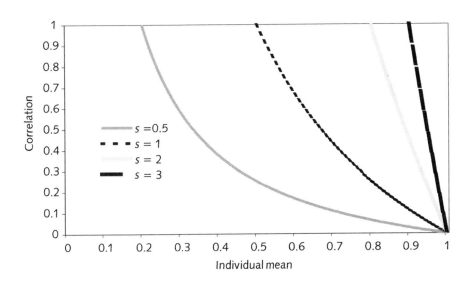

Maximum s for tripolar distribution

TWO-POINT AND NEARLY TWO-POINT SOLUTIONS

The previous chapter showed that a pure two-point solution for sums of uncorrelated variables attaches probability $\dfrac{1}{s^2 + 1}$ to an s-tail. For a nearly two-point solution, the corresponding probability is $q = \dfrac{1 - \epsilon}{s^2 + 1 - \epsilon}$ where $\epsilon \equiv \dfrac{r(1 - r)(1 - q)}{\sigma_{SUM}^2}$ and r is whatever value between 0 and 1 that makes $s' = \dfrac{1 - \epsilon}{s} + \dfrac{1 - r}{\sigma_{SUM}}$ correspond to an integer.

These equations continue to apply when the underlying variables are correlated. Hence, the maximum risk for a proper s-tail is always smaller for a nearly two-point solution than for a two-point solution. However, the gap is typically small in both absolute and relative terms. The only exceptions occur when the Bernoulli sum has a nearly degenerate distribution, either because μ is very close to 0 or 1, n is very small, or ρ is very negative.

Virtually the same arguments apply for minimum risks of improper tails, since these correspond to (one minus) the maximum risks of proper upper tails. Simply replace s with $-1/s$, so the probability $\dfrac{1}{s^2 + 1}$ becomes $\dfrac{1}{s^{-2} + 1} = \dfrac{s^2}{s^2 + 1}$.

FEASIBLE RANGE FOR TWO-POINT AND NEARLY TWO-POINT SOLUTIONS

For a pure two-point solution to be feasible, the two points s and $s' = -1/s$ must lie between 0 and n. This implies restrictions of:

$$0 < -\frac{1}{s_n} = \sqrt{\frac{\tilde{\rho}\mu}{1 - \mu}} \leq s \leq \sqrt{\frac{\mu}{\tilde{\rho}(1 - \mu)}} = s_0 \quad \text{for proper tails}$$

$$s_n = -\sqrt{\frac{1 - \mu}{\tilde{\rho}\mu}} \leq s \leq -\sqrt{\frac{\tilde{\rho}(1 - \mu)}{\mu}} = -\frac{1}{s_0} < 0 \quad \text{for improper tails}$$

The range between $-1/s_0$ and $-1/s_n$ is precisely the no-zero-tails range.

In addition, a pure two-point solution must satisfy integer constraints. In deriving the maximum tail risk, s should be chosen to correspond to the largest integer T in the tail, in which case s' will correspond to:

$$T' = \mu_{SUM} + \frac{\sigma_{SUM}}{\mu_{SUM} - T} = n\mu + \frac{n\sqrt{\tilde{\rho}\mu(1 - \mu)}}{n\mu - T}$$

For the minimum tail risk, s should correspond to the smallest integer $T + 1$ beyond the tail, so just substitute $T + 1$ for T in the formula above.

If T' is not an integer but the other constraints hold, a nearly two-point solution applies. For randomly chosen parameters, nearly two-point solutions will be far more common than two-point solutions. Indeed, for a given ρ and μ, T' may not be an integer for any n and T, ruling out any two-point solution.

GREATEST LOWER BOUNDS FOR TAIL RISK

We can summarize the greatest lower bounds for tail risk as follows, where T refers to the largest integer in the tail.

- 0 if $T + 1 \leq \mu_{SUM} - \dfrac{\sigma^2_{SUM}}{n - \mu_{SUM}}$

- $\dfrac{n(T + 1) + \mu^2_{SUM} + \sigma^2_{SUM} - (T + 1 + n)\mu_{SUM}}{n(T + 1)}$

  if $\mu_{SUM} - \dfrac{\sigma^2_{SUM}}{n - \mu_{SUM}} < T + 1 < \mu_{SUM} + \dfrac{\sigma^2_{SUM}}{\mu_{SUM}}$

- $\dfrac{(T + 1 - \mu_{SUM})^2}{(T + 1 - \mu_{SUM})^2 + \sigma^2_{SUM}}$ plus some generally small positive

  margin if $\mu_{SUM} + \dfrac{\sigma^2_{SUM}}{\mu_{SUM}} \leq T + 1 \leq n$

- 1 if $T \geq n$

LEAST UPPER BOUNDS FOR TAIL RISK

Similarly, we can summarize the least upper bounds for tail risk as:

- 0 if $T < 0$

- $\dfrac{(T - \mu_{SUM})^2}{(T - \mu_{SUM})^2 + \sigma^2_{SUM}}$ less some generally small positive margin

  if $0 \leq T \leq \mu_{SUM} - \dfrac{\sigma^2_{SUM}}{n - \mu_{SUM}}$

- $1 - \dfrac{\mu^2_{SUM} + \sigma^2_{SUM} - T\mu_{SUM}}{n(n - T)}$

  if $\mu_{SUM} - \dfrac{\sigma^2_{SUM}}{n - \mu_{SUM}} < T < \mu_{SUM} + \dfrac{\sigma^2_{SUM}}{\mu_{SUM}}$

- 1 if $T \geq \mu_{SUM} + \dfrac{\sigma^2_{SUM}}{\mu_{SUM}}$

FEASIBLE RANGE IF n UNBOUNDED

Using formulas given earlier, the preceding values can be converted to measures in μ, $\tilde{\rho}$, and the standard deviations represented by T or $T + 1$. If n can range upward without limit (which rules out negative ρ), the feasible range for s-tails works out to:

- 0 if $s > \sqrt{\dfrac{\mu}{\rho(1-\mu)}}$

- $\left[0, \dfrac{1}{1+s^2}\right]$ if $\sqrt{\dfrac{\mu}{\rho(1-\mu)}} \geq s \geq \sqrt{\dfrac{\rho\mu}{1-\mu}}$

- $\left(1 - \mu - \dfrac{(1-\rho)\mu(1-\mu)}{\mu - s\sqrt{\rho\mu(1-\mu)}}, \; 1 - \mu + \dfrac{(1-\rho)\mu(1-\mu)}{1 - \mu + s\sqrt{\rho\mu(1-\mu)}}\right)$

  if $\sqrt{\dfrac{\rho\mu}{1-\mu}} > s > -\sqrt{\dfrac{\rho(1-\mu)}{\mu}}$

- $\left[\dfrac{s^2}{1+s^2}, 1\right]$ if $-\sqrt{\dfrac{\rho(1-\mu)}{\mu}} \geq s \geq -\sqrt{\dfrac{1-\mu}{\rho\mu}}$

- 1 if $s < -\sqrt{\dfrac{1-\mu}{\rho\mu}}$

BOUNDS WHEN μ CAN VARY

The previous bounds apply for a fixed ρ and μ. When μ can vary, $\sqrt{\dfrac{\mu}{1-\mu}}$ and $\sqrt{\dfrac{1-\mu}{\mu}}$ can get arbitrarily small or large, so that the bounds are set by two-point distributions regardless of ρ which takes us back to the uncorrelated case. The range will be $\left[0, \dfrac{1}{1+s^2}\right]$ for a proper tail and $\left[\dfrac{s^2}{1+s^2}, 1\right]$ for an improper tail.

5 | The Creation of Correlation

The next morning Devlin did not come by Conway's office, so after lunch Conway sought him out. "How are the infinite triangles going?"

Devlin smiled. "Only finitely fast. I haven't figured them out yet. But I have made some progress. One of your questions I can answer already."

"Which question is that?"

"You asked whether excluding distributions that can't be extended by extra rows narrows the feasible range for tail risk a lot or just a little. I found that in an unbiased, uncorrelated game, it narrows them a lot."

Now that is good news. "For example?"

"I worked out the extreme tails for combinations of 16 variables from a pool of 32 unbiased, uncorrelated, exchangeable Bernoulli variables. In other words, starting with our previous 16-variable unbiased, uncorrelated Bernoulli game, I sifted out the distributions that could not be extended to embrace 32 variables. The bounds turn out to bracket the binomial much more closely than without the extra sieve. Here, look at this." Devlin brought up a chart on his computer screen.

Conway was jubilant. "Thank heavens. You had me thinking the tail risks wave around like octopus tentacles. But now I see the core risks are pinned to the binomial. So we can continue using the standard formulas as the base case."

"You think so? I'm not so sure. I wouldn't say this chart pins the tail risk to the binomial. To begin with, the range of variation remains substantial. The worst case gives a 2.9% chance of a 4-standard deviation event."

"But surely that shrinks further if you add more rows."

"Yes, it does. Here is another chart comparing the feasible tail risks for 16 unbiased, uncorrelated, exchangeable Bernoulli variables drawn randomly without replacement from pools of 16, 32, and 48 such variables. It focuses on tail risks of two standard deviations and more."

Extreme tail risks for 16 unbiased, uncorrelated Bernoulli variables

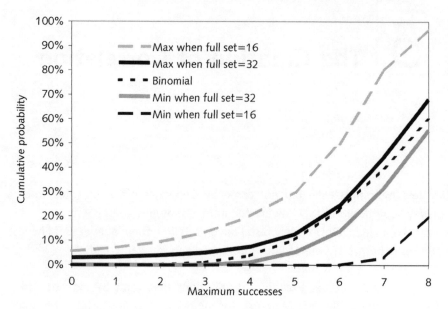

Extreme tail risks for 16 unbiased, uncorrelated Bernoulli variables

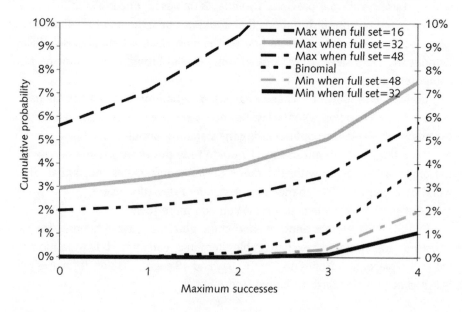

"So you agree. The mountain you made has shrunk back to being a molehill."

Devlin was piqued. "No I do not agree. Despite the shrinkage, the outer tail risks can remain quite high in this example even with a large pool of variables."

"And if the pool is infinite?"

"I can't answer that question yet. I suspect the bounds would narrow to the binomial distribution. But let's not overstate the implications. Unlimited exchangeability is a strong assumption. In practical finance it's violated all the time. For example, it prohibits negative correlations. And even if we accept the assumption, it doesn't rule out extremely un-binomial tails."

Poor Devlin. He's so attached to his problem he doesn't want to solve it. "Listen to yourself, my friend. You've just conceded that extending the degree of exchangeability shrinks and possibly eliminates un-binomial tails for uncorrelated variables. And yesterday you claimed that the risk bounds tend to be narrower for correlated variables than uncorrelated variables. Put the two together. Isn't it obvious where we're heading? To infinity and beyond!" Conway grinned at Devlin, looking for a laugh.

How can you go beyond infinity?"

"I was joking. It's a line from a movie. A fun movie. You should watch one now and then."

Devlin was embarrassed but held his ground. "Maybe" he murmured unconvinced. "The last movie I went to see was *Titanic*. I thought it was way too contrived. Those two leaning over the bow of the ship. Just didn't seem probable. From your statement, however, I take it you expect infinite exchangeability to get rid of distributions with unusually fat tails."

"Don't you?"

"I thought it might. But my results about relative correlated/uncorrelated risk bounds applied only for the bottom rows of my triangles. I couldn't extend them to intermediate rows."

"It must be complicated. But don't get too lost in theory. I suggest you just introduce correlation into your linear programming models and work out the resulting risk bounds for various values of n. I am sure you will find the ranges narrow."

"Well, I did and they don't."

"There must be some mistake."

"I checked. I checked a lot. Then it flashed on me."

"Devlin, could you please get to the point? What flashed?"

"A simple way to model symmetrically correlated Bernoulli variables, regardless of whether they're finitely or infinitely exchangeable. A way that always yields fat tails."

"What way is that?"

"Imagine that nature randomly takes one of two states. In the first state, which occurs with probability ρ, the Bernoulli variables are perfectly correlated. In the other state they are perfectly independent. In either state the mean is $\frac{1}{2}$. It is easy to check that the unconditional correlation is ρ, and that the Bernoulli sum has far too lumpy a tail to be captured by a binomial distribution. Here is a histogram for the two-state scenario with 16 unbiased variables and a correlation of 0.1. Each of the extreme points represents a 2.5 standard deviation event, yet has a 5% probability." Devlin brought up another chart on the screen.

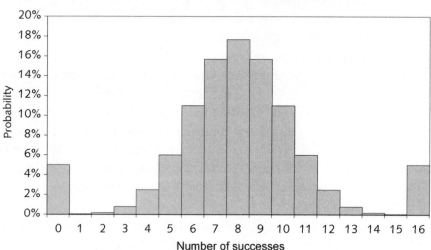

An unbiased, 0.1 correlated, infinitely exchangeable game

One look at the chart confirmed for Conway what he most feared. *Devlin is right.* "I see," he said a bit sheepishly. "By interpreting correlation as a lottery between independence and perfectly aligned movements, you end up with a fat-tailed mixture of a bipolar distribution and a binomial distribution. Yet in either state you can have unlimited exchangeability."

"Bingo."

"I presume you can apply this approach to biased variables as well."

"Yes. Just set the mean of the exchangeable Bernoulli variables at μ in both the uncorrelated and the aligned states. Then the unconditional mean will equal μ, and the unconditional correlation will equal the probability of being perfectly correlated."

"So should I take it that this distribution rather than a straight binomial is the appropriate limiting distribution?"

"No. Once I saw that the distribution above was feasible, I realized there are many, many others. For a sample of n infinitely exchangeable Bernoulli variables, any mixture of binomial distributions of order n is potentially feasible. You just have to make sure that the first two moments of the mixture match the values implied by μ and ρ."

"How do you know these mixtures are feasible?"

"One way is to use my triangles. We know that any binomial probability distribution can be extended indefinitely without violating a summation rule or implying a negative probability. So let us indefinitely extend a mixture of binomial distributions by taking the mixture of each of the extensions. A mixture is a valid probability measure and preserves the summation rules. Hence, all of the conditions are satisfied. However, a math proof is not the most intuitive way to appreciate these results."

"What is?"

"Conditional independence. Assume that the variables are independent given their common mean, but that nature randomly shifts the mean. Clearly, such variables are infinitely exchangeable and a binomial distribution applies in every state. The distribution of the mixture is just the mixture of the distributions."

"So where does the correlation come from?"

"From the changes in the common mean. Recall that the unconditional covariance equals the sum of the mean conditional covariance and the covariance of the conditional means. The first component is zero thanks to conditional independence. The second component is positive thanks to exchangeability, unless the mean is fixed. The unconditional correlation indicates how much of the aggregate variance of an exchangeable variable stems from the variance of its conditional mean."

"Can you give me an example?"

"I already did. We just need to reinterpret it. Perfectly correlated Bernoulli variables can be viewed as reflecting a mixture of two degenerate, conditionally independent binomial distributions: one where success is certain and the other where failure is certain. So the chart above can be interpreted as a mixture of binomial distributions having mean 0 with probability 5%, mean 1 with probability 5%, and mean $\frac{1}{2}$ with probability 90%."

"Degenerate variables are weird. How about an example with full-fledged binomial distributions?"

Devlin nodded, and clicked on another chart. "Here is another mixture that implies the same overall mean and correlation as the previous chart, but looks quite different. It represents a weighted average of two binomial distributions having means 4 and 9.6 respectively. You can interpret it as follows. With 28.6% probability, the 16 Bernoulli variables are independent with common mean. Otherwise they are independent with common mean $\frac{9.6}{16} = 0.6$."

Another unbiased, 0.1 correlated, infinitely exchangeable game

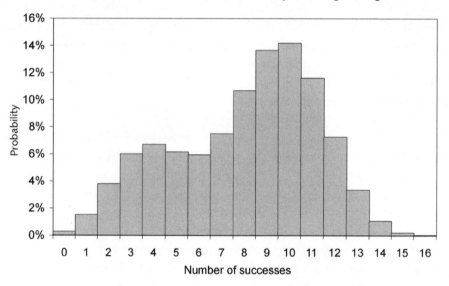

Conway was impressed. "Without your explanation I never would have figured out this represented a feasible, infinitely exchangeable game."

"Nobody could. Not from looking at this chart. What's the probability of 16 successes?"

"Nearly zero. So close to zero I can't see a bar."

"I can't either. But if it really were zero, this histogram couldn't represent an infinitely exchangeable game."

"Why not?"

"If a sample of 16 variables has to contain at least one failure, no matter how big the pool it is drawn from, then the pool itself can never contain more than 15 successes. The only infinitely exchangeable variables that meet that requirement are degenerate failures."

"Can we at least tell from inspection whether a histogram at least resembles a binomial mixture?"

"Sometimes. If you know that the variables are uncorrelated it's easy. If the means of the binomials are distinct, their variance will be positive, and hence the implied correlation between the variables will be positive. So the only valid binomial mixture for uncorrelated variables is a pure binomial."

"Suppose I know the variables are correlated, or have to figure it out from the histogram."

"Then look at how sharply the distribution undulates. If a binomial mixture places a lot of weight on a point k that is not an extreme, it has to place substantial weight on $k - 1$ or $k + 1$ and usually both. So except at the end points a binomial mixture can't undulate too sharply."

"Or too little, I would guess. Binomial mixtures amount geometrically to an overlay of mountain peaks. So they can't be too even."

"You'll be surprised," said Devlin. He pulled up another chart on his computer screen. "Where do you place the peaks in this 50-variable binomial mixture?"

Binomial mixture without peaks

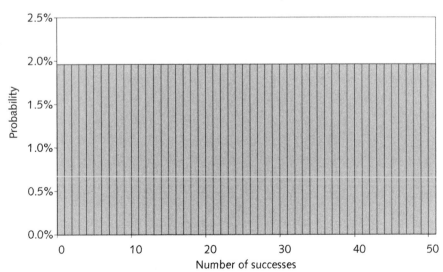

Oh very funny. "You must be pulling my leg. This isn't a binomial mixture."

"Yes, it is. You generate it by assuming that every possible conditional mean is equally likely. The unconditional Bernoulli variables are unbiased with correlation $\frac{1}{3}$. You can also generate the distribution using my triangles without reference to binomials. Just assume that the probability of zero successes equals $\dfrac{1}{n+1}$ for every n and work out the other elements using the summation rule."

"It may check out mathematically but it's preposterous. If you have 50 coins there are $\binom{50}{25}$ distinct ways for 25 tails to turn up." Conway reached over Devlin to do a quick calculation on his computer. "That's more than 126 trillion ways. In contrast, there is only one way for 50 tails to turn up. There is also only one way for 50 heads to turn up. But your distribution indicates the three combinations are equally likely. It's wholly unnatural."

"It's not unnatural at all. Without that distribution, the whole universe might collapse."

"What in the world are you talking about, Devlin? I want us to focus on realistic distributions, not story lines from a B-grade science fiction movie. And please cut out the dramatics."

"No really, it's all about photons, as well as ions containing an even total number of protons and neutrons. Look, suppose you have 50 identical such particles whizzing around two equally likely halves of a small space. The probability that exactly k particles fall in the first half is given by the histogram above. The generalization to multiple regions is called the Bose-Einstein distribution. It makes each combination equally likely rather than each permutation."

"That is very strange."

"Very. Apparently, most physicists were shocked when they first encountered it. It seemed as unnatural to them as it does now to you. But they had to adjust, because that's what the evidence kept showing. In fact, hardly any random behavior of elementary particles appears to be explained by single binomial distributions or approximations to them. So physicists had to introduce more complicated distributions."

"Thank you for this fascinating glimpse into quantum mechanics, Devlin. Fascinating, but surely irrelevant. Physicists take exceedingly refined measurements under carefully controlled conditions. Even the uncertainty they face is precisely defined. We deal with assets that reflect all sorts of unknown or poorly understood factors. The relevant influences keep changing and are virtually impossible to replicate."

"What's your point, Conway? That financial risk managers need measures robust to large misspecifications and uncertainties?"

"Absolutely. At last you are getting there. That is why I wanted you to deal with infinitely exchangeable variables. Not to describe reality, but to describe our uncertainty about reality. When we can't distinguish one variable well from another, we might as well assume symmetrical dependence. And if we don't know the mean, we have to make a guess."

"Could you ever be so uncertain about the mean that you feel any value is equally likely?"

"I doubt it, but wouldn't reject it as a stylized modeling assumption. It is certainly far more realistic than these exotic distributions you keep peddling. Bose-Einstein indeed!"

"Then we're not so far apart after all. A Bose-Einstein distribution is precisely what you get if you assume symmetric dependence with a uniform distribution on the common mean."

Devlin wrote down some equations for Conway and explained them. They discussed things for a few minutes until Conway understood. Then Conway laughed, and Devlin laughed, and they laughed at each other's laughter.

"You win," said Conway, "I bow to Bose-Einstein, and to any other binomial mixture you care to present. But I need to take a break. Ideas are scattered around my brain like photons. And I don't want them to collapse. Can I take a copy of your spreadsheet so that I can get a feel for the various distributions?"

"Sure. You can use it here if you like. I'm going fishing in the library for more insights about infinitely exchangeable Bernoulli variables. I still don't know whether binomial mixtures capture the full spectrum of potential dependence."

Let's use the break to elaborate some properties of mixtures of binomial distributions. These mixtures may contain an uncountable number of elements, so I will begin by reviewing standard notation for dealing with probabilities in such cases. Then I will derive a formula relating the moments of a binomial mixture to the moments of its Bernoulli variable counterparts. Finally, I will verify that a uniform mixture of binomial distributions generates a uniform Bose-Einstein distribution.

Despite the intimidating look of some of the integrals, the math is simpler in this section than it was in the preceding two chapters. Do check that you understand it, because subsequent chapters will build a lot on these foundations.

PROBABILITY MEASURES ON A CONTINUUM

So far we have dealt only with discrete outcomes, which can be numbered using integers. If a continuum of outcomes is possible, then the probability $p(x) \equiv Pr\{X = x\}$ that a single point x occurs will equal zero almost everywhere. Indeed $p(x)$ may be zero for every point x, even when the probability of any interval stretching between two points is strictly positive. In such cases, theory focuses on the analogue $f(x)$, known as the probability density.

For purely continuous probability measures, $f(x) \geq 0$ for all x and the integral $\int_{-\infty}^{\infty} f(x)dx = 1$. The expectation $E[X]$ is defined as $\int_{-\infty}^{\infty} xf(x)dx$. It follows that $E[h(X)] = \int_{-\infty}^{\infty} h(x)f(x)dx$ for all functions h of X.

MIXED PROBABILITY MEASURES

A "mixed" probability measure refers to a mixture of discrete and purely continuous probability measures. Given a weight λ between 0 and 1 on the discrete measure, the expectation under the mixed measure is

$$\lambda \sum_{k \in K} x_k p(x_k) + (1 - \lambda) \int_{-\infty}^{\infty} xf(x)dx. \text{ Clearly,}$$

$$E[h(X)] = \lambda \sum h(x)p(x) + (1 - \lambda) \int_{-\infty}^{\infty} h(x)f(x)dx.$$

A UNIFIED TREATMENT

Probability point mass and probability density are linked through the cumulative probability distribution $F(x) \equiv Pr\{X \leq x\}$. Its definition does not depend on whether the feasible set is discrete or continuous. Note that F always reaches or asymptotically approaches zero as X gets unboundedly negative, and one as X gets unboundedly positive. I will write this as $F(-\infty) = 0$ and $F(\infty) = 1$. Moreover, F is monotonic in X: it must never decrease as X rises, though it might stay the same. It follows that:

- F is differentiable almost everywhere, and the derivative
  $$\tilde{f}(x) \equiv \frac{dF}{dx} \equiv \frac{dF}{dX}\bigg|_{X=x} \quad \text{is nonnegative wherever it exists.}$$
- Wherever F is not continuous, the jump $\tilde{p}(x) = F(x) - F(x^-)$ is strictly positive. Here $F(x^-)$, also known as the "lower limit" of F at x, denotes the limiting value of $F(z)$ as z approaches x from below.

- The sum of the integral $\int_{-\infty}^{\infty} \tilde{f}(x)dx$ and all jumps $\sum_{k \in K} \tilde{p}(x_k)$ equals 1.

We can extend both $\tilde{f}$ and $\tilde{p}$ to cover all real values by defining functions f and p such that $f(x) = \tilde{f}(x^-)$ and $\tilde{p}(x) = F(x) - F(x^-)$ for all x. These functions match $\tilde{f}$ and $\tilde{p}$ wherever possible, never take negative values, and maintain the property that the sum of the integral and the jumps equal 1. Hence f and p jointly define a probability measure, with f as the probability density and p as the probability point mass.

To obtain a unifying notation, define $dF(x)$ as $F(x) - F(x^-)$ where F has jumps and $\dfrac{dF}{dx^-}dx$ where it does not. More precisely,

$$\int_J h(x)dF(x) \equiv \sum_J h(x)\left(F(x) - F(x^-)\right) + \int_J h(x)\frac{dF}{dx^-}dx$$

for all intervals J and functions h. This integral is known as the Reimann-Stieltjes integral. Every monotonic F such that $\int_{-\infty}^{\infty} dF(x) = 1$ can be associated with a probability measure. It follows that $E_F[h(X)] = \int_{-\infty}^{\infty} h(x)dF(x)$ given a probability measure F.

CONDITIONAL AND MARGINAL PROBABILITIES ON A CONTINUUM

Let X and Y be two random variables characterized by a joint cumulative distribution function F, such that $F(x, y) = Pr(X \le x, Y \le y)$. If the joint density $f(x,y) = \dfrac{\partial^2 F(x,y)}{\partial x \partial y}$ is well-defined everywhere, then the marginal density of Y can be defined as

$$g(y) \equiv \int_{-\infty}^{\infty} f(x,y)dx = \int_{-\infty}^{\infty} \frac{\partial^2 F(x,y)}{\partial x \partial y} dx = \frac{\partial F(\infty,y)}{\partial y}$$

the conditional density as

$$f(x\mid y) = \frac{f(x,y)}{g(y)}$$

and the cumulative conditional distribution as

$$F(x\mid y) = \int_{-\infty}^{\infty} f(z\mid y)dz = \frac{\int_{-\infty}^{\infty} f(z,y)dz}{g(y)} = \frac{\partial F(x,y)}{\partial y} \bigg/ \frac{\partial F(\infty,y)}{\partial y}$$

The formulas are essentially the same as for discrete probabilities except that integrals and derivatives replace sums and differences. For mixed distributions we should use sums and differences where there are jumps and differentials where there are no jumps. This can be written as a two-dimensional Riemann-Stieltjes integral but I will not bother, due to the awkward terminology needed to distinguish increments in the X and Y directions.

MIXTURES OF BINOMIAL DISTRIBUTIONS

As we have seen, the sum of n independent Bernoulli variables, each having a probability θ of success, is distributed binomially, with a probability $\binom{n}{k}\theta^k(1-\theta)^{n-k}$ of sum k. Now let θ be a random variable with cumulative probability distribution G. That is, model the outcome as a two-stage lottery in which:

- the first stage chooses a value θ between 0 and 1, where $G(x)$ denotes the probability that θ does not exceed x;
- the second stage generates n independent outcomes, each with probability θ of success.

The distribution of the sum will be a mixture of binomials with mixing distribution G. The probability of k successes will be given by:

$$P(n,k) = \int_0^1 \binom{n}{k} \theta^k (1-\theta)^{n-k} dG(\theta)$$

The corresponding element $p(n,k)$ of Devlin's triangle – the probability of a given permutation of k successes – equals $\int_0^1 \theta^k (1-\theta)^{n-k} dG(\theta)$

$\int_0^1 \theta^k (1-\theta)^{n-k} dG(\theta)$. The summation rule is readily confirmed:

$$p(n,k) + p(n,k+1) = \int_0^1 \theta^k (1-\theta)^{n-k} dG(\theta)$$

$$+ \int_0^1 \theta^{k+1} (1-\theta)^{n-k-1} dG(\theta)$$

$$= \int_0^1 [1 - \theta + \theta]\theta^k (1-\theta)^{n-k-1} dG(\theta)$$

$$= \int_0^1 \theta^k (1-\theta)^{n-k-1} dG(\theta) = p(n-1,k)$$

MEAN AND VARIANCE OF A MIXTURE OF BINOMIALS

A pure binomial distribution has mean $n\theta$ and variance $n\theta(1-\theta)$. A mixture of binomials with mixing distribution G has mean $nE_G[\theta]$. The variance of the mixture equals the mean of the conditional variance plus the variance of the conditional mean, or:

$$E_G[n\theta(1-\theta)] + n^2 Var_G[\theta] = nE_G[\theta] - nE_G[\theta^2] + n^2 Var_G[\theta]$$

$$= nE_G[\theta] - n(E_G[\theta])^2 - nVar_G[\theta] + n^2 Var_G[\theta]$$

$$= nE_G[\theta](1 - E_G[\theta]) + (n^2 - n)Var_G[\theta]$$

Now, the sum $\sum_{i=1}^n X_i$ of n exchangeable Bernoulli variables with mean μ and pairwise correlation ρ will have a mean of $n\mu$ and a variance of $n\mu(1-\mu) + (n^2 - n)\rho\mu(1-\mu)$. These calculations will match the preceding if and only if:

$$E_G[\theta] = \mu \quad ; \quad Var_G[\theta] = \rho\mu(1-\mu) = \rho Var[X]$$

In other words, if the sum of exchangeable Bernoulli variables is distributed like a mixture of binomials, the mixing distribution will have the Bernoulli mean and a variance that equals the correlation times the Bernoulli variance.

ALTERNATIVE INTERPRETATION OF CORRELATION

Rearranging the last equation, $\rho = \dfrac{Var_G[\theta]}{Var[X]}$. We can view X as the sum of the conditional mean θ and a random deviate that equals $1 - \theta$ with probability θ and $-\theta$ with probability $1 - \theta$. Then ρ indicates how much the variance of θ contributes to the total variance of X.

Devlin's first example of a feasible mixing distribution attaches probability $\rho(1 - \mu)$ to 0, probability $\rho\mu$ to 1, and probability $1 - \rho$ to μ. This can be interpreted as a probability ρ of perfect correlation and $1 - \rho$ of zero correlation, with both states having mean μ.

BOSE-EINSTEIN DISTRIBUTION

Suppose that the mixing distribution in a mixture of binomials is uniform, so that $G(\theta) = \theta$. The corresponding Bernoulli variables will have mean $\frac{1}{2}$ and correlation $\frac{1}{3}$. For any integer k between 0 and $n - 1$,

$$P(n, k) = \int_0^1 \binom{n}{k} \theta^k (1 - \theta)^{n-k} d\theta$$

$$= \binom{n}{k} \frac{\theta^{k+1}}{k+1} (1 - \theta)^{n-k} \Big|_0^1 - \int_0^1 \binom{n}{k} \frac{\theta^{k+1}}{k+1} (k - n)(1 - \theta)^{n-k-1} d\theta$$

$$= 0 + \int_0^1 \binom{n}{k} \frac{n - k}{k+1} \theta^{k+1} (1 - \theta)^{n-k-1} d\theta$$

$$= \int_0^1 \binom{n}{k+1} \theta^{k+1} (1 - \theta)^{n-k-1} d\theta = P(n, k + 1)$$

so the histogram must be flat with height $\dfrac{1}{n+1}$.

For a more intuitive proof, suppose that $n + 1$ numbers are picked at random (with a uniform distribution) from the interval [0,1]. If the last number equals θ, the probability that k numbers lie below it and $n - k$ lie above it equals $\binom{n}{k} \theta^k (1 - \theta)^{n-k}$. Hence the unconditional probability that the last number has rank $k + 1$ from the bottom is $\int_0^1 \binom{n}{k} \theta^k (1 - \theta)^{n-k} d\theta$. By symmetry, any feasible ranking is equally likely, so the integral must equal $\dfrac{1}{n+1}$.

INTERPRETATION OF BOSE-EINSTEIN DISTRIBUTION

Conditional on k successes in n trials, the probability that the next trial brings success is:

$$\frac{p(n+1, k+1)}{p(n, k)} = \frac{P(n+1, k+1) \big/ \binom{n+1}{k+1}}{P(n, k) \big/ \binom{n}{k}}$$

$$= \frac{\dfrac{(k+1)!(n-k)!}{(n+2)!}}{\dfrac{k!(n-k)!}{(n+1)!}} = \frac{k+1}{n+2}$$

which always exceeds $\dfrac{k}{n}$. So the Bose-Einstein distribution represents a case of "success breeding success", or at least this is how it might be viewed in sequential sampling.

Indeed, a sampling game known in statistics as "Polya's urn problem" gives precisely this distribution. Suppose an urn initially contains one red ball and one black ball, and that every time a ball is drawn, two balls of the same color are put back in the urn. The conditional probability of drawing another red ball, given that k red balls and $n - k$ black balls have already been chosen, is $\dfrac{k+1}{n+2}$. Hence, one possible interpretation of Bose-Einstein statistics is that some particles attract other particles toward them.

However, the modeling as a mixture of binomials shows that no causality need be involved. Rather, $\dfrac{k+1}{n+2}$ could just be viewed as a revised estimate of the mean given a uniform initial estimate and k subsequent successes in n trials.

6 | Defining Moments from De Finetti

For the second morning running, there was no sign of Devlin. *He must not have landed any great catches. Otherwise he would have been back in a flash to display them.* After lunch Conway found Devlin at his desk, mumbling "definitely, definitely" as he tinkered with a spreadsheet. "Definitely what?" Conway asked.

"Not 'definitely'. De Finetti. Bruno de Finetti. He identified all the feasible distributions for infinitely exchangeable Bernoulli variables. His theorem is well known among professional statisticians. But most statistics courses ignore it, and I had forgotten about it myself."

"I can't remember whether it slipped my mind or never entered. So what feasible distributions are there, apart from the binomial mixtures we already discussed?

"There aren't any. All compatible distributions are binomial mixtures. In other words, given the conditional mean θ, the Bernoulli variables must be independent. But the conditional mean can change across states according to a mixing distribution G."

"Why are these the only feasible types? In English please."

"The proof isn't very intuitive, at least not in the versions I saw. So I started playing with Pascal's and my triangles again until it hit me. We can use these triangles to construct G."

"How?"

"Start by collecting information on the probabilities of perfect successes $p(n, n)$ for all values of n. This identifies the right edge of one of my triangles, or perhaps I should say cone because the triangle stretches to infinity. Since each row adds only one degree of freedom, these values uniquely determine the whole. So to prove de Finetti's Theorem we just have to find a mixing distribution G that correctly specifies the right edge,"

"What is so special about the right edge?"

"For a binomial mixture, each $p(n, n)$ represents the nth moment of G. It's reasonably straightforward to work out a distribution that generates a given set of moments. For example, one can construct the moment-generating function directly, and then invert it to obtain G."

"Not so fast. How can you be sure the resulting G will be a probability distribution on the unit interval?"

"By construction, each of the elements $p(n, k)$ defines the expectation of $\theta^k(1 - \theta)^{n-k}$. If G weren't a probability distribution or attached probability outside the unit interval, at least one of these elements would be negative."

"I'm not sure I buy that. And what if I don't know how to invert the moment-generating function?"

"You can also construct approximations using the rows of the cone. For every row n, calculate the probability distribution G_n as a step-function of the relative frequency. That is, $G_n(\theta)$ denotes the probability of $n\theta$ or fewer successes out of n outcomes, and is flat except at integer multiples of $1/n$. These G_n will converge to the G you need."

"This may be obvious to you but I still don't get it. Could I ask you to walk me through an example?"

"Sure. Let's go back to our perfectly even histogram, where $P(n, n) = \dfrac{1}{n + 1} = p(n, n)$ for all n. The only distribution whose nth moment equals $\dfrac{1}{n + 1}$ for all n is the uniform distribution $G(\theta) = \theta$. Alternatively, look at $G_n(\theta)$, which equals $\dfrac{1}{n + 1}$ times the smallest integer exceeding $n\theta$. As n gets large, this approaches θ."

Conway wrote down a few of the rows for Devlin's triangle and mulled this over. After a few minutes he spoke. "You managed to extend your triangles to infinity after all. Congratulations."

"Thanks. But the real credit goes to de Finetti."

"Well I never! So there are indeed some authorities you respect."

Devlin blushed. "Didn't you know that?"

"I am just pulling your leg," assured Conway, though he wasn't. "What i really want to know is what happens to the range for tail risk. There must be some restrictions compared with the finitely exchangeable case."

"There are. The distributions that bound the tail risks of infinitely exchangeable Bernoulli variables are mixtures of two or three binomials rather than two-point or three-point distributions. The extra restriction depends on how well or poorly a binomial distribution can approximate a single-point distribution. Sometimes the feasible range gets trimmed a lot." Devlin pulled a chart up on the screen.

Maximizing the odds of ≤ 2 successes for $n = 16$, $\mu = 0.5$, $\rho = 0.1$

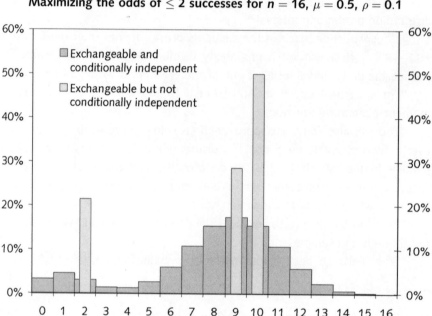

"Each of these histograms," continued Devlin, "depicts 16 unbiased exchangeable Bernoulli variables with correlation 0.1. The light histogram gives the unrestricted maximum risk of two or fewer successes, which represents a 1.90 standard deviation tail. The dark histogram gives the maximum when the variables are conditionally independent. The maximum tail risk is barely half as much in the second case as in the first: 10.8% versus 21.4%."

"Why is the gap so large?"

"Each of the two binomials in the mixture consumes a lot more variance than a distribution concentrated around the two conditional means. Consequently, a lot less variance is available to 'finance' probability mass in the tail."

"I notice the conditional means or peaks of the distributions don't line up either. Why not?"

"The lower binomial peak is shifted to the left so that less probability mass spills over the threshold. While this consumes even more variance, up to a point it's worth it. In this example, the optimal mean for the lower binomial is 1.27, which gives a 75% conditional probability of staying inside the threshold versus the 50% conditional probability that would apply if the mean were 2.00."

"And the upper peak?"

"If the lower peak shifts away from the mean, then in order to satisfy the mean and variance constraints, the upper peak must shift toward the mean and become more likely. Hence both peaks shift to the left."

"You said that the risk bounds were roughly halved. Is that a general result?"

"No, the impact varies with the parameters. For example, the risk bounds don't get affected proportionately as much for extreme tails as for intermediate tails because binomials with extreme peaks don't create much variance. Take a look at the tail risk bounds for the scenario we've been discussing." Devlin brought up another chart on the screen.

Extreme tail risks for $n = 16$, $\mu = 0.5$, $\rho = 0.1$

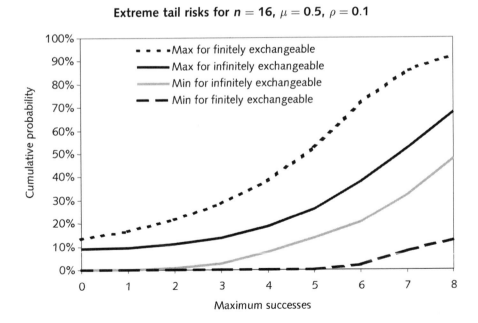

"How many standard deviations do zero successes represent in this chart?"

"Just over 2.5. The maximum probability shrinks from 13.3% to 9.1%. The minimum probability expands to 1 in 16,000 from zero. Note that conventional mean/variance-based risk analysis estimates the probability of a 2.5 standard deviation event at 0.6%."

Conway sighed. "I suppose I should be grateful that 2.5 standard deviation events are only 15 times as frequent as conventionally assumed and not 20."

"Unfortunately, you can't rule that out. As the number of variables n increases, the restriction to binomial mixtures matters less. In the limit there's no significant difference at all, provided the correlation ρ is positive."

"How can that be? We just saw that binomial mixtures dissipate more variance than point distributions with the same conditional means, and that this dissipation trims the feasible range for tail risk. The variance of a binomial rises with n. So why doesn't the dissipation worsen?"

"In absolute terms, you're right. Binomial mixtures dissipate variance in direct proportion to n. However, the total variance of a Bernoulli sum also includes a term in ρn^2. That term eventually dominates the sum if ρ is even mildly positive. So the dissipation shrinks as a fraction of the whole variance, roughly in proportion to $1/n$."

"I'm not arguing with the math. I just don't see intuitively why we should focus on the relative dissipation rather than its absolute amount."

"Then draw a picture. Chart total successes so that the width of the chart remains constant regardless of n. Then each standard deviation of a binomial with mean rate of success θ will have width $\dfrac{\theta(1-\theta)}{\sqrt{n}}$. As n grows, each binomial will look more and more concentrated around its peak. Hence, if n gets large enough, we can center a binomial several standard deviations inside the threshold – to keep the spillover across the threshold very small – without dissipating a significant fraction of the variance."

"Aha. I am beginning to understand. Can you walk me through another example?"

"No problem. Let's stick with unbiased, 0.1-correlated variables but quadruple the number of variables to 64. This will halve the standard deviation of a binomial relative to the feasible range. And let's choose 11 or fewer successes as the tail event. That represents a 1.94 standard deviation tail, the closest analogue to the 1.90 standard deviation tail in my previous example. Here are the distributions that maximize the tail risks." Devlin brought up another chart on the screen.

Maximizing the odds of ≤ 11 successes for $n = 16$, $\mu = 0.5$, $\rho = 0.1$

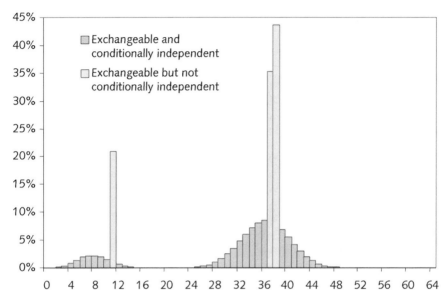

"You said the binomials would be more concentrated. So why are the peaks lower than before?"

"The peaks are lower because there are four times as many feasible outcomes. The counterpart to 9 successes out of 16 is something like 36 to 39 successes out of 64. And whereas the probability of 9 successes in the first chart was 17%, the probability of 36 to 39 successes in this chart is nearly 33%. To confirm the higher concentration, just compare the valleys between the peaks. In this chart, the space between 14 and 24 successes is nearly empty: the probability of landing in that range is less than 0.5%. In contrast, the binomials visibly overlap in the first chart at 4 successes out of 16."

"It looks like spillover is less as well."

"Yes. Conditional on the lower binomial applying, the probability that the sum exceeds the threshold is less than 9%, compared with 25% for the corresponding 16-variable case. Expanding to 64 variables also allows the lower binomial to carry slightly more weight – 14.9% instead of 12.4%, for this example – because relatively less variance is dissipated.

"So how much closer does this get you to the unrestricted range?"

"With 64 variables of 0.1 correlation, the maximum probability of a 1.94 standard deviation or higher shortfall is 13.6% when infinite exchangeability is required versus 20.9% when it isn't. So infinite exchangeability shaves the maximum by just over a third, versus half for the closest 16-variable counterpart."

"One-third is still substantial. How many variables do you need before finite and infinite exchangeability generate roughly the same bounds on tail risk?"

"That depends again on the parameters, but given positive correlation you're typically talking in the hundreds or thousands rather than dozens. Convergence is slow because it depends on $1/\sqrt{n}$ vanishing."

"And if the correlation is zero or negative?"

"We saw that already. The correlation is a positive multiple of the variance of the conditional means. So it can't be negative, and if it's zero there's only one state, implying unconditional independence."

"So the uncorrelated case really stands out as exceptional."

"Extremely. No matter how many independent Bernoulli variables you have, the tail risks must be binomial. In contrast, for every other feasible correlation, no matter how small, the s-tail risks can vary over a range that in the limit extends from 0 to $\dfrac{1}{s^2 + 1}$."

Conway was now thoroughly confused. "But you told me before that 0 to $\dfrac{1}{s^2 + 1}$ provides the limiting bounds on s-tail risk for any probability distribution! Doesn't infinite exchangeability do anything to narrow the bounds?" he asked despondently.

"Not unless you have perfectly uncorrelated variables or only a limited pool of correlated variables."

"And how in practice would I know that?"

"You wouldn't. You couldn't. Your estimates would always have a significant margin of error."

"So we are back to the general 0 to $\dfrac{1}{s^2 + 1}$ bounds."

"I'm afraid so."

Conway frowned and began to pace back and forth beside Devlin's desk. *This is terrible. How am I ever going to explain this to the Risk Oversight Committee?*

While Conway frets, let's take a closer look at de Finetti's Theorem and its implications.

DE FINETTI'S THEOREM

De Finetti's Theorem says that any set of infinitely exchangeable Bernoulli variables must be conditionally independent given their common mean. Formally, the probability $P(n, k)$ successes out of n outcomes must equal

$$\int_0^1 \binom{n}{k} \theta^k (1 - \theta)^{n-k} dG(\theta)$$

for some probability distribution G on $[0,1]$. The corresponding element $p(n, k)$ of Devlin's triangle equals $\int_0^1 \theta^k (1 - \theta)^{n-k} dG(\theta)$. In particular,

$$p(n, n) = \int_0^1 \theta^n dG(\theta) \equiv E_G[\theta^n].$$

An elaborate proof of de Finetti's Theorem can be found in William Feller's classic text on probability theory. Feller constructs what amounts to the step functions G_n defined by

$$dG_n\left(\frac{k}{n}\right) \equiv P(n, k) = \binom{n}{k} p(n, k)$$

Feller uses a version of Devlin's triangle to show that the moments of G_n converge to the set $\{p(0,0), \ldots, p(n, n), \ldots\}$, and then shows that the moments uniquely define G.

To repeat Devlin's illustration, $P(n, k)$ for the Bose-Einstein distribution is independent of k. Defining $Int(n\theta)$ as the least integer not greater than $n\theta$, $G_n(\theta)$ equals $\dfrac{Int(n\theta) + 1}{n + 1}$ and hence converges to a uniform distribution. For another illustration, if $p(n, k) \equiv \theta^k (1 - \theta)^{n-k}$ for all n and k, G_n corresponds to a binomial distribution with n variables and mean $n\theta$, except that the probabilities assigned to k successes in a binomial are assigned under G_n to k/n. As n increases, G_n will shrink toward a point distribution on θ, which indeed correctly defines G.

DEMONSTRATION OF CONVERGENCE TO G

Let $\tilde{P}_n(n, \lambda n)$ denote the probability of λn successes in n trials, assuming the distribution is generated by mixture G_n. Then:

$$\tilde{P}_n(n, \lambda n) = \int_0^1 \binom{n}{\lambda n} \theta^{\lambda n}(1-\theta)^{n-\lambda n} dG(\theta)$$

$$= \sum_\theta \binom{n}{\lambda n} \theta^{\lambda n}(1-\theta)^{n-\lambda n} P(n, \theta n) \equiv \sum_\theta A(n, \lambda, \theta) P(n, \theta n)$$

where the summations are taken over θ in $\{0, 1/n, 2/n, \ldots, 1\}$. Next I apply Stirling's formula, which says that $\dfrac{n!}{\sqrt{2\pi n} \cdot n^n e^{-n}} \cong 1$ for large n. Hence if neither λn nor $n - \lambda n$ is small,

$$A(n, \lambda, \theta) = \binom{n}{\lambda n} \theta^{\lambda n}(1-\theta)^{(1-\lambda)n} = \frac{n! \theta^{\lambda n}(1-\theta)^{(1-\lambda)n}}{(\lambda n)!(n-\lambda n)!}$$

$$\cong \frac{\sqrt{2\pi n} \cdot n^n e^{-n} \theta^{\lambda n}(1-\theta)^{(1-\lambda)n}}{\sqrt{2\pi \lambda n} \cdot \lambda^{\lambda n} n^{\lambda n} e^{-\lambda n} \sqrt{2\pi(1-\lambda)n} \cdot (1-\lambda)^{(1-\lambda)n} n^{(1-\lambda)n} e^{-(1-\lambda)n}}$$

$$= \left(2\pi \lambda(1-\lambda)n\right)^{-1/2} \left[\left(\frac{\theta}{\lambda}\right)^\lambda \left(\frac{1-\theta}{1-\lambda}\right)^{1-\lambda} \right]^n \equiv B(n, \lambda) \cdot [C(\lambda, \theta)]^n$$

Now look at the term $C(\lambda, \theta)$. It is less than 1 unless $\theta = \lambda$, as can be readily verified by maximizing $ln(C)$ with respect to θ. Hence C^n converges to 1 at $\theta = \lambda$ and 0 when $\theta \neq \lambda$. Furthermore $B(n, \lambda)$ is a sort of integrating factor, intended to deal with the cases where θ is only infinitesimally different from λ. Since B is independent of the values of P, and since $\tilde{P}_n$ must always have the same aggregate measure as P, B must amount in effect to 1. This demonstrates, albeit not rigorously, that $\tilde{P}_n(n, \lambda n)$ converges to $P(n, \lambda n)$.

MOMENT-GENERATING FUNCTIONS

The expectation of $e^{\gamma X}$, considered as a function $\mathcal{M}$ of γ, is known as the moment-generating function for the random variable X. It is readily established that the nth derivative of $\mathcal{M}$, evaluated at $\gamma = 0$, is just the nth moment of X. That is,

$$\mathcal{M}_F^{(n)}(0) \equiv \frac{d^n \mathcal{M}_F}{d\gamma^n}\bigg|_{\gamma=0} = \int X^n e^{\gamma X} dF(X)\bigg|_{\gamma=0} = \int X^n dF(X) = E_F[X^n]$$

Given all the values for the derivatives of $\mathcal{M}$, we can use a Taylor series expansion to reconstruct $\mathcal{M}$. Subject to certain restrictions, $\mathcal{M}$ can then be inverted to reveal the function F that generated it. Provided $\mathcal{M}_F(0) = 1$, F will have measure 1. However, F will not be a valid probability measure (that is, dF might occasionally be negative) unless the moments are internally consistent. For example, the second moment cannot be less than the square of the first moment or the implied variance would be negative.

To apply moment-generating functions to justify de Finetti's Theorem, use the elements $p(n, n)$ to construct the moment-generating function for G and then invert it. The nonnegativity of the associated Devlin's triangle guarantees that G is monotonic.

The preceding "proof" doesn't address the possible non-existence or non-invertibility of $\mathcal{M}$. For a more rigorous treatment, we should switch to some close relatives of the moment-generating function like the Laplace transform or the characteristic function. However, the core of the argument remains the same.

TYPES OF BINOMIAL MIXTURES GENERATING EXTREME RISKS

For a binomial mixture, the tail risk for T or fewer successes out of n tries is:

$$Pr(k \leq T) = \sum_{k=0}^{T} \int_0^1 \binom{n}{k} \theta^k (1 - \theta)^{n-k} dG(\theta)$$

Given a mean μ and positive correlation ρ for the Bernoulli variables, we know from the previous chapter that G must have mean μ and variance $\rho\mu(1 - \mu)$, in which case the second moment of G will equal $\rho\mu + (1 - \rho)\mu^2$. Hence, by direct analogy with the treatment for finitely exchangeable Bernoulli variables, the problem of determining the feasible range for tail risks of binomial mixtures can be posed as a constrained optimization with Lagrangean:

$$\sum_{k=0}^{T} \int_0^1 \binom{n}{k} \theta^k (1-\theta)^{n-k} dG(\theta) + \tau_0 \left(\int_0^1 dG(\theta) - 1 \right)$$

$$+\tau_1 \left(\int_0^1 \theta dG(\theta) - \mu \right) + \tau_2 \left(\int_0^1 \theta^2 dG(\theta) - \rho\mu - (1-\rho)\mu^2 \right)$$

$$+ \int_0^1 \nu(\theta) dG(\theta)$$

where τ_i is the multiplier on the ith moment and $\nu(\theta)$ is the multiplier on each $dG(\theta)$ satisfying the complementary slackness conditions $\nu(\theta) \geq 0$, $dG(\theta) \geq 0$, and $\nu(\theta)dG(\theta) = 0$.

The solution for an optimal G requires that at every θ:

$$\sum_{k=0}^{T} \binom{n}{k} \theta^k (1-\theta)^{n-k} + \tau_0 + \tau_1\theta + \tau_2\theta^2 \equiv Q(\theta) \begin{cases} = 0 & \text{if } dG(\theta) > 0 \\ < 0 & \text{if } dG(\theta) = 0 \end{cases}$$

This nth-degree polynomial equation in θ looks daunting. Nevertheless, we can tease out sufficient information to establish that solutions for G are either two-point or tripolar distributions. To see this, differentiate Q three times to obtain:

$$Q'(\theta) = -n \cdot \binom{n-1}{T} \theta^T (1-\theta)^{n-T-1} + \tau_1 + 2\tau_2\theta$$

$$Q''(\theta) = n \cdot \binom{n-1}{T} \theta^{T-1} (1-\theta)^{n-T-2} [(n-1)\theta - T] + 2\tau_2$$

$$Q'''(\theta) = n \cdot \binom{n-1}{T} \theta^{T-2} (1-\theta)^{n-T-3}$$

$$[(n-1)(n-2)\theta^2 - 2T(n-T)\theta + T(T-1)]$$

Note that every interior zero of Q must represent a local maximum, while every pair of local maxima must be separated by a local minimum. Hence, if an optimal G attaches positive probability to two interior points and one or more other points, Q' would have to change signs at least four times. Since the derivatives are continuous, Q'' would have to change signs at least three times, and Q''' would have at least three interior zeros. In fact, Q''' has by inspection at most two interior zeros.

Therefore the support for an optimal G must consist of either two interior points or one interior point plus poles.

GEOMETRIC INTERPRETATION

Earlier I portrayed the feasible first and second moment pairs for sums of n finitely exchangeable Bernoulli variable as a convex hull $Conv(L)$ of a set L of $n + 1$ points representing degenerate distributions. We can do the same for the moment-pairs of G, except now the set L corresponds to the quadratic curve (θ, θ^2) between $(0,0)$ and $(1,1)$. Suppose that, for a specified tail, G generates an extreme risk within the class $\Phi(M)$ of distributions having a moment-pair M. Furthermore, suppose that G has the thinnest support in $\Phi(M)$. I will proceed to show that G has at most three points in its support.

Denote by H the subset of L that corresponds to the support of G. Since M lies in $Conv(H)$, by earlier discussion M must also lie in the convex hull of a three-or-fewer-point subset H^* of H. Hence $\Phi(M)$ must contain a distribution G^* having support H^*. Moreover, some other distribution G^{**} must exist such that G is a mixture of G^* and G^{**}. It is readily verified that G^{**} also belongs to $\Phi(M)$, and that the tail risk of G is a weighted average of the tail risks of G^* and G^{**}. Since the tail risk of G is extreme in $\Phi(M)$, G^* and G^{**} must have the same tail risk as G, and G must not have a larger support than G^*.

Convexity also provides some intuition for why optimal distributions with three points are tripolar. In the chart below, O denotes the origin, C the other pole $(1,1)$, M the constraint on the moments, and A and B two points on L such that OPB and APC are straight lines. Let X denote a candidate (θ, θ^2) for an optimal distribution. It must be associated with one or two other points on L such that M is contained in their convex hull. To dissipate the least variance, choose the point $X^* = (\theta^*, \theta^{*2})$ where the line through XM intersects L. A two-point distribution is feasible for any point lying in the segments OA or BC of L. However, if X lies in the segment AB, a two-point distribution is not feasible, and the best way to maximize or minimize tail risk is to associate it with the two poles O and C.

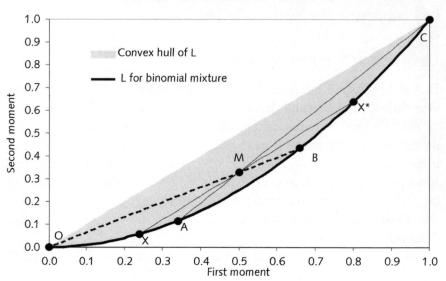

Convex hull for binomial mixture

ESTIMATING THE FEASIBLE RANGE

The preceding geometric characterization identifies every interior θ with a single two-point or tripolar binomial mixture G_θ satisfying the constraints on the moments. Indeed, it suffices to consider only those θ corresponding to points in the region OB, since every point in the region BC is twinned with a point in OA. The associated mixing distribution works out to:

$$dG_\theta(\theta) = \frac{\rho\mu(1-\mu)}{\rho\mu(1-\mu) + (\mu-\theta)^2}$$

$$dG_\theta(\theta^*) \equiv dG_\theta\left(\frac{\mu[(1-\rho)\mu - \theta]}{\mu-\theta}\right) = \frac{(\mu-\theta)^2}{\rho\mu(1-\mu) + (\mu-\theta)^2} = 1 - dG_\theta(\theta^*)$$

whenever $\theta \leq (1-\rho)\mu$. The region AB corresponds to $(1-\rho)\mu < \theta < \rho + (1-\rho)\mu$ where:

$$dG_\theta(0) = \frac{(1-\mu)[\theta - (1-\rho)\mu]}{\theta}$$

$$dG_\theta(\theta) = \frac{(1-\rho)\mu(1-\mu)}{\theta(1-\theta)}$$

$$dG_\theta(1) = \frac{\mu[1-\theta-(1-\rho)(1-\mu)]}{\theta} = 1 - dG_\theta(\theta) - dG_\theta(0)$$

We can then calculate the tail risk associated with each candidate G_θ and look for the extreme values. There is no explicit analytic solution valid for all T and n. However, it is easy to calculate numerical solutions.

ASYMPTOTIC LIMITS FOR THE FEASIBLE RANGE

Since the variance of the conditional mean of each variable equals $\rho\mu(1-\mu)$, the variance of the sum of the conditional means is $\rho n^2\mu(1-\mu)$. The total variance of the Bernoulli sums is $(1-\rho+\rho n)n\mu(1-\mu)$. The remainder $(1-\rho)n\mu(1-\mu)$ is the expected conditional variance. To confirm the latter figure, note that the conditional variance of the sum is $n\theta(1-\theta)$, and then take the expectation with respect to G.

Hence, the variance of the conditional mean sum accounts for $\frac{\rho n}{1-\rho+\rho n}$ of the whole variance, regardless of μ. As n rises, then unless G is degenerate, its variance will approach 100% of the total. Intuitively, it follows that for very large n, we can treat the tail risks as if the sums were concentrated at n times the values in the support of G.

Devlin identified the asymptotic feasible range as $\left[0, \dfrac{1}{s^2+1}\right]$. That is correct if we want a limit valid for all μ. The bounds when ρ and μ are known are given at the end of Chapter 4 and will be repeated here for lower s-tails:

- 0 if $s > \sqrt{\dfrac{\mu}{\rho(1-\mu)}}$

- $\left[0, \dfrac{1}{1+s^2}\right]$ if $\sqrt{\dfrac{\mu}{\rho(1-\mu)}} \geq s \geq \sqrt{\dfrac{\rho\mu}{1-\mu}}$

- $\left(1-\mu-\dfrac{(1-\rho)\mu(1-\mu)}{\mu-s\sqrt{\rho\mu(1-\mu)}}, 1-\mu+\dfrac{(1-\rho)\mu(1-\mu)}{1-\mu+s\sqrt{\rho\mu(1-\mu)}}\right)$

  if $\sqrt{\dfrac{\rho\mu}{1-\mu}} > s > 0$

A PHYSICAL ANALOGY

In a stationary container of gas, ignoring quantum effects, virtually any spatial distribution of molecules within the container is feasible. Nevertheless, unless the gas is ultra-sparse, the probability of the gas being significantly denser in one part of the container than another is infinitesimal. In other words, the overwhelming majority of distributions cluster tightly around the average distribution, which is uniform within the container. Ludwig Boltzmann proved this over a century ago and thereby founded the field of statistical thermodynamics, whose development has been crucial to modern chemistry, physics, and communications.

How is this analogous? Our Bernoulli variables correspond to ideal gas molecules, and the conditional Bernoulli mean to a uniform distribution within the container. The distribution G corresponds to probabilities that the container sits in various possible locations. Physics usually ignores G, because the experimenter can easily control the environment or simply measure the location relative to the container. If portfolio investors could easily control the environments they invest in, they could afford to ignore G too.

7 | Big Risks in Values at Risk

Of all the manners that Conway had acquired in English boarding school, by far the most redeeming was tact. Granted, tact was hard to maintain in the swashbuckling environment of a trading floor, and sometimes a harsh word was needed for credibility. Ms Manners would never survive on the Jolly Roger without mastering a few good curses and an occasional kick to the groin. Still, Conway tried to be gentle when he could and had been rewarded well for the effort. To help maintain his own cool in meetings, he tried to imagine the controversies that might arise beforehand and how he might defuse them.

But now Conway was troubled. For try as he might to visualize himself tactfully explaining Devlin's latest findings to the Risk Committee, he never finished his imaginary presentation before getting tossed out on his imaginary ear. How do you tell a Master of the Universe, for whom leverage is ambrosia, that Megabucks should occasionally keep 10 standard deviations' worth of returns as reserves in order to keep insolvency risks below 1%? *Ouch. Chalk off that approach too.* Suddenly Conway realized why his presentations were doomed to fail. It wasn't just that he wouldn't get a fair hearing. It was that he could already envisage the obvious rebuttal and couldn't counter it. "Devlin, something smells fishy."

"It's probably my left-over gefilte fish taco. I should have wrapped it better."

"Gefilte fish taco?" Conway shuddered. "Devlin, please bin that. And please will your stomach to science. Somewhere in the linings there lurks a good substitute for asbestos. But I was referring to your findings, not your leftovers."

"What findings? We've gone thru this lots of times."

"You tell me that large, highly diversified portfolios can bear a nearly 4% probability of a five standard deviation tail. Most other analysts would adamantly deny that. Is it not possible they see something you don't?"

"Sure it's possible. My estimates assume a bare minimum of information. Additional information can pin down the tail risks more precisely. In some situations five standard deviation outliers are rare. In others they're not. But analysts who claim such outliers are always rare aren't drawing on special insight. They're just ignorant or confused."

"One thing I have always admired about you, Devlin, is your deep respect for your colleagues. Would you like to have them drawn and quartered, or will hanging suffice?"

"I'm not criticizing anyone in particular. I'm just telling you how it is."

"How it is in theory, that is. Perhaps you've overlooked some factor that dampens tail risks in practice. I find it hard to believe that thousands of trained analysts could so drastically miss the boat."

"Well, they can and they did. Don't forget what happened to our predecessors. They completely misgauged Asian credit risks in 1997. Otherwise they'd still have their jobs and we wouldn't be discussing these issues now."

"That was different, Devlin. Their model was OK. They just used the wrong parameters. The default risk and the correlation turned out a lot higher than they thought."

"It wasn't just the estimates, Conway. It was also how they thought about the problem. Conventional mean-variance analysis straitjacketed their minds."

"What do you mean?"

"Crisis destabilizes core parameters and makes them hard to forecast. Factoring in that uncertainty would have forced a big hike in loss provisions. But conventional analysis doesn't make any provision for that. Its forecasts depend only on your best estimate of the mean, variance, and correlation, regardless of how unsure you are."

"Can we not incorporate the higher risk directly by upping the mean default rate?"

"That's not enough. For one thing, measured correlations tend to rise in crisis. That's a thorn in the side of conventional analysis."

"So how would you explain it?"

"I'm not sure I can explain all of it. But at least part of it stems from uncertainty. Recall that for infinitely exchangeable Bernoulli variables, the correlation is directly proportional to the variance of the mean default risk. The more uncertainty there is, the higher the estimated variance tends to be, so the estimated correlation rises."

"Interesting. So I take it we should revise the correlation estimate in line with the mean and variance of the conditional default risk."

"Unfortunately, that's still not enough. Even using the correct first and second moments, the standard model still understates the outer tail risks. Indeed, unless the variance of the conditional default risk is very low, the understatement tends to be severe. I've set up a spreadsheet that compares the actual and estimated tail risks under various assumptions. Care to run some simulations?"

"Sure. Suppose 1,000 different emerging Asian corporations each borrow $1 million for one year. If any default, we end up recovering half of what we're owed. Ordinarily, default rates are 3% per annum but in crisis, which occurs on average once every twenty-five years, default rates jump to 50%. Apart from the common default rates, repayments are uncorrelated. What's our value at risk with 99% confidence? That is, where's the threshold for a lower tail bearing 1% risk?"

"What's your assumption about lending spreads?" asked Devlin. "I'll need that to calculate losses net of profits."

"Forget about it. Assume a worst case where default occurs immediately after the money is lent rather than the day the loan comes due. While it is not very realistic, it is how regulators typically assess the value at risk for bank loans."

Devlin opened the spreadsheet, entered the numbers, and read off the results. "In calm times, our bank would stand a 1% chance of losing $21 million or more exclusive of profit. In crisis, the corresponding value at risk would be $268 million. If we didn't know whether we were heading for crisis, but assessed its probability at 4%, the value at risk would be $255 million."

True 1%-ile values at risk

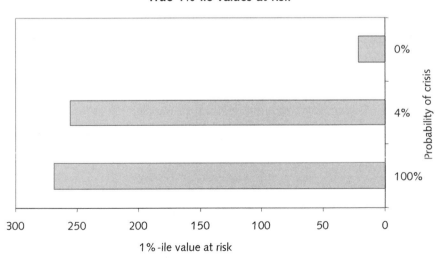

Assumes 1,000 conditionally independent assets each lose 0.5 in default, with risk 3% in calm and 50% in crisis.

"$255 million is very close to $268 million. Why is there so little difference in risk limits between a 4% probability of crisis and a 100% probability?"

"Under your assumptions, the chances of losing over $100 million in calm times are infinitesimal. So essentially every event in the 1%-ile occurs during crisis. If we know a crisis is coming, we should look at the 1%-ile of the crisis distribution. If there's only a 4% chance of a crisis, we should look at the 25%-ile of the crisis distribution. These points lie respectively 2.33 and 0.67 conditional standard deviations below the conditional mean. But, conditional on a crisis occurring, the standard deviation is small relative to the mean loss: $8 million versus $250 million. That's why there's not much practical difference between the two estimates."

"So if I understand you correctly, given a 4% chance of crisis, a 3.9%-ile estimate of value at risk would also lie near to $250 million."

"That's right. Since 3.9% equals 97.5% of 4%, the 3.9%-ile will lie nearly 2 standard deviations above the conditional mean. Let's see ..." Devlin did some quick calculations. "That works out to $235 million, which lies just over 4.5 unconditional standard deviations below the unconditional mean. That's close to the 4.6% maximum possible risk for such an outlier."

"Interesting. Your upper bounds are looking less outlandish than I thought. What are the corresponding values at risk implied by standard mean-variance analysis?"

"If you're absolutely certain what state you're entering, you get the right answers: $21 million in calm and $268 million in crisis to cover the 1%-ile. But a 4% probability of crisis really screws up the estimates. Let's start with the naïve approach, where you correctly forecast the probability of crisis but assume the correlation stays constant at zero. The 1%-ile loss works out to $32 million, or only one-eighth of the true value."

"What if the unconditional correlation is calculated correctly?"

"For a 4% probability of crisis, the unconditional correlation works out to 0.183. Standard mean-variance analysis will then re-estimate the 1%-ile value at risk at $132 million. That's a lot better than before but still barely half of what is needed."

"Those are huge discrepancies," said Conway. "Maybe my example was too stark. In practice, we don't know the true default risk in either state. Instead of a mean 3% default risk in ordinary times, let's assume the mean risk is distributed uniformly between 0% and 6%. And instead of a mean 50% default risk in crisis, let's assume the mean risk is distributed uniformly between 25% and 75%. How does that affect the 1%-iles?"

Estimated 1%-ile values at risk

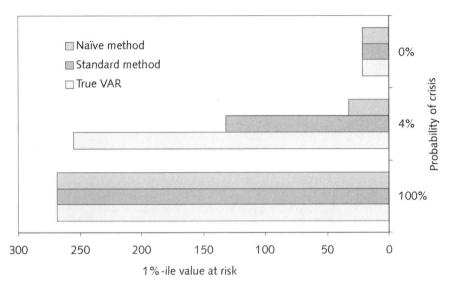

Assumes same as before. Standard method uses true first and second moments. Naïve method ignores correlation.

Devlin entered the new parameters and read off the results. "The true 1%-iles are $40 million in calm, $383 million in crisis, and $313 million with a 4% chance of crisis. The values at risk are larger than before, with a bigger gap between a certain crisis and a 4% chance of crisis."

"Why is that?"

"Each 1%-ile value at risk slightly exceeds the average loss given the corresponding 1%-ile of mean default risk. So the extra uncertainty breeds higher but more diverse risk limits."

"How about the estimates based on conventional mean-variance analysis? Are they any closer to the true values than before?"

"Not if you ignore the correlations induced by uncertainty. That would take you back to the naïve estimates from the previous case of $21 million in calm, $268 million in crisis, and $32 million with 4% chance of crisis from the previous case. The naïve estimates will understate the true values at risk by 30% to 90%."

"And if you calculate the first two moments correctly?"

"If you know whether crisis or calm applies, mean-variance analysis performs reasonably well. It estimates value at risk at $36 million in calm and

$419 million in crisis. Those values represent, respectively, a 9% underestimate and a 9% overestimate. Once again, however, mean-variance analysis handles skewed risks very badly. It estimates value at risk given a 4% chance of crisis as $139 million. That's barely more than in the first example and less than half of the true value."

Re-estimated 1%-ile values at risk

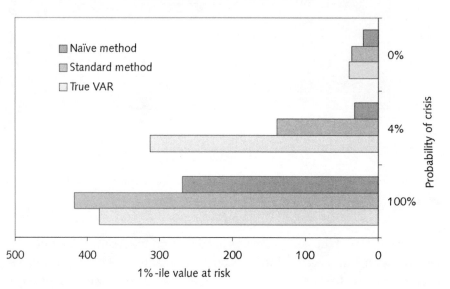

Assume mean default risk is uniformly distributed between 0% and 6% in calm and between 25% and 75% in crisis. Other assumptions remain as before.

"So what's the bottom line, Devlin?"

"I haven't got to the bottom, Conway. There's a lot more I don't understand."

"And I've got a business to run that needs answers."

"Nonsense, you've got lots of answers. Mean-variance analysis churns out answers all the time. But they tend to be answers to the question: 'What's the worst I should reasonably expect in the current state of the world?'"

"What's wrong with that question?"

"Nothing, if the chances of crisis are remote. But if the risks of crisis are significant, then what happens in the current state is basically irrelevant to the 1%-ile. You have to focus on the big risks."

"And if you're not sure what the big risks are?"

"Then you should take account of your uncertainty. Although uncertainty *per se* doesn't change the mean, it will generally breed higher perceived correlation. And in a diversified portfolio, correlation is crucial to value at risk."

Conway nodded slowly and reflected. It was at least getting clearer now why things were so unclear. The main unspoken rule at Megabucks was never to admit to ignorance about risks. Buy them, sell them, slice and dice and repackage them. But if you admit you don't know what the risks really are, you'll lose face with clients and colleagues and someone who claims to know better will stake claims on your turf. Better to pretend to know and blame subsequent outliers on Fate. That was a no-brainer for anyone savvier than Devlin.

But what Conway had never understood was why the outliers tended to be so high. Devlin's methods were offering two simple but powerful answers. First, the objective risk bounds were far higher than standard approximation suggested. Second, ignorance made the perceived risk bounds even higher.

"Devlin, is there any way to trim the uncertainty surrounding the tail risks? We could make high s-tail risks a lot more palatable to the Risk Committee if we could also identify ways to rule them out."

"You mean like 'Buy lots of disaster insurance' or 'Sell claims to big windfalls'?"

"No, I don't mean how to handle an existing tail risk. I mean how to specify more precisely what the tail risk is."

"Have you thought about measuring higher-order moments?" asked Devlin with a mischievous grin.

"Well, I suppose . . .," said Conway, and caught himself. *Whenever he gets that look in his eyes he can't be trusted. This must be some kind of test.* "Wait a second. I thought you told me we'd need the cross moments too."

"Yes, you would," said Devlin, grinning more broadly. "But computing power is cheap nowadays. And it's just the sort of thing to appeal to number-counting bureaucrats."

"But hardly anybody will understand what the higher-order cross moments mean."

"They don't need to understand them. Why don't you get a computer to estimate the maximum and minimum feasible values of s-tail risk compatible with a given set of moments and cross moments. Report that range only, and don't trouble about the individual moments."

"Good idea. So how much computing resources do we need to pin down the s-tail risks of portfolios containing, say, 1,000 credit assets?"

"Hmm. To get any s-tail exactly right, given that you haven't specified whether the assets are exchangeable, we'd need to measure the probability of every possible joint outcome. That's because the probability that only the first two assets default need not equal the probability that only the last two assets default, and so on. The number of distinct joint outcomes is 2^{1000}, or 1 followed by 434 zeroes. Of course, that assumes each asset is Bernoulli, with only two possible outcomes, which is a gross oversimplification. But it doesn't really matter since the amount of storage you'd need far exceeds the number of particles in the known universe."

"You know what Devlin" said Conway with a half smile. "There's something in you that's just plain mean," and they both laughed. "OK, let me simplify. Suppose that various credit assets are exchangeable with others, so we have only 40 distinct classes to deal with. Let's confine ourselves to moments of order five and less. How many moments will we have to keep track of?

Devlin typed in a few numbers and instantly got an answer. "1,221,758."

"Over a million? How can that be?"

"Each distinct mth-order moment is represented by a distinct combination of m numbers, where each number refers to a class and may or may not be repeated. So let's start counting. There are $\binom{40}{5}$ combinations of five numbers out of 40 in which no number is repeated. That's over 650,000, or more than half of the total we need. Similarly, there are $\binom{40}{4}$ or over 90,000 combinations of four distinct numbers out of 40. There are also $4 \times \binom{40}{4}$ or over 360,000 combinations of five numbers in which only four numbers are distinct, because any one of the four numbers can be repeated without creating a duplicate combination. So we're already up to 1.1 million and we haven't touched combinations of three, two, or one distinct numbers."

"How much more do we have to amalgamate classes or shave moments before this gets manageable?"

"It depends what you mean by manageable. Here, let me compose a table for you." Within a few minutes Devlin printed out the following sheet.

Conway gaped at the numbers. "They're overwhelming."

"Most likely. If you have 20 assets and don't request anything higher than a kurtosis or co-kurtosis, you have roughly 10,000 moments to track. That's not infeasible with today's technology, and tomorrow's will make it easier. But even there you run into a problem."

Number of distinct *m*th-order moments given *n* assets

	$m = 2$	$m = 3$	$m = 4$	$m = 5$	$m = 6$
$n = 5$	15	35	70	126	210
$n = 10$	55	220	715	2,002	5,005
$n = 15$	120	680	3,060	11,628	38,760
$n = 20$	210	1,540	8,855	42,504	177,100
$n = 30$	465	4,960	40,920	278,256	1,623,160
$n = 40$	820	11,480	123,410	1,086,008	8,145,060
$n = 50$	1,275	22,100	292,825	3,162,510	28,989,675
			including lower-order moments (except $m = 0$)		
$n = 5$	20	55	125	251	461
$n = 10$	65	285	1,000	3,002	8,007
$n = 15$	135	815	3,875	15,503	54,263
$n = 20$	230	1,770	10,625	53,129	230,229
$n = 30$	495	5,455	46,375	324,631	1,947,791
$n = 40$	860	12,340	135,750	1,221,758	9,366,818
$n = 50$	1,325	23,425	316,250	3,478,760	32,468,435

"Which is?"

"The precision of your estimates. In classical statistical theory you ought to have more observations than the number of parameters you're trying to estimate. But it's rare with daily financial data to have 10,000 observations that are considered relevant."

Conway threw up his hands. "So there are too many moments to remember, and if we could remember we probably couldn't measure them well anyway. I give up. The Risk Committee isn't going to buy any of this." *Not in the 30 seconds I'll get before they hang me out to dry.* "I'm going back to my office, grabbing a bottle of 100 aspirin, and counting out two tablets. Those are numbers I can deal with!"

While Conway treats his headache, I will flesh out the formulas that Devlin used.

IMPACT OF UNCERTAINTY

Higher uncertainty can generally be viewed as adding to the variance Var_G of G without changing its expected value E_G. However, Var_G divided by $E_G(1 - E_G)$ equals the correlation of the corresponding Bernoulli variables. From this perspective, uncertainty breeds higher correlation and can drastically increase the estimated value at risk.

For a more detailed derivation of the same result, consider the following:

- For exchangeable variables, the unconditional correlation ρ^U equals the unconditional covariance Cov^U divided by the unconditional variance Var^U.
- Cov^U always equals the mean conditional covariance $E[Cov^C]$ plus the covariance of the conditional mean $Cov[E_G]$. That includes the special case $Var^U = E[Var^C] + Var[E_G]$.
- Conditional independence implies $Cov^C = 0$.
- For exchangeable variables, $Cov[E_G]$ equals the variance of the conditional mean Var_G.
- For Bernoulli variables, Var^U equals the probability of success times the probability of failure or $E_G(1 - E_G)$.

It follows that $\rho^U = \dfrac{Var_G}{E_G(1 - E_G)}$ for conditionally independent Bernoulli variables. The higher is the perceived variance of G holding the mean fixed, the higher will be the perceived correlation.

USING HIGHER MOMENTS TO DEMARCATE TAIL RISK

Devlin's triangle shows us that N moments are generally needed to completely define the tail risk of a portfolio of N Bernoulli assets. If variables are not confined to binary outcomes, even higher moments will be needed. However, information on even a single higher moment will often help narrow the feasible s-tail risk. To take a simple though extreme example, information that the kurtosis is very close to -2 indicates that the risk of 2-tails is negligible, because the only distribution having a kurtosis of -2 puts all its weight equally ± 1 standard deviation from the mean.

To maximize or minimize tail risk subject to constraints on higher moments, we can simply append the constraints to the Lagrangeans we worked with earlier in Chapter 4. For example, if the constraints apply to skewness and kurtosis, then denoting their multipliers by τ_3 and τ_4 respectively, the necessary conditions for a maximum work out to:

$$-\tau_0 - \tau_1 k - \tau_2 k^2 - \tau_3 k^3 - \tau_4 k^4 \equiv Q(k) \begin{cases} = 1 & \text{if } p_k > 0 \quad \text{and} \quad k \leq T \\ \geq 1 & \text{if } p_k = 0 \quad \text{and} \quad k \leq T \\ = 0 & \text{if } p_k > 0 \quad \text{and} \quad k > T \\ \geq 0 & \text{if } p_k = 0 \quad \text{and} \quad k > T \end{cases}$$

So again the restrictions require that a polynomial Q lie on or above two line segments at levels 1 (in the tail) and 0 (outside the tail) respectively, with positive probabilities only where Q is touching the segments. The only difference is that Q is no longer quadratic but quartic. The interesting solutions come in two forms, depending on whether the quartic points upward or downward. See the diagrams below.

Maximal supports given restrictions on first four moments

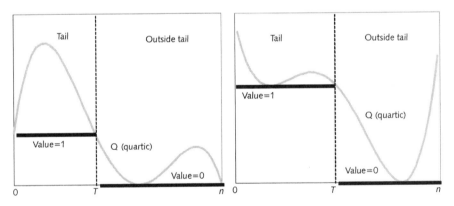

Clearly, the maximum s-tail risks given constraints on the third and fourth moments will be characterized by a support that is not larger than three or four points: T, a point between T and n, and either 0 and n or else one point between 0 and T. In either case this yields five degrees of freedom. There are also five constraints: the four moments plus the 0th moment or adding-up constraint on probabilities. Hence we simply need to work out the two sets of parameters and determine which one is feasible, according to whether a higher kurtosis would ease or tighten the constraint. An analogous procedure allows us to determine the minimum, or greatest lower bound if there is no definite minimum. For completeness, let me note that if the extreme probabilities are either 0 or 1, the optimal Q can be a straight line and there will usually be more degrees of freedom.

The preceding technique is readily extended to higher moments. Q becomes a polynomial of degree equal to the highest constrained moment m. The candidate solutions come in two variants depending on the sign of the constraint on the mth moment. In each variant, $m + 1$ constraints exhaust the $m + 1$ degrees of freedom. So there are at most two solutions, but in fact only one is feasible.

REVIEW: WHY CROSS MOMENTS MATTER

The preceding technique hinges on knowledge of the moments of the portfolio. For any given portfolio these can be calculated directly, given sufficient relevant data, and no cross moments are needed. However, what if we want to calculate the mth moment $E\left[\left(\sum_{i=1}^{n} w_i X_i\right)^m\right]$ of any portfolio of a given set $X_1, \ldots, X_n$ of assets? The expression in brackets expands to the sum of a lot of terms of the form $X_1^{i_1} X_2^{i_2} \ldots X_n^{i_n}$, indeed of every combination (possibly with a zero coefficient) for which the i_js sum to m. To calculate the mth moment of any portfolio, we will thus need to know all the mth-order moments of the n assets, both the own moments and the far more numerous cross moments.

COUNTING MOMENTS AND CROSS MOMENTS

How many distinct mth-order moments and cross moments are there? Here's one way to count them, courtesy of Feller. Arrange the numbers 1 to n from left to right, and insert m zeros somewhere to the right of 1. Identify the location of each zero by the nearest positive number to the left, and combine the locations into an m-tuple. For example, the series "1200304450" can be summarized as the quadruple $\{2,2,3,5\}$. Each m-tuple can be identified with an mth-order moment, unique up to permutation. The number of distinct combinations is clearly $\binom{m + n - 1}{m}$, since there are m zeros and $m + n - 1$ places to put them.

To count the distinct moments of order m or less, extend Feller's method by allowing zeros to be placed to the left of 1. For example, the series "012003450" can be summarized as the quadruple $\{0,2,2,5\}$. In this way moments of order less than m are uniquely identified too. Since there are now $m + n$ places to put the zeros, the number of distinct combinations is $\binom{m+n}{m}$. However, one of these combinations, where the zeros all lie to the left of 1, refers to the 0th-order moment, which is usually ignored.

8 | Good Approximations Behaving Badly

"You have convinced me," Conway said to Devlin a few days later over lunch. "No more 'one size fits all' risk analysis. From now on, we shall distinguish between credit risk and short-term market risk. I shall call it 'Devlin's Divide'. For credit risk, the $\dfrac{1}{s^2 + 1}$ rule will provide the upper bound. We will assume normality only for market risk."

Devlin nearly choked on his sandwich. He gulped down some water to clear his throat. "Conway, would you mind leaving my name out of this?"

"Don't be modest. You deserve it. And it's important that you re-establish your credibility within the firm. Without your help, I hardly could have realized credit risk was fundamentally different from the rest. Besides, I'm not going before the Committee without at least some vicarious backup from you. We're a team."

"But hold on just a second. I never told you credit risk was fundamentally different."

"Of course you did. All the variables we have examined pay either a fixed amount or nothing. That's nothing but credit risk."

"It's not just credit risk. Bernoulli variables can be building blocks of other risk processes too. For example, the average of a large number of independent, exchangeable Bernoulli variables converges to a normal distribution. That's just an application of the Central Limit Theorem. So if you want, you can model market risk as a collection of zero/one outcomes." Devlin bit into a pickle and some pickle juice dribbled down his chin.

Conway smiled. *Ah ha! For once I've got him.* "Have you not forgotten something, Professor? Something basic?"

Devlin looked around. "Gee, I forgot my napkin. Wait a second while I get one."

"Take this." Conway handed Devlin a napkin. "You always forget your napkin so I always pick up an extra. But it wasn't the napkin I was referring to. It was the fundamental difference between market risk and credit risk."

Devlin wiped his chin. "And what difference is that?"

"The obvious one. The range. An independent Bernoulli average will have a binomial distribution. And while a binomial might resemble a normal through much of the range, it can never match at the tails. A binomial distribution takes only positive values. A normal distribution is unbounded."

"You're right. The Central Limit Theorem doesn't apply to the extreme tails. You remember more of our statistics courses than I thought."

Conway nodded in satisfaction. He didn't often catch Devlin making a mathematical error and decided to forgive the backhanded compliment. Then Devlin added, "But that doesn't really matter. When the standard deviation gets small enough, a normal distribution with positive mean return is so unlikely to generate negative total wealth that you may as well ignore that possibility."

Trying to wriggle out of it, aren't you? "Wait a second Devlin. For weeks you have been warning me not to judge the tails of the distribution by its first two moments. Now you tell me I can and should. I just don't see the logic."

"We've already seen the logic. Even with credit risk there was one situation where we could effectively ignore the higher moments: infinitely exchangeable Bernoulli variables with zero correlation. By de Finetti's Theorem, such variables have to be unconditionally independent."

"Are you suggesting to draw a divide between dependent and independent risks rather than between market risk and credit risk?"

"In principle, yes. In practice, there's always a judgment call. Full independence is a myth. But sometimes it's a useful myth."

"Myth? What kind of myth? I am talking about reality. Suppose you and I go to a casino and play at two different roulette wheels. What possible connections are there between the two outcomes?"

"Lots. First, we might have an accident that prevents us from reaching the casino, or the power might go off. Taking that possibility into account, I'm less likely to play when you don't play and vice versa, so our outcomes are not independent."

"Let us ignore null outcomes."

"You're imposing a condition."

"A trivial one."

"That depends. But if you want to impose it, fine. Let's go back to the casino. You and I are placing bets at adjoining roulette wheels. Suddenly the police raid the casino, arrest me, and seize my money. Most likely you'll be arrested too. That makes our potential earnings dependent."

"The chances of a raid will be remote."

"Not in all countries at all times. Rule out the possibility and you impose another condition."

This is getting ridiculous. Accidents. Police raids. Next comes alien invasions. "Stop splitting hairs, Devlin. I am talking about fair games played by the rules."

"There aren't many of those. Even without raids, customers' expected returns from gambling will be negative. The customers' losses represent revenue to the casino operator, who has to cover costs to stay in business and wants to earn a profit. Some casinos charge higher spreads than others, say due to taxes. So if the odds are stacked unusually high against players at your wheel, they'll likely to be stacked unusually high against players at my wheel too."

"More nitpicking. Most roulette wheels are standardized, except for fraud."

"You keep acknowledging more qualifying conditions. But I agree that it's often reasonable to disregard them. I said you have to make a judgment call about whether to assume independence. That's all I meant."

Conway thought it over. When he spoke again he was softer. "Can you not test for independence?"

"Yes, if you have a representative sample or can run controlled experiments with all but a few factors held constant. But there's the rub. In practical finance, the relevant conditions are nearly always changing. No amount of trawling through data on prior emerging Asian securities' performance alone could have prepared you for the market crash in 1997. You would have had to realize that emerging Asia had entered an overinvestment crisis, and look for analogies to Japan in the late 1980s and to Britain and the US in the early 1890s."

"I get your point about Asia. Either you saw the crisis coming and adjusted your model's risk parameters or you didn't see it coming and took a beating."

"Or both. Even a good model can suffer big losses."

Conway nodded in agreement. "But I'm still trying to figure out when a model is good enough. Suppose most of the portfolio assets really are independent. Can we then safely use a normal approximation for the portfolio as a whole?"

"For the central tendencies, yes. Not for the tails though. The divergence from a normal distribution can be huge in the tails."

"Even if, say, 95% of the assets are independent?"

"Even if the proportion is higher. Let's work through an example." Devlin took out his pen and jotted down some numbers on the cleaner bits of his napkin. "Suppose you own 2,500 fair Bernoulli assets, each with default risk of 2%. Assume 98% of the assets are independent of every other, while the remaining 2% are perfectly correlated with each other. The expected number of defaults is 50, while the standard deviation works out to just under 10. Yet 2% of the time the number of defaults will lie in the neighborhood of 100, which is 5 standard deviations away from the mean."

"Ouch. So much for normal approximations."

"Not quite. A single normal approximation won't do the trick in this example. But two will."

"What do you mean?"

"I mean you need a weighted average of two normal distributions. The first, which carries a 98% weight, is conditioned on no defaults in the perfectly correlated group of assets. It will have a mean of 49 defaults, with a standard deviation slightly less than 7, the square root of the mean. The second normal distribution, which carries only a 2% weight, is conditioned on default in the perfectly correlated group. It will have a mean of 50+49=99 defaults, again with a standard deviation slightly less than 7."

"I'm afraid you're losing me." *Again.*

"Are you finished eating? If so, let's go back to the office and I'll draw you a proper picture." They cleared their trays and went back to Devlin's desk. Devlin quickly produced the following chart on his computer.

"I see," said Conway. "A small number of highly correlated assets can drastically change the tail risks. We ought to view their behavior as a conditional shift in the portfolio mean. But what if none of the assets is highly correlated? Can we use a single normal approximation then?"

"Not necessarily. Suppose we own 50 assets. The returns on each of these assets represent the average of 50 different Bernoulli factors with common mean 0.98. Of the 50 factors, all but one are independent of each other and of the factors influencing other assets. The remaining factor is common across assets. What's the correlation between any two assets?"

"0.02, which will be difficult for most tests to distinguish reliably from zero."

"That's right. Yet the distribution of returns on the aggregate portfolio will remain as before. All we've done is rename the 2,500 original assets as factors and rearrange them into 50 exchangeable assets."

Probability distribution of defaults

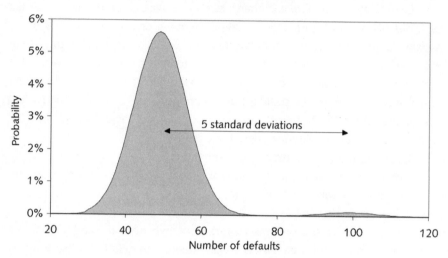

2,500 Bernoulli assets each have 2% mean default rate. 2% of assets perfectly correlated. The rest are independent.

"Hence a small correlation across a lot of assets can wreak as much damage as a lot of correlation across a few assets."

"Yes, provided a common or largely common factor is driving the small correlation."

Conway felt like a horse training for a show jumping event. Every time he jumped a fence, Devlin raised the pole higher. "What difference does that make?"

"It keeps diversification from diluting the aggregate contribution to risk."

"Is that not taken care of in the correlation?"

"Not necessarily. If we recast the previous example to maintain the 50 exchangeable assets, the 0.98 mean and the 0.02 correlation but get rid of the common factor, portfolio returns will look much more normally distributed."

"How can you get rid of the common factor without altering the correlation?"

"Let the factor m affecting asset n be the same as the factor n affecting asset m, for every m and n. Otherwise let all the factors be independent with mean 0.98. You can readily check that the correlation remains 0.02, without a single factor affecting three or more assets."

Conway borrowed a pen and paper from Devlin. "So instead of $50 \times 49 = 2450$ factors appearing once and one factor appearing 50 times, you have $50 \times 49 \div 2 = 1225$ factors appearing twice and 50 factors appearing once. The variance of the portfolio must remain the same, since that depends only on the variance and correlation of the factors. Hence $2450 \times 1 + 1 \times 50 \times 50$ must equal $1225 \times 2 \times 2 + 50 \times 1$. Yes, both expressions equal 2950."

"How about the tail risks?"

"They must be smaller now, because it takes at least 25 independent factors to trigger 50 'defaults', whereas before a single factor could suffice."

"Exactly. The aggregate portfolio distribution should look much smoother, without a double peak." After a few minutes Devlin produced another chart:

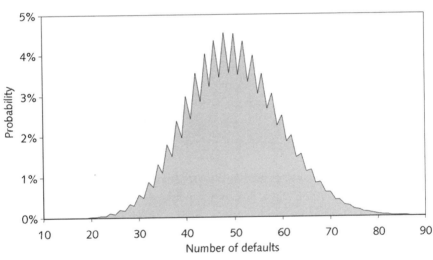

Alternative probability distribution of defaults

2,500 Bernoulli exchangeable assets have mean default rate 2% and correlation 2%. No single factor affects three or more assets.

"Smoother? That looks like a porcupine under a blanket. Are you sure you calculated this right?"

Devlin laughed. "I forgot. Given the changed assumptions, most defaults will come in pairs. That makes the surface jagged. But it's a lot closer to a normal distribution in the upper tail than it was before. Before you had a 1% chance of 100 or more defaults, a 5 standard deviation event. Now you don't have a 1% chance of even 75 or more defaults, a 2.5 standard deviation event."

"That's remarkable. Even though the first two moments and cross-moments are held constant, the presence or absence of a common factor changes the tail risk. Why didn't anyone ever tell me that before?"

"I don't know. Maybe others didn't notice, or maybe it wasn't relevant for the distributions they were using."

"Oh really? You mean there are some portfolios that common factors don't affect, other than via volatility and correlation?"

"Yes. Normally distributed portfolios. The first two moments of their independent and common factors must determine the aggregate mean and variance, so nothing else matters."

"I see. What others are there?"

"There aren't any. Every other kind of portfolio distribution is susceptible to the presence of a common factor, above and beyond pairwise correlation. It's easy to prove using moment-generating functions. Want me to show you?"

"For the moment I'll concede the point. But don't you think it's strange?"

"What's strange about a common factor affecting tail risk more than the correlation suggests? Seems perfectly natural to me. Correlation is only a pairwise measure. A common factor affects everything."

"I mean it's strange that the normal distribution is the only case that makes the one reducible to the other. I would have expected normal random variables to be more ... well, more *normal*. Why call them normal if they behave so exceptionally?"

"The term 'normality' refers to the trend behavior of large numbers of independent random variables. But common and partially common factors are precisely what interfere with independence. And when they interfere, normality may not be even approximately correct. Like I said, there really is a huge divide between dependence and independence!"

Conway scowled. If what Devlin was saying was right, most of what they had learned in statistics was irrelevant to the problems Megabucks was facing. *But let's not throw out the baby with the bathwater.* "Calm down, Devlin. I grant you're on to something. I just doubt the differences are as stark as you're making them out. How about showing me that proof now?"

Before Conway tackles the proof he could use a brief refresher on normality. Devlin will probably explain something along the following lines.

NORMALITY

X is said to have a standard normal distribution, denoted $\mathcal{N}(0,1)$, if the probability density $f(x)$ equals $(2\pi)^{-1/2}\exp(-\frac{1}{2}x^2)$. This density has a well-known bell shape, as shown in the chart below.

Standard normal distribution

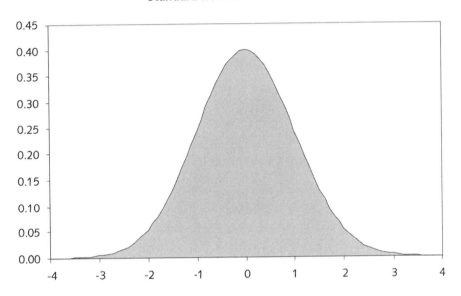

$\mathcal{N}(0,1)$ is symmetric around the origin, so the mean and all odd-ordered moments (which turn out to be well-defined) will be zero. For n even, the nth moment equals the product $(n-1)(n-3)\cdots 3\cdot 1$ of all the odd numbers less than n. In particular, the variance equals one and the kurtosis zero. I'll show you a neat way to calculate that later.

If X has a standard normal distribution, then $X' = \sigma X + \mu$ will have probability density $(2\pi\sigma)^{-1/2}\exp\left(-\frac{1}{2}\left(\frac{x'-\mu}{\sigma}\right)^2\right)$ with mean μ and variance σ^2. This is called the general normal distribution – or "Gaussian" if you are trying to avoid confusion with other uses of the word "normal" – and is denoted $\mathcal{N}(\mu,\sigma^2)$. Note that, when measured in standard deviations from the mean, any normal random variable has the density $\mathcal{N}(0,1)$.

Tail Risks for Normal Distributions

The s-tail risk $\int_{-\infty}^{-s} (2\pi)^{-1/2} \exp\left(-\frac{1}{2}x^2\right) dx$ for the cumulative normal distribution cannot be solved analytically except for a few values. However, it is readily calculated to high precision for any s. Here is a table of representative values.

Normal tail risks for $s = 0$ to $s = 6$

Standard	Tail risk	1/Tail risk
0	0.500000000	2.0
0.5	0.308537539	3.2
1.0	0.158655254	6.3
1.5	0.066807201	15
2.0	0.022750132	44
2.5	0.006209665	161
3.0	0.001349898	741
3.5	0.000232629	4.3 thousand
4.0	0.000031671	32 thousand
4.5	0.000003398	294 thousand
5.0	0.000000287	3.5 million
5.5	0.000000019	53 million
6.0	0.000000001	1.01 billion

Note that the tail risk drops off more and more rapidly as one moves away from the mean. Shifting the s-threshold to 2 from 1 cuts the risk by a factor of 7. Shifting the s-threshold to 6 from 5 cuts the risk by a factor of nearly 300, or over 40 times as much.

Central Limit Theorem

The normal distribution derives its name and fame mostly from its excellent approximation to the distributions of the sums and averages of most large sets of independent random variables. The classic expression is the Central Limit Theorem, which says that all s-tail risks of all sums of n independent, identically distributed variables with finite mean and variance converge to the s-tail risk of a standard normal distribution.

Moreover, the Central Limit Theorem can be extended to cover independent variables that are not identically distributed, provided that no small subgroup completely dominates the rest. There are even extensions that deal with infinite variance.

While the shape of the underlying distributions does not affect the ultimate convergence – that's the point of the Theorem! – it does affect the speed of convergence. The more the individual tail risks deviate from a normal, the longer convergence tends to take. The differences in speed can be quite striking, so what is large enough to warrant a normal approximation in one context may be way too small in another.

EXAMPLES OF BINOMIAL CONVERGENCE TO NORMALITY

Here are a few binomial examples intended to illustrate both convergence and its variations in speed. I begin by charting the distribution for 13 fair coin tosses. It looks about as bell-shaped as a 14-point distribution can be. The difference between the corresponding cumulative binomial and normal probabilities at half-integers is at most 20 basis points. (I use half-integers rather than whole integers to compensate for the difference between discrete and continuous distributions.)

Probabilities of heads with 13 independent coin tosses

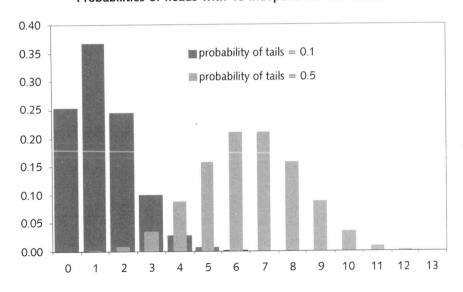

probability of tails = 0.1
probability of tails = 0.5

Now let's reduce the probability of tails to 0.1. Here the normal approximation for 13 coin tosses fares much worse. The mean of the sum is 1.3, and lies so close to the origin that the bell shape has to be severely clipped. Even if we toss 5 times as many coins, so that the mean is 6.5 like before, the resulting distribution is still visibly skewed to the right. To show this more clearly, I superimpose a discrete normal approximation, calculated as the integral of the corresponding normal distribution between $k - \frac{1}{2}$ and $k + \frac{1}{2}$, and omit the graph beyond 16 heads because the corresponding odds are less than 0.02%.

Binomial distribution versus normal approximation for $\mu = 0.9$, $n = 65$

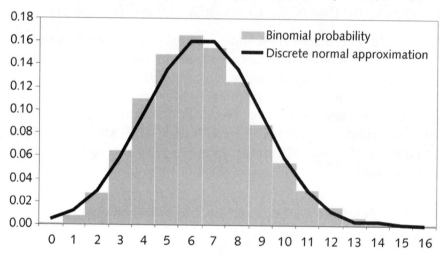

MOMENT-GENERATING FUNCTION OF A NORMAL DISTRIBUTION

The moment-generating function (MGF) for $\mathcal{N}(\mu, \sigma^2)$ takes a very neat form: $\mathcal{M}(\gamma) = \exp(\gamma\mu + \frac{1}{2}\gamma^2\sigma^2)$. To confirm that, calculate:

$$\mathcal{M}(\gamma) = \int_{-\infty}^{\infty} \exp(\gamma x) \cdot \frac{1}{\sigma\sqrt{2\pi}} \cdot \exp\left(-\frac{(x-\mu)^2}{2\sigma^2}\right) dx$$

$$= \int_{-\infty}^{\infty} \frac{1}{\sigma\sqrt{2\pi}} \cdot \exp\left(\frac{-x^2 + 2\mu x - \mu^2 + 2\gamma\sigma^2 x}{2\sigma^2}\right) dx$$

$$= \int_{-\infty}^{\infty} \frac{1}{\sigma\sqrt{2\pi}} \cdot \exp\left(-\frac{-(x-\mu-\gamma\sigma^2) + 2\gamma\mu\sigma^2 + \gamma^2\sigma^4}{2\sigma^2}\right) dx$$

$$= \exp\left(\frac{2\gamma\mu\sigma^2 + \gamma^2\sigma^4}{2\sigma^2}\right) \cdot \int_{-\infty}^{\infty} \frac{1}{\sigma\sqrt{2\pi}} \exp\left(-\frac{(x-\mu-\gamma\sigma^2)^2}{2\sigma^2}\right) dx$$

$$= \exp\left(\gamma\mu + \tfrac{1}{2}\gamma^2\sigma^2\right)$$

where the last step follows from the unit measure of the total normal density. For a standard normal distribution, $\mathcal{M}(\gamma) = \exp(\tfrac{1}{2}\gamma^2)$. To verify the first four moments, we can calculate:

$$\mathcal{M}'(\gamma) = \exp\left(\tfrac{1}{2}\gamma^2\right) \cdot \gamma \Rightarrow \mathcal{M}'(0) = 0$$

$$\mathcal{M}''(\gamma) = \exp\left(\tfrac{1}{2}\gamma^2\right) \cdot (\gamma^2 + 1) \Rightarrow \mathcal{M}''(0) = 1$$

$$\mathcal{M}'''(\gamma) = \exp\left(\tfrac{1}{2}\gamma^2\right) \cdot (\gamma^3 + 3\gamma) \Rightarrow \mathcal{M}'''(0) = 1$$

$$\mathcal{M}''''(\gamma) = \exp\left(\tfrac{1}{2}\gamma^2\right) \cdot (\gamma^4 + 6\gamma^2 + 3) \Rightarrow \mathcal{M}''''(0) = 3$$

Note that all MGFs with quadratic exponents correspond to a normal distribution, because if any additional constant appeared in the quadratic, the measure $\mathcal{M}(0)$ would not equal 1.

MOMENT-GENERATING FUNCTIONS OF SIMPLE PORTFOLIOS

Taking the multiple α of an asset is equivalent in MGF terms to multiplying γ by α. Taking the sum of independent assets is equivalent in MGF terms to multiplying the individual MGFs together. Denoting the MGFs by $\mathcal{M}_i$ for asset X_i and $\mathcal{M}_P$ for the portfolio $\sum_{i=1}^{n} \alpha_i X_i$,

$$\mathcal{M}_P(\gamma) \equiv \int \cdots \int \exp\left(\gamma \sum_{i=1}^{n} \alpha_i x_i\right) dF_1(x_1) \cdots dF_n(x_n)$$

$$= \left(\int \exp(\gamma\alpha_1 x_1) dF_1(x_1)\right) \cdots \left(\int \exp(\gamma\alpha_n x_n) dF_n(x_n)\right)$$

$$= \mathcal{M}_1(\alpha_1\gamma) \cdot \mathcal{M}_2(\alpha_2\gamma) \cdots \mathcal{M}_n(\alpha_n\gamma)$$

Alternatively, we can say that the logarithms of the MGFs of portfolios of independent assets are additive in the logarithms of the individual MGFs, with each γ rescaled to reflect individual quantity.

WHEN MEAN AND VARIANCE SUMMARIZE THE COMMON FACTORS

Suppose every asset's returns can be decomposed linearly into a common group of independent factors $\{Z_i\}$, each with mean μ_i and variance σ_i^2. Then any aggregate portfolio can be treated as a linear combination $\sum a_i Z_i$ with mean $M = \sum a_i \mu_i$ and variance $V = \sum a_i^2 \sigma_i^2$. Furthermore, suppose the common factors don't influence the portfolio other than via M and V. What does that tell us about the common factors?

For any given γ, let us choose the $\{a_i\}$ to maximize or minimize the logarithm of the portfolio MGF, subject to M and V being held constant. The associated Lagrangean is:

$$\sum \ln\big(\mathcal{M}_i(a_i\gamma)\big) + \tau_1\big(M - \sum a_i\mu_i\big) + \tau_2\big(V - \sum a_i^2\sigma_i^2\big)$$

with first-order conditions of:

$$\frac{d \ln\big(\mathcal{M}_i(a_i)\big)}{da_i} = \frac{\tau_1\mu_i}{\gamma} + \frac{2\tau_2\sigma_i^2}{\gamma}a_i$$

Given three or more common factors there will be a continuum of feasible $\{a_i\}$ associated with a given M and V. Each of these must satisfy the first-order conditions, which implies that the derivative of $\ln(\mathcal{M}_i(a))$ must be linear in a. Only MGFs of normal distributions possess that property. Hence every common factor Z_i will have to be normal.

A CHARACTERISTIC FUNCTION PATCH

The preceding demonstration applies only to distributions with a well-defined MGF. It doesn't cover densities like $f(x) = 2x^{-3}$ for $x \geq 1$, whose third and higher moments are infinite. For a comprehensive proof, we need to call on the MGF's big brother, the characteristic function.

Characteristic functions, which I will denote by $\mathcal{C}$, embrace all probability distributions. Anything MGFs can do, characteristic functions can do as well or better. However, they are defined in terms of complex numbers. Specifically,

$$\mathcal{C}(\gamma) \equiv \mathcal{M}(i\gamma) \equiv E\big[\exp(i\gamma X)\big] = E\big[\cos(\gamma X)\big] + iE\big[\sin(\gamma X)\big]$$

where $i \equiv \sqrt{-1}$. While complex numbers aren't much harder to deal with than real numbers, they can be intimidating to the novice. I used

MGFs instead as a proxy. The more rigorously inclined should substitute $i\gamma$ for γ.

NORMAL COMPONENTS OF NORMAL PORTFOLIOS

Actually, it's not necessary to assume the existence of three or more common factors. Any time a normal random variable can be decomposed into independent factors, those factors must indeed be normal. The proof requires more advanced analysis of characteristic functions than I will attempt here.

To summarize, if first and second moments tell you all you need to know about underlying common factors, both the portfolio and its common factors must be normal. Conversely, if the portfolio isn't normal, you can't identify underlying common factors just by looking at the first two moments.

9 | The Abnormality of Normality

Conway was shaving a few days later when the thought hit him. It was simple. So simple that he could have kicked himself for not having thought of it earlier. *Talk about not seeing the forest for the trees!* But at least he realized now. Best of all, he had the satisfaction of realizing before Devlin did. *No, wait, the best part will be watching Devlin eat some humble pie.* Conway dressed quickly and hurried to the office, more cheerful than he'd been in weeks.

At the office, Conway walked casually by Devlin's desk. *Don't give it away too soon.* "Oh, Devlin, if you have some free time later, why don't you drop by my office. Nothing urgent. Just a few thoughts I'd like to bounce off you." *Like a colossal counterexample to your claim.*

When Devlin came by, Conway ushered him in and closed the door behind him. "Please sit down. Make yourself comfortable. Can I get you some coffee?"

"Cut the air hostess routine, Conway. What's the bad news?"

"Don't be paranoid. I just wanted to pick up on an earlier conversation in a more relaxed fashion. Now, where had we left off?"

"Dependence versus independence. The Great Divide."

"Yes, the Great Divide. If I recall correctly, did you not place normality on the independent side?"

"Yes, normality is ultimately the statistics of independent variables."

Good. Now for the refutation. "Then why do we bother to calculate correlations between assets assumed to be normal?"

"For the same reason we calculate correlations between any assets: to help work out the variance of portfolios."

"But if assets are correlated they can't be independent. So the Divide can't be 'Great'. Normality bridges it." *Triumph at last.*

Devlin started to object and then caught himself. He reflected a while and began again. "I see the bridge you're driving towards. But it doesn't go where you think. The dependence that normality can handle is just a concealed form of independence."

"Why is it that whenever I win an argument you redefine the terms? And stop speaking gobbledygook. Concealed independence?"

"OK, let's start with a simple example. You divide up your portfolio equally between two lousy traders, Punch and Judy. Each of them earns normal, uncorrelated, identically distributed returns, with zero mean excess return 0 and a variance that we can re-measure as $\frac{1}{2}$. What are the odds of a portfolio loss exceeding 4?"

"That's easy. The portfolio will be normally distributed with mean 0 and variance 1, so the odds are 1 in 30,000."

"Wrong. You forgot to ask me about common factors."

"Why should I ask? You yourself said they don't matter for normal portfolios."

"They don't. But normal assets don't always add up to normal portfolios. They certainly don't for Punch and Judy."

"Why not?"

"Because Punch and Judy have a strange relationship. Half the time they completely agree so hold the same portfolios. Half the time they completely disagree so just go long and short against each other. But neither has consistently superior judgment."

"Sounds like a few traders I know."

"I've disguised the names to protect the guilty." Devlin returned Conway's grin. "Anyway, in aggregate Punch and Judy earn either nothing at all or exactly twice their lone returns, with even odds of either. So the probability of an aggregate 4-tail is half the probability that Judy loses at least 2. The latter represents a 2.8-tail for Judy alone, since her standard deviation is 0.7. Work thru the calculations and you get odds exceeding 1 in 1,000. That's over 30 times what you estimated."

"I see. The aggregate distribution becomes an equal mixture of two normals, one of which is degenerate. But the 4-tail risk is still small. How much worse can it get?"

"About ten times worse. Suppose you divide your assets between a thousand Punches and Judies, each of whom always holds standard normal portfolios. With probability 9% the traders pool their information and decide on identical portfolios. Otherwise they act independently. The variance given a pooled decision accounts for nearly all the aggregate variance, so the latter will be roughly $9\% \times 1000^2 = 90{,}000$ and the aggregate standard deviation will be 300. When a 4-tail occurs, then almost certainly the traders hold identical portfolios and are losing at least $4 \times 300 \div 1000 = 1.2$ each. Multiply the 9% probability of collusion by a roughly 11% individual chance of losing 1.2 to obtain an overall risk of 1%. That's about the highest 4-tail risk you can get given a mixture of normal distributions with a common mean."

"A 1% 4-tail risk is a lot less than the 6% you can approach when the means vary."

"Still, it's significant. Big or small, it shows that aggregate portfolio normality requires both individual asset normality and stable portfolio variance. Only one type of distribution satisfies both these conditions: multivariate normal."

"I thought multivariate normal just meant you have multiple normal variables with possible correlation."

"So do most folks. They either never saw or don't remember the counter-examples in their statistics texts. That's hardly surprising. The formula for a multivariate normal density looks innocent enough, apart from the messy correlations. To really appreciate what multivariate normality imposes, you need to think geometrically. May I use your computer to compose some charts?"

"Be my guest".

"Let's go back to the first Punch-and-Judy example and think about what the joint probability density looks like. Measuring Punch's returns along the X-axis and Judy's returns along the Y-axis, it's clear that all the positive probability is scrunched into two diagonals. One diagonal represents equal returns, the other opposite returns. Within each diagonal the probability density is normal, so the joint density is just the crossing of two flattened bells."

Conway studied the chart. "What do the bands represent?"

"The vertical zigzags don't mean anything. They just provide a sort of scaffolding for the density perched on top. As for the horizontal lines, they connect the level curves or points of equal probability density. Each level curve consists of four distinct but symmetric points, one in each quadrant, with nothing in between."

"OK, I understand the chart. I take it each level curve for multivariate normal variables is connected?"

"Yes, and more symmetric too. Here's the joint probability density for two standardized independent normal variables, the so-called standard bivariate case. It looks like a regular three-dimensional bell, with level curves that are circles."

Probability density for 1st Punch-and-Judy example

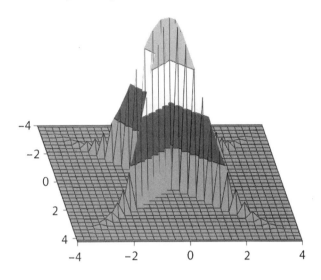

"So it's completely symmetric around the vertical axis."

"Exactly. That's called rotational symmetry. The probability of a given deviation depends only on its distance from the origin, not its direction."

"So I take it that the level curves for *n* standard independent normal

Probability density for standard bivariate normal

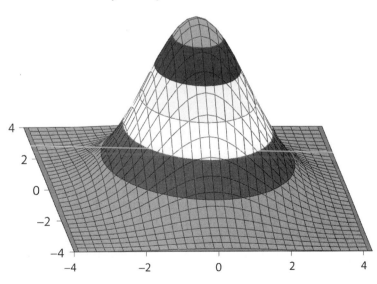

variables are the surfaces of n-dimensional spheres, which again makes the density rotationally symmetric within its defining space."

"Great, Conway, you're getting it. Now think of each observation as a record of random motion in n orthogonal directions. If the motion is standard multivariate normal, would you agree that any movements at right-angles to each other must be independent?"

"Yes. Otherwise the graph of the density would depend on the orientation of the right-angles, and wouldn't be rotationally symmetric."

"Exactly. Now what physical entity most behaves like this?"

"I don't know. A chicken with its head cut off? Mind you, it's too big and floppy to pinpoint to one location."

Devlin grinned. "That's the right idea. The answer is: an isolated container of gas. The gas molecules amount statistically to sub-microscopic headless chickens, flitting around in space. So given the right time scale their motion is standard multivariate normal."

"Wait a second. Why does it have to be standard multivariate normal? Don't any other distributions have independent and rotationally symmetric components?

"No, only rescalings of standard multivariate normality. That's how Maxwell derived the velocity distribution of gas molecules in the first place."

"Rotational symmetry sounds very reasonable for gases, apart from gravitational asymmetries. But surely it's too rigid for finance."

"I wouldn't say that. You can shift, stretch, and slant it if you want."

"What do you mean by that?"

"Start by associating each measure of rotationally symmetric motion with a different ruler. Then shift, stretch, and slant the rulers. Shifting a ruler's origin changes the mean of the associated measure. Stretching or compressing a ruler by a constant proportion changes the volatility of the associated measure. Slanting a ruler changes the mean and volatility of the measure and its correlation with other measures. But the measures remain multivariate normal. They'll just have means, variances, and covariances that differ from the standard zeroes and ones."

"How about an example?"

"Sure. Starting with the standard bivariate normal, let me shift the X-axis origin two units to the right, halve the size of the Y-ruler, and rotate the Y-axis 45 degrees clockwise." Devlin drew two sets of rulers. "The new rulers define $X' = X - 2$ and $Y' = \sqrt{2}X + \sqrt{2}Y$. So X' has mean -2 and variance 1, Y' has mean 0 and variance 4, and the covariance is $\sqrt{2}$."

Original and revised rulers for example

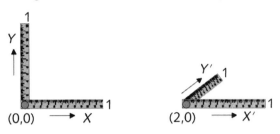

$$Y \qquad 1$$
$$(0,0) \longrightarrow X \qquad\qquad (2,0) \longrightarrow X'$$

"What happens to the standard bell when you remeasure?"

"It starts looking like a traffic cone that's seen too much traffic. Circular level curves get transformed into ellipses, while spheres get transformed into ellipsoids. Here's what they look like for the transformation above."

Conway wasn't sure whether he was eyeing the level curves or the level curves were eyeing him. "Thanks for the pictures, Devlin. But I'm disappointed with the kind of dependence they're associated with. By reversing the transformation, you can explain everything in terms of independent variables again. Granted, the independent variables will generally be portfolios rather than single assets, but that's just an accounting issue."

"That's right. Here the reverse transformation is $X = X' + 2$ and $Y = \sqrt{\frac{1}{2}Y' - X'} - 2$. But countless other transformations will work as well. Just rotate the X-axes and Y-axes by the same angle to preserve a right-angle between them. Given rotational symmetry, that has to keep the resulting variables independent."

"Yes, and that's what's bothering me. I want some examples of multi-variate normality that can't be reinterpreted so easily as independence."

"There aren't any. Every single portfolio of multivariate normal assets can be decomposed in countless ways into independent normal building blocks."

"No exceptions?"

"None."

Devlin's declaration didn't leave Conway much hope of rebuttal. "OK. Let me grant you the theoretical point. What kind of discrepancies are we talking about in practice?"

"I'm not sure. Why don't we examine some data?"

"Sounds good. But let's not get too complicated. Can you obtain monthly equity returns for the US, the UK, France, Germany, and Japan over the past 30 years?"

"I can get that. You want the returns gross or net?"

Density and level curves for revised measure

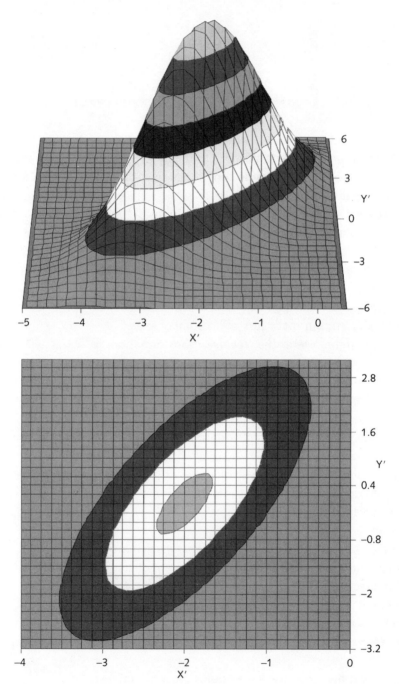

"Include the dividends and take out the returns in local currency. That way we strip out most of the influence of dividend, inflation, and exchange rate fluctuations."

While Devlin prepared the series, Conway asked him what kind of test he planned.

"First I'll calculate the means vector and the covariance matrix. I'll use that to standardize the data in terms of five uncorrelated, zero-mean, unit-variance series. Then I'll measure the squared distance from the origin of each standardized observation, which is just the sum of the squares of each component. If multivariate normality applies, the squared distance should follow a chi-squared distribution with five degrees of freedom."

"And if the data passes the chi-squared test, can we accept it as multivariate normal?"

"Not quite. The chi-squared test looks only at the distance from the origin, not at rotational symmetry. If the data were all bunched in one cone, they might pass the chi-squared test, but some portfolios of assets would still be blatantly non-normal. But let's not worry about that yet. I suspect the data won't come close to passing the chi-squared test."

Conway agreed and set off on his daily walkabout on the trading floor while Devlin processed the data. When he returned, Devlin pointed proudly to the chart displayed on the monitor. "What do you think of this fit?"

Comparative histograms

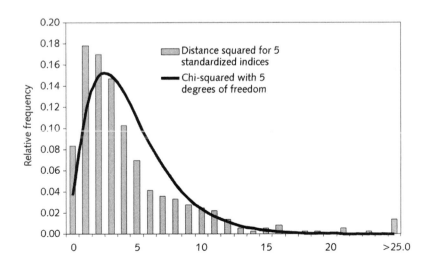

"Not too good. Compared with the histogram for the corresponding multivariate normal distribution, there's too much probability mass near the origin, too little in the middle, and way too much far away. How much higher than 24 do the values get?"

"Nearly 80 for January 1975, when UK equities jumped by half in a month, French equities rose 22%, and the other indices changed only modestly. The chances that 360 observations from a five-variate normal distribution would show an outlier of that magnitude or higher are around 1 in three trillion."

"Obviously a one-time event or a mistake. Let's ignore it. What's your next-worst outlier?"

"35 in October 1987. If you could observe a 5-variate normal distribution once a month for the next 40,000 years, you'd expect roughly a single outlier of that magnitude or higher."

"That crash was a fluke. Let's ignore that observation too."

"Conway, you can't just keep cutting out the outliers to create a normal distribution. It's like trying to create a woman by castrating a man. Sometimes the parts you lop off are symptoms of a more fundamental condition."

Conway laughed. "Come on, you have to admit those were extremes. I want you to take those two months out and reestimate the fit. Where does that leave us?"

Devlin did as Conway asked. "The worst outlier now has a value of 46.6. In a 5-variate normal world, a monthly deviation that bad or worse should occur about once every 12 million years. There are also outliers at 33 and 27, which are roughly 1 in 200,000 and 1 in 20,000 events under normality. The odds that three outliers of those magnitudes or higher will occur in our purged sample, assuming independent observations on a 5-variate normal distribution, are less than one in 16 billion."

"One in 16 billion? After purging the sample of the two worst outliers?

"I haven't mentioned four more outliers which represent 1 in 1,000 events. If we include those ..."

Maybe if I shut my eyes and think happy thoughts this will all go away ...
"Enough. I never imagined the fit would be that bad. How does that compare with the odds that each series individually is normal?"

"Ignoring the observations in January 1975 and October 1987, the worst outlier in each series lies between 3.6 and 4.3 standard deviations from the mean. If the series were normally distributed, the odds of that occurring would range from 1 in 18 to 1 in 318. The chances that a normal distribution would have three outliers worse than the three worst outliers observed range from 1 in 2,000 to 1 in 200,000."

"So if ordinary normality compares the observed outliers to the odds of, say, a sunny month in London, multivariate normality compares them to a snowball's chance in hell."

"In physics, no. In finance, yes."

"How do you propose to deal with that?"

"I'm switching to physics. Just after lunch. Care to join me?"

"I don't know much physics."

"I meant lunch."

"Oh, sure. There's a small chance I'll even pick up your tab."

"A normal chance?"

"More like a multivariate normal chance."

I hope Devlin takes his wallet with him. While they're out let's bone up on the mathematics of multivariate normality. First, I shall briefly review basic matrix theory, which we can no longer conveniently avoid. The payoff will be large in terms of simplified expression and sharper intuition. I will especially emphasize the geometric interpretation of matrices.

MATRICES

A matrix A of size $m \times n$ is a rectangle of numbers having m rows and n columns:

$$A = \begin{pmatrix} a_{11} & \cdots & a_{1n} \\ \vdots & \ddots & \vdots \\ a_{m1} & \cdots & a_{mn} \end{pmatrix}$$

Sometimes it is identified as $A \equiv [a_{ij}]$. A matrix with all zero elements is called a zero matrix and denoted $\mathbf{0}$. Two matrices are equal only if they have the same size and all their corresponding elements are equal.

When $m = n$, A is called a square matrix of order m. Its m elements a_{ii} are called its diagonal elements. If all off-diagonal elements are zero, a square matrix is called diagonal. A diagonal matrix with all diagonal elements equal to one is called an identity matrix and denoted I.

MATRICES AS BUNDLES OF VECTORS

A matrix having only one column is called a column vector or simply a vector. A matrix having only one row is called a row vector. Note that a matrix can be viewed as a row of column vectors or a column of row vectors.

A row or column vector with m elements is called an m-vector. Geometrically, an m-vector corresponds to a straight arrow in m-dimensional space, with the ith element representing the element's extension in the ith dimension. Hence, a matrix is a bundle of arrows: either m arrows in n-dimensional space or n arrows in m-dimensional space. The vector components of square matrices can be viewed as defining the edges of a parallelepiped (a multi-dimensional parallelogram).

CALCULATION SHORTCUTS

Matrix calculations can be quite cumbersome. Fortunately there are some well-established shortcuts to simplify and speed them. It's easy nowadays to get a computer to do the calculations quickly for you.

ADDITION AND SCALAR MULTIPLICATION OF MATRICES

Two matrices can be added only if they have the same size. To form a sum $A + B = C$, add the corresponding elements: $c_{ij} = a_{ij} + b_{ij}$. Geometrically, matrix addition corresponds to placing the tails of the component B vectors at the heads of the A vectors and defining the C vectors as the arrows stretching from the tails of A to the heads of B.

To multiply a matrix by a scalar s, multiply each matrix element by s: $sA \equiv [sa_{ij}]$. Geometrically, scalar multiplication multiplies the length of each vector arrow by the same amount without changing its direction.

All of the basic properties of scalar addition and multiplication apply to addition and scalar multiplication of matrices.

MATRIX MULTIPLICATION: SIMPLEST CASE

Matrix multiplication is tricky. Let's start with the simplest case: namely, a row vector $R \equiv [r_1 \dots r_m]$ multiplied by a column vector

$$C \equiv \begin{bmatrix} c_1 \\ \vdots \\ c_m \end{bmatrix}$$ of the same size. By definition the result is a scalar

$r_1 c_1 + r_2 c_2 + \ldots + r_m c_m$. Apart from the row versus column rule, this is the same operation as a vector dot product. It works out to the length of R times the projection of C on R. The projection tells us how far C extends in the direction of R. Hence an equivalent expression for dot product is the product of the length of the two vectors and the cosine of the angle between them.

Vector projections

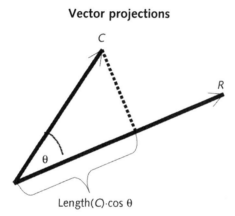

Length(C)·cos θ

GENERAL MATRIX MULTIPLICATION

For general matrix multiplication, the first matrix A has to have the same number of columns n as the second matrix B has rows. The resulting matrix AB will have as many rows as A and as many columns as B, with every $\langle i, j \rangle$ element calculated as the ith row vector of A times the jth column vector of B, or $\sum_{k=1}^{n} a_{ik} b_{kj}$.

Geometrically, matrix multiplication rotates, stretches, and squashes each vector separately, but in a way that preserves linear scaling relations. That is, while a ruler transformed by matrix multiplication may be longer or shorter than before and point in a new direction, it will still measure lengths in a straight line and divide them evenly. The mathematical shorthand for this is "linear transformation".

   Pre- or post-multiplying A by a complementary identity matrix I yields A. Matrix multiplication also satisfies $(AB)C = A(BC)$ and $A(B + C) = AB + AC$. However, the product AB does not generally equal BA, even when A and B are square matrices of the same order.

TRANSPOSITION

Switching the rows and columns of a matrix A, so that the $\langle i,j \rangle$ element becomes the $\langle j,i \rangle$ element, creates a so-called "transpose" matrix A'. The transpose is the reflection of a matrix in a strange kind of mirror. Only square matrices that are symmetric along the main diagonal equal their transpose. Yet all matrices equal the transpose of their transpose.

   The transpose of a sum equals the sum of the transposes: $(A + B)' = A' + B'$. The transpose of a matrix product equals the product in reverse order of the transposes: $(AB)' = B'A'$.

   Products of a matrix with its transpose are the matrix counterparts of squares, and see a lot of use. $X'X$ measures the squared length of the vector X, while XX' gives the crossproducts of all the elements of X. Note that matrix squares are always symmetric.

ORTHOGONALITY

Two nonzero vectors B and C will be orthogonal if and only if the cosine of the angle between them is zero, which in turn requires $BC' = B'C = \mathbf{0}$. If each vector also has unit length they are called orthonormal.

   All the vector components of matrix A will be orthonormal to each other if and only if $A'A = I$. You would think that such matrices would be called orthonormal, but most texts call them orthogonal instead. I am tempted to buck convention here but won't.

   Geometrically, multiplication by an orthogonal matrix A corresponds to a fixed rotation, because it preserves all distances and all angles between vectors:

$$(AX_1)'AX_2 = X_1'A'AX_2 = X_1'X_2$$

Hence, a mathematical structure is rotationally symmetric around the origin if and only if multiplication by orthogonal matrices preserves it.

DETERMINANTS

The determinant $|A|$ of a square matrix A of order m (non-square matrices don't have determinants) amalgamates $m!$ different products. Each product contains exactly one element from each row and one element from each column: i.e., $a_{1i_1} a_{2i_2} \cdots a_{mi_m}$ where $(i_1, i_2, \ldots, i_m)$ is a permutation of the set of integers 1 through m. Each permutation is classified as odd or even depending on how many pairs of elements have to be interchanged in order to restore the ordering $(1, \ldots, m)$. The determinant sums all the even-permutation products and subtracts all the odd-permutation products.

The determinant of a product of square matrices equals the product of its determinants. Transposing a square matrix doesn't change its determinant. Hence an orthogonal matrix must have a determinant of one.

Geometrically, the determinant measures the volume (apart from sign) of the parallelepiped associated with the square matrix. The volume will be zero if and only if at least one of the component vectors lies in the hyperspace spanned by the others, or equivalently, is a linear combination of the others.

MATRIX INVERSION

Any matrix B such that $AB = I$ is called a right inverse of A, in which case A is a left inverse of B. With a square matrix A, the only type we will be interested in inverting, the inverse A^{-1} exists and is unique if and only if $|A|$ is nonzero. This is consistent with the notion of determinant as volume. A zero determinant means that the corresponding linear transformation eliminates at least one dimension of information, and you can't restore something from nothing. However, if the information still exists, inversion just runs the original transformation in reverse. Algebraically, the inverse is readily expressed in terms of determinants and sub-determinants.

QUADRATIC FORMS AND POSITIVE DEFINITE MATRICES

The product $\omega' A \omega$ of a vector ω and symmetric square matrix A of the same order is called a quadratic form. If all possible quadratic forms using A are positive (nonnegative), A is called positive definite (positive semi-definite). If A is non-symmetric, the symmetric matrix $(A + A')/2$ will yield exactly the same quadratic forms as A.

A symmetric positive definite matrix A will have a positive determinant $|A|$ and a positive definite inverse A^{-1}. It will also have an invertible matrix square root $A^{1/2}$.

Multivariate Moments in Matrix Form

Now we can begin to exploit the main advantage of matrices, namely the incredible simplification of notation and derivation. Let $X = [x_1 \ldots x_n]'$ denote a vector of n scalar random variables and let $M \equiv E[X]$ denote the corresponding vector of means. Then the matrix $\Sigma \equiv [\sigma_{ij}]$ of covariances equals $E[(X - M)(X - M)']$. For any vector ω of n constants, also note that the variance of the linear combination $\omega'X$ will equal the quadratic form $\omega'\Sigma\omega'$:

$$Var[\omega'X] = E[\omega'(X - M)(X - M)'\omega]$$
$$= \omega'E[(X - M)(X - M)']\omega = \omega'\Sigma\omega$$

Since variance can never be negative, Σ must be positive semi-definite. Assuming no component of X is a linear combination of the others, the variance will never be zero except in trivial cases. In that case, Σ will be positive definite.

Multivariate Normality

An n-vector X is multivariate normal if its density takes the form:

$$f(X) = \frac{1}{\sqrt{2^n \pi^n |\Sigma|}} \exp\left(-\tfrac{1}{2}(X - M)'\Sigma^{-1}(X - M) \right)$$

The vector mean and covariance matrix work out to M and Σ respectively. Standard multivariate normality is characterized by mean $\mathbf{0}$ and variance I. Every multivariate normal distribution can be standardized by performing the transformation $Y = \Sigma^{-1/2}(X - M)$.

INDEPENDENCE + ROTATIONAL SYMMETRY = STANDARD MULTIVARIATE NORMALITY

Suppose the components x_i of X are mutually independent, which implies $f(X) \equiv f_1(x_1) \ldots f_n(x_n)$ for component densities f_i. Suppose also that X is rotationally symmetric, so that $f(X) = f(AX)$ for any orthogonal matrix A. It follows that the various components $A_i x_i$ will be independent too, implying $f(AX) = f_1(A_1 x_1) \ldots f_n(A_n x_n)$. Again, the physical analogy is ideal gas molecules without gravity, whose movements along three orthogonal axes are considered independent no matter how the axes are drawn.

Combining these equations, taking logarithms, and defining $h_i \equiv \ln(f_i)$, we see that:

$$h_1(x_1) + \cdots + h_n(x_n) = h_1\left(\sum_{j=1}^{n} a_{1j}x_j\right) + \cdots + h_n\left(\sum_{j=1}^{n} a_{nj}x_j\right)$$

Next, differentiate with respect to x_1 and any other variable x_k to obtain:

$$0 = h_1''\left(\sum_{j=1}^{n} a_{1j}x_j\right) a_{11}a_{1k} + \cdots + h_n''\left(\sum_{j=1}^{n} a_{nj}x_j\right) a_{n1}a_{nk} \equiv B'A_k$$

where $B_i \equiv h_i''\left(\sum_{j=1}^{n} a_{1j}x_j\right) a_{i1}$. Since B is orthogonal to every vector A_k that is orthogonal to A_1, it must be a scalar multiple of A_1. This can occur only if h_i'' takes a single value regardless of X or I, in which case each f_i is normal with the same variance. Furthermore, by rotational symmetry f_i must be centered at the origin, as otherwise it would have multiple peaks. It follows that X is a scalar multiple of a standard multivariate normal random variable.

While the preceding proof assumes the density is differentiable, it can be extended to cover all cases by comparing characteristic functions. Full rotational symmetry isn't needed either, just symmetry under one sufficiently complex rotation.

CHI-SQUARED TESTS FOR MULTIVARIATE NORMALITY

The sum z of the squares of n standard independent normal variables has a chi-squared density $\chi^2(n)$ given by:

$$f(z) = \frac{z^{(n/2)-1}e^{-z/2}}{2^{n/2}\Gamma(n/2)}$$

Here $\Gamma(n/2)$ is the gamma function defined to make the density integrate to 1, with value $\left(\frac{n}{2} - 1\right)!$ for n even and $\frac{1}{2} \cdot \frac{3}{2} \cdot \frac{5}{2} \cdots \frac{n-1}{2} \cdot \sqrt{n}$ for n odd.

A general multivariate normal X can be transformed into a vector $\Sigma^{-1/2}(X - M)$ with standard independent normal components, whose sum of squares equals $(X - M)^T\Sigma^{-1}(X - M)$. This is the statistic Devlin used to test for multivariate normality.

DERIVATION OF CHI-SQUARED DENSITY

A standard independent n-variate normal density will be directly proportional to $\exp\left(-\frac{1}{2}\sum_{i=1}^{n} x_i^2\right) \equiv \exp\left(\frac{1}{2}r^2\right)$, where r denotes the distance from the origin. The points lying r away from the origin form the surface of an n-dimensional spheroid, and hence have a measure proportional to r^{n-1}. So the probability of lying between r and $r + dr$ from the origin will be proportional to $r^{n-1}e^{-r^2/2}dr$. To find the probability that the squared distance from the origin lies between z and $z + dz$, substitute z for r^2 and dz for $2r \cdot dr$ to obtain $z^{(n/2)-1}e^{-z/2}dz$. Therefore the sum of the n squares obeys a $\chi^2(n)$ distribution.

APPLICATION OF CHI-SQUARED TEST

Devlin calculated the probability that the same number of independent samples from $\chi^2(5)$ would produce equal or worse outliers. For multiple outliers at different values, this calculation gets quite complicated, so Devlin approximated it as the product of the tail risk for each outlier times the number of feasible permutations of the outliers. This approximation is an overestimate. For example, with outliers at 46, 33, and 27, Devlin effectively counted the combination (46,34,34) twice – once as (>46,>33,>27) and once as (>46,>27,>33).

From another angle, Devlin's categorization of "worse outliers" is an underestimate. For example, Devlin did not count (27,32,50) as worse than (27,33,46), although its probability density is less. However, remember that the purged sample contained four more outliers whose associated tail risks were each less than 1 in 1000. Incorporate these into your calculations and you'll find that the odds are even more remote than Devlin claimed.

10 | Dependent Independence

Enlightenment? Or disillusionment? The words evoke such contrasting emotions that we often forget they refer to the same thing: the abandonment of a hopeless hope. Conway, who had just abandoned a hopeless hope about statistics, felt neither enlightened nor disillusioned. He felt relieved. He would have felt even more relieved had Devlin stopped slurping his spaghetti. When Devlin paused for water Conway seized the opportunity for conversation. "I have to hand it to you, Devlin."

"That's all right. I can reach the glass myself."

I hope that was intended to be a joke. "I meant thanks for showing me the Great Divide. On one side, normality and independence, the twin towers of classical statistics. On the other side, the kind of dependency we meet in practice. Too bad there's no bridge between them."

Devlin felt so awkward at being agreed with that he didn't know what to say. Besides, when he heard his thoughts reflected back to him, he wasn't sure he agreed with himself. "Maybe I was too extreme," he said after a pause to wipe spaghetti sauce off his shirt. "Maybe the bridge is under our nose. A Cheshire Cat bridge."

Conway tapped on his wristwatch and raised it toward his ear. "I'm sorry, Devlin. My Universal Speech Translator has broken down. Your last phrase sounded like 'Cheshire Cat bridge'. Until I get this fixed I'll have to ask you to speak directly in English."

Devlin was too lost in thought to hear. He flashed back to his childhood in New Mexico, and the many hikes he used to take in the mountains near his home. The trails snaked in and out of danger, and sometimes banked so sharply he felt sure they would lead him off the edge. But every turn brought a new vision of the path ahead. "Yes, that's it," he said, nodding to himself. "A Cheshire Cat bridge."

"Devlin!" said Conway in exasperation. "What on earth are you talking about?"

"I mean a bridge that comes and goes and reappears in new places, like the Cheshire Cat in *Alice in Wonderland*."

"Thank you. That was in English. Too bad I don't have a clue about what this means for statistics."

"Oh, I think you do. We've already seen one Cheshire Cat bridge. It's called de Finetti's Theorem. Comprende?"

"I'm not sure. De Finetti's Theorem associates dependent Bernoulli variables with mixtures of conditionally independent variables. So the conditionality serves as a kind of bridge between dependence and independence. Oh, I get it now. A Cheshire Cat bridge is a conditional bridge, and so is de Finetti's Theorem."

"Bingo. And what's the best continuous analogue to independent Bernoulli sums?"

"Normal sums. So are you suggesting that we model dependent continuous variables as mixtures of normal variables?"

"Mixtures of conditionally multivariate normal variables, to be precise."

"That's a mouthful. Sounds terribly complicated."

"Not conceptually. It simply amounts to dividing a complex dependence into perfectly dependent and independent parts."

"Where's the perfect dependence?"

"The common conditioning event or regime. By definition, it's the same for all the variables. And once the regime is set, the variables are multivariate normal, which we've seen already can be transformed into independent components."

"That's neat. So what classes of dependent variables can be modelled this way?"

"They all can. At least I think so."

"Wait a second. De Finetti's Theorem applied only to symmetrically dependent Bernoulli variables. So why does your continuous analogue apply to all dependent variables?"

"Because, unlike de Finetti's Theorem, I'm not forcing the components to be symmetric. While I don't have a rigorous proof, I can't think of a likely counterexample. Geometrically, it just amounts to modelling a given terrain as a mixture of squeezed bell-shaped mountains"

"What about distributions with sharp edges?"

"We already looked at one example."

"We have?"

"Sure. Remember the uniform Bose-Einstein distribution for Bernoulli sums? We saw how to express it as a uniformly distributed mixture of binomial sums. As the number of variables rises, each binomial converges to a normal distribution."

"I see. But that requires a continuum of conditional states. How good an approximation can you get with just a few states?"

"I don't know. But I like the question. Give me a couple hours to work on this and I'll get back to you." They cleared their trays and went back to work.

Conway figured Devlin wouldn't finish that quickly and he was right. Devlin didn't turn up until the next day at 11 a.m., when he stumbled into Conway's office clutching a sheaf of papers.

"Up all night, were you Devlin?"

"How'd you know?"

"You still have a spaghetti stain on your shirt."

"Look, I have some neat results. Do you want to see them or be my mother?" While Devlin could think math without sleep, he couldn't stay civil without sleep.

"Alright, alright. Of course I want to see them. Keep your hair on."

Devlin handed Conway a chart. "Let me start with an approximation to a standard uniform distribution using a mixture of 8 normals."

Approximating a uniform distribution with 8 normals

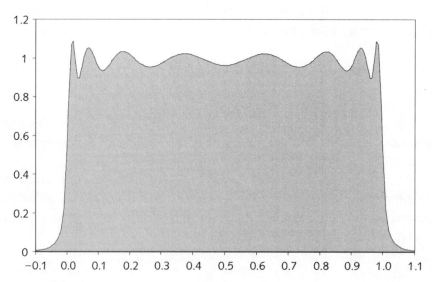

"Not bad. Not bad at all. But a bit too wavy. I can clearly distinguish 8 peaks. The walls at 0 and 1 aren't steep enough either."

"I know," said Devlin. "Here's a redo with 16 normals."

Approximating a uniform distribution with 16 normals

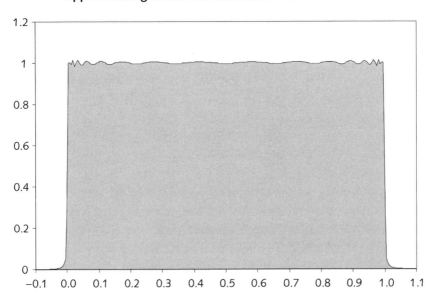

"Wow. That's impressive. I can just barely pick out the separate peaks and the slant at the walls."

"I thought you'd like it." Devlin was feeling quite pleased with himself, like a preschooler who has just learned to draw a square. "Now let's move on to a uniform bivariate distribution on the unit square. Modeling this as a mixture of conditional bivariate normal distributions amounts geometrically to squeezing bells and packing them neatly into a cube. That's harder than the univariate analogue, especially at the corners. Plus you need roughly n^2 normal distributions to get the same evenness of coverage on a unit square as you get with n normals on a unit line segment."

"So you're saying that 64 bivariate normals aren't going to fit a cube as well as 8 normals fit a square."

"That's right. And even that assumes a best-case scenario, where we select the best possible parameters. Since I haven't worked out a formula for the optimal fit, I have to rely on trial and error. The more variables we have to search, the more likely even our best answer is to fall well short of the optimal."

Conway did some mental arithmetic. "Wait a second. Each bivariate normal is characterized by 2 means, 2 variances, 1 covariance, and 1 probability weight. You searched by trial and error for combinations of 384 continuous-valued parameters?"

"Actually, I used 80 bivariate normals to get a better fit. But it was a lot easier than you make it sound. First of all, I took advantage of symmetries. A uniform square is symmetric along its vertical axis, its horizontal axis, and both its diagonal axes. So I concentrated only on solutions that share those symmetries. That left me 10 bivariate normals to search, with each distribution replicated 8 times through reflection along an axis of symmetry. And the probabilities on those 10 normals had to sum to $\frac{1}{8}$. That cut the degrees of freedom to $6 \times 10 - 1 = 59$."

"That's still far too many for a reasonable grid search. How'd you manage?"

"Computer sex."

Conway turned pale. *Oh no. I haven't been trained to deal with this. This is way out of my league.* "Look Devlin, eh, I do appreciate that this is important and complex work you're doing here and I appreciate your dedication, but everybody has his limits and I think you may have gone beyond them. I'll tell you what. Take a few days off. Start rebuilding your social life. If you want, I can put you in touch with some specialists I know who . . ."

"Shut up, Conway," Devlin snapped. "This has nothing to do with me and the computer. I'm talking about a kind of sex game that the computer plays. It picks some candidate solutions at random, lets the best ones reproduce by exchanging the 'genes' that code different parameters, and allows occasional mutations. The point is to improve on blind trial and error by mimicking biological evolution. The techniques are called 'genetic algorithms', and they're easy to implement. One night sufficed to breed a few thousand generations."

Sounds like the computer had a lot more fun than Devlin. He's getting more wound up every day. Pretending to be unfazed, Conway said nonchalantly, "So you solved the problem after all."

"Hah! I seriously doubt it. You never know for sure with genetic algorithms, but a few thousand generations are highly unlikely to solve a problem of this magnitude."

"So what did you, or should I say Mother Computer, come up with?"

Devlin handed Conway another chart. "Here's a cutaway view of the first quadrant, assuming the unit cube is centered at the origin."

Approximating a uniform bivariate with 80 bivariate normals

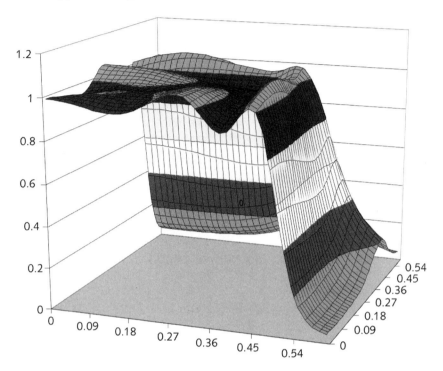

"Kind of droopy, isn't it? Looks like a wrinkled tablecloth. Or maybe a dentist's view of a sick molar."

"Sorry," Devlin apologized. "I was hoping for something better myself." His face drooped like the chart. Lack of sleep always brought out the manic depressive in Devlin.

"Come on, Devlin, please don't take this so personally. Whether the fit is good or bad doesn't reflect on you."

For weeks Devlin had been leading the charge, dragging Conway along. Now he was losing heart. "I was just hoping conditional multivariate normality would prove useful. I am tired of discovering things that don't work."

Whether consciously or unconsciously, partners tend to compensate for each other. So it was that Devlin's despair tapped a gusher of enthusiasm in Conway. "But it does work. Remember this is a closeup view, which focuses on imperfections. The interior of the square has a density close to one, while most of the exterior has a density nearer zero. That's the essence of what we're after. Only the boundaries are giving us trouble."

"Yes, even with an 80-state mixture that a computer took all night to weave into a pseudo-uniform density. I'm afraid this isn't tractable after all."

"Devlin, how often do we deal practically with probability densities that have perfectly flat tops and vertical cliffs? Apart from occasional binary options, I can't think of any."

"I agree that rounded tops and tapered tails will be much easier to fit using conditionally multivariate normal densities. But fit them with just a handful? I doubt it. They'll all look like wrinkled tablecloths or teeth with cavities. Or worse."

"But maybe that's good enough, Devlin. For the practical problems we face, we don't need a perfect fit. I'll be happy if they pass the squint test."

"I don't know that test."

"It's my favorite. Chart the empirical frequencies against the predicted probabilities and check the resemblance when you squint your eyes."

"Oh, that's very scientific," said Devlin, dripping with sarcasm.

"You can make it more scientific if you want. Yesterday you checked the likelihood of multivariate normal outliers using the chi-squared test. That's a kind of squint test. As you pointed out, passing it doesn't guarantee rotational symmetry. But I'd be willing to give any sample that does pass the benefit of a multivariate normal doubt."

"Well, I wouldn't."

"I know that. And you're a better scientist than me for it. But it makes you too much a perfectionist in practice. At least in our kind of practice."

"You guys aren't perfectionist enough."

"No, we're not. We squint too hard or keep our eyes wide shut. Thanks for opening my eyes, Devlin. I appreciate it. I really do. But now I want to squint them again while you run another test."

"What test is that?" asked Devlin, sullen and suspicious.

"I want you to try to fit a mixed multivariate normal distribution to the stock index data we looked at yesterday."

"Good luck squinting. The data comes in 5 dimensions. You'll need supernatural vision."

"Touché. My vision is only ordinary. I just want to know how many states you need to mix before no outlier looks too outrageous."

"How far is outrageous?"

"You tell me."

"How am I supposed to tell you when you're the one squinting?" Devlin's face turned red. "This is a farce. I've had it."

Conway spoke calmly, but couldn't hide his sarcasm. "I'm very sorry if you feel it beneath you to develop your clever theories into something of practical use."

"Maybe it's over my head."

"Maybe you should try to help before you say you can't."

"Maybe you should answer your own ridiculous questions."

"Enough!" snapped Conway, who then immediately softened his tone. *Remember he's been up all night.* "Devlin, let me remind you that I am both your colleague and your manager. However, as your friend, I will chalk this up to exhaustion. Go home and get some sleep. Tomorrow we shall forget this ever happened."

The next day a chastened Devlin turned up bathed and in fresh clothes, with his hair combed and his shirttail tucked in tightly. No spaghetti sauce in sight. He hadn't looked like that since his second day on the job. "Conway, I took the index data home and fitted mixed multivariate normals to it. The best answer I can give you is two."

"You can fit the data with two multivariate normals? Including January 1975 and October 1987?"

"Yes, including everything. At least I can do it well enough to pass a squint test. I divided the observations into two regimes. If the observations in each regime had been generated by a conditionally multivariate normal distribution with the same means and covariances as the sample, the radii squared ought to follow in each case a chi-squared distribution with 5 degrees of freedom. Take a squint at these histograms."

Conway looked over the charts "This is much better than before. But why are there so many gaps for Regime 2?"

"Small number problem. I only put 24 of the 360 observations into Regime 2. With so few entries it's not so odd to have gaps."

"Why didn't you split the regimes up more evenly?"

"It was easier not to. I was just looking for a simple way to reduce outliers. So first I tried to identify the largest sample I could that wouldn't include wild outliers. The chi-squared boundary I ended up settling on was 16, which corresponds to a 0.7% tail probability. The chances that none of 360 multivariate normal observations will land in such a tail are only 10%, so in at least one respect I am being conservative."

"How did you know that the outliers could be embraced by a single additional regime?"

A crude mixed multivariate normal fit

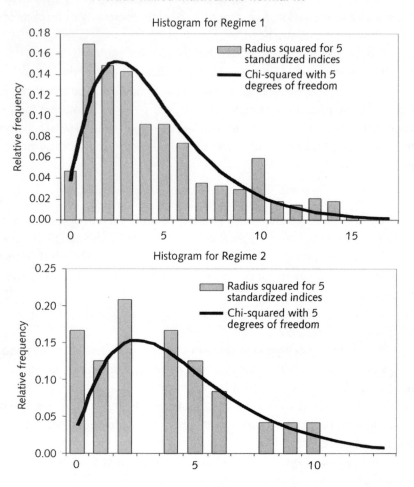

Histogram for Regime 1

Histogram for Regime 2

"I didn't. I was prepared to exclude outliers again and form a third regime, or even more. But I didn't need to. Assuming the observations in Regime 2 faithfully reflect the underlying mean and covariance matrix of a multivariate normal distribution, even the worst outlier represents a tail probability of more than 5%. The chances that 24 observations wouldn't yield any outliers in such a tail are only 28%, so two regimes have indeed eliminated fat tails."

"This is amazing. Even you must be impressed with the fit."

"I kind of am. It's light years ahead of the conventional approach. But ..." Devlin stopped himself, mindful of yesterday's scolding.

"But what?"

"Never mind."

"Devlin, I know what you're thinking. You're thinking I don't want to hear any criticisms. But that's not it. I just don't want the criticisms to paralyze us. Now that you've come up with something, you're more than welcome to point out its shortcomings. What don't you like?"

"Well, for one thing, Regime 2 is fairly amorphous. The main common denominator is high volatility, ranging from 29% to nearly 58% on an annualized basis. Maybe for some purposes, like estimating tail risks, a turbulent catch-all regime like that is good enough. For other purposes, maybe we should subdivide more. For example, simply by reclassifying the October 1975 observation as an oddball, the maximal volatility in what's left of Regime 2 drops to under 45%. Or maybe we should distinguish 'fly' scenarios from 'dive' scenarios."

"Fair enough. Anything else you don't like?"

"Yes, I don't think these histograms indicate a great fit. There's not enough density in the 3 to 8 region compared with closer in or farther out. That's another indication we should add more regimes."

"Why not just reclassify some observations from Regime 1 to Regime 2?"

"I tried that but it didn't work. It tends to create even more observations with unusually low chi-squared statistics, and also swells the chi-squared stats for the far outliers in Regime 2. I kept depleting the middle region of the histogram for Regime 2 more than I was filling it for Regime 1."

"So how many regimes do you think are appropriate?"

"I don't know. I'm not even sure that two regimes aren't enough. Maybe I just didn't sort the observations correctly. Or maybe I was too harsh in forcing the regime parameters to match the respective sample means and covariances."

"Have you thought about just maximizing the overall likelihood of the sample observations? That way you wouldn't need to sort the observations by regimes or match a particular parameter."

"Actually I tried that a few times. It was a disaster. The likelihood estimate kept diverging to infinity. Then I realized why."

"A computer glitch, obviously."

"I wish. No, unfortunately the computer was fine. It just kept trying to assign a zero variance to one of the conditional regimes, with a mean equal to one of the observations. The density at that observation would then become infinity, maximizing the likelihood."

"That's strange," said Conway, who didn't quite understand the result. "Why doesn't that happen with ordinary distributions?"

"Because with an ordinary single-point distribution, the gain in fitting one observation is offset by the losses in fitting others. In contrast, a mixture of a single-point distribution and a distribution that spans the whole space can achieve an infinite likelihood at one outcome without approaching minus infinity anywhere else."

"I see. You need to impose some extra restrictions to rule out implausible answers."

"If we try to maximize the likelihood, yes. But I'm not sure where to draw the line or why. Or how to measure the degree of confidence in a given model. Or how to be sure the search algorithms haven't missed a much better model. Or . . ."

"OK, OK I get the point. There's a lot left to sort out. I still think we've made a lot of progress. Thanks a lot, Devlin."

"For what? For opening up more cans of worms?"

"For introducing me to a neat way to think about the world. It doesn't assume that all changes are analogous to independent ones. It doesn't rule out regime switches. It isn't irreconcilable with empirical evidence. Yet it doesn't force us to directly estimate all the higher moments and cross-moments. It even embraces the conventional approach as a special case."

"But it raises more questions than it answers," said Devlin, despondently.

"I thought you liked questions."

"I used to. Now I'd like a few answers for a change. I don't know anything any more."

"Don't be ridiculous."

"I guess I am." Devlin dropped his head, turned around, and walked out the door.

A stunned Conway took a moment to realize what had happened. Then he got up and followed after Devlin, calling "Wait, I didn't mean it that way . . ."

I am afraid Devlin is seriously depressed. While Conway tries to console him, let's fill in a few mathematical gaps in their discussion.

CONDITIONAL MULTIVARIATE NORMALITY

Suppose a random n-vector X has probability p_k of being in one of K regimes, so that $\{p_k\}$ denotes the mixing distribution over regimes. In each regime k, suppose X is multivariate normal with mean M_k and covariance matrix Σ_k. Then the unconditional density is given by:

$$f(X) = \sum_{k=1}^{K} \frac{p_k}{\sqrt{2^n \pi^n |\Sigma_k|}} \exp\left(-\tfrac{1}{2}(X - M_k)'\Sigma_k^{-1}(X - M_k)\right)$$

A shorthand for a mixture of conditionally multivariate normal regimes is "mixed multivariate normal".

DEGREES OF FREEDOM FOR MIXED MULTIVARIATE NORMAL

Each multivariate normal regime will be characterized by one mixing probability, n means, and $\tfrac{1}{2}n(n+1)$ distinct variances and covariances for a total of $\tfrac{1}{2}(n+1)(n+2)$ degrees of freedom. Allowing for K regimes multiplies this by K except that that one degree of freedom is used to make sure the mixing probabilities sum to one. We thus have $\tfrac{1}{2}K(n+1)(n+2) - 1$ degrees of freedom in total.

For comparison, directly specifying all first three moments and cross-moments requires the estimation of $\binom{n+3}{3} - 1$ parameters. Mixed multivariate normal will be a more parsimonious specification if and only if $K < \dfrac{n}{3} + 1$. Similarly, mixed multivariate normal will be a more parsimonious specification than the first four moments and cross-moments provided $K < \left(\dfrac{n}{3} + 1\right)\left(\dfrac{n}{4} + 1\right)$.

GOODNESS OF FIT

Fitting a probability distribution to empirical data raises a host of issues. Should we measure deviations in terms of densities or cumulative distributions? Should we focus on maximum divergence, average absolute divergence, average divergence squared, or something else? Should divergence in the tails count for more than divergence in the center? Each choice has pros and cons, with no universally favored standard.

When Devlin fitted a mixed multivariate normal density to a uniform density, he used a blend of absolute divergence and divergence squared because he liked the visual results. In most practical work, visual appeal is less important than tractability.

Maximum Likelihood

Maximizing the likelihood is usually the most convenient way to fit complicated distributions. The likelihood is the joint probability of the observations as a function of the choice parameters θ. That is, if X_j denotes the vector of outcomes for observation j (not the jth component of X), then the likelihood is $\prod_j f(X_j; \theta)$ assuming the observations are independent. In practice it is easier to work with the logarithm, known as the "log likelihood", since it converts the product into a sum without changing the optimal choice of θ.

Unfortunately, that won't work for mixed multivariate normal distributions. By identifying one of the sample observations as the mean M_k of one of the regimes and shrinking the determinant $|\Sigma_k|$ of the associated covariance matrix, a maximizing algorithm can make the density at M_k infinitely large. This effect will dominate the rest as long as the rest of the mixture keeps the other densities bounded. To get a more plausible answer, you need to place a floor under each $|\Sigma_k|$ or impose some other restriction with this effect.

Grid Search

Imagine you're leading a team that aims to hike in dense fog toward the highest summit in a given area. If there's only one summit and the terrain slopes smoothly toward it, you can find your way efficiently just by taking the steepest path up. If there are a lot of summits in the area, however, that approach might lead you to a secondary peak. Given a large enough team, you might prefer to begin with a grid search. Divide your terrain methodically into sectors, send out search parties to check the height at some point in the sector. Then refocus all your efforts on the best or a few best sectors, subdivide the sectors into subsectors, and survey again. Eventually you should feel confident enough to focus your efforts on one small sector, and take the steepest path up from there.

Maximizing a complicated function is so similar to hiking in a fog that mathematicians often call their solution techniques "hill-climbing algorithms". Like hill-climbing, these techniques are simplest and most reliable when there is only one hill, so that any local maximum is the global maximum. If you have more than one hill, you might prefer a comprehensive grid search. However, a comprehensive grid search often isn't practical, as each free variable adds another dimension to the search. Just allowing four variants each for twenty variables makes for a trillion combinations.

GENETIC ALGORITHMS

Genetic algorithms offer an alternative to comprehensive grid search. They mimic natural evolution by choosing a few random candidate solutions, pruning out the least effective, and choosing random offshoots of the rest for further testing. In a conscious analogy to sexual reproduction, the offshoots typically mix parameters of two parent candidate solutions plus an occasional random mutation.

Like natural evolution, genetic algorithms are both unreliable and miraculous. On the one hand, thousands of generations can pass without significant progress, and not even local optimality can be guaranteed. On the other hand, genetic algorithms generally improve dramatically on purely random search, and occasionally devise combinations that are hard not to describe as ingenious.

Genetic algorithms can often be usefully combined with other methods. The genetic algorithms identify core elements of a solution, while local optimization provides fine-tuning. Some manual tweaking can help too. Recall, for example, the mixed bivariate normal approximation to a uniform distribution that Devlin generated using genetic algorithms. You can improve on it by consolidating some regimes that nearly coincide, adding new regimes near the edges, and then optimizing locally. Here is one resulting revision, again in cutaway view. It undulates much less than the other.

ACTUAL VERSUS ESTIMATED TAIL RISKS

Devlin noted that even crude mixed multivariate normal models might provide reasonable estimates of tail risks. The chart below presents an example using an equally weighted basket (rebalanced every month) of the five equity indices Devlin was examining. The crooked line shows the actual frequencies for tails with thresholds ranging from 2.5 to 5.0 standard deviations below the mean. The dotted curve shows the risks

Approximating a uniform bivariate: revised version

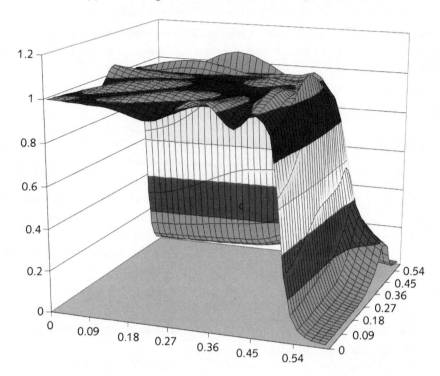

Tail risks for an equal basket of five equity indices

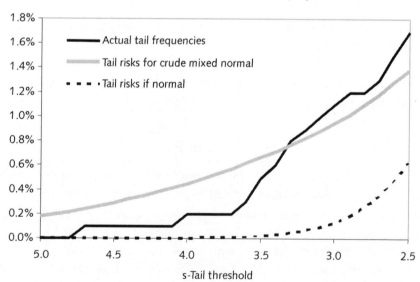

Actual tail frequencies

Tail risks for crude mixed normal

Tail risks if normal

s-Tail threshold

for a normal portfolio. The solid curve uses Devlin's crude mixed normal estimate.

The crude mixed normal estimate looks much better than the standard normal estimate in the range of tail risks we would normally be interested in. However, it overestimates the risks of very large outliers. While these calculations may not be representative, they illustrate both the promise and the perils of crude mixed multivariate normal estimation.

11 | Just Desserts

While tensions eased over the following week, Conway and Devlin continued to drift further apart. Oddly, they had never seen more eye to eye over theory. Both viewed conditional multivariate normality as a great improvement in assumptions over unconditional normality. Where they disagreed was over the implications.

Conway saw tremendous opportunities for practical estimation. "I don't see why you're so gloomy," he told Devlin on one occasion. "If two regimes don't provide a good fit, try three or four regimes. If one fitting method isn't tractable, try another. One way or another we'll make headway."

Devlin, ever more anxious, saw perils looming everywhere. "Yes, you'll make headway. So do lemmings on their way to the ocean. How are we to identify the various regimes or even to figure out which regime currently prevails? All our confidence intervals are shot. Don't you realize that a little knowledge is a dangerous thing?"

"It's 'a little learning is a dangerous thing'; Alexander Pope," replied Conway, instantly regretting his smugness. "I'm surprised you think that. Next you'll be telling me that ignorance is bliss."

"No, ignorance isn't bliss. Ignorance is blight. Ignorance is blunder. And do you know why? Because people pretend they know more than they do!"

Careful. He's starting to lose it again. "OK OK, I agree with you there. That's why mean-variance analysis gets you into trouble at the tails. It presumes to give you more insight than it can. Conditional normality peels away the blinders."

"In principle, yes. But how can you legitimately apply something you can't reliably estimate?"

"And just how reliable are the estimates for mean-variance analysis? They rest on assumptions of regime stability that you've shown are indefensible. I'd rather be approximately right than precisely wrong."

"So would I, Conway. So why don't we just reveal that s-tail risks can range from 0 to $\frac{1}{s^2 + 1}$?"

"Of course we'll reveal that. Only not that alone. It's too wide a range. You know we need to provide more guidance."

"But at this point I don't think we can provide more guidance. Let's not pretend we can."

"We can provide some guidance now. Do we need to provide better guidance in the future? Definitely. But let's not make the better the enemy of the good."

"And let's not fake the good with a façade."

After that they just agreed to disagree. Conway decided to press ahead, and had Devlin lecture to the rest of the group on his findings. Devlin, to his credit, was concise and clear and entertaining. Soon, the whole risk group was abuzz with debate about the reestimation of risk limits. Some were optimists like Conway about the prospects of applying mixed multivariate normality. Others were pessimists like Devlin. All agreed that the new theoretical perspective was far more in tune with what they observed in practice than the mean-variance analysis they had been trained in.

Conway was delighted at the new enthusiasm in the ranks. And while he didn't feel ready to take on the whole Risk Committee at once, he thought he could win over a couple of senior managers to the new approach. *Let them soften up the others.*

A few days later Conway got his chance. He was out on the trading floor reviewing major position limits with the head trader when his secretary rushed up. "Conway, I've been looking all over for you. The Controller called. He wants you."

"What about?"

"He didn't say. He never says. He just asked you to drop by when you're free."

"That's Controller-speak for 'come here immediately'."

"I know. That's why I've been looking for you."

Conway excused himself from the trader, hurried back to his office, grabbed his suit jacket and a stack of Devlin's charts, and hurried off again to the elevators. When Conway arrived at the executive floor, he gave his name to one of the immaculately groomed receptionists and sat down. While he waited, he marveled again at the contrast between the executive floor and the rest of Megabucks: richly upholstered chairs, plush carpet, and fine paintings hung on mahogany panels. Most of all he marveled at the quiet. So far removed from the constant hum and cackle of a trading floor.

"The Controller will see you now." The receptionist led Conway to what must have been the quietest alcove on the floor, knocked once softly on the door, and opened it halfway. As soon as Conway entered she shut the door quietly behind him.

A trim and distinguished-looking man with silver hair was sitting behind an expansive and uncluttered desk. He eyed Conway calmly and spoke in an eerily even voice. "Good afternoon, Conway. It's nice to see you again." The Controller smiled and his voice dissolved into the still.

"Good afternoon, Mr Ford. It's nice to see you too." Conway was getting uneasy. He hesitated about ten feet away from the desk.

"I hope I didn't interrupt you."

"Not at all, sir. I was just having a discussion about risk limits."

"With Devlin?"

"No, not with Devlin. I didn't realize you knew him."

"I don't. I just know of him. He has created quite a stir. Please, Conway, sit down and make yourself at home."

As Conway made his way to the chair, he spied a small glass paperweight on the Controller's desk, bearing the inscription "Ignorance is Bliss". Conway read it and shuddered.

"I take it you've seen this?" The Controller brandished the auditors' report.

Conway gulped. "Yes, sir, I have. But I don't recall it mentioning Devlin's name."

"It doesn't. But it wasn't hard to find out whom the auditors were referring to. They want his head on a platter. I take it you know that too."

"Yes," Conway admitted sheepishly. "But I tell you: they're wrong about Devlin. He is by far the cleverest person on my staff, myself included. And he was right about the issue they disagreed on."

"I figured that as soon as I heard about the auditors' grudge." He looked Conway straight in the eyes. "Mediocrities like them can forgive your being wrong. They can never forgive your being right."

Conway was shocked. He would never have imagined the Controller speaking so frankly, much less taking Devlin's side. "You mean you agree with Devlin?"

"On the risk of no winners out of three unbiased, uncorrelated Bernoulli variables? Yes. It needn't be $\frac{1}{8}$. It can be any number between 0 and $\frac{1}{4}$, depending on the third cross-moment."

"That's exactly what Devlin discovered. I can't tell you how relieved it makes me feel that a senior executive like yourself appreciates the problem."

"Why do you attach such importance to such an odd problem?"

"Because it turns out to be the tip of an iceberg. An iceberg of risk that mean-variance analysis can't detect."

The Controller raised his eyebrows. "Are you sure?"

"I didn't believe it myself at first but Devlin kept exposing more and more of it."

"What made Devlin able to see what other smart people missed?"

"I'm not sure, sir. He tends to look at things a bit like a child: naive enough to admit what he doesn't know, and curious enough to keep trying to find out."

The Controller raised his eyebrows. "With your encouragement?"

"Not at first. It was more something he had to do for himself. But gradually he convinced me that most of conventional risk analysis is unreliable. In many cases, burning a risk report will shed more light than reading it."

"Delightful. That has long been my conviction. In the winter, I take some reports home just to use as fire-starters." The Controller laughed, only with eyes so cold that Conway didn't dare join in. "But I imagine Devlin would have offered a more quantitative assessment. What exactly did he find?"

"In a nutshell, that risks of an s-standard deviation tail, or what we call 's -tails', can vary from 0 to $\frac{1}{s^2 + 1}$. So a 5-tail can have up to a 4% probability."

"And a 10-standard deviation tail up to a 1% probability. I recall reading the formula once in an old statistics book. But it's almost purely theoretical, is it not? Those outer bounds reflect some very peculiar distributions. Surely the base case remains a normal distribution."

"That's what I thought too. But these wide bounds kept reappearing even after Devlin took various measures at my request to exclude oddball cases."

"What kind of measures?"

"To begin with, I had Devlin look only at sums or averages of exchangeable Bernoulli assets. Each asset can take only the values 'success' or 'failure' and has to be statistically interchangeable with every other asset. Each setup or 'game' is defined by the number of assets in the pool and by a fixed, internally consistent set of probabilities for the various outcomes."

"What do you mean by 'internally consistent'?"

The Controller's tone was disturbingly clinical. *Why are you interrogating me this way?* But he was asking such good questions that Conway continued answering them as best he could. "Just the standard restrictions. Each probability must be nonnegative, the probability of any set of outcomes equals the sum of the probabilities of every distinct outcome it entails, and the probability of the whole must be one."

"That still must leave a huge number of possibilities to juggle."

"It does. Each additional asset adds a degree of freedom. Devlin showed this by building triangles that are complements to Pascal's Triangle. The only difference is that neighboring row elements add up to the element above rather than the element below. Every nonnegative Devlin's triangle turns out to specify an exchangeable Bernoulli game and vice versa. The kth element on the nth row tells you the probability of $k - 1$ successes followed by $n - k$ failures."

"And what did you do with these degrees of freedom?"

"We used them to maximize or minimize the tail risks under a variety of restrictions: numbers of assets, means, correlations, and so on. Devlin's triangles indicated how to pose these as straightforward linear programming problems. But at first we weren't quite sure how to interpret the solutions."

"Why not?"

"It was my fault, really. I had asked Devlin to focus on uncorrelated assets, which I thought would be simpler to deal with. But when you expand the pool of uncorrelated Bernoulli assets, two opposite patterns emerge. One suggests a very narrow range for tail risk, the other a very wide range."

"What patterns are those?"

"On the one hand, the probability distribution for any fixed number of variables converges toward a binomial distribution with the same mean. For example, if we choose three coins at random from a pool of four unbiased, uncorrelated, exchangeable coins, the probability of all tails will range from $\frac{1}{12}$ to $\frac{1}{6}$. That's tighter than the 0 to $\frac{1}{4}$ range that applies with a pool of three such coins. As the pool expands, the probability of three tails will converge to $\frac{1}{8}$."

"So a wide range for tail risks seems to be a small numbers problem."

"In one way, yes. However, if we focus on the bottom row of Devlin's triangle, which encompasses all the variables in the pool, we get a very different answer. The bigger the pool, the more the tail risks can flop around."

"What if you control for variations in means and standard deviations?"

"Then the feasible range for uncorrelated s-tails is always 0 to $\dfrac{1}{s^2 + 1}$, apart from integer constraints on the numbers of successes and failures. Those constraints typically don't matter much as long as the tails embrace more than a handful of outcomes."

"So what happens when you allow for correlation?"

"Nothing in aggregate. The range doesn't get any wider or narrower. If you fix the correlation but not the means, the range doesn't change either. Provided the correlation is feasible of course."

"Why wouldn't a correlation be feasible?"

"Geometry. For example, three variables can't all be perfectly negatively correlated with each other. That's like asking three people to all look in opposite directions."

"I see. Isn't it similar to the requirement that no portfolio ever have a negative variance?"

"It's actually the same requirement. You've clearly studied a lot of statistics."

"Too much. I didn't realize then that Mark Twain was right."

"Right about what?"

"He said there are three kinds of lies: lies, damned lies, and statistics." Seeing Conway blanch, the Controller hastened to add, "Obviously Mark Twain did not have the opportunity to participate in discussions like this. The research you are describing is fascinating."

"Thank you, sir. I shall relay your compliment to Devlin. Unless you prefer to speak with him yourself."

"That isn't necessary. Your explanations are excellent. But I seem to have lost the thread of your story. If feasible correlation doesn't matter, why do you single it out for special treatment?"

"Because correlation does matter if the mean is also fixed. It then limits the maximum standard deviation outlier from the origin, which in turn rules out whole ranges for feasible tail risk. Tail risk estimates based on normality can be too low to be feasible or too high to be feasible, depending on other parameters."

"That's very interesting. I would never have thought of checking."

"Nor I. Devlin's good about that sort of thing. Even he had trouble, however, checking for feasibility when the pool size is unbounded."

"I can appreciate that. How do you examine the last row when there isn't one?"

"By examining an edge of the triangle instead. One edge completely determines every other element. But Devlin didn't think about that at first. He was happy to find even one class of Bernoulli assets that he could demonstrate was infinitely exchangeable."

"What class was that?"

"Assets that are independent given their common mean, even though the mean itself may fluctuate. Their probability distributions are binomial mixtures. And their feasible tail risks span the full range I mentioned, except when the correlation is zero."

"What's so special about zero correlation?"

"It allows only a trivial mixture, consisting of one pure binomial distribution, with s-tail risks like those of a normal distribution."

"I see. Binomial mixtures lead to completely bifurcated results. Did Devlin ever find any other infinitely exchangeable Bernoulli variables?"

Conway shook his head. "No. He found something better: a proof that there aren't any. It's called de Finetti's Theorem. Furthermore, as Devlin studied the proof, he realized that it simply worked through the calculations that are implicit in his triangles."

"What good is that?"

"Aesthetic for one. It shows there's a uniform, easy-to-understand treatment. It also showed how to read off the parameters of the mixing distribution from the probabilities along the right edge, by way of a moment-generating function."

"You're getting a bit detailed. I doubt I'll remember all this."

"You don't have to. You only need to remember two things. First, the sharp bifurcation in feasible tail risks between pure binomials and binomial mixtures. Second, the interpretation of pure binomials and binomial mixtures as independence and conditional independence respectively."

"That's a striking contrast. But how much does it hinge on assets having only binary payoffs?"

"In form a lot. In content only a little."

"What do you mean?"

"A binomial distribution presumes a portfolio of identical independent assets. To allow a continuum of outcomes and a wider variety of assets, you need a more flexible distribution. But the pure distribution is still linked to independence and the mixture to conditional independence, with vastly different implications for risk tails."

"What flexible distribution are you thinking of? Normal?"

"Not quite. Multivariate normal. It just means that all portfolios consist of independent normal components."

The Controller looked puzzled. "Hold on, Conway. Multivariate normal assets don't have to be independent. They can have any feasible covariance matrix."

"Believe me, I had the same initial reaction when Devlin told me. But those independent components don't have to be the assets themselves. They can be portfolios in their own right."

"A lot of random variables can be decomposed into independent components. Why are multivariate normal ones so special?

"Because they can be reorganized into independent scalar components in so many different ways. Moreover, each scalar component is normal, and hence can be viewed as the limit of any sum of independent random variables with the specified total mean and variance. Multivariate normal variables are independent to their core."

"Is that realistic?"

"That depends what part of reality you're looking at. If you can completely stabilize the external environment, like a physicist studying gas in a bottle, then multivariate normality is very realistic. Otherwise you need to distinguish between common and independent influences. That's what conditional multivariate normality does."

The Controller looked around the room as if he were checking for imaginary bottles. He then turned his gaze back to Conway. "I look at financial reality. Which modeling approach do you think is better and why?"

"That depends. It's a lot easier to extract insights assuming pure multivariate normality. Nearly all the classic results of finance theory depend on it. I'll probably always look for answers there first because that is how I was trained. But I'll never trust them again like I used to. Especially not for risk analysis."

"So you think conditional multivariate normality is better for financial risk analysis."

"It has to be better. Pure multivariate normality is preposterous." Conway then thought of Devlin's hesitations. "I grant you, there are a few practical difficulties to sort out."

"Oh, really? What kind of practical difficulties?"

"It's just not so easy to fit a mixed multivariate normal distribution as it is to fit the pure version. We're not sure how to estimate the confidence intervals either."

"So if you wanted to be absolutely sure not to understate the s-tail risks, would you opt for $\dfrac{1}{s^2 + 1}$?"

Conway tried to dodge the barbed question. "No, sir, I wouldn't. As long as I had any relevant data, I would try to fit a mixed multivariate normal distribution and infer the tail risks from it."

"But you just said it was difficult to fit a mixed multivariate normal distribution or estimate the confidence intervals."

Conway stammered a bit. "Ye .. yes, that's true. But we could always fit a few mixed multivariate normal distributions and calculate their average s-tail risk, or their worst s-tail risk if you prefer."

The Controller did not reply. His gaze was fixed on Conway, who dared not move, and the room regained its former still. After a long silence he spoke. "Conway, that was one of the most illuminating discussions on risk that I have ever had. I always wondered why high standard deviation events occur so much more frequently than standard theory predicted. Now, thanks to your account of Devlin's work, I know."

"I am glad you see it that way, sir."

"Your account also confirms my initial hunch on how to deal with this pending disciplinary action against Devlin." He opened up a folder, signed a document, and called his secretary on the intercom. "Ms Stephenson, could you please come in?"

Conway's eyes grew wide. "Disciplinary action? What disciplinary action?"

"I told you the auditors wanted Devlin's head on a platter. They took advantage of Devlin's probationary status, itself a reflection of past run-ins with authorities and colleagues, to demand that he be dismissed. Normally in a situation like this, they would get their way. However, some of the disciplinary committee regard Devlin as a provocative lateral-thinker whom Megabucks should cherish. I was asked to cast the deciding vote."

"Thank heavens we had a chance to talk first." Conway sighed with relief.

Just then Ms Stephenson walked in. "What can I do for you, Mr Ford?"

"Ms Stephenson, please take this folder on Devlin Advogado to Security. It contains all the necessary materials authorizing his dismissal. I would like him removed from the premises immediately."

"Yes, Mr Ford." She took the folder and left.

Conway felt his stomach tearing apart. All the blood drained from his face, and he felt paralyzed.

"I take it you are surprised," said the Controller. Summoning every muscle at his command, Conway managed a weak nod. "Trust me. I bear him no ill will. This is purely a business decision."

Conway regained control over a few vocal chords. "Why?" he rasped.

"For repeated dereliction of his primary duty as a risk analyst."

A surge of anger brought Conway back to his senses. "I strongly disagree, sir. Devlin always calls the risks as he sees them."

"I have no doubt that he does," said the Controller, calmly. "But that is not his primary duty. His primary duty is to see the risks as he calls them."

"See the risks as he calls them? What on earth does that mean?" Conway could barely contain himself.

"It means that a risk analyst should be able to clearly justify to third parties whatever risk rating he assigns. If the analyst can't make up his mind, or offers too convoluted reasoning, he adds to the perceived risk of whatever he's monitoring. No serious investment bank can tolerate that."

"But it's not Devlin's fault if he uncovers extra complications."

"No, it isn't. He can uncover all the complications he wants. He just needs to cover them up when he finishes. Or resolve them if he can. I ask you: what would you think of an architect who designed all the toilets out in the open, and with no doors to boot?"

Conway couldn't stand to hear his friend ridiculed. "If that's the way you feel about Devlin, then you may as well sack me too."

"That would be unprofessional. For while Devlin betrayed his primary duty as an analyst, you upheld your primary duty as a risk manager."

"How can you tell me that I managed risks well when we're not close to sure what they are?"

The Controller shook his head. "I'm afraid you still don't get it, Conway. I never claimed you managed risks well. But you managed the appearances of risk well. And that is your primary duty as a risk manager."

"I can't believe I'm hearing you say that. You, the Controller. You're courting disaster for Megabucks."

Don't let your passions blind you," said the Controller, unflappable as ever. "We always court disaster, if it pays. Especially if everyone else is courting the same disaster, because if we all go down the Fed will bail us out. But Devlin's approach courts a disaster only we will pay for."

"In what way?"

"To begin with, the Bank for International Settlements forces us to ratchet up all our estimated risk coverage by a factor of roughly three. So suppose you and Devlin investigate using mixed multivariate normality and report that the BIS is roughly correct. Happy resolution, right?

"Maybe."

"Wrong. The very act of reporting triple risks will force Megabucks to adopt your more cautious system. And the BIS rules will in turn force us to ratchet up our risk coverage. Since total assets are limited, Megabucks will have to slash risk exposures and cut bonuses, causing top staff to leave. Its stock plummets and investors call for a major overhaul. Do you think that's justified? All because you and Devlin have an attack of compulsive honesty?"

"Surely the BIS can't be that mechanical. And investors can't be that short-sighted."

"You are an optimist, aren't you? Maybe you're right. But why take the risk, when the mushroom treatment works so well?"

"Mushroom treatment?"

"Feed them bullshit and keep them in the dark." The Controller cracked a smile. Conway felt utterly repulsed. "Mr Ford, you are the most cynical man I have ever met."

"I am realistic," said the Controller, slowly, as if teaching a foreign language. "I am also rich. Thanks to years of faithful service to Megabucks."

"And you expect me to serve in the same spirit?"

"No, I don't. Something in Devlin has rubbed off on you. And I don't want you stirring up trouble."

"I see. You're going to fire me too."

"No, you would be too visible that way. And given your excellent prior record, it would look bad. I have arranged for a transfer instead."

"A transfer? To where?"

"To the asset management side. I think you'll enjoy it. It will give you a chance to develop your theories without risking Megabucks' own capital. Of course, you can't expect the same bonuses going forward. Retail fund management is a low margin business."

"And when is this transfer supposed to occur? Immediately, like Devlin's dismissal?"

"No, in two months. It is only your current duties that terminate today. I have arranged for you to draw your full salary in the interim and would encourage you to take a long vacation. It's always best to start a new job rested and relaxed."

"You've worked this all out, haven't you?"

"I've tried. That's my job."

Conway refused to return the Controller's smile. "If you're through with me, I'd like to go."

"I'm glad you see it that way. Good luck, Conway."

In the few seconds it took to leave the Controller's Office, Conway felt like an underwater diver straining to regain the surface. He took a big gulp of fresh air as soon as got outside. He then thought of Devlin. Devlin! He rushed back to his office, his head spinning, hoping to find Devlin before he left. But he was too late. The security guards had even cleared out Devlin's cubicle. The only sign of the former occupant was a message scrawled in black marker across the desk:

Ignorance is Blight

PART II

Insights into Ignorance

Introduction: "More Dollars than Sense"

While the psychiatric community continues to debate the efficacy of Dr Donald Dementi's novel treatments, no one denies his marketing genius. By chopping up traditional psychotherapy into soundbites and bundling them with complementary goods and services, he recaptured market share for shrinks that most industry analysts had permanently written off to Prozac. Dr Dementi first came to popular attention in 1992 when he launched Mad Donald's™, the world's first burger chain to offer seasoned counselling while you waited for your meal. Reviews were rave, especially for a double-burger combo with French Fries, soft drink, and primal scream therapy. While pricey at $49.95, The Big Mad™ became a best seller once insurance companies accepted it as a legitimate medical expense.

Unfortunately, just as the one hundredth franchisee signed on, the British government confirmed that some zealously vegetarian cows had gone completely bonkers after being fed diseased sheep offal, and threatened to infect predators further up the food chain. The resulting hysteria forced the whole Mad Donald's chain to shut down, despite an exemplary health record. As *Forbes* magazine would later put it, it had succumbed to the madness of crowds and cows.

A lesser man would have given up, cursing European agricultural standards. Not Dr Dementi. While vacationing in the Caribbean with his wife and lover, unable to keep the pair from squabbling, he had a flash of inspiration. Legions of well-off, stressed-out Baby Boomers were forking out big bucks for rest and recuperation without getting enough of either. A combination of leisure with therapy would be far more potent, not to mention lucrative, than lunch and therapy had ever been.

Hurrying back home, Dr Dementi quickly found some venture capitalists willing to back his concept. Club Mad™ proved a runaway success. No thick-walleted status seeker could resist the advertising lures of a place "For People With More Dollars Than Sense"™. Lawsuits from an ageing French chain of similar appellation were settled by a leveraged buyout that left French investors very happy and dotted Club Mad resorts around the globe.

Critics charge that Club Mad is just a ploy to get medical insurance to subsidize rich folks' vacations. But undercover sleuths sent by TV networks found no evidence of fraud. The global accounting monolith PriceErnst-Deliotte&Others audits all overheads and bills insurance companies and Medicare only for the expenses that meet their approval. All therapists are fully credentialed and must pass a rigorous in-house training course.

Moreover, waiting lists are by far the longest at two resorts that offer the least in the way of conventional holiday comforts. The Palm Beach Club Mad, just opened in December 2000, does not even boast a beachfront. Instead, an old warehouse was carved into rooms that are spitting imitations of polling places, county electoral commission offices, court chambers, and media assembly halls. In addition, every guest is allowed to supervise at least one mock election, with rights not only to fine-tune the chad punches but also to set the number of perforations needed to constitute a valid vote. These are essential props for Club Mad's banner therapy, called Lose That Loser's Feeling™, which encourages guests to replay painful experiences until they get them right.

The other Club Mad in top demand lies on the New Jersey banks of the Hudson, an easy ferry ride from Wall Street and the financial district. The therapeutic *pièce de résistance* is an enormous trading room filled with what at first glance looks like ordinary Bloomberg screens, Reuters terminals, and PCs. In fact, the machines have been ingeniously reengineered to allow users to turn back the clock and insert new data. It is possible for example, to replay October 1987 so that the US market crash never happens, or to allow it to happen but load up on shorts first, all in plain view of Manhattan.

The results are remarkable. According to independent medical tests reported in the *New England Journal of Medicine*, 25% of severely depressed ex-traders recovered normal serotonin brain levels within one month. Within three months, over 80% claimed to be Masters of the Universe again. Such is the demand to play on BloomAgain™ screens that the mock trading room is kept open around the clock, and residents are limited to 30-minute sessions at peak times.

Critics charge that Lose That Loser's Feeling alumni confuse ersatz cures with the real thing. However, as Dr Dementi explained to talk show hosts Larry King and Oprah Winfrey, the critics' argument rests on disrespect for the sanity-challenged. If a person who thought he was crazy no longer thinks he is, who is to say whether he was right in both cases, wrong in both cases, or right in one case and wrong in the other?

Unfortunately, some losers never lose that losing feeling. Granted, "never" is a loaded term. The more upbeat Dr Dementi concedes only that some nuts are harder to crack than others. Privately, however, Club Mad staffers admit to frustrations.

To better appreciate what makes a so-called Lost Loser, let us whisk ourselves over to Club Mad on the Hudson and eavesdrop on a therapy session . . .

"I don't know," says a familiar voice.

"But if you don't know, who will?" asks the doctor.

"I don't know."

The doctor, who has been taking notes, snaps his pencil in exasperation. "if you can't think of any good alternative," he says in the gentlest voice he can muster, "will you consider giving BloomAgain another chance? Thirty minutes, that's all I ask. At night, if you prefer, away from the crowds."

"It won't help. It won't be the same."

"You can make it the same if you want. Or you can make it different. That's the whole point. All the odds are user-controlled."

"It still won't be the same. I'll know the odds, whereas in real life I didn't."

"That's why it's better. It will help you hone your trading skills playing the odds."

"But I wasn't a trader. I was a risk analyst. It was my job to guess the odds. If I know what they are, how will that improve my guessing?"

"Then just spin the risk dial without looking, and try to guess what the odds are from the outcomes."

"Too easy. I'll still know exactly when I spun the risk dial. That tells me to ignore previous data as irrelevant. Work was never that simple. Was the Nasdaq's near-doubling in 1999 a sign that Nasdaq would continue to soar in 2000, a sign that it would likely retreat, or not a sign of anything at all? I didn't know. Actually, I don't even know now."

"Devlin, please don't exaggerate. Of course you know now. Nasdaq retreated." The doctor remembered this quite well, having watched his stock accounts wither.

"But I don't know why. I mean it's always tempting, all else being equal, to favor the hypothesis that best predicts the data. But that doesn't always work. You do believe in blind luck, don't you, doctor?"

"Oh, yes." Of course he believed in blind luck. Especially blind bad luck: the kind that assigned Devlin to him. "But I'm afraid we've wandered far beyond my professional expertise. Do you mind if we shift topics? I would like to ask you more about your childhood."

Devlin squirmed on the sofa. "Sure. Go ahead."

"Last time you said you identified with everyone and no one. What do you mean by that?"

"My mother was a mix of every kind of blood she knew of. Apache, Navajo, Chinese, Mexican, English, you name it. She taught me to think of myself as part of one big global family. But everyone else in our little town seemed to identify with one particular branch. In a way that made me the biggest outcast of all."

"And your father?"

"I don't know."

"You don't know his nationality?"

"I don't know my father. He left before I was born. But I think he might have been Jewish, because I really like gefilte fish tacos."

The doctor winced but kept writing. "Anything else you know or guess about your father?"

"He was good at math. At least that's what my mother says. She said he could add up customers' bar bills faster than any calculator she ever knew."

"Your dad worked in a bar?"

"No, but my mother did. She was a cocktail waitress. Chatted up the guys to encourage them to buy a few. Every once in a while she went out with one. That's how I came about."

"Did you ever try to find your father?"

"No, I didn't have enough information."

At last the doctor spied a clue. "Aren't you denying something, Devlin?"

"Like what?"

"Like whether you could find your father? A Jewish guy who's good at math in a small town?"

"We lived near Los Alamos. The weapons lab there employs I don't know how many hundreds of physicists, and I don't know how many hundreds more pass through as visitors. It won't release personnel records unless you're hunting a Chinese spy."

"Never mind," said the doctor. "So how do you feel about your father abandoning you?"

"He didn't. Not completely. Every year a fat envelope full of money got pushed under our door, with 'For Devlin's Education' written across the top. My mother took that seriously. Spent it on books and tutoring and stuff like that, and when I was 12 we moved to Los Alamos so I could attend a better school. At graduation I got a scholarship to Stanford. That's when I met Conway."

"Your former boss."

"My former friend. Funny, I nearly didn't give him a chance to be friends. Too much of a Zim."

"A Zim?"

"A white settler in Zimbabwe. His parents were well-to-do farmers. At least they were in the days when Zimbabwe had well-to-do farmers. Anyway, his parents sent Conway off to English boarding school, hoping he'd continue on to Oxford or Cambridge. But Conway decided he'd like more adventure and went to Berkeley instead. The first time I met him I figured he was just a colonialist white boy. But I was wrong. You shouldn't judge a book by its cover."

"So why do you call him a former friend?"

""It was my fault. I let him down really badly. I even cost him his job."

"How did you do that?"

"By saying 'I don't know' too much, until he himself didn't know."

The doctor immediately felt a huge sympathy for Conway. "And why did you do that?"

"I don't know. Too many doubts, I guess."

The doctor looked at his watch. Thank heavens. It was 4:30 already. He had a tennis game in 15 minutes. "Devlin, I'm afraid that's all we have time for today. I'll see you tonight at samba class."

"Sorry, I won't be there. I've signed up for the night dive in the Hudson. See you tomorrow in group therapy."

Meanwhile, across the Hudson and halfway to the East River, Devlin's former friend is getting briefed on his new job.

"Welcome to Megabucks Asset Management, Conway. We don't see many transfers from the sell-side over here, but I'm delighted you're here. My brother speaks very highly of you. Your experience in risk management could be a real boost for us."

"Thank you, Mr Ford." *What did he really say about me?*

"Please, call me Jim. No need for formalities around here, except for the occasional investor conference. Life on the buy side's a lot more relaxed. You'll hardly ever need to work late or on weekends."

"I'm looking forward to that, sir."

"I told you. It's Jim. I hope you're not confusing me with my brother." He smiled warmly at Conway.

Conway guardedly returned the smile. "Maybe so. I'll try to remember. Just let me know the drum beat you want me to march to."

Jim laughed. "My brother really got to you, didn't he? Look, whatever happened to you over there, try to forget about it. Folks around here don't march. They just kind of collectively amble."

"How's performance?"

"Not bad. We have over $100 billion of assets, growing at about 12% per year. Average management fees are 200 basis points, for $600 million gross. Of course, we pay out most of that to the brokers bringing us business, and other overheads are high too, but that still leaves a tidy profit."

"I meant: how's fund performance?"

"That's not bad either. The managers generally beat their benchmark indices by a percent or so."

"Is that raw or inclusive of fees?"

"Raw. Look, Conway, how about I guess what you're thinking, and if I win, you lighten up. Is that a deal?" Conway nodded. "I think you're wondering why people invest with us, given that net of fees we don't beat the index."

Conway laughed. "OK. Jim, you win. So why do people invest with us?"

"Hand holding, largely. People tend to need some coaxing to look after their long-term interests, and some help in weighing risks versus rewards. That's why you need a sales force to sell insurance or mutual funds. You can't just display the prospectuses on a shelf or a website."

"Aren't you concerned about the competition?"

"I'm very concerned. The margins are getting tighter all the time and our clients more demanding. And despite our growth, we're losing market share. I'm expecting the next bear market to trigger a big shakeout. That's why I want to tap your expertise."

"Look, Jim, I'm no expert in calling bear markets. I just tried to manage people who were experts, or at least who claimed to be."

"I still think you can help."

"How? You said that people here just collectively amble. I don't even know which direction you want them to go in."

"Frankly, I'm not sure myself. Everyone's using different maps, so we can't communicate very well and I don't know how to judge whether someone's on a path or off it. I want you to give me advice."

Conway liked the sound of that. *Work directly for the boss and stay out of office politics.* "What kind of advice?"

"I want you to draw some useful practical lessons from portfolio theory for how we manage our funds."

"I'm no longer sure the standard theory is that useful. Its assumptions are too extreme."

"Always?"

"No, not always."

"Then just tell me what you think is useful and why. If you want to change the assumptions to make them more realistic, fine. That's why I hired you and not some pointy-head. Just don't make this any more complicated than it needs to be. My eyes glaze over very quickly."

"So do mine, to be honest. And I had some super help before that I don't have now."

"Just do your best then. I appreciate a man who knows his limitations. Some of my fund managers don't."

Conway was liking Jim more and more. *Maybe this transfer will work out after all.* "You just made me an offer I can't refuse. Where would you like me to begin?"

"With the single measure that you think best summarizes the risk/reward tradeoffs in a portfolio. I want you to explain that measure and tell us how to use it to better manage our asset allocation."

"Oh, that's simple. I can tell you now. It's . . ."

Jim cut him off. "Not now. Tomorrow afternoon at 3:00. In a meeting of all the senior fund managers. It will give me a chance to introduce you."

Conway gulped. "Don't you think I should run this by you first?"

"I don't see why. You said it was simple, and they're not going to bite. I'm sure you'll do fine."

Conway didn't share Jim's confidence but hadn't left himself much scope to object. He excused himself and went off to prepare.

We've entered a new phase of the adventure now. You might call it a witty phase: Conway has to test his wits while Devlin has to collect his. But I prefer to call it reconstruction. Sometimes life forces us to rebuild before the master plan is ready. How should we respond? The best one-word answer I can give is "experiment".

Experiment doesn't please everyone. It implies tentativeness, disorder, and upheaval. It's not just conformists who object to this. World War II caused far more devastation in the Soviet Union than in any other country, yet the Soviet Union recovered first. How did the beacon of world revolution manage this astounding feat? Largely by rebuilding every factory it had to the letter of the original blueprints. These blueprints, usually dating from the 1930s, were themselves often imitations of American and British factories built a decade or more prior. In contrast, West Germany and Japan rebuilt using pioneering new technology. No wonder that by the 1960s the Soviet Union was losing steam, while West Germany and Japan were charging ahead.

But I'll still give the Soviets credit for eventually throwing in the towel. Contrast that with, say, London public transport, which seems to sink to ever-deeper levels of disgrace. Not that the dithering authorities wanted this. They just got too wrapped up in debates about whether and how to privatize, how much to invest, where to get the money from, when to avoid disruption, and above all how to shift the blame for inaction to someone else. What started as a battle between the better and the good has seen nothing triumph over anything. Fear of experimentation has caused paralysis.

So I ask readers in this section not to judge Conway too harshly. He's groping for answers he can't see and sometimes has to grab what he can get. Personally I'm optimistic, because Conway's job will keep his feet on the ground while the spirit of Devlin will keep him reaching for the stars. It's a long stretch, though. The best you can hope for is a bit of stardust.

As for Devlin, I hope he survives the night dive. He was never much of a swimmer.

12 | Teaching Elephants to Dance

The portfolio managers gathered together the next day to meet their new head of portfolio risk management. While polite, they were a bit subdued, despite Jim's attempts at levity. Conway wasn't surprised. No one wants a troubleshooter pointed at him. Conway fiddled with the connections between his laptop and the projector he was planning to use.

After introducing everyone, Jim said, "As you know, I've asked Conway to give us a seminar on the single most important lesson he's learned for portfolio management."

"Oh, I know that already," piped up one manager. "Make the other guy take the blame." Everyone laughed.

"That probably is the most important lesson," said Conway, "but I can't say I've fully learned it. Otherwise, I'd still be on the sell side." Everyone laughed some more, and the mood became more relaxed. After a pause he continued. "So I'm going to talk today about the second most important lesson, one thing I have learned, even though I can't say I always apply it well. Now if I can just get this projector to work, I'll post it on the screen." He found the right switch and a slide flashed into view:

"What the heck is that?" asked someone.

"Oops, operator error. Wait just a second." Conway flipped the slide over. "There, that's better."

"Henry, that looks just like you!" someone said. More laughter.

"Great slide," said Jim. "What does it mean?"

"Two things mostly. First, that standard portfolio allocation is like a lumbering elephant. Movements require a lot of energy to proceed step by cumbersome step. However, once under way, movements aren't readily reversed and tend to demolish every sapling of an objection."

"Why do you think that is?"

"Various reasons. Portfolio theory is generally perceived to work best over long time periods, when the law of large numbers can prevail over short-term deviations. Most investment advisors caution clients to maintain broadly stable allocations, so as not to lose their bearings or chase endlessly after last year's best trades. Fund managers too tend to stick to familiar patterns, partly because that's what they know how to do best and partly because that's what their clients and bosses expect from them. But eventually some new consensus emerges, and drags asset allocation along."

"That sounds like a fair depiction," said a manager. "But I don't see what's so bad about it. Better than flitting around like night bugs from one lantern to the next. That's a sure recipe for getting burned."

"I'm not criticizing allocation for being an elephant. I agree stability's a plus. But I do think that risk forecasts need to be updated a lot more frequently than most people seem to think, and that new information sometimes calls for dramatic changes in allocations. That's my second point. The elephant needs to dance."

"There's no point in needing something that can't be had. Elephants can't dance."

"I partly agree. They don't dance easily, and they'll never be as nimble as you'd like. One thing's for sure. Without good incentives and a culture of learning you won't see the least trace of a tango, let alone a whole routine."

The managers mulled this over. Conway had made a good impression but they still weren't sure what he meant. One of them spoke up. "Where's the music?"

"Excuse me?"

"I said, where's the music? We elephants can't dance without music. How will we know when to make our moves? And when we do move, how will we know whether to twist or to waltz?"

"Those are good questions. I wish I had half as good answers. All I can offer you are the basics. Our music consists of risk and reward assessments. Our choreography is optimization based on those assessments."

"That's a shame. I was hoping for Swan Lake."

Conway smiled and shook his head. "We'll never come close to Swan Lake. Our music has too much background noise and the choreography will look slipshod. I doubt we'll ever host a performance without some dancers bumping into each other or falling off the stage. Fortunately, our audience is pretty tolerant of mistakes, as long as they're not too gross."

"What kind of optimization do you have in mind?" asked someone else.

"I haven't worked that out in the detail it needs. But there is one basic measure we can use for a rough approximation. And it also illustrates the need for dancing. It's called the Sharpe ratio."

"Isn't that the mean return of a portfolio divided by its standard deviation?"

"Not quite. The numerator is the mean excess return relative to a risk-free benchmark, usually assumed to be short-term Treasury bills. Moreover, we want to use the expected excess return going forward, not the historical return which will usually differ due to random errors or regime change."

"How are we supposed to measure this expected excess return?"

"You can't measure it. You have to forecast it. And you forecast it the same way you forecast anything else, namely by mixing historic data with subjective judgment about what data is relevant and how things may have changed."

"And if our data or judgment isn't good?"

"Then the forecast will probably be lousy. Garbage in, garbage out. That's the fundamental law of forecasting. Playing with Sharpe ratios can't repeal that. The best it can do is to help you use good forecasts well."

Conway doubted he had said anything the managers didn't already know. They were just testing him on whether he knew the limits of his profession. Looking around the room for signs of objections, he decided it was safe to press on. "Now let me ask all of you a question. Why do you think I'm focusing on the Sharpe ratio and not some other measure?"

After a brief pause, answers began to trickle in. "It's simple." "It's easy to work with." "You can't goose it through leverage." "It's the best target to maximize."

"Excellent," said Conway. "You're all right. To help appreciate why, let's take a look at this chart." He flashed another slide on the screen.

Sharpe ratio maximization

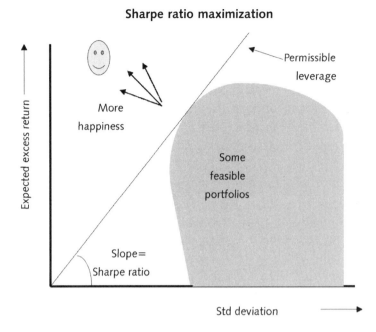

"Let's look at the tombstone first," continued Conway. "Each shaded point indicates the risk/reward combination for some feasible portfolio, where the horizontal coordinate marks the standard deviation and the vertical coordinate the expected excess return. But these aren't the only feasible points. Can someone tell me why not?"

Nobody answered, but Conway could tell that a lot of them knew. Finally the guy they called Henry spoke up. "As long as you can invest in risk-free securities, you can always move radially toward the origin. That's because the investment shaves the excess returns and the standard deviation by exactly the same proportion, so the Sharpe ratio doesn't change. And, if you can borrow risk-free securities you can move radially outward from the origin too."

"Thanks, Henry. The Sharpe ratio of a portfolio equals its vertical coordinate divided by its horizontal one, which is precisely the slope of a line from the origin to the point. Hence the ray running from the origin tangent to the tombstone represents the highest feasible Sharpe ratio. Leverage can take you anywhere below that ray but nowhere above it."

"What does the smiley represent?" asked Jim.

"Investor happiness. Normal investors like reward and dislike risk, all else being equal. So if the mean and the standard deviation are the only portfolio information at hand, they will prefer more northwesterly bundles. And that means that out all of the feasible portfolio locations, investors will always prefer the diagonal, where the Sharpe ratio is highest."

"Where on the diagonal?"

"We don't know. It depends on how enticing rewards are relative to risk and may vary for each investor. The beauty for portfolio managers is that it doesn't matter. They can just focus on delivering high Sharpe ratios and reporting the expected coordinates. Individual investors can then lever or dilute as they please."

"What if investors have more information at hand than just the mean and standard deviation?"

"Then this approach won't necessarily work. And, frankly, I'm not sure what will. I said before this is a rough approximation."

"Fair enough," said Jim. "Let's stick with the Sharpe ratio for now. Suppose we try to maximize it. What does that mean for our asset allocation?"

"Mathematically, there's a very simple recipe for maximizing a Sharpe ratio." Conway changed slides. "Here it is:"

SHARPE RATIO MAXIMIZATION FOR RISKY ASSETS
**Set the portfolio weights proportional to the
inverted covariance matrix times the expected excess returns vector.**

"Here 'inversion' means matrix inversion and 'times' refers to matrix multiplication. If we use algebraic symbols, the recipe is even shorter and sweeter. Now can anyone tell me what obvious practical implication follows from this recipe?"

Conway looked around, but this time everyone seemed clueless. "Good. We seem to agree again. No implication seems obvious, apart than the demonstration that what's easy to express in math can be hard to grasp intuitively. So let's try to tease out insights from some simpler examples. What's the most intimidating part of the formula? The matrix inverse, right?"

Everyone nodded. Conway continued, "Fortunately, it isn't always intimidating. Suppose all the assets are uncorrelated. Then both the covariance matrix and its inverse will be diagonal. Each diagonal element in the inverse will equal one over the respective variance. So what will each asset's optimal weight be proportional to in that case?"

"Its expected excess return divided by its variance," someone said.

"Exactly. And that choreography already hints at some lively dancing.

Suppose your portfolio contains two uncorrelated assets and you upgrade your forecast dollar return on one of those assets to a 9% mean from 6% without changing any other forecast. Sharpe ratio maximization tells you to roughly double the relative weight of that asset in your portfolio."

"Why double? The returns only rose by a third."

"That's because we need to look at excess returns over and above the roughly 3% return on US T-bills."

"Excuse me, Conway," interjected Jim, "but that doesn't seem so remarkable to me. In a large portfolio of uncorrelated assets, I could imagine modest changes in forecasts causing a considerable fluctuation in portfolio weights were it not for transaction costs. Granted, I'm not sure. We don't see many cases where correlations are negligible."

"I concede that. At this stage we're only getting hints. Let me introduce another example that may impress you a bit more. Suppose investors' only risky asset is one mega-fund run by one star portfolio manager. Suppose also that statistical analysis has detected a reliable alpha, beta, and residual error *vis-à-vis* Nasdaq, and that you adjust the Nasdaq exposure optimally by buying and selling Nasdaq futures. Does this sound more realistic to you?"

"Yes, although I should probably warn you that we don't do a lot of hedging here. I could blame it on the regulators, but in truth we could do more if we wanted, either directly or indirectly."

"Maybe we should do more. Let's see what the analysis tells us. Returning to the example, let me ask everyone to mentally rearrange the individual stock holdings and the long or short positions in Nasdaq futures into two uncorrelated components. The first component is the net Nasdaq exposure. The second is the combination of the manager's alpha and the residual. Is everyone still with me?"

"Are you measuring alpha including or net of nominal rates?" asked Henry.

"Net. From here on let's measure everything in terms of excess returns, so that we don't have to keep remembering to subtract the T-bill rate. Now imagine we're managing asset allocation for this mega-fund from mid-October 1999 when the Nasdaq is soaring until mid-March 2000 when the Nasdaq is still flying high but suffering much more turbulence. How would our forecasts be likely to change over this period?"

"That's a tough question," said Jim. "Now that we know what happened, it's hard to remember what seemed reasonable at the time. It's awfully tempting to substitute a hindcast for a forecast."

"Granted. But let me ask you this. Would it be reasonable to become more bullish or less bullish on Nasdaq's prospects, given that Nasdaq had rocketed 75% in five months?"

"Less bullish, of course."

"Would it also be reasonable for analysts to change their view on Nasdaq's future volatility roughly in line with the implied volatility on Nasdaq options?"

"That seems as good an assumption as any."

"And do you recall what happened to implied Nasdaq vols over that period?"

"They got higher, I recall, but not by how much."

"Up by 1500 basis points, to 50% instead of an already high 35%. The implied variance doubled. So Sharpe ratio maximization would tell you to at least halve your relative Nasdaq exposure in mid-March 2000 compared to six months prior, even before you trim your forecast of the mean. Granted, this presumes the manager's alpha and residual variance stay constant."

"Wow," said Jim. "That would have been a huge leap. I'm sorry you weren't around then. What else does theory tell us?"

"It tells us the marginal contributions of different uncorrelated assets or subportfolios to overall performance. The results can be summarized in four rules." Conway flashed a new slide:

SHARPE-SQUARED RULES FOR UNCORRELATED ASSETS

1. The optimal weights are directly proportional to the Sharpe ratio per unit of risk (volatility).
2. The square of the Sharpe ratio on the optimal portfolio equals the sum of squares of the individual Sharpe ratios.
3. Each optimally weighted asset contributes to mean portfolio return in direct proportion to the square of its Sharpe ratio.
4. Each optimally weighted asset contributes to mean portfolio variance in direct proportion to the square of its Sharpe ratio.

"This confirms that diversification across uncorrelated assets or trading strategies always helps in a mean/variance world. More importantly, it tells you how much it helps. Doubling the Sharpe ratio of an uncorrelated asset or subportfolio warrants roughly quadrupling its fair share of risk. An uncorrelated asset with triple the Sharpe ratio of others is worth roughly nine of the latter."

"Very interesting. Too bad it's not very useful. I've never seen a real-life portfolio without some highly correlated assets. Lots of times we want highly correlated assets to help track a benchmark."

"Actually, portfolios that are heavily benchmarked to tradable indices are where Sharpe-squared rules come in most handy. We just need to remeasure each asset's or strategy's Sharpe ratio to focus on the component that's uncorrelated with the benchmarks, the way we did in the preceding example. The Sharpe ratio of the residual is often called the asset's 'information ratio', because it measures a signal relative to noise. But if you don't mind, I'd rather call it 'sharpness', because that helps you remember what it means."

"Suit yourself. What do you do with it?"

"Easy. Assuming the residuals are independent of each other, use the Sharpe-squared rules to build a portfolio that maximizes the aggregate sharpness. Then go long or short enough index futures to achieve the desired benchmark exposure."

"Can we always find an uncorrelated residual?"

"Yes. Imagine a hyperspace in which each dimension measures a possible set of market returns. Drop a perpendicular from the vector that represents the asset to the hyperplane that represents linear combinations of the benchmark indices. Then the perpendicular describes the residual, while the vector extending on the hyperplane from the origin to the perpendicular describes the best index fit. Here's how it looks for three dimensions and two benchmark indices."

Decomposing assets into orthogonal components

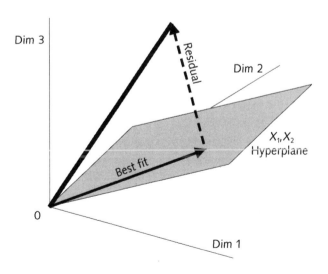

"How hard is this to calculate?"

"Not hard at all if you have representative data. Just regress the asset's excess returns against the indices' excess returns and a constant. The beta estimates tell you the best linear fit, while the sharpness is just the intercept divided by the standard error of the fit.

"How can we be certain that the residuals for different assets will be independent of each other?"

"We can't be. But the more market drivers the benchmark encompasses, the less unreasonable it becomes to treat the residuals as normal and independent. It's a bit like bleaching: the more colors you wash out, the whiter the clothes look. Only here we're talking about statistical white noise. If that's what the residuals amount to, the portfolio that maximizes the aggregate sharpness will be most likely to outperform the benchmark it tracks. Would you like me to walk you through a hypothetical example?"

"That would be great."

"Suppose in autumn of 2000 you are running a global equity fund with tech and nontech subportfolios. When regressed against Nasdaq percent returns and a tradable proxy for MSCI World percent returns, your sub-portfolio returns yield the following annualized decomposition." Conway brought up a fresh slide on the screen:

HYPOTHETICAL TECH AND NON-TECH SUBPORTFOLIOS
$$Tech = 0.06 + 0.5 \cdot Nasdaq + 0 \cdot MSCI + 0.15 \cdot \epsilon_{tech}; \quad S_{tech} = 0.4$$
$$Nontech = 0.03 - 0.1 \cdot Nasdaq + 0.8 \cdot MSCI + 0.1 \cdot \epsilon_{nontech}; \quad S_{nontech} = 0.3$$
$$\epsilon_{tech} \text{ and } \epsilon_{nontech} \text{ independent, standard normal variables}$$

"That is, your tech subportfolio has an alpha of 6%, a Nasdaq beta of 0.5, an MSCI beta of 0, and a residual vol of 20%. Your nontech subportfolio has an alpha of 3%, a Nasdaq beta of −0.1, an MSCI beta of 0.8, and a residual vol of 10%. The sharpnesses S work out to 0.4 for tech and 0.3 for nontech. That gives an aggregate sharpness of 0.5, which implies a 69% chance of outperforming the benchmark on a one-year horizon."

"Regardless of the benchmark?"

"The benchmark doesn't matter, as long as it's some mixture of Nasdaq and MSCI that you can buy or hedge out in the market. That's the beauty of sharpness analysis. It lets you answer some questions even while you're wrestling with others."

"So how do you construct the optimal portfolio?"

"Start with the desired index benchmark. Reallocate 25 units away from spare cash toward 16 units of the tech subportfolio and 9 units of the nontech. Then neutralize the change in Nasdaq and MSCI exposure by selling off $16 \times 0.5 + 9 \times (-0.1) = 7.1$ units of Nasdaq and $16 \times 0 + 9 \times (0.8) = 7.2$ units of MSCI. That will help replenish your cash."

"What scale of trades are you talking about?"

"That can vary with how much risk and leverage you can tolerate. Sharpness can't tell you that on its own."

"But you can still decide the relative allocation between tech and nontech?"

"Yes, provided you're tracking a benchmark, and provided you believe the residuals are white noise."

Jim leaned back in his chair and stroked his chin. "You know, this has some interesting management implications. To the extent the assumptions are valid, we could divide the group into 'alpha' teams, a 'beta' team, and an 'omega' team. Each alpha team could concentrate on maximizing its sharpness. The beta team could try to track the desired benchmark. The omega team would allocate assets between the teams to handle risk and leverage concerns. While we'd still want the teams to communicate, they could operate relatively autonomously, without being dragged down to the level of the slowest, or being overwhelmed with irrelevant information."

"You mean fewer meetings where we address everything and decide nothing?" someone asked. Everyone laughed.

"Yes," said Jim. "But then we'll have to stay awake in the ones we do attend. I don't see anyone asleep here, so that's a good start. Thanks Conway. This has been very helpful."

"Wait a second, don't you want to hear about allocation with correlated assets?"

"I thought you addressed everything by breaking them down into common and independent components."

"I did, but that only works for the alpha teams. If your beta team is managing both Nasdaq and MSCI exposures, and is aiming for outperformance rather than just passive tracking, you need to take the correlations between Nasdaq and MSCI into account."

"I see. But I'm afraid my brain can't handle any more sharpness today. How about we meet again tomorrow? Same time and place."

Others nodded in agreement and the meeting adjourned. Conway was overjoyed. *No icebergs. No professional doubters. Just a nice normal discussion.*

What a relief to find some simple models that seem to work! Here are some notes reviewing the basic math of Sharpe ratio maximization, to help readers get more comfortable with the results. I also identify some inherent ambiguities in measurement, not to discourage potential users, but to help them better distinguish between good approximations and lousy ones.

EXCESS RETURN

The excess return is typically defined as the nominal percentage return on an asset less the risk-free interest rate, as if the investors borrowed money at the risk-free rate, bought the asset, repaid the loan out of the proceeds, and then measured the net profit as a share of the initial investment. That's the right idea, except that it's better to measure net profit in present value terms before taking its ratio to the initial investment.

$$E[\text{ExcessReturn}] = \frac{E[\%\text{Return}] - \text{RiskfreeRate}}{1 + \text{RiskfreeRate}}$$

This approach makes the ratio nearly independent of the currency used to measure it. For example, when Turkish T-bills were earning 100% due to high inflation, an asset promising 110% in Turkish lira, or 1000 basis points (bps) in nominal excess return, wasn't as juicy as an asset promising 600 bps excess return in dollars or marks. Granted, no sensible investor regarded such T-bills as a risk-free asset! But the problem crops up on a smaller scale even in more developed markets. In effect, the focus on excess returns presumes that portfolio investors hedge out all extraneous inflation and currency risk, except insofar as they explicitly buy this risk as an asset.

If we measure expected excess returns logarithmically, that is, as $\ln(1 + E[\%\text{Return}])$, they should scale linearly in time (as long as the regime stays the same). Percentage returns need to be compounded. In either case they are typically reported on an annualized basis.

VOLATILITY

The volatility or "vol" refers to the annualized standard deviation. To annualize the standard deviation of an investment measured every T

trading days, you might multiply it by $\sqrt{252/T}$, where 252 represents the average number of trading days in a year. While there's nothing sacred about 252 or the exclusion of non-trading days, the multiplication by a square root rests on a simple, powerful, and often plausible assumption: namely, that the returns across holding periods are uncorrelated. That makes the standard deviation of log returns (and, for the most part, of percentage returns) scale with the square root of time.

When returns are serially correlated, the use of standard annualization formulas can be misleading. Perhaps the most extreme example concerns a currency trading in a narrow band around some foreign currency anchor. Intra-day fluctuations might rival those of a floating exchange rate, implying a high vol, even though the actual standard deviation of yearly movements will be negligible as long as the band holds. Fortunately, apart from currencies, few securities show much serial correlation given holding periods ranging from a few days to a few months, where this book focuses.

PORTFOLIO MEASURES

Let M denote the vector of expected excess returns. Let ω denote the vector of portfolio weights, defined as shares of base investment. The expected excess return μ on the portfolio can be calculated as $\omega'M$, provided M is measured over the whole period and the portfolio isn't adjusted along the way.

Forgetting the caveats can cause a lot of confusion. To take an extreme example, suppose your $100 portfolio is originally equally divided between cash and a risky asset that every six months either triples or nearly vanishes. Clearly, you have equal odds of gaining $100 or losing $50 in the first six months, for an expected return of 25%. How about your yearly return? If you restore your original portfolio shares for the second six months, you'll have an expected return for the year of $1.25 \times 1.25 - 1 = 56.25\%$. In contrast, if you hold on to the original bundle for the whole year, you'll have a 25% chance of earning $400 and a 75% chance of losing $50, for an expected return of +62.5%.

Denoting the covariance matrix of excess returns by Σ, the variance σ^2 of the portfolio's excess return will equal $\omega'\Sigma\omega$. Again, this formula is exact only for a single holding period.

Sharpe Ratio

The Sharpe ratio, named after the finance professor who popularized it, indicates how many standard deviations returns need to fall below their mean before the investor earns less than the risk-free rate. I will denote it by S. It equals the expected excess return μ of a portfolio divided by the standard deviation σ of that excess return:

$$\text{Sharpe ratio } (S) \equiv \frac{\mu}{\sigma} = \frac{\omega'\text{M}}{\sqrt{\omega'\Sigma\omega}}$$

The Sharpe ratio typically scales with roughly the square root of time. Like the mean and the standard deviation, it is typically reported on an annualized basis to avoid confusion.

Invariance to Leverage

Note that the share of the portfolio devoted to the risk-free asset does not affect either the mean or the standard deviation, except insofar as it constrains the sum of the other shares. So leverage or dilution at the risk-free rate doesn't affect the Sharpe ratio.

Assuming unlimited potential investment or borrowing at the risk-free rate, it is convenient to ignore the risk-free investment in our matrix calculations. That allows us to drop any restriction on the sum of the remaining portfolio shares. We can still back out the implied risk-free share as $1 - \omega'\mathbf{1}$; that is, as one less the sum of the remaining shares.

Any function g of the mean and standard deviation that is invariant to leverage is a function of the Sharpe ratio. To verify this, note that $g(\mu, \sigma) = g(k\mu, k\sigma)$ for all k, and in particular for $k = 1/\sigma$. So if we define a new function $h(y) \equiv g(y, 1), g(\mu, \sigma) = g\left(\frac{\mu}{\sigma}, 1\right) \equiv h\left(\frac{\mu}{\sigma}\right) = h(S)$.

Matrix Derivatives

To derive the portfolio weights that maximize the Sharpe ratio, it's handy to apply matrix calculus. Matrix calculus is just like regular calculus except that it uses matrix notation to keep track of the results. The basic rule is that the derivative of a column m-vector with respect to a row n-vector is an $m \times n$ matrix, whose $\langle i, j \rangle$ element equals the derivative of the ith element of the column vector with respect to the jth element of the row vector. The two main results we need concern the derivatives of standard matrix products and quadratic forms:

$$\frac{d}{dx}x'M = M$$

$$\frac{d}{dx}x'\Sigma x = 2\Sigma x$$

for any vector M or symmetric matrix Σ. The only difficulties involve keeping track of transposes and the order of multiplication.

SHARPE RATIO MAXIMIZATION

Let's now apply the preceding formulas to maximize the Sharpe ratio. Since the Sharpe ratio is invariant to leverage, let's constrain the excess return to equal or exceed some target $\bar{\mu}$ and look for the minimum-variance portfolio in that class. Form the Lagrangean

$$\omega'\Sigma\omega - \eta(\omega'M - \bar{\mu})$$

with η positive (since the constraint will always be binding) and differentiate with respect to ω to obtain the matrix first-order condition:

$$2\Sigma\omega - \eta M = 0$$

This has a unique interior solution only if Σ is invertible (so that no portfolio of risky assets is ever completely risk-free), in which case:

$$\omega^* = \tfrac{1}{2}\eta\Sigma^{-1}M$$

Hence any positive multiple of $\Sigma^{-1}M$ is a stationary point for some $\bar{\mu}$. Convexity arguments (if you graph the variance in ω space, tangents to the curve must lie below it) confirm that the stationary point minimizes the variance. The maximum Sharpe ratio works out to:

$$\frac{\omega^{*\prime}M}{\sqrt{\omega^{*\prime}\Sigma\omega^*}} = \frac{M'\Sigma^{-1}M}{\sqrt{M'\Sigma^{-1}\Sigma\Sigma^{-1}M}} = \frac{M'\Sigma^{-1}M}{\sqrt{M'\Sigma^{-1}M}} = \sqrt{M'\Sigma^{-1}M}$$

SHARPE RATIO AND HOLDING PERIOD

To the extent that the holding period changes the relative means, it alters the optimal strategy. This may seem strange, since the Sharpe formulas don't explicitly refer to holding periods. But there's no inconsistency. Remember that the optimization doesn't look at every possible portfolio strategy. Rather, it selects from strategies that rebalance the portfolio as frequently as the returns are compounded. Also, changing the holding period implicitly changes the definition of the means and covariances. In practice, ambiguity about the holding period is a trifling issue compared with forecasters' uncertainty about the portfolio risks to expect looking forward.

SHARPE-SQUARED RULES FOR UNCORRELATED ASSETS

If assets are uncorrelated, Σ will be a diagonal matrix, in which case the optimal weight on each asset will be proportional to $\dfrac{\mu_i}{\sigma_i^2} = \dfrac{S_i}{\sigma_i}$. The contribution of asset i to the expected aggregate excess return will be proportional to $\mu_i \cdot \dfrac{\mu_i}{\sigma_i^2} = S_i^2$, while its contribution to the aggregate volatility will be proportional to $\left(\dfrac{\mu_i}{\sigma_i^2}\right)^2 \sigma_i^2 = S_i^2$. Finally, the square of the aggregate Sharpe ratio will equal $\sum_i \dfrac{\mu_i^2}{\sigma_i^2} = \sum_i S_i^2$.

BENCHMARK COMPARISONS

Consider a portfolio consisting of a benchmark plus a subportfolio of multivariate normal assets. The subportfolio will be normally distributed with an expected excess return μ and volatility σ that depend on the subportfolio weights ω. The risk that the portfolio underperforms the benchmark equals the cumulative normal probability of $-\dfrac{\mu}{\sigma} = -S$. To minimize that risk, invoke the Sharpe rules above to maximize S.

REGRESSIONS

A regression of Y on X approximates Y by a linear combination $X\beta$. Here Y is a J-vector, X is a $J \times m$ matrix (equivalently, an m-vector of J-vectors), and β is an m-vector, where J is the number of observations and m is the number of explanatory variables. The residual $R = Y - X\beta$ measures the fit.

Ordinary least squares regression minimizes the sum of squared residuals. Differentiation with respect to β yields the solution

$$X'Y - X'X\beta = 0 \Leftrightarrow \beta = (X'X)^{-1}X'Y$$

If X and Y are measured as deviations from their respective means, or if one of the explanatory variables is a constant, $R = (I - X(X'X)^{-1}X')Y$ will be uncorrelated with X, because

$$Cov[X, R] = E[X'R] - E[X']E[R] = E[X'(I - X(X'X)^{-1}X')Y] - E[X'] \cdot 0$$
$$= E[(X' - X'X(X'X)^{-1}X')Y] = E[(X' - X')Y] = 0$$

SHARPNESS ("INFORMATION RATIO")

Suppose that Y effectively consists of a linear combination of tradeable indices X and an uncorrelated residual with mean α and volatility ν. The sharpness with respect to X is defined as the Sharpe ratio α/ν of that residual. Neither overall leverage nor hedges in the components of X can change the measured sharpness. But changing X generally will change the sharpness, and may even reverse its sign. The standard Sharpe ratio is a special case of sharpness with a purely risk-free benchmark.

The Sharpe-squared rules also apply to sharpness. For example, if asset sharpnesses are uncorrelated, the sum of their squares equals the square of the optimal portfolio sharpness. Standard finance literature uses the phrase "information ratio" instead of sharpness. I prefer to use "information ratio" more generically, the way statisticians do, to refer to statistical evidence bearing on a hypothesis. Besides, I think "sharpness" more clearly reminds you what it is. But suit yourself. A statistical rose by any other name ...

MIXTURES OF IDIOSYNCRATIC AND CORRELATED EFFECTS

If all constructed residuals, including exposures to core traded indices, are independent of each other, we can invoke the Sharpe-squared rules to set optimal relative weights. If we can disentangle some exposures but not others, we can still invoke Sharpe-squared rules for part of the portfolio. Suppose the reconstructed subportfolios have covariance matrix

$$\tilde{\Sigma} = \begin{pmatrix} \Sigma_R & 0 \\ 0 & D \end{pmatrix}$$

where D is a diagonal matrix but the residual covariance Σ_R is not. Then the inverse of the revised covariance matrix takes the form

$$\tilde{\Sigma}^{-1} = \begin{pmatrix} \Sigma_R^{-1} & 0 \\ 0 & D^{-1} \end{pmatrix}$$

Since D^{-1} is also diagonal, it follows that the Sharpe-squared rules apply among the assets that D covers. Note, however, that reconstructed assets should be independent of every other asset and not just of those covered by D.

13 | Betting on Beta

"Thanks to all for showing up again," said Jim, convening the next day's meeting. "Yesterday, as you recall, Conway presented a vision of portfolio elephants swaying to Sharpe music. But he focused on the case where each elephant hears its own independent music. Today he's going to examine a more advanced choreography, where the main tunes are correlated. At least that's what I think he's going to do. Take it away, Conway."

Okay, here we go. I hope yesterday wasn't just beginner's luck. "Thanks. You summed it up correctly, Jim. But I have to warn you all: I'll be leading you in a circle. First I'll explore core differences in Sharpe ratio analysis between correlated and uncorrelated assets. Or to use Jim's proposed management scheme, I'll explain how the beta team has to differ from alpha teams. Then I'll show you a trick that lets you treat all the assets as uncorrelated, so that the beta team turns into an alpha team after all. Are you ready to roll?"

Everyone nodded. "Good. Let's start by reviewing the two basic techniques for reducing risk without crimping reward. The first technique is diversification, or spreading your eggs among different baskets. The second technique is long/short hedging, where you short one asset as a proxy for another. What factors influence your choice of technique?"

"Sharpe ratios for one," said Henry. "It's hard to benefit from shorting an asset with a high Sharpe ratio, or from buying an asset with a low or negative Sharpe ratio."

"Right. What else?"

"Correlation. Diversification works best when the different baskets thrive in contrasting environments, or failing that when the baskets thrive more or less independently of each other. That means negative or low correlation. Long/short hedging works best when the risks are highly correlated."

"Right again. To illustrate this, I have graphed the aggregate Sharpe ratio versus portfolio shares for a basket of two assets, for correlation ranging from −0.4 to +0.9. Each graph assumes excess expected returns of 4% for the first asset and 8% for the second, with a 20% vol for each." Conway switched on the projector and flashed a slide from his PC. "By the way. Thanks to whomever left the overhead projector instruction manual on my desk last night. Very helpful."

Influence of correlation on a two-asset portfolio

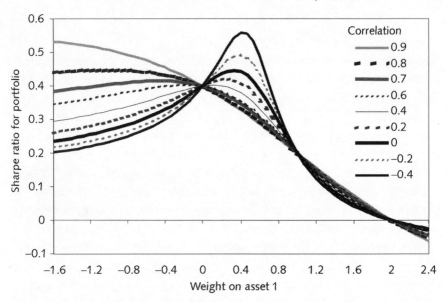

Mean$_1$ = 0.06, Mean$_2$ = 0.12, Vol$_1$ = Vol$_2$ = 0.20.

"Anyway, as you can see, all the graphs intersect at three points: where you hold one or the other asset only or where you hold a portfolio with zero mean. And all the graphs flatten out at the extremes with one interior maximum. But otherwise the shape varies a lot. When the correlation is low, it's always worthwhile to hold some of asset 1, even though it gives only half the reward as asset 2 for the same direct risk. When the correlation is high, however, it's better to short asset 1 and overload on asset 2."

"Now at first glance the formula for Sharpe ratio maximization we saw yesterday, which sets the portfolio weights to a multiple of the inverse of the covariance matrix times the expected excess returns, doesn't say anything about either Sharpe ratios or correlations. But we can rewrite it in a way that does." Conway flashed the next slide.

SHARPE RATIO MAXIMIZATION REPHRASED
Set the portfolio weight times the volatility proportional to the inverted correlations matrix times the vector of Sharpe ratios.

The maximum Sharpe ratio squared will equal a quadratic form in the asset Sharpe ratios and the inverted correlations matrix.

"Now we see very clearly that the correlations and Sharpe ratios are central to the allocation scheme. But their interaction is complicated. To gain more insight we have to plunge into the calculations. Here's the result for two assets.

SHARPE RATIO MAXIMIZATION WITH 2 ASSETS
Set the portfolio weight times the volatility proportional to the asset's own Sharpe ratio less ρ (the correlation) times the other asset's Sharpe ratio.

Raising an asset's Sharpe ratio improves the aggregate Sharpe ratio if and only if the asset's optimal portfolio weight is positive.

"That's not so bad, is it? Given the Sharpe ratios, raising the correlation increases the incentive for long/short hedging as opposed to diversification. Given the correlation, raising an asset's Sharpe ratio helps if you're already long the asset and hurts if you're short. And if the correlation is zero, we get yesterday's Sharpe rules again. I can't think of any simpler formula that generates all these results."

"How about more than two assets?" asked Jim. "What's the most interesting thing Sharpe ratio maximization tells us then?"

"That diversification shrinks in usefulness relative to long/short hedging when you're facing a lot of correlated assets. If you can't short but are confident about the risk parameters, then unless the correlations are small it's probably not worth your while to hold more than a dozen assets."

"Really? Most US mutual funds are founded on just the opposite principle: investing in dozens of moderately correlated assets without short hedges."

"I realize that. But there's no doubt about the key mathematical result. If you hold probabilistically exchangeable assets with a common correlation ρ, you can never multiply your initial Sharpe ratio by more than $\sqrt{1/\rho}$."

"What if ρ is negative or zero?"

"You can't have too many assets with a negative ρ. If ρ is zero, then – as we've seen – the square of the aggregate Sharpe ratio keeps rising by the square of the Sharpe ratio of the next asset you buy. But the limit kicks in very fast as ρ rises, as the next slide shows.

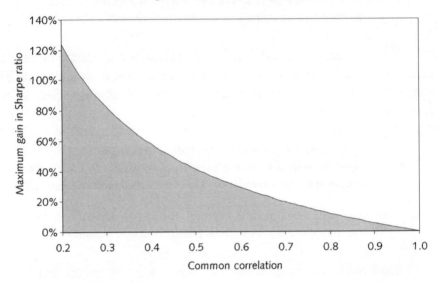

Limits on gains from simple diversification

"Already at $\rho = 0.25$ you can at best double your initial Sharpe ratio. At $\rho = 0.7$ you can't improve the initial Sharpe ratio by 20% even with an infinite number of assets. Moreover, the higher the correlation is, the more quickly diminishing returns set in when you add assets one by one. Here is a table indicating the size of the portfolio basket at which the marginal gain in Sharpe ratio from adding another asset falls below 1%. It also indicates how close that basket comes to achieving the maximum possible diversification benefit."

When is a basket of exchangeable assets big enough?

Correlation	Basket size where marginal Sharpe improvement <1%	Sharpe ratio improvement as % of maximum
0	50	0
0.1	17	81%
0.2	12	84%
0.3	10	89%
0.4	8	91%

0.5	7	93%
0.6	5	93%
0.7	4	94%
0.8	3	95%
0.9	2	97%

"That's a lot less than I would have guessed," said Jim. "What's the intuition?"

"Think of each asset as containing two components. One component, accounting for a fraction ρ of the variance or $\sqrt{\rho}$ of the volatility, generates the same returns for all assets. The other component is independent. In a large portfolio the independent components wash out but the common component never does. So a mixture never reduces the variance to less than ρ of the original, and the Sharpe ratio never improves by more than a factor $\sqrt{1/\rho}$. Moreover, the larger ρ is, the smaller the independent components are, so stopping your diversification at a handful of assets doesn't leave much undone."

"What if the correlation doesn't stem from a single common component?"

"As long as we're doing mean-variance analysis, the results will be the same. So we may as well assume the simplest possible causal structure. Mind you, the causal structure may change the third and higher moments."

"OK. I think I see why diversification doesn't help you much when the correlations are high. But I don't see how long/short hedges help you either. How can you make money arbitraging completely exchangeable assets?"

"You can't. The assets need to have at least slightly different Sharpe ratios. But if they do, long/short hedges can create a new series of profitable, uncorrelated asset bundles. The more of these we have the merrier, with no inherent ceiling on the aggregate Sharpe ratio."

"Can you give an example?"

"Sure. Suppose assets come in two types. Each type has a volatility of 20% and is perfectly correlated with the other. However, if the first type has 100 bps higher expected return than the second, then a bundle of one unit long the first type and one unit short the second type will have an expected return of 1% with no volatility."

Jim spotted a problem. "One bundled asset with an infinite Sharpe ratio? Surely that's too extreme."

"It is. I just wanted to demonstrate the long/short effect in full force. If in the previous example the various assets had only 50% correlation with each other, each long/short bundle would have a volatility of 20%, for a Sharpe ratio of 0.05. But each bundle would still be uncorrelated with each other, so by spreading your portfolio among more and more such bundles you could raise your aggregate Sharpe ratio *ad infinitum*."

"You might need a huge portfolio before that long/short combo beats the Sharpe ratio on the best individual asset."

"Agreed. As I said, for a given correlation, large portfolios are more likely than small portfolios to favor long/short hedging over simple diversification. But in practice, where a lot of correlations across major market indices exceed 0.7 and individual Sharpe ratios diverge by hundreds of basis points, prohibitions on shorts or related derivatives will cripple your ability to manage risk."

"Maybe you should write a letter to the SEC," said Jim. "Although I wouldn't bet on a quick reply. The public associates derivatives more with risk than with risk reduction, and the SEC seems more geared toward managing the appearance of risk than risk itself. But for now let's assume we have the regulatory authorization. How should we manage the beta team?"

"One approach is to have the beta team maximize the aggregate Sharpe ratio for a portfolio composed of the various market indices, while instructing the alpha teams to neutralize any net index exposure. The omega team then allocates funds to the alpha teams and the beta team in direct proportion to their reported sharpnesses per unit of volatility risk. The omega team also buys the benchmark index or some proxy for it."

"Doesn't that threaten wasteful trading, where different teams are long and short the same indices?"

"Just agree to net out trades internally before trading on the external market. For example, if the alpha team is 0.2 units short the Nasdaq 100, the beta team is short 0.1 units, and the benchmark is 0.3 units long, no Nasdaq futures need to be bought or sold externally."

"You'll need an extra layer of accounting to track the various exposures. Maybe even internal audits." Jim's observation prompted a collective groan.

"It's not a complicated layer," said Conway. "In the previous example, one trader entrusted to handle all Nasdaq futures could easily manage it. And it needn't stifle your initiative. It just enhances your accountability. No firm can decentralize effectively without accountability."

Jim smiled. "We fund managers like that in the companies we invest in. I'm not so sure we like applying that to ourselves. But go on. What did you mean by the differences between beta and alpha management? The way you've been talking they sound the same."

"If you are managing multiple correlated indices, you have to decide the relative exposures jointly. That requires solving several simultaneous equations, which is what multiplying the inverse forecast covariance matrix by expected excess returns does. Moreover, you'll need to forecast the indices more carefully, as high correlations make the weightings very sensitive to errors."

"Why not break the beta team into multiple teams, each managing a single index exposure?"

"That won't help much for correlated indices, as each beta team would still need the other forecasts to decide its own relative shares. But there is a way to make this approach work."

"Namely?"

"Reconstitute the indices into uncorrelated components. Then the beta teams really would resemble alpha teams."

"And how do you propose to reconstitute the indices?"

"Here's one way that's particularly easy to grasp. Rank the indices in the order of their perceived importance to your portfolio. The premier index will usually be the index for the market as a whole, say MSCI World if you're managing a global fund. Assign it to the first beta team to manage. Then regress the second index against the premier index and a constant, and assign the residual (including the constant) to the second beta team to manage."

"Like the way you suggested assigning a sector residual to an alpha team?"

"Just like that," agreed Conway. "Next regress the third index against the first two indices and a constant, and assign the residual (including the constant) to the third beta team to manage. Continue until you've run out of indices. By construction each beta team's component will have been uncorrelated historically with every other beta or alpha team's component. With luck the indices will stay uncorrelated, and perhaps even be mutually independent."

"And if they don't?"

"Then tweak them until you expect them to be uncorrelated, report the relevant parameters, and invest your allocation as you've pledged. That's what managing an alpha or beta component means."

"What if some of the residual sharpnesses are so tiny that they hardly affect the aggregate Sharpe ratio?"

"Then disband the teams managing those residuals. For example, if you're managing a global equity fund, and if you expect the French and German indices to basically move in synch, then one team might suffice to manage both exposures. Another team might be better deployed to manage, say, Asian versus European exposures."

"That sounds very subjective."

"It is. But there's a tool you can use to help make it more objective. It's called principal component analysis. To understand the motivation, take a look at this chart of monthly excess returns in French and German stock markets from 1986 thru 1999. While both French and German returns vary a lot, most of the variation runs along the diagonal axis I've drawn. If you defined one index to measure along that axis, and if past trends persist, it would capture 88% of the total French and German variance."

Monthly German vs. French excess returns 1986–1999

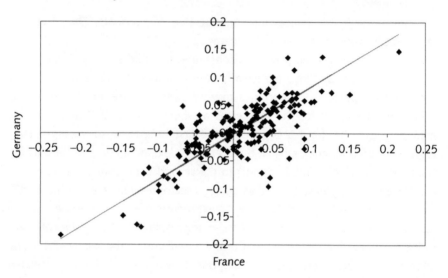

"I used principal components analysis to pick the axis. Eyeballing this graph I would have picked roughly the same one. But eyeballs don't work so well in higher dimensions. Principal components analysis uses eigenvalues and eigenvectors to identify the orthogonal axes that explain the most variance between them. If you want, you can assign the first principal component to the first beta group, the second principal component to the second beta group, and so on until most of the variance is accounted for."

"Why didn't you suggest that in the first place?"

"I nearly did. I just worry that in some cases forecasters might find it intimidating, and the mass of detail in a multivariate index might blind them to some fundamental change. Also, managing a detailed non-standard index can add significant transaction costs."

"So how do you suggest using principal components?"

"Like a torch. Illuminate the main trends, and try to find some index that captures their essence but is easier to deal with. For example, the aggregate world index is nearly always very highly correlated with the first principal component of the various country and sectoral indices. That's why I suggested assigning it to the lead beta group. Other principal components tend to resemble 'US versus non-US', 'Europe versus Asia', 'new-tech versus old-tech', and so on. I would prefer to use the latter as a proxy for the principal components than the principal components as a proxy for the latter."

"So if I understand you correctly, you'd like to carve out uncorrelated alpha and beta teams using some combination of what people feel comfortable forecasting and what seems to account for most of the variance."

"That's right."

"What if people aren't comfortable forecasting uncorrelated residuals?"

"Then we may need to divide the teams along other lines. But I'd prefer to try this first. In a previous job I once had to forecast interest rate premia for emerging market dollar bonds. Like nearly all my counterparts at other firms, I focused on analyzing individual country developments. But it quickly became clear that fluctuations in US stock markets drove over half of total variance. Most of what we emerging market analysts were doing was just predicting the performance of the residual. I think that's true for most specialized analysts."

Jim nodded. "I see your point," he said. "And I understand, or I think I understand, how to manage the alpha and beta teams along the same lines. Maybe we should give this a whirl. Let me just ask you one question first."

"Sure. Go ahead." *It's such a pleasure to deal with a reasonable man.*

"How do you propose to deal with iceberg risks?"

Conway froze inside. "I ... uhh ... I'm not sure what you mean," he stammered.

"I mean the big dangers that you never clearly see, but can't afford to ignore. Like market crashes that seem to defy the laws of averages."

"Or sudden changes in regimes," said Henry.

"Or risk parameters that are stable only you're not sure what they are," added another voice from the back of the room.

Conway felt like a kid caught with his hands in the cookie jar. *Better confess now and ask for mercy.* "Yes, I know those kinds of risks. On my last job I had a colleague who hardly talked of anything else. Drove himself nuts."

"And not thinking about them can drive you bankrupt," said Jim. "I want us to have a balance. Can your Sharpe ratio approach provide it?"

Conway paused, searching for a clever reply. He didn't find one. "I don't know. I hope so."

"Have you thought about how to provide it?"

"Some. Not enough."

"Well, I suggest you think about it some more. I appreciate what you've done so far, Conway. I really do. But I'm reluctant to revamp our system without more insight on where we're heading."

Everyone else agreed. "So am I." "Likewise." "Why rush?" The meeting adjourned soon afterward, leaving Conway to nurse his wounds. *You can run but you can't hide.*

While Conway ponders what to do next, let's work thru some more matrix math.

The "diag" Operator

The "diag" operator converts a vector or square matrix A into a diagonal matrix. If A is a vector, then the ith element of A becomes element $\langle i, i \rangle$ of diag(A). If A is a square matrix, diag(A) just "zeroes out" the off-diagonal elements of A. These operators are useful in certain kinds of multiplication. For example, if $A = [a_1 \cdots a_n]'$ and $B = [b_1 \cdots b_n]'$, the vector with elements $a_i b_i$ can be expressed as either diag(A)B or diag(B)A.

Reformulation of Sharpe Ratio Maximization

Let P denote the matrix of correlation coefficients and $H \equiv \text{diag}(\Sigma)$ denote the diagonal matrix of variances. Note that $\Sigma = H^{1/2}PH^{1/2}$ where $V^{1/2}$ denotes the diagonal matrix of volatilities. Also, $H^{-1/2}M$ equals the vector S of Sharpe ratios. Hence the optimal portfolio weights ω are proportional to $\Sigma^{-1}M = H^{-1/2}P^{-1}H^{-1/2}M = H^{-1/2}P^{-1}S$, and the weights times the volatilities are proportional to $H^{1/2}H^{-1/2}P^{-1}S = P^{-1}S$. The maximum squared Sharpe ratio $M'\Sigma^{-1}M$ can be rewritten as $M'H^{-1/2}P^{-1}H^{-1/2}M = S'P^{-1}S$.

SHARPE RATIO MAXIMIZATION WITH TWO ASSETS

With two assets the inverse correlation matrix P^{-1} equals

$$\frac{1}{1-\rho^2}\begin{bmatrix} 1 & -\rho \\ -\rho & 1 \end{bmatrix}$$

which implies that $\dfrac{w_1^*\sigma_1}{w_2^*\sigma_2} = \dfrac{S_1 - \rho S_2}{S_2 - \rho S_1}$. The maximum Sharpe ratio works

out to $\sqrt{\dfrac{S_1^2 - 2\rho S_1 S_2 + S_2^2}{1-\rho^2}}$.

THE GEOMETRY OF SHARPE RATIO MAXIMIZATION

Recall that the correlation between two vectors can be interpreted geometrically as the cosine of the angle between them. Sharpe ratio maximization with two assets can also be interpreted geometrically as follows. In the diagram below, **AB** and **AC** are line segments of lengths S_1 and S_2 respectively with an angle $\theta = \cos^{-1}(\rho)$ between them. **BD** is a perpendicular from **B** to **AC**, while **CE** is a perpendicular from **C** to **AB**. Since the length equals S_1 times $\cos \theta = \rho$, **CD** must have length $S_2 - \rho S_1$. Similarly, **BE** must have length $S_1 - \rho S_2$, so the two lengths are proportional to the optimal volatility contributions.

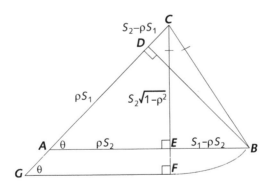

The segment **CE** has length S_2 times $\sin \theta = \sqrt{1 - \cos^2\theta} = \sqrt{1-\rho^2}$. By Pythagoras' Theorem, the side **CB** must have length $\sqrt{(S_1 - \rho S_2)^2 + (1-\rho^2)S_2^2} = \sqrt{S_1^2 - 2\rho S_1 S_2 + S_2^2}$. Now extend **CE** to a point **F** such that **CF** has the same length as **CB**. Draw a line thru **F**

parallel to **AB**, and extend **CA** until it meets that line at **G**. Since the angle between **GAC** and **GF** equals θ, **CG** must have the length of **CB** divided by $\sin \theta$, which equals the maximum Sharpe ratio.

LIMITS OF DIVERSIFICATION WITH EXCHANGEABLE ASSETS

By symmetry an optimal portfolio of n exchangeable assets will hold a $1/n$ share of each asset. The portfolio mean will equal μ while the portfolio variance will equal $\left(\dfrac{1-\rho}{n} + \rho\right)\sigma^2$, which is bounded below by 0 or $\rho\sigma^2$. If ρ is positive, the Sharpe ratio of the portfolio will never exceed $\sqrt{1/\rho}$ times the individual Sharpe ratio S.

Moreover, unless ρ is very close to zero, the marginal gain drops off quickly with n. The logarithm of the aggregate Sharpe ratio equals its upper bound $\ln S - \frac{1}{2}\ln \rho$ less $\frac{1}{2}\ln\left(1 + \dfrac{1-\rho}{\rho n}\right)$, which for $\rho n > 5$ is close to $\dfrac{1-\rho}{2\rho n}$. For example, if $\rho = 0.5$, then 10 assets brings you to within 5% of the maximum Sharpe ratio achievable through diversification, and doubling the number of exchangeable assets to 50 from 25 ups the Sharpe ratio by only 1%. In practice, the lowering of asset quality in the second 25 assets would likely swamp the diversification gains, unless the assets are nearly uncorrelated. Unfortunately for their clients, few long-only mutual fund managers seem to realize this.

THE OPTIMALITY OF LONG-SHORT HEDGES IN LARGE PORTFOLIOS

If P is an $n \times n$ matrix with all off-diagonal elements equal to ρ, it is readily checked that all the diagonal elements of P^{-1} equal $\dfrac{1 + (n-2)\rho}{(1-\rho)(1+(n-1)\rho)}$, while all the off-diagonal elements equal $\dfrac{-\rho}{(1-\rho)(1+(n-1)\rho)}$. Again, ρ must exceed $-\dfrac{1}{n-1}$ to keep variances positive, so if n can rise without limit ρ cannot be negative.

Denoting by Δ_i the difference between the individual Sharpe ratio S_i and the average Sharpe ratio for all assets, the optimal weight times the volatility must be proportional to:

$$\left(1 + (n-2)\rho\right)S_i - \rho \sum_{j \neq i} S_j = (1-\rho)S_i + \rho\left(nS_i - \sum_j S_j\right)$$

$$= (1-\rho)S_i + \rho n \Delta_i$$

Hence, if n is sufficiently large, the optimal portfolio strategy will always short positively correlated assets with Sharpe ratios below the mean.

UNBOUNDED GAINS FROM LONG-SHORT HEDGING

Continuing the previous example, suppose that assets come with two equally prevalent Sharpe ratios S_1 and S_2. The maximum squared Sharpe ratio works out to:

$$\frac{(1-\rho)\frac{n}{2}(S_1^2 + S_2^2) + \rho\frac{n^2}{4}(S_1 - S_2)^2}{(1-\rho)(1+(n-1)\rho)}$$

which as n grows large approaches:

$$\frac{S_1^2 + S_2^2}{2} + \frac{n(S_1 - S_2)^2}{4(1-\rho)}$$

Unlike diversification, the maximum Sharpe ratio from hedging grows without limit as n increases. To appreciate why, imagine you held the superior and inferior assets in optimal long/short pairs, with the same volatility for each holding. The Sharpe ratio of each pair will be $\frac{|S_1 - S_2|}{\sqrt{2(1-\rho)}}$, and since the $n/2$ pairs are uncorrelated the aggregate squared Sharpe ratio will be $\frac{n(S_1 - S_2)^2}{4(1-\rho)}$, capturing most of the feasible gains.

GENERATING UNCORRELATED COMPONENTS THROUGH REGRESSIONS

Let $\{X_i\}$ denote a set of random variables for which there are J observations. Set $X_0 = 1$, and consider the residuals R_j formed sequentially from $i = 1$ to m by regressing X_i on $X_{i-1}, \ldots, X_0$. By the nature of a linear regression, each R_i will be a linear combination of $X_0, \ldots, X_i$ that is uncorrelated with $X_1, \ldots, X_{i-1}$. By construction, it will also be uncorrelated with any preceding residual. Hence no residual will be correlated with any other.

EIGENVECTORS AND EIGENVALUES

A nonzero vector z is an eigenvector for a square matrix A, with associated scalar eigenvalue λ, if $Az = \lambda z$. While any scalar multiple of an eigenvector is also an eigenvector (with the same associated eigenvalue), I will focus on eigenvectors of unit length, where $z'z = 1$. I will also focus on real symmetric matrices A. To convert a non-symmetric matrix into a symmetric one yielding the same quadratic forms, average it with its transpose.

The eigenvector/eigenvalue relation can be rewritten as $(A - \lambda\mathrm{I})z = \mathbf{0}$, which has a nonzero solution for z if and only if the determinant $|A - \lambda\mathrm{I}|$ vanishes. This yields a polynomial equation in λ of degree n. I will assume the n solutions are distinct, ignoring the minor complications that duplicates pose.

A portfolio with weights proportional to an eigenvector z of the asset covariance matrix Σ will have a variance that is a positive multiple of $z'\Sigma z = z'\lambda z = \lambda z'z = \lambda$. Hence no covariance matrix can have negative eigenvalues. Neither can the correlation matrix.

EIGENVECTORS AND EIGENVALUES OF REAL SYMMETRIC MATRICES

Let A be a real symmetric matrix with distinct eigenvalues $\{\lambda_i\}$ and associated unit-length eigenvectors $\{z_i\}$. Then every eigenvector will be orthogonal to every other, since

$$\lambda_i z'_i z_j = z'_i A' z_j = z'_i A' z_j = z'_i \lambda_j z_j = \lambda_j z'_i z_j \Leftrightarrow z'_i z_j = 0$$

Let $\Lambda \equiv \mathrm{diag}([\lambda_1 \cdots \lambda_n])$ denote the diagonal matrix of eigenvalues and $Z \equiv [z_1 \cdots z_n]$ denote the square matrix of associated eigenvectors. The orthogonality of distinct eigenvectors implies that $Z'Z = \mathrm{I}$ and $Z'AZ = \Lambda$. Moreover, $Z\Lambda Z' = ZZ'AZZ' = A$. Other implications include:

- **Λ and Z must be real.** Complex eigenvectors, like complex eigenvalues, come in conjugate pairs of the form $A \pm B\sqrt{-1}$. But

$(A + B\sqrt{-1})'(A - B\sqrt{-1}) = A'A + B'B$, which cannot be zero unless both A and B are.

- **A will be positive (semi-)definite if and only if all eigenvalues are positive (nonnegative).** Since $w'Aw = w'Z\Lambda Z'w$, any quadratic form in a vector w and A can be rewritten as a quadratic form in $w'Z$ and Λ. That form is a positively weighted sum of the eigenvalues, and hence can be negative if and only if at least one of the eigenvalues is negative.

- **If A is positive definite, it will have a positive definite inverse and square root.** The inverse A^{-1} equals $Z\Lambda^{-1}Z'$ since $Z\Lambda^{-1}Z'Z\Lambda Z' = Z\Lambda^{-1}\Lambda\,Z' = ZZ' = I$. The square root $A^{1/2}$ equals $Z\Lambda^{1/2}Z'$ since $Z\Lambda^{1/2}Z'Z\Lambda^{1/2}Z' = Z\Lambda^{1/2}\Lambda^{1/2}Z' = Z\Lambda Z' = A$. This confirms an earlier claim.

IDENTIFYING THE MAIN PRINCIPAL COMPONENT

For a set of vector observations X with mean M, the components in direction z are given by $X'z$, with variance $z'E[(X - M)(X - M)']z = z'\Sigma z$. The principal component has the maximum variance controlling for the length of z. To identify it, solve the constrained maximization problem with Lagrangean $z'XX'z - \lambda(z'z - 1)$. The first-order condition $2\Sigma z - 2\lambda z = 0$ shows that z must be an eigenvector of Σ. Which one? Since the variance will be $z'XX'z = z'\lambda z = \lambda z'z = \lambda$, the principal component must be the eigenvector associated with the maximum eigenvalue of Σ.

If X is measured in standard deviations from the mean to control for differences in measurement units, $E[(X - M)(X - M)']$ will correspond to the correlation matrix P instead of Σ. Principal components can be calculated with respect to either.

OTHER PRINCIPAL COMPONENTS

Among the unit-length components y that are not correlated with the first principal component z, the one that explains the most variance is the second principal component. The associated Lagrangean is $y'\Sigma y - \eta(y'y - 1) - \nu(y'z - 0)$ with first-order condition:

$$2\Sigma y - 2\eta y - \nu z = 0$$

in addition to the feasibility constraints. Pre-multiply this equation by z' and use the information about the orthogonality and unit length of eigenvectors to simplify as follows:

$$0 = 2z'\Sigma y - 2\eta z'y - \nu z'z = 2\lambda_{max}z'y - 0 - \nu = -\nu$$

Hence $\nu = 0$, and the first-order conditions indicate that y must be an eigenvector of Σ distinct from z. The constrained maximum variance is η, so y must be associated with the second-largest eigenvalue. A similar logic applies to subsequent principal components.

14 | Relief through Beliefs

Every Saturday is Visitors' Day at Club Mad. Children and parents, spouses and lovers, friends and business partners can come for a few hours or the whole day. They can schmooze with the convalescents or snooze with them, attend lectures or use the sports facilities, and eat and drink to their hearts' content. All for a modest $100 fee, with toddlers admitted free.

Not everyone likes this policy. Far more screaming, fisticuffs, slit wrists and attempted stranglings occur on Saturdays than on the rest of the week combined. Club staff demand triple pay to work on Saturdays. Insurance providers have offered to halve the Club's liability premia if Visitors' Days cease. The most severe critics of the policy are the people the visitors come to see. "Let the hideaway stay hidden" they cry. As a concession, Club Mad has established safe zones where visitors are prohibited, guarded by bouncers recruited from local nightclubs. But these zones are cramped and miserable on Saturdays, causing residents to compare them to refugee camps in Bosnia.

Why in the face of all this opposition does Club Mad retain Visitors' Days? The Club brochure emphasizes the therapeutic rationale: to maintain residents' ties with the "mainland", Club-speak for the outside world. However, over cocktails with Wall Street analysts prepping for a Club Mad IPO, Dr Dementi once revealed the real reason. "It's an incredible marketing tool," he said. "Our records show that residents who receive visitors stay an average 25% longer than those who don't. I guess it reminds the homesick why they're sick of home. Plus, when the visitors see all the amenities, many of them want to make bookings for themselves. A few check themselves in right on the spot!"

A few analysts remained skeptical, and snuck back the next Saturday afternoon as visitors. On their way in they passed a mother and her daughter who were leaving. "That was so much fun, Mommy," said the girl, beaming. "Can I stay at Club Mad when I grow up?" "If you're good and make lots of money," said the mother. The analysts revised their recommendations to "Must Buy", and the IPO was oversubscribed by half.

Conway didn't know why Club Mad allowed visitors, but he was glad they did. "Welcome to Club Mad," said the receptionist. "May I take your name please and the name of the person you're visiting?"

"Conway Wisdon. I'm here to see Devlin Advogado."

The receptionist checked her guest list. "Yes, he is expecting you. He paid your visitor's fee as well. Sherri will show you the way."

Sherri was a svelte blonde, dressed like a cross between a dental hygienist and a real estate broker. Her jacket sported a large yellow button with a lavender inscription: "We heal the well-heeled." "Can I get you something to drink?" she asked. "A glass of fresh-squeezed orange juice?"

"No thank you. I just had breakfast."

"What a shame. Devlin must have forgotten to tell you about our champagne brunch. Can I sign you up for a massage or a manicure while you're here?"

"No thank you. I don't have time."

"Not even for a quick tour of the facilities?"

"Perhaps later. I'm eager to see Devlin. It's been months. How is he?"

"Oh, he's making excellent progress," Sherri gushed. "He's extremely self-motivated, yet sensitive to others' needs and never foists his views on others."

"I'm so glad to hear that." *It is Devlin I'm coming to see, right?* They entered a large, elegantly furnished lounge. Some people were reading by themselves, or using the internet on the computers planted around the room. Others sat chatting in twos and threes. Conway spied a hand waving. It was Devlin. Conway thanked Sherri and walked over. "It's great to see you Devlin."

"You too." They shook hands warmly and patted each other on the shoulder.

"I hear you're doing well."

"Not bad. Mostly I keep to myself and study quantum mechanics. If anybody asks or request something I say either 'I don't know,' 'I don't care', or 'Whatever you want.' "

So that's what she meant. Conway laughed. "I'm proud of you Devlin. You're finally mastering the social graces."

Devlin smiled. "It keeps life simple. I love reading about scientists who acknowledged the uncertainties at the core of what they thought they knew and rebuilt a more powerful theory on that basis."

"Like you?"

"I wish. I'm only good at the first part."

"How do you know?"

"I'm plumb out of ideas. There's a Russian saying: you can't squeeze blood from a turnip."

"You don't look like a turnip to me. How about letting me stick a few thought needles in to check?"

Devlin tried to suppress a smile. "No offense, Conway, but I never thought of you as needle-sharp."

Conway laughed. "Touché. Thanks for reminding me of the benefits of not working with you every day. But actually I have come up with a few sharp ideas. Or at least, ideas about sharpness. I was hoping you might help me refine them."

Devlin, who was starved for serious conversation, couldn't resist the appetizer. "What does sharpness have to do with finance?"

Conway pretended not to hear. "Of course, if you're too busy with physics, I understand . . ."

"Unless you mean something like Sharpe ratios. Very useful in a mean-variance world. Too bad they can't handle iceberg risk."

"That's what I thought too. After all, Sharpe ratios are functions of the first two moments only, whereas iceberg risk lurks among the higher moments."

"And what do you think now?"

"That we can incorporate at least some iceberg risk by distinguishing between conditional and unconditional Sharpe ratios."

Devlin perked up. "What do you mean?"

"A big part of iceberg risk is uncertainty. We're not quite sure our estimates for first and second moments really applied in the past. We have even more doubts over whether they apply going forward. But the standard procedures just rely on your best estimates. They don't take your degree of doubt into account."

"So how do you propose to take it into account?"

"By modelling your doubts as a probability distribution over parameters. Each belief 'outcome' represents a conditionally valid parameter estimate."

"There's nothing wrong with that. Even the best econometric estimates allow for errors. But what does it buy you?"

"It lets you form unconditional estimates that combine your conditional estimates and your uncertainties."

"Big deal. Whether the mean excess return really is 4%, or whether it's just normally distributed around 4%, the unconditional mean is still 4%."

"Granted. But the unconditional covariance matrix is more than the mean conditional covariance matrix. You have to add in the covariance matrix of the conditional means. For any portfolio, the unconditional variance will always equal or exceed the conditional variance."

"So what? How does that help you deal with iceberg risk?"

"Well, for one thing, it can steer you away from allocations that look good on paper but aren't robust."

"Such as?"

"Suppose you are choosing between two assets that are essentially the same, except for slight differences in tax treatment. Since the correlation in each tax regime is near 100%, conventional theory tells you to go long the asset with the higher expected return and short the other."

"And how is your approach different?"

"Uncertainty about which tax regime applies will raise the unconditional vol of each asset but won't change their covariance much. So the unconditional correlation will drop, making a long/short combo more risky. If it drops enough, you won't short the lesser asset but instead buy it for diversification."

"Could you walk me through some calculations? I want to make sure I understand."

Thank heavens! Conway pulled some papers out of his satchel and handed them to Devlin. "I was hoping you'd say that. Here's an example I worked out."

EXAMPLE: ASSET ALLOCATION WITH HIGH UNCERTAINTY

- Two assets 1 and 2 have 10% conditional volatility and 90% conditional correlation.
- Means are uncertain. Beliefs can be expressed as independent probability distributions with means 5% and 3% respectively and standard deviation δ.
- Unconditional variance $= 10\% \times 10\% + \delta^2 = 0.01 + \delta^2$.
- Unconditional covariance $= 0.9 \times 10\% \times 10\% = 0.009$.
- Unconditional correlation $\rho = \dfrac{9}{10 + 1000\delta^2}$.
- Optimal asset allocation ratio $= \dfrac{5 - 3\rho}{3 - 5\rho}$, so short asset 2 if and only if $\rho = 0.6$, which in turn holds if and only if $\delta < 7.07\%$.

Sensitivity of asset share 2 to uncertainty

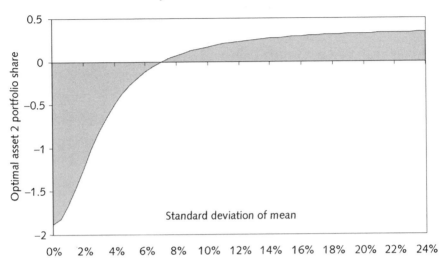

"I see how this could be useful," Devlin commented after studying the example. "But does uncertainty always dispose you against shorts?"

"Not necessarily. Suppose the uncertainty pertains to a common disaster. The more likely the disaster, the lower the unconditional mean and the higher the unconditional correlation. Both of these will incline you to short the weaker assets. Suppose I modify the previous example so that there's no conditional correlation, but a small chance of a common disaster that knocks 30% off both assets. Here's what happens." Conway handed over more papers.

EXAMPLE: ASSET ALLOCATION WITH COMMON DISASTER RISK

- Two assets, 1 and 2, have 10% conditional volatility and no conditional correlation, with known conditional means 5% and 3% respectively.
- A common "-30%" disaster strikes with probability $q < 10\%$.
- Unconditional means = $0.05 - 0.3q$ and $0.03 - 0.3q$ respectively.
- Unconditional variance = $10\% \times 10\% + q(1-q) \times 30\% \times 30\%$ $= 0.01 + 0.09q(1-q)$.
- Unconditional covariance = 0 + covariance of disaster
  = variance of disaster = $q(1-q) \times 30\% \times 30\% = 0.09q(1-q)$.

- Unconditional correlation $\rho = \dfrac{9q(1-q)}{1+9q(1-q)}$.

- Optimal asset allocation ratio $= \dfrac{5 - 30q - \rho(3 - 30q)}{3 - 30q - \rho(5 - 30q)}$, so short asset 2 if $\rho > \dfrac{3 - 30q}{5 - 30q}$, which requires $q > 6.4\%$.

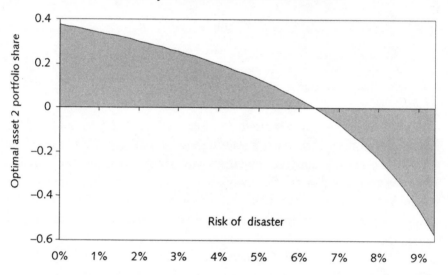

Sensitivity of asset share 2 to disaster risk

Devlin worked through the calculations and shook his head. "The numbers are right but I have qualms about the setup."

"I grant you, you won't know exactly how harsh the disaster will be. But we could allow for uncertainty about that too."

"I don't mean that. I mean the focus on mean and variance in an extremely non-normal environment. I suspect most investors would gladly sacrifice some Sharpe ratio to trim the disaster risk. But by your metric it doesn't matter."

Conway nodded. "You're right. I saw the problem myself and was stumped. So I went to the library and started scouring the literature, to see what other remedies were on offer."

"And?"

"I'm still stumped. But I did find a neat way to incorporate uncertainty when everything is multivariate normal. It's called the Black-Litterman approach."

"What's so neat about it?"

"Well, for one thing, you don't need to have an opinion about everything. It's OK to be clueless."

"I like that. But if you don't have an opinion, whose opinion does it use?"

"The market's. Or rather, the market's view as implied by the model."

"How do you calculate that?"

"Think of the market as a unified decisionmaker, choosing optimal risky portfolio weights to maximize the Sharpe ratio. The excess returns will be directly proportional to the covariance matrix times the weighting vector. But we know the market's weighting vector: it's just the relative capitalization of the assets. Assuming the world is stably multivariate normal, the covariance matrix is easy to identify too. We can infer the constant of proportionality from other data, for example, the long-term Sharpe ratio. Multiply those three together and you get the implied excess returns."

"What if the market expects the covariance matrix to change?"

"In principle, we could use the implied vols from options markets to identify the variances. If varied enough basket options are available, we could identify covariances too. Otherwise I guess we have to draw on historical correlations."

"Why not use historical data on means to impute the covariances?" Devlin grinned.

It's nice to see you getting back in form. "Come on, Devlin, you know very well why not. The relative market caps of *n* different assets suffice to identify only *n* other variables. That's enough to identify relative excess returns but not to identify the covariances. And in any multivariate normal world, you need a lot longer historical series to identify the means than the covariances. So Black-Litterman just assumes your covariance estimates are valid."

"I'm not too keen on that, but go on. What else is neat about the Black-Litterman approach?"

"It lets you specify your beliefs very flexibly. Instead of predicting European and Japanese markets separately, for example, you might just predict that Europe is, say, likely to outperform Japan by 5% on average with a standard deviation of 5%. Alternatively you could say there's a 16% chance that Japan will outperform Europe, and another 16% chance that Europe outperforms Japan by 10% – from that you could work out the implied mean and standard deviation of 5% each."

"What if your belief concerns a weighted average basket?"

"No problem. The belief just needs to pertain to a linear combination of asset returns, with the uncertainty expressible as a normal distribution."

"How about multiple beliefs?"

"No problem there either, provided each belief pertains to a linear combination, and the joint uncertainty can be expressed in terms of a multivariate normal distribution."

"And how do you combine the market consensus and the forecaster's beliefs?"

"For the expected excess returns you just take a weighted average, where the weights are proportional to the inverse of the covariance matrix, also known as the precision. Intuitively, the less diffuse the estimate, the more you want to weight it."

"Why weight by the precision instead of something else?"

"Here's one way to make sense of it. Think of every belief of precision j as based on j independent observations or 'measurements', where each measurement has a precision of one."

"What are these observations measuring?"

"The true mean, which none of us know for sure. You don't have to think about beliefs that way, but it's useful."

"OK, go on."

"Anyway, in combining two beliefs, each underlying measurement should be weighted equally. That means each belief gets weighted by its precision, and the aggregate precision equals the sum of the individual precisions."

"I see. So is that all you need to work out the optimal portfolio weights given the various beliefs?"

"Absolutely. While the calculations look intimidating, they're straight-forward and easy to computerize. Best of all they give you wiggle room in case the initial recommendations look ridiculous. Cut the precision of your own belief and you contract the recommended weights back toward the benchmark."

"Why not just average your recommendations with the benchmark directly?"

"That's not nearly as sophisticated. Besides, the contraction isn't always linear. I've prepared an example if you care to see it."

"Please."

"The Barra consulting group tabulates separate indices for Growth and Value components of the S&P 500, where Growth stocks are defined to have higher P/E ratios than Value stocks. Since 1993 Growth and Value returns have been 80% correlated with vols of 18.4% and 14.4% respectively. For an equal allocation to be optimal assuming a long-term Sharpe ratio of 0.3, the market must be expecting an excess return of 5.3% for Growth and 4.0% for Value, for a difference of 1.3%. Now suppose that privately you feel 95% certain the true difference in expected returns lies between −3% and +5%, for a mean of 1% and standard deviation of 2%. How will your asset allocations vary with the credence you attach to the market's views relative to your own?"

"Let's see. If I don't have any respect for my own views, presumably I will just hold the 50/50 benchmark. If at the other extreme I believe the market consensus is worthless, I won't worry about its view at all. Instead I will load my portfolio with the best bet I know, namely a long growth/short value combo."

"What if you attach just a little credence to your own view?"

"I suppose I might underweight growth stocks because my estimate of the mean difference in returns is lower than the market's. But as I get more confident about my views, eventually I will start to focus on the long/short position."

"Bingo! Here's the chart. Actually the curve starts to steepen as soon as you're even one-tenth as confident in your own views as the market's. And once it does steepen the rise is nearly linear in the relative weight attached to your private belief. While not all set-ups show a turning point, the near-linearity for high confidence levels is typical. Ascribing equal weights to your private beliefs and the market's is a decent rule of thumb for avoiding extremes without mimicking the market allocation."

Optimal growth stock share in Black-Litterman example

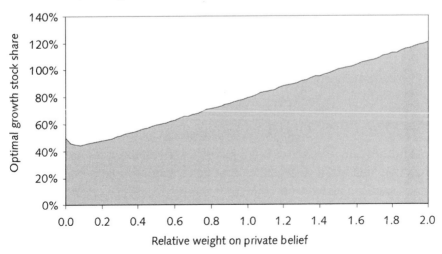

"Clever," said Devlin, nodding. "But it's too razzle-dazzle for my taste. Your view on how to weight your private belief versus the market's is also a private belief, so I'm not sure how you maintain a distinction. And while the contraction toward a benchmark pulls us out of trouble, it doesn't explain why trouble pulls us in."

"Why do you think trouble pulls us in?"

"Because Black-Litterman compresses all our uncertainty into one bell-shaped mountain of conditional means. What if markets sling you from one mountain to another, like a tech boom that goes bust? You'll be a bloody pulp long before anyone notices a supposed 2% outperformance of conditional means."

"I agree. The first model I showed you handles regime change but loses the optimality of Sharpe ratio maximization. The Black-Litterman approach lends itself to Sharpe ratio maximization but rules out major regime changes. How are we going to reconcile the two?"

Devlin didn't respond. He sat silently, diving deeper and deeper into his thoughts. Seconds ticked into minutes.

"Devlin, are you there?" Still no answer.

I've lost him. Conway was about to leave when he felt a tap on his shoulder. He spun around to see a raven-haired woman dressed in black. She was beautiful, but with the saddest eyes Conway had ever seen. "Pardon me for eavesdropping," she said, "but if Dr Know-Nothing can't help you, maybe I can."

"Go away, Misery Girl," snapped Devlin. "We don't need you."

"Oh, I think you do," she said.

While Devlin fends off this intrusion, let's work through some of the math of adjusting for beliefs.

BELIEFS AS PROBABILITIES

Probabilities are measures of objective risk. Beliefs are measures of subjective uncertainty. Whether the latter can be identified with the former was for generations the single most divisive issue in statistics. Orthodox statisticians say no. They are determined to root out subjectivity, which they feel can only sully the science. They concede that a human observer may have only imperfect observations on a probability measure. But the measure itself should be precise, not subject to the vagaries of human judgment.

Supporters of subjective probability are known as Bayesians, after the Reverend Bayes who originated this approach over two centuries ago. Bayesians are often agnostic about the existence of an objective risk measure. Rather, they focus on the inference process for combining old information with new and forming judgments under uncertainty.

To impose structure, both camps require that certain axioms be satisfied. Orthodox statistics imposes these axioms on the probability measure itself. Bayesians either impose a similar structure on beliefs or derive it from axioms about sensible gambling behavior: basically that the gambler does not willingly lose money.

ACKNOWLEDGING UNCERTAINTY

Fifty years ago, Bayesian statistics seemed doomed to extinction. But a few Bayesians soldiered on. They showed how in principle to address the uncertainties inherent in various sciences and gradually garnered support. On the practical level, they could solve only relatively simple problems, as Bayesian updating tends to be computationally demanding. Their successors have harnessed advancing computer power to vastly extend the scope of Bayesian analysis.

Academic bookshelves bear witness to the growing acceptability of subjective probability. Many more textbooks in Bayesian methods are available than there were ten years ago. Moreover, mainstream texts increasingly include favorable references to the Bayesian approach.

Finance, of course, is all about people who think their investments follow certain probability laws, aren't sure which, and are trying to guess. That would seem to make it Bayesian territory *par excellence*. Nevertheless, most academic finance remains wedded to the classical approach. Strange, isn't it?

BAYES' RULE

The most important equation in Bayesian statistics is known as Bayes' rule. It describes how to use observations x to update beliefs about phenomena Y_i that you don't directly observe. By repeatedly invoking the rules of conditional probability, we can write:

$$P(Y_j|x) = \frac{P(Y_j \cap x)}{P(x)} = \frac{P(x|Y_j)P(Y_j)}{\sum_i P(Y_i \cap x)} = \frac{P(x|Y_j)P(Y_j)}{\sum_i P(x|Y_i)P(Y_i)}$$

Here $P(Y_i)$ denotes the (subjective) probability that Y_i occurred, prior to or without knowledge of x occurring. $P(Y_i|x)$ denotes the updated probability given that x occurs. For example, suppose a village that always makes hay when the sun shines also makes hay a quarter of the time it's shady. If you started out deeming sun and shade equally likely, then the probability it is sunny given that the village is making hay is given by:

$$P(Sun|Hay) = \frac{P(Hay|Sun)P(Sun)}{P(Hay|Sun)P(Sun) + P(Hay|Shade)P(Shade)}$$

$$= \frac{1 \cdot \frac{1}{2}}{1 \cdot \frac{1}{2} + \frac{1}{4} \cdot \frac{1}{2}} = \frac{4}{5}$$

No orthodox statisticians object to Bayes' rule *per se*. They just object to the use of Bayes' rule to describe beliefs and other things they don't regard as objective measures of risk. Again, Bayesians claim it doesn't matter, and indeed question whether any observer can ever completely distinguish between objective risks and beliefs.

INCORPORATING UNCERTAINTY INTO COVARIANCES

In calculating optimal relative portfolio weights using the $\Sigma^{-1}M$ rule, most people use their best unbiased point estimates for the mean M conditional on the variance and the variance Σ conditional on the mean. Conway wants to revise this allowing for uncertainty, which he models Bayesian-style as a probability distribution over the mean and variance.

A wobbly variance doesn't typically change the estimate of the mean (more formally "the unconditional mean of the conditional mean"), unless the weights on different observations change. However, a wobbly mean does change the overall or unconditional variance, even when it doesn't change the conditional variance. The difference between the two is the variance of the conditional mean, which is never negative.

The corresponding matrix formula is:

$$Cov_u[X] = E_u[Cov_c[X]] + Cov_u[E_c[X]]$$

where X is a vector and the subscripts u and c denote unconditional and conditional respectively. For off-diagonal covariances, the unconditional value can fall below the corresponding expected conditional values. For any portfolio, however, the unconditional variance must equal or exceed the expected conditional variance, since:

$$\sigma_u^2 - \sigma_c^2 = \omega' Cov_u[X]\omega - \omega' E_u[Cov_c[X]]\omega = \omega' Cov_u[E_c[X]]\omega \geq 0$$

IMPACT ON CORRELATIONS, SHARPE RATIOS, AND PORTFOLIO WEIGHTS

Suppose two assets have equal conditional variances σ_c^2, equal variances σ_m^2 of their conditional means, correlation ρ_c of their conditional variances and correlation ρ_m of their conditional means. The unconditional correlation ρ_u works out to:

$$\rho_u = \frac{\rho_c \sigma_c^2 + \rho_m \sigma_m^2}{\sigma_c^2 + \sigma_m^2} = \theta \rho_c + (1 - \theta)\rho_m \quad \text{where} \quad \theta \equiv \frac{\sigma_c^2}{\sigma_c^2 + \sigma_m^2} = \frac{Var_c[X]}{Var_u[X]}$$

In other words, ρ_u is a weighted average of ρ_c and ρ_m, with weights determined by the ratio of conditional to unconditional variance. If the uncertainties about the conditional means are independent of each other, $\rho_m = 0$ and $\rho_u < \rho_c$. If a common underlying factor drives all the uncertainties about the conditional means, $\rho_m = 1$ and $\rho_u > \rho_c$.

Uncertainty reduces Sharpe ratios of individual assets because it raises their perceived variance without changing their excess returns. To determine the relative portfolio weights, we need to factor in their correlation too. Conway's examples show that the impact can be striking.

CAVEAT IN APPLYING SHARPE RATIO ANALYSIS

Once you incorporate uncertainty in the mean or variance, the distribution of returns typically ceases to be multivariate normal. Absent multivariate normality, it will generally not be possible to rank portfolios' desirability in terms of mean and variance alone. Still, it's better to be approximately right than precisely wrong. The patches described above for uncertainty can help warn against extreme risks.

BLACK-LITTERMAN APPROACH

The Black-Litterman approach rests on five tenets:

1. The world of excess market returns is multivariate normal, with an unknown mean M and a known covariance matrix Σ.
2. Forecasters have beliefs about various linear combinations QM of expected returns M. Q has as many rows k as the forecaster has beliefs and as many columns n as there are variables. For example, if $Q = \begin{bmatrix} 1 & -1 & 0 \\ \frac{1}{3} & \frac{1}{3} & \frac{1}{3} \end{bmatrix}$, then the forecaster has two beliefs about three variables, of which the first concerns the difference of the first two expected returns and the second concerns the simple average expected return.
3. Beliefs can be expressed as a multivariate normal distribution for QM having mean q and covariance matrix Ω. Usually Ω is taken as diagonal, implying zero correlation among beliefs, but this isn't essential.
4. The vector of market benchmark weights w_m, calculated using current capitalizations, can be treated as an optimal portfolio choice given the market consensus view R_m. Hence w_m must be proportional to $\Sigma^{-1}R_m$, so that $R_m = k\Sigma w_m$ for some scaling factor k. This factor can be calculated as:

$$k = \frac{w_m'R_m}{w_m'\Sigma w_m} = \frac{\text{Market excess return}}{\text{Market variance}} = \frac{\text{Market Sharpe ratio}}{\text{Market volatility}}$$

5. The market view R_m is itself random, with a mean equal to the true expected return M and a variance $\tau\Sigma$ for some positive scalar τ. The scaling factor indicates how strongly the forecaster rates his private beliefs relative to the consensus.

The rest of this chapter works through the implications of these tenets.

CONDITIONAL MULTIVARIATE NORMALITY OF MEAN RETURNS

Bayes' rule tells us that the probability density p_1 of M given the market consensus R_m, is directly proportional to the density p_2 of the market's beliefs about R_m given M times the density p_3 of the forecaster's beliefs about M:

$$p_1(M|R_m) \propto p_2(R_m|M) \cdot p_3(M)$$

$$\propto \exp\left(-\tfrac{1}{2}(R_m - M)'(\tau\Sigma)^{-1}(R_m - M)\right)$$

$$\cdot \exp\left(-\tfrac{1}{2}(QM - q)'\Omega^{-1}(QM - q)\right)$$

$$\propto \exp\left(-\tfrac{1}{2}\left((R_m - M)'(\tau\Sigma)^{-1}(R_m - M)\right.\right.$$

$$\left.\left. + (QM - q)'\Omega^{-1}(QM - q)\right)\right) \equiv \exp(-\tfrac{1}{2}\Upsilon)$$

To establish the multivariate normality of p_1 with mean M^* and variance V, we need to show that Υ differs by at most a constant from the quadratic form $Y \equiv (M - M^*)'V^{-1}(M - M^*)$. (The constant washes out because in any case the probability density has to integrate to 1). Now Y is minimized at $M = M^*$, whereas Υ can only be minimized there if

$$-(\tau\Sigma)^{-1}(R_m - M^*) + Q'\Omega^{-1}(QM^* - q) = 0$$

$$\Leftrightarrow \left((\tau\Sigma)^{-1} + Q'\Omega^{-1}Q\right)M^* = (\tau\Sigma)^{-1}R_m + Q'\Omega^{-1}q$$

$$\Leftrightarrow M^* = \left((\tau\Sigma)^{-1} + Q'\Omega^{-1}Q\right)^{-1}\left((\tau\Sigma)^{-1}R_m + Q'\Omega^{-1}q\right)$$

Furthermore, Υ and Y must have the same second derivatives with respect to M, so that

$$V^{-1} = (\tau\Sigma)^{-1} + Q'\Omega^{-1}Q \quad \Leftrightarrow \quad V = (\tau^{-1}\Sigma^{-1} + Q'\Omega^{-1}Q)^{-1}$$

Under these conditions, Υ and Y do indeed match up as required.

INTERPRETATION IN TERMS OF INDIVIDUAL MEANS AND PRECISIONS

If Q is invertible, the forecaster's beliefs can be recast as mean $Q^{-1}q$ for M with precision $Q'\Omega^{-1}Q$. The aggregate mean M^* is then indeed a weighted average of market view R_m and forecaster belief $Q^{-1}q$, with weights equal to the precisions (note that $Q'\Omega^{-1}QQ^{-1}q = Q'\Omega^{-1}q$). Furthermore, the precision of the joint estimate is the sum of the individual precisions, as it must always be for two uncorrelated estimates weighted by their precisions V_i^{-1}:

$$Var\left[(V_1^{-1} + V_2^{-1})^{-1}(V_1^{-1}X_1 + V_2^{-1}X_2)\right]$$

$$= (V_1^{-1} + V_2^{-1})^{-1} \cdot$$

$$(V_1^{-1}Var[X_1]V_1^{-1} + V_2^{-1}Var[X_{1/2}]V_2^{-1} + \text{covariances})$$

$$\cdot (V_1^{-1} + V_2^{-1})^{-1}$$

$$= (V_1^{-1} + V_2^{-1})^{-1}(V_1^{-1} + V_2^{-1} + 0)(V_1^{-1} + V_2^{-1})^{-1}$$

$$= (V_1^{-1} + V_2^{-1})^{-1}$$

In general Q need not be invertible, but we can still make the same interpretation by augmenting Q with extra rows that make it invertible, carrying through the calculations above, and then stripping out the extra rows.

OPTIMAL PORTFOLIO WEIGHTS GIVEN BELIEFS

The unconditional covariance matrix of asset returns equals the conditional covariance matrix Σ plus the covariance matrix V of M given R_m. To maximize the Sharpe ratio, set portfolio weights proportional to $(\Sigma + V)^{-1}$ times the unconditional mean M^*. Substituting and simplifying,

$$(\Sigma + V)^{-1}M^* = (\Sigma + V)^{-1}V\left((\tau\Sigma)^{-1}R_m + Q'\Omega^{-1}q\right)$$

$$= (V^{-1}\Sigma + I)^{-1}\left((\tau\Sigma)^{-1}k\Sigma w_m + Q'\Omega^{-1}q\right)$$

$$= \left((\tau^{-1}\Sigma^{-1} + Q'\Omega^{-1}Q)\Sigma + I\right)^{-1}(\tau^{-1}k w_m + Q'\Omega^{-1}q)$$

$$= \left((1 + \tau^{-1})I + Q'\Omega^{-1}Q\Sigma\right)^{-1}(\tau^{-1}k w_m + Q'\Omega^{-1}q)$$

This is the summary Black-Litterman formula. Standard Sharpe ratio maximization is a special case with $Q = I$, $q = M$, $\Omega = \Sigma$, and $\tau = \infty$.

15 | Rating Risks without Regret

Devlin squared off with the intruder. "Go away, Misery Girl. We're not talking about failed relationships so this can't possibly interest you."

"That's an awfully strong opinion you're expressing, Dr Know-Nothing. Congratulations. Too bad it's wrong."

Oh no. I've landed in a soap opera. Please, both of you, hold your fire. "I take it you know each other," said Conway pleasantly.

"We're in group therapy together," said the woman. "Twice a week for two hours."

"Twice a week for eternity is more like it," said Devlin. "It's like a scene from Sartre's play about hell."

"You've read *No Exit*? I'm impressed, Know-Nothing. There's not an equation in it."

"What do you have against equations, Misery Girl?"

"Nothing. I just don't think group therapy is an appropriate place to discuss them. You're supposed to talk about what's ailing you."

"Well, uncertainty is ailing me just like lost love is ailing you. At least I'm focused on the present, which is more than I can say for you."

Misery Girl's eyes welled up with tears. Conway felt sorry for her. "Don't mind my friend," he said softly, "Sometimes he gets carried away. Hi, I'm Conway. What's your name?"

"Regretta," she said. "And unfortunately your friend is right. I do focus too much on the past. That's why I don't trade any more. But I know the principles you ought to trade by. I think they can help you in asset allocation too."

"Like 'Buy low, sell high'?"

"That's part of it. But I mean something more general. It's the theory of economic rationality."

"What would you know about that?" asked Devlin, suspicious.

"More than you think. I studied two years for a PhD in Behavioral Economics before deciding that an academic life wasn't for me. But I found a very practical use for what I learned, namely, trading against people who hadn't learned it."

"And what was it you knew that they didn't?"

"That it's awfully easy to take sucker bets. And very important not to. You have to be coolly rational."

"You, coolly rational? Ha!" snorted Devlin.

Regretta's eyes turned to steel. "I told you I don't trade anymore, Know-Nothing. Just like you don't answer anything. But for your information, they used to call me Icewoman. Now are you willing to hear me out, or this is just a debate for dickheads?"

Devlin shrivelled up instantly, and his ears turned red. *She's got his number. And Devlin knows it.* "Since you express the choice so delicately," said Conway after a pause, "we would love to hear you out. Wouldn't we, Devlin?" Devlin glowered but said nothing.

"Thank you," said Regretta. "Now here's what I think you need to do. First measure every outcome in terms of its gross percentage return, like 1.05 if you've had a 5% gain. Second, square that return and take the negative inverse. Third, form the probability-weighted average of the various negative inverses. Fourth, pick the portfolio that generates the highest probability-weighted average. Am I being clear?"

Devlin and Conway were blown away. "She does math," mumbled Devlin to himself. "Maybe too clear," replied Conway. "Where'd you get the square from?"

Regretta smiled. "Actually I don't know about the square. Theory just says to use a power that varies with your risk aversion. Two's probably not the right number. I just think it's not far wrong."

"Why use a power function at all? And why weight by the probabilities?"

"The first depends on what you don't know. The second on what you don't want to find out."

"You've lost me, Regretta. And I thought Devlin was hard to understand. Do you mind starting again from the beginning?"

"With economic rationality?"

"Why not? How's that different from ordinary rationality?"

"I'm not sure it is. It's just that I want to focus on economic decisionmaking under uncertainty: rational gambling if you prefer. And there rationality boils down to one simple rule: don't be a sucker."

"Don't be a sucker? What do you mean by that?"

"Don't make bets, or sequences of bets, that are bound to leave you worse off."

"How do you define worse off?"

"Pretty liberally. More is always better than less. But a bird in hand may be worth more or less than two birds in a bush. That depends on how you feel about risk."

"If the definition is so liberal, why can't I just define worse off to make all bets rational?"

"Good question. There are just a few things that aren't allowed. First, you have to be willing to meaningfully rate every bet – and by bet I mean any choice with uncertain outcome – against every other. If you strictly prefer bet A to bet B, you can't in the same breath say you prefer B to A under the same conditions. You have to make up your mind. Otherwise a clever trader could sucker you into trading A for B and then paying extra money to buy back A again. That's the axiom of completeness."

"Those are obvious," said Conway. "What else?"

"Your choices have to be transitive. If you prefer bet A over B and bet B over C, you can't strictly prefer C to A under the same conditions. Otherwise, a clever trader could sell you B in exchange for C, sell you A in exchange for C, and then get you to pay extra money to buy back C again for A."

"That's obvious too. What else?"

"Your choices have to be convex. Convexity means that uncertainty *per se* won't reverse your rankings. So if you prefer A to B given either probability distribution p or probability distribution q, you'll also prefer A to B if p or q applies but you're not sure which. Otherwise, a clever trader might rig up a lottery between p and q, get you to trade in A plus cash for B, and then get you to trade back B for A once the lottery is completed."

"I don't have any problem with that either. But why do you call it convexity? Isn't that a geometric concept?"

"It is. Let me draw you a picture. You wouldn't have any colored pens, would you?"

"I've got a blue felt-tip and yellow highlighter in my bag." Conway fished them out for her, along with some blank paper.

Regretta talked as she drew. "Let's assume nature has only three possible states. Then I can graph the space of feasible probability measures as a right-angled triangle extending one unit horizontally and one unit vertically from the origin. The horizontal coordinate measures the first probability p_1, the vertical coordinate measures p_2, and p_3 is defined implicitly as $1 - p_1 - p_2$. Now suppose I color all the points at which A is weakly preferred to B in blue, and all the points at which B is weakly preferred to A in yellow. Then green will mark all the points at which A is indifferent to B. How wild can the resulting pattern be?"

"I don't know. I guess it depends on the specific preferences."

"Wrong. If they're convex, the pattern can't be wild at all. The green bit has to be a straight line segment dividing the triangle into a blue part and a yellow part. And any straight line segment connecting two points of the same color must stay within that color."

Preferences between two acts in three states

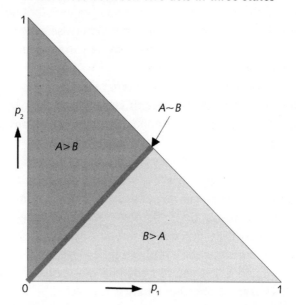

"And that's true no matter how many states and choices you have?"

"Absolutely. We'll need a lot more colors and dimensions to mark off every distinct preference region. But if preferences are convex, every region will have to contain every straight line segment connecting two of its points."

"Neat. So are completeness, transitivity, and convexity all that not being a sucker entails?"

"Just about. Theorists generally posit a stronger condition, namely that exchanging one lottery prize for something you like just as much doesn't worsen your opinion of the lottery as a whole. Philosophically, that's more controversial than convexity, because some people argue that valuation shouldn't be separated from context."

"I'm inclined to agree. What's wrong with preferring pretzels to water when you're hungry and water to pretzels once you're thirsty?"

"Nothing. Real-life preferences are nearly always in flux. It's still useful to speak about them as if they're momentarily stable and well-defined. Otherwise even the axiom of order fails."

"Granted. I'm still not sure whether it's reasonable to compare lottery prizes out of context."

"You and a lot of others. But you did accept convexity, and in practice there's not much difference between the two. Basically, if you have completely ordered, transitive, convex preferences, and know the relevant odds, you can't be made a sucker, and vice versa. Am I making myself clear?"

Conway wrinkled his brow. "About economic rationality? I think so. But what does that have to do with the portfolio rating system you propose?"

"Simple. Economic rationality allows you to assign a utility score to each outcome and rank bets by their expected utility. That's a crucial part of my rating system."

"Are you suggesting that people quantify every outcome?"

"Of course not. But economically rational people must act as if they do. That's called 'behaving according to expected utility theory'."

"That's remarkable. Thanks, Regretta. I didn't realize how easy it was to justify this."

"From one angle, yes. Unfortunately, there's overwhelming evidence that expected utility theory is wrong and Barnum was right."

"Barnum?"

"P.T. Barnum, the famous circus impresario. Over a century ago he said there's a sucker born every minute. He also said you can fool all of the people some of the time and some of the people all of the time."

"So which axiom of rationality do people violate?"

"Take your pick. For example, people are very sensitive to the way choices are posed. It's called the 'framing effect.' If you canvas opinions on a risky new medication, you'll get more support if you formulate the question in terms of expected lives saved than expected lives lost, even though the probabilities you present are identical. Also, hardly anyone can keep all her choices transitive when dealing with very small odds of very large payoffs or penalties."

"Sounds like they succumb to emotional appeals in the former case and arithmetic errors in the latter."

"Maybe, but it's awfully widespread. Without it, businesses would employ a lot fewer salespeople, and public mega-lotteries wouldn't sell nearly so many tickets."

"How about violations of convexity?" asked Conway.

"They're more subtle but possibly just as rampant. For example, retailers find that consumers faced with too many choices will often refuse to buy, even when individual items sell well on their own."

"Maybe consumers just want to defer their decision until they gather more information."

"Sometimes that happens. Other times they act like they want less information. For example, people generally dislike hearing about the success of investments they could have made but didn't. In fact, some people argue that fear of future regret – that is, of discovering you could have consumed something you didn't – is a more important motivator than satisfaction in what you directly consume."

"Can't that be reconciled with expected utility theory?"

"Not easily. Convexity basically denies any value to information other than in improving consumption. Regret theory cedes information a value in its own right."

"But what if information about what you didn't consume helps you refine your consumption choices in the future?"

"Good point. I'm sure you can explain a lot of apparent irrationality that way. For example, imagine a mother with two kids has only one lollipop to give them. She might reasonably prefer to decide through a fair coin toss rather than a biased coin toss, so as not to show any favoritism. In the short run such a choice clearly violates convexity. But the mother may clearly derive a longer-term value, in terms of discipline and loving relations, from cultivating perceptions of her fairness."

"So you think that taking future payoffs into account makes it easier to defend economic rationality?"

"To defend, yes. To refute alternative views, no. It's harder to test theories geared to long-term outcomes, both because it takes longer and because preferences may evolve over time."

"So how do you justify expected utility theory in finance?"

"Two ways. The first is evolution. Rational traders who study irrational traders ought to have some success in fleecing them. I know I did. Over time that ought to shift wealth toward economically rational investors, though there may be some dissipation as well."

"And the second?"

"Fiduciary responsibility. When you're managing funds, you're supposed to be looking after your clients' best interests. Presumably those best interests don't include getting taken for a sucker, or taking the client for a sucker, even when the client is a sucker. In fact, maybe that's why investors came to the funds manager in the first place, to avoid being taken for suckers."

Conway mulled over Regretta's arguments. *It all sounds quite reasonable. But maybe I'm missing something.* "You make a strong case, Regretta. So strong that I wonder why this approach isn't used much."

"But it is used, Conway. Surely you're familiar with VAR analysis, for value-at-risk."

"Of course. We used it all the time at Megabucks. We had to. The regulators made us."

"Well, VAR is just the simplest possible application of expected utility theory, where the utility score takes only two possible values. Here, look at this." Regretta made a quick drawing. "What's the expected value under this utility function?"

VAR utility function

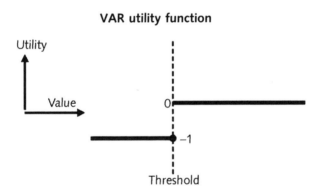

"Let's see. It's minus one times the probability of falling at or below the threshold. I get it. Maximizing the expected utility works out to minimizing the tail risk."

"Exactly. Simple, isn't it? And kind of stupid. I mean: why shouldn't big losses worry you more than small ones, or big gains ease your mind? And why such a jump at the threshold?"

"I think the regulators are just trying to capture the risk of needing a public bailout."

"But VAR doesn't capture that. A public bailout will only be needed if other private lenders won't step to the plate through lines of credit or equity infusions. And that depends crucially on the size of the losses and prospects for big gains."

"Maybe other potential lenders will be in crisis too, and unable to step to the plate. I think that's what regulators are most concerned about."

"Then why don't they focus on the losses that are highly correlated with other banks' losses, or say with the stock market if they need a proxy? At the very least they should promote risk aversion. The aggregate portfolio should never be worth more than its mean, but under VAR criteria it can be. That's just bound to promote extra risk-taking and manipulation of the books."

"I don't know, Regretta. I've always marveled at the power of bureaucracy to transform a mass of bright individuals into one collective idiot. But what kind of utility function is needed to promote risk aversion?"

"It just has to be concave. You know, where the first derivative is positive and the second derivative is negative, without jumps. Like this:" She sketched another curve.

Concave utility function

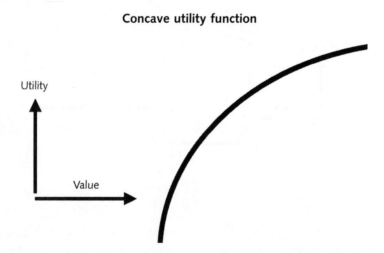

Devlin, who had been silent ever since Regretta chewed him out, finally piped in again. "Look, Conway, I buy her expected utility approach. But that's the easy part. I still want to hear how she justifies her choice of a negative inverse square."

"Listen, Know-Nothing. If you have a problem with something I'm saying, how about asking me directly? Anyway, you're wrong. Justifying the expected utility approach is the hard part. The rest is easy. And if you'll spare me half an hour to do some calculations I'll show you. Excuse me, boys." And with that she strode off.

Conway watched Regretta leave. "She cuts quite a figure, doesn't she?" he asked Devlin.

Devlin, whose ears had turned red again, shook his head. "I can't believe I never noticed before ..."

"You never noticed how attractive she is?"

"I never noticed her drawing math figures. You know, Conway, maybe I underrated her."

Conway laughed. "Only maybe?"

"She can talk the talk. Let's see whether she walk the walk. In the meantime, how about I show you around the club?"

While Conway and Devlin are taking their tour, let's review expected utility theory.

Rational Gambling

People feel all kinds of ways about risk, and don't always act how they feel. That makes it really hard to model risk preferences. To make things tractable, you want to exclude enough behavior to make things tractable but no more. In finance, that means excluding suckers. Suckers occasionally take bets that are certain to lose them money. Everyone else is a "rational gambler". I don't know anyone, including myself, who's never been a sucker. Still it's a fitting exclusion for finance theory, both because the market tends to squeeze suckers dry and because you don't necessarily serve suckers well by respecting their preferences.

Expected Utility Maximization

Consider another class of people known as expected utility maximizers. They act as if they assign a numeric score or utility to every possible outcome, calculate the expected score for every risky choice, and opt for whichever choice promises the highest expected score. How is this class related to rational gamblers?

Clearly, expected utility maximizers have to be rational gamblers. A sucker bet or sequence of bets will lower their expected utility, so they will reject it. It's far less obvious that rational gamblers have to act as if they're maximizing expected utility. But essentially they do. This is one of the most fascinating results in microeconomic theory.

CHOICES BETWEEN LOTTERIES

To appreciate this near-equivalence, let's reformulate rational gambling in terms of a few axioms of choice. Let's start with choices between lotteries. A lottery is defined by payoffs and probabilities of obtaining those payoffs. For any two lotteries L and M, let $L \succeq M$ denote the relation "L is weakly preferred to M". Also, let $L \succ M$ denote the relation "L is strictly preferred to M", where $L \succeq M$ but not the converse. Let $L \sim M$ denote indifference, where $L \succeq M$ and $M \succeq L$. The most basic axioms postulate:

- **Completeness:** Either $L \succeq M$ or $M \succeq L$.
- **Transitivity:** If $L \succ M$ and $M \succeq N$, then $L \succ N$.

These axioms are essential to consistently order preferences. And clearly, without them you can't be a rational gambler. But neither specifically addresses risk. To do that, the standard treatment offers a substitution axiom couched in terms of compound lotteries. A compound lottery $\overline{L, M; \lambda}$ offers a payout L with probability λ and M with probability $1 - \lambda$. The substitution axiom says that replacing one of the mutually exclusive prizes in the lottery with a better prize can only improve the overall lottery.

- **Substitution:** If $L \succeq M$, $\overline{L, M; \lambda} \succeq M$ for any positive probability λ.

STANDARD DERIVATION OF EXPECTED UTILITY THEORY

Suppose (this is not essential, but simplifies the derivations) the set of lotteries contains a most-preferred element L_{best} and a least-preferred element L_{worst}. Assign a utility score of 1 to the best and 0 to the worst; i.e., $U(L_{best}) \equiv 1$ and $U(L_{worst}) \equiv 0$. For any other lottery M, completeness and transitivity imply there is exactly one probability λ_M for which $\overline{L_{best}, L_{worst}; \lambda_M} \sim M$. Define $U(M) \equiv \lambda_M$. Expected utility theory will hold if and only if for any two lotteries L and M and any probability λ, $U(\overline{L, M; \lambda}) = \lambda U(L) + (1 - \lambda)U(M)$. Now by the substitution axiom, we can replace both L and M by lotteries in L_{best} and L_{worst}, so that

$$\overline{L, M; \lambda} \sim \overline{\overline{L_{best}, L_{worst}; \lambda_L}, \overline{L_{best}, L_{worst}; \lambda_M}; \lambda}$$

$$\sim \overline{L_{best}, L_{worst}; \lambda\lambda_L + (1 - \lambda)\lambda_M}$$

But this implies $U(\overline{L, M; \lambda}) = \lambda\lambda_L + (1 - \lambda)\lambda_M = \lambda U(L) + (1 - \lambda)U(M)$ as required.

CHOICES BETWEEN ACTIONS

As Regretta mentioned, the substitution axiom takes a lot of flak because it seems to separate valuation from context. To avoid that, you can compare actions rather than lotteries. An action specifies outcomes in different states of the world without specifying the probability $p \equiv (p_1, p_2, \ldots)$ of those states. So whether you prefer one action or another will typically vary with p.

For any two actions A and B, let $A \succeq_p B$ denote the relation "A is weakly preferred to B at probability p". Similarly, let $A \succ_p B$ and $A \sim_p B$ denote respectively strict preference and indifference. Again the most basic axioms postulate:

- **Completeness:** Either $A \succeq_p B$ or $B \succeq_p A$.
- **Transitivity:** If $A \succ_p B$ and $B \succeq_p C$, then $A \succ_p C$.

In this framework, no one is ever asked to rate one probability measure relative to another or actions in one probability context relative to actions in another context. But some axiom is needed to connect different risks. The most natural axiom is convexity:

- **Convexity:** If $A \succ_p B$ and $A \succeq_q B$, then $A \succ_{\lambda p + (1-\lambda)q} B$ for any probability λ.

Think of λ as the probability of heads in a coin toss. If the outcome is heads, probability measure p will apply, and you'll strictly prefer A. If the outcome is tails, probability measure q will apply, but you'll still weakly prefer A. Convexity means that you'd be willing to choose A over B even before you learn the outcome of the coin toss. In other words, if knowing something won't affect your behavior, then not knowing it won't affect your behavior either.

THE GEOMETRY OF CONVEXITY

In geometry, a set is convex if and only if it contains every straight line segment running from one point in that set to another. Regretta's graph demonstrated convexity between two acts in three states. The extension to higher-dimensional spaces is straightforward. With $n + 1$ states, the feasible probabilities map out an n-dimensional subspace known as the unit simplex. If preferences are convex, the strict preference regions for every action will be convex and n-dimensional, unless they're empty (in which case you might as well ignore that action because it will never be chosen).

Strict preferences between any two actions will be separated by $(n - 1)$-dimensional hyperplanes whose intersections with the unit simplex represent the indifference. Without loss of generality we can extend those separating hyperplanes through the origin, making them n-dimensional. Each extended hyperplane is completely defined by a unit vector v_{AB} orthogonal to it. That is, $q'v_{AB} = 0$ whenever $A \sim_q B$.

USING CONVEXITY TO CONSTRUCT A UTILITY MEASURE

Expected utility measures are always complete, transitive, and convex. To verify the last property, note that if U_A and U_B denote vectors of utility scores for A and B respectively, $p'U_A > p'U_B$ and $q'U_A \geq q'U_B$ imply $(\lambda p + (1 - \lambda)q)'U_A > (\lambda p + (1 - \lambda)q)'U_B$ for any probability λ.

Now suppose we are given a preference mapping and asked to find expected utility measures consistent with it. At any point q where $A \sim_q B$, we must have $q'U_A = q'U_B$ or $q'(U_A - U_B) = 0$. We know that this will work if $U_A - U_B$ is a multiple of v_{AB}. And it can't work otherwise, because otherwise $U_A - U_B$, v_{AB}, and the various q would have to span $n + 1$ dimensions, one more than the simplex allows. So we can construct utility measures as follows:

- Set $U_A = 0$ for some A.

- If v_{AB} defines the hyperplane of indifference between A and B, set U_B equal to plus or minus v_{AB}, with the sign chosen to make $p'(U_A - U_B)$ positive at a point where $A \succ_p B$.
- If v_{BC} defines the hyperplane of indifference between B and C, and if q is some point where A is viewed indifferently to C but not to B, then set $U_C = U_B - \dfrac{q'U_B}{q'v_{BC}} v_{BC}$.
- Proceed in this fashion until utility vectors have been defined for every action.

USING TRANSITIVITY TO ESTABLISH EXISTENCE

I haven't yet shown this construction method will work. What if some of the indifference and preference regions are defined incorrectly? Here's where transitivity comes in.

To illustrate this, let's return to a three-state world, with preferences marked out between A, B, and C. (To simplify, I ignore the boundaries of the simplex.) The construction method above correctly defines all the preferences between A and B, the line of indifference $B \sim C$, and one point q on the line $A \sim C$ that is not on the other two indifference lines. But by transitivity, the intersection of $A \sim B$ and $B \sim C$ also lies on $A \sim C$, and the expected utility comparison calls that second point correctly too. Since expected utility is a convex measure, it must correctly specify the whole line $A \sim C$.

Convexity with and without transitivity

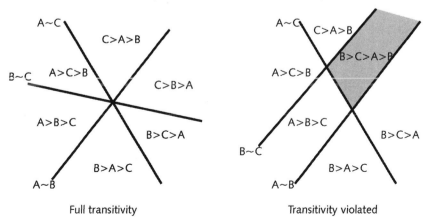

Full transitivity   Transitivity violated

Next let's check whether the utility construction misspecifies any strict preferences between B and C. Given convexity and the correct placement of the line $B \sim C$, the utility construction must in fact get either all those preferences right or all of them wrong. But anywhere on the line $A \sim C$ it must get the preferences between B and C right, because it gets the preferences between A and B right and respects transitivity. A similar argument shows that the utility construction correctly specifies all strict preferences between A and C.

With more than three states, verifying that the utility construction implies the correct hyperplane of indifference is more complex. I won't pursue it here, however, partly because the logic is similar and partly because the logic is flawed.

FLAW IN PRECEDING ARGUMENT

What if in the preceding graph the intersection of the lines $A \sim B$ and $B \sim C$ falls outside the unit simplex? Then transitivity won't force $A \sim C$ to pass through that intersection, even though expected utility theory would insist on this. So in some cases preferences can be complete, transitive, and convex without being amenable to expected utility maximization.

These cases may have some relevance to choices between a few discrete alternatives, like whether or not to build a nuclear power plant. When it comes to optimizing financial portfolios, however, each choice typically has neighbours with very similar payoffs. This packs the hyperplanes of indifference very close together, so that violations of transitivity outside the simplex will almost surely cause violations of transitivity within the simplex. Certainly, none of the conventionally mooted alternatives to expected utility theory respect convexity within the simplex. In practice, completeness, transitivity, and convexity are nearly tantamount to expected utility maximization.

RISK AVERSION

Let's imagine we're all hard-core rational investors, caring about nothing but financial wealth W. If more is always better than less, our utility score U will be increasing in W. If we rate risk worse than certainty given equal expected payoffs, any line segment S connecting two points on U has to pass below U. That's because given a lottery in the two outcomes associated with those points, the height of S at the expected wealth will equal the expected utility. Conversely, if we love risk, the set above U will be convex, which makes U what is known as a convex function.

Note that convexity and concavity of utility functions have nothing to do with the convexity of preferences. Convexity of preferences refers to sets defined in probability space, without explicit mention of the quantitative payoffs. Convexity and concavity of utility functions refers to sets defined over quantitative payoffs, without regard to probability. Economically, it's just the difference between maximizing expected utility and seeking or avoiding risk.

Algebraically, a wealth-loving, risk-averse U is continuous and almost everywhere twice differentiable, with U' positive and U'' negative. To verify the last point, let's consider a lottery that pays $W + \delta$ or $W - \delta$ with even odds for some small positive δ. Taking a second-order Taylor series' expansion, expected utility works out to approximately $U(W) + \frac{1}{2}U''(W)$, so U'' must be negative for this to be worth less than the expectation W.

16 | Unusually Useful Utility

Regretta returned an hour later clutching a few charts. "Sorry to keep you waiting. I was rustier at spreadsheets than I thought."

"That's OK," said Conway. "It gave Devlin and me some time to catch up. And one of us made a small profit betting you'd return. Didn't we, Devlin?"

"I'll have to owe you," muttered Devlin to Conway. "I don't have my wallet with me."

Regretta turned to Devlin. "Oh really?" she asked solicitously. "Another strong opinion? And here I thought the group therapy sessions hadn't helped you."

"The ones you're at don't."

"That's funny. I feel the same way. So we have something in common after all."

I don't know whether to fence them apart or lock them up together. "Please, both of you," said Conway. "Can we get back to utility functions? Regretta, what makes you opt for a power function of gross percentage returns?"

"I'll gladly consider a broader range if you're willing to track clients' total wealth."

"Clients' wealth? I won't know that. And why should it matter? Fund managers just take the funds invested with them and allocate them among assets."

"So each client receives a prorated portion of the fund, with the same percentage breakdowns as every other investor."

"Of course. Any other division would get absurdly complicated and drag you into litigation. But I'm sure you know that, Regretta. What are you driving at?"

"Only one kind of utility function implies optimal relative portfolio allocations that are independent of wealth, regardless of the distribution of returns. So you might as well assume it applies. It's characterized by something called constant relative risk aversion, or CRR for short. The CRR indicates what multiple percentage of wealth you'd be willing to relinquish per small percentage reduction in variance."

"So do CRR functions equal gross percentage returns raised to a power?"

"Not quite. You have to sign the result to make sure that more is better than less. The CRR equals one less the power, so if people dislike risk the power can't exceed one. A CRR of zero corresponds to logarithmic utility. Moreover, as with any expected utility function, you can always add a constant or multiply by a positive constant without changing the implied preferences. Here are two charts I prepared."

Two views of CRR functions

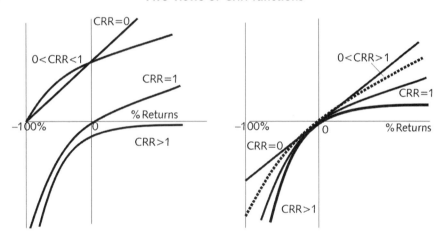

Regretta explained. "On the left, I've just drawn the CRR functions as signed power functions. A CRR of 0 denotes indifference to risk and corresponds to a straight line. When the CRR is positive but less than one, the investor is willing to risk everything for a sufficiently promising payoff. With any higher CRR, the disutility of total loss is unbounded, so the agent will never willingly risk everything. Indeed, with a CRR greater than one, the utility of positive returns is strictly bounded, so that even an infinite gain may not compensate for the risk of a given finite loss. On the right, I've rescaled everything so that zero returns deliver a utility of zero and a marginal utility of one. That makes it clearer that higher CRR corresponds to increased convexity; that is, more rapidly decreasing marginal returns."

"I don't know any investors who'd willingly risk total ruin," said Conway. "Not if it's truly total."

"I don't either. So that argues for a CRR of at least one."

"But what makes you think that two is a good number?"

"I didn't say two. I said to raise returns to the minus-two power, which corresponds to a CRR of three."

"OK, why three?"

"I did a few thought experiments. The first was to consider the maximum risk you'd be willing to bear of a given loss, even if the upside were infinite. For example, how much risk do you think most people would willingly tolerate of losing half of their wealth?"

"I'm not sure. More than 5%, I would think, but less than 50%. I guess that doesn't provide much guidance."

"You'll be surprised. Your estimates bracket the CRR between two and a bit over five. Here's a chart."

Maximum tolerable risk with CRR functions

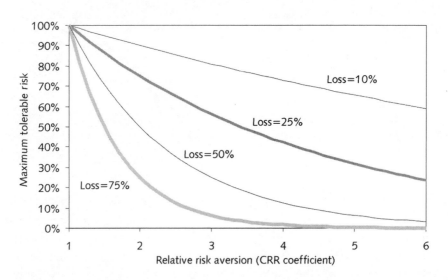

"That's interesting," said Conway. "But I'm having second thoughts. I don't know how reliably I can compare huge losses to infinite gains."

"Fair enough. So let's try another thought experiment. Suppose people are offered even odds of doubling their total wealth. How much of their wealth do you think they would be willing to risk for that opportunity?"

"Hmmm. I don't feel very confident about that either. Off the top of my head I'll guess somewhere between 20% and 40%."

"Well, that brackets the CRR between 1.5 and 3.8. Here's another chart if you're interested. Putting the two tests together, it looks like you think CRR deserves a handle of 2 or 3."

Willingness to risk for even odds of doubling wealth

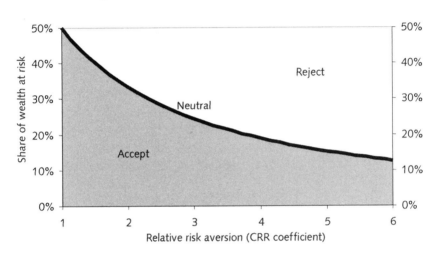

Devlin spoke up. "Do you mean stock market wealth or total wealth?"

"That's a good question. In theory, it ought to include all wealth, human capital too. But in practice, we're interested in responses to changes in financial assets. What do you think, Conway?"

Remarkable. You didn't snap at Devlin. "Oh, excuse me, my mind was wandering. Think about what, Regretta?"

"Which were you thinking about when you gave me your estimates? Total wealth or just financial wealth?"

"Financial wealth. I guess I had in mind investors whose wealth is largely financial. They're the ones who seem to dominate our markets."

Regretta nodded. "Some of the literature estimates CRR at over ten. But those estimates are geared to total wealth. If your non-financial wealth is uncorrelated with your financial wealth and of comparable size, then CRR calculated with respect to your financial wealth alone is roughly a quarter of your total CRR. I suggest we just focus on changes in financial wealth, which is all we tend to measure. And that leads us to the second way to estimate CRR."

"Which is?"

"Using data on long-term financial market performance to out investors' risk profiles. Investors presumably adjust their portfolios until their marginal expected utility from securities purchases or sales fails to cover the transaction costs. So if in the long run markets behave roughly how investors expect, the average historical utility should proxy for the expected utility. We can then just look for the CRR that zeroes out the average historical marginal utility."

"Which history? Average excess returns relative to volatility are a lot higher if you focus on US markets since World War II than if you include the Depression or world experience as a whole."

"I agree. Most likely the US market has outperformed postwar expectations, because threats of world war, hyperinflation, or severe depression didn't materialize. And surely it underperformed expectations in the Depression. So I favor including both major bull markets and major bear markets."

"How do you know average risk aversion has been stable for that long?" interrupted Devlin again.

"I don't. I'm only advocating this for ballpark estimation. Are you saying that's not worthwhile, Know-Nothing?"

Uh-oh. She's getting irritated. Normal service resumed. This time Conway decided to stay out of it.

"It depends how wide the ballpark is," said Devlin.

"In principle I suppose it does. In practice, I don't find it changes the CRR estimate by more than a couple of units. If I recall correctly, the implied CRR for a pure S&P 500 portfolio held since the series began in 1871 is about 2.1. Looking only at the postwar period the implied CRR is about 3.5."

"I thought your baseline CRR estimate was three."

"That's because I think an S&P portfolio is too narrowly concentrated. If you allow for some cash and bonds, the implied CRR is higher."

"Why only a unit higher?"

"On a whim. Look, I told you I wasn't claiming three was right, just that it wasn't badly wrong."

Conway nodded in approval. *A woman after my own heart. Too bad I'm married.* "So, Devlin, what do you think?"

"I'm not sure about the parameter estimates ..."

"No surprise there, Know-Nothing," said Regretta. "Is that all you can say?"

"No it isn't, Regretta. Can you please let me finish my sentence?"

Regretta was taken aback. Devlin had never called her by her name before, much less said please. "Sure, Devlin, go ahead."

"I'm not sure about the parameter estimates but I like the math. Too bad I can't mix CRR utility with normal probability distributions."

"Why can't you?" asked Conway. "Is the expectation that hard to solve?"

"Worse," said Regretta. "It's not even defined for a normal distribution. Normal distributions are unbounded, whereas CRR utility won't let wealth drop below zero. If you tried to calculate the expectation anyway you'd come up with minus infinity."

"How about truncating a normal distribution so wealth never sinks too low? That's more realistic anyway."

"I suppose we could," said Devlin. "But I'm not sure where to truncate, and it's messy to calculate when I do. I'd like to find something cleaner."

"Well," said Regretta, "there is a utility family called CAR that's a negative exponential in returns. That will allow for negative wealth. Furthermore, it turns the expectation into a moment-generating function, which is usually easy to calculate."

"Great," said Devlin. "What's the CAR stand for?"

"Constant absolute risk aversion. It means you're willing to relinquish a constant amount per small reduction in variance, regardless of your base wealth."

"That's not too realistic, is it? The richer I am, the more willing I'll be to sacrifice a million dollars to reduce risk. And if I don't have a million dollars, which I don't, forget it."

"I realize that. That's another reason to favor CRR utility."

"How about a compromise?" ventured Conway. "Keep the exponential form, but use percentage returns instead of absolute returns."

"Nice try," said Regretta, "but forget it. That may look like an expected utility format, but it's not. It can't be. If preferences depend only on relative returns, the utility function has to be CRR. And that rules out normality."

"Too bad. But I guess we have to adjust. If wishes were horses, beggars would ride."

No one spoke for a while. Then Regretta piped up. "How about allowing another distribution besides normal? Something that generates a simple form for expected CRR utility."

"Fine, but I don't know one. What do you suggest?"

"I don't know either. How about you, Devlin? Do you have any ideas?"

"Why yes, I do. It's ..." Suddenly Devlin's eyes glazed over and he started talking to himself. "Wait, will that work for portfolios? ... Oh, I guess not. Too bad ... Hey, what kind of distributions are those portfolios, anyway? ... Let's see. If we take a simple Taylor series ... Why, that's just the same as ... Maybe this works after all ... Then again, maybe the approximation isn't ..."

Regretta waved a chart in front of Devlin, trying in vain to get his attention. "We've lost contact with him," she told Conway. "Do you think I should call a nurse?"

"No, that's normal for Devlin. He must be getting back to his old self. Let him be."

A short while later Devlin came to, and his eyes regained their focus. "Interesting. I think you both may be right."

"About what?"

"About how to make CRR expectations tractable."

"But we don't know how. That's why we asked you."

"Look, I don't want to argue with you now. Maybe I'm mistaken. Give me some time to think this through more clearly. Can you come back next Saturday, Conway?"

"Absolutely. Regretta, will you join us?"

"I'll need to check my social calendar," said Regretta, smiling. "But I think I can fit it in."

"Good. I'll see you both then. Good luck, Devlin. I'm counting on you."

While Devlin goes to work, let's explore these CRR and CAR utility functions.

EQUIVALENCE ACROSS UTILITY FUNCTIONS

Given any utility function U, any scalar a, and any positive scalar b, $a + bU$ defines the same risk preferences under expected utility maximization as U. That's because for any two actions A and B, $E[U(A)] > E[U(B)]$ if and only if $a + bE[U(A)] > a + bE[U(B)]$.

The converse is true as well. Suppose that for any two actions A and B, two sets of utility functions U and V rank preferences the same regardless of the underlying distribution. That is, $E[V(A)] \geq E[V(B)]$ if and only if $E[U(A)] \geq E[U(B)]$. Defining u and v as the vectors whose components are the various values of $U(A) - U(B)$ and $V(A) - V(B)$

respectively associated with different outcomes, then $v'p = 0$ if and only if $u'p = 0$. That is, v is orthogonal to all the vectors that are orthogonal to u and therefore must be a scalar multiple b of u. Moreover, b must be positive to preserve the sign of the inequalities. It follows that $V(B) - bU(B) = V(A) - bU(A)$ regardless of the outcome. Since this holds for any pair of actions, $V - bU$ must be constant.

Hence, utility functions come in equivalent families, where every member of the family equals a scalar plus a positive multiple of every other.

CURVATURE AND RISK AVERSION

Recall from the previous chapter that, for small risks, the gap between the expected utility $E[U(A)]$ and the utility $U(E[A])$ of the expected outcome is approximately $\frac{1}{2}U''(E[A])$. So at first glance risk aversion varies directly with U''. However, since multiplying U by a positive number doesn't change the implied risk preferences, risk aversion must vary with the ratio of U'' and higher derivatives to U' rather than with U'' directly. These are measures of curvature controlling for scale. The more curved U is, the more risk aversion it implies.

CERTAINTY EQUIVALENCE

To investigate the relation between curvature and risk aversion more closely, let's measure how much guaranteed return a risky lottery L is worth. This is known as the certainty equivalent. The certainty equivalent can in turn be decomposed into two parts: the expected return $E[L]$ less a risk premium R. In general, R varies not only with the characteristics of the lottery but also with other wealth W, because other wealth affects one's ability to bear risk. The basic formula is $U(W + E[L] - R) = E[U(W + L)]$.

This formula is easier to use than it looks. Consider again, for example, an even-odds bet of making or losing a small amount δ. The expected return is zero, so we can write:

$$U(W - R) = \tfrac{1}{2}U(W + \delta) + \tfrac{1}{2}U(W - \delta)$$

Taking a second-order Taylor series' expansion and simplifying,

$$-RU'(W) + \tfrac{1}{2}R^2 U''(W) \cong \tfrac{1}{2}\delta^2 U''(W)$$

As δ approaches zero, R is roughly linear in δ^2 while R^2 approaches zero much faster. So we can ignore the R^2 term in approximation and write:

$$R \cong \tfrac{1}{2}\delta \cdot \frac{-U''(W)}{U'(W)}$$

This confirms R's dependence of risk aversion on the ratio $-U''/U'$, which is known as the coefficient of absolute risk aversion.

CONSTANT ABSOLUTE RISK AVERSION

If R is independent of W, $\dfrac{U''}{U'} \equiv \dfrac{d \ln U'}{dW}$ must be a constant $-\kappa$, where κ is positive given risk aversion. Integrating, $\ln(U')$ must equal $-\kappa W$ plus some constant, so that U' is proportional to $\exp(-\kappa W)$. It follows that U must give the same rankings as $-\exp(-\kappa W)$. This is called CAR utility, for constant absolute risk aversion. Here are some graphs for a few values of κ.

CAR utility function

While the CAR parameters κ in these graphs are all on the order of a few percent, that's not essential. Depending on the unit of measurement for W, it may not even be appropriate.

RELATIVE RISK AVERSION

If the risk premium R is expressed as a fraction r of W, and the risk δ as a fraction ϵ of W, the equation relating the risk premium to the risk can be rewritten as:

$$r \cong \tfrac{1}{2}\epsilon^2 \cdot \frac{-WU''(W)}{U'(W)}$$

The ratio $\dfrac{-WU''}{U'}$ is known as the coefficient of relative risk aversion.

If r is independent of W, $\dfrac{WU''}{U'} \equiv \dfrac{d \ln U'}{d \ln W}$ must be a constant $-c$, where c is positive given risk aversion. Integrating, $\ln(U')$ must equal $-c \cdot \ln(W)$ plus a constant, so that U' is proportional to W^{-c}. It follows that U must give the same rankings as $\dfrac{W^{1-c}}{1-c}$ when $c \neq 1$ and as $\ln(W)$ when $c = 1$. This is called CRR utility.

WHEN ONLY RELATIVE WEALTH MATTERS

With CRR utility, dividing all wealth outcomes by a scalar doesn't affect the relative rankings of lotteries or actions. In particular, you can divide through by base wealth, so that all wealth returns become gross percentage returns: i.e., $1 + x$, where x is the percentage return. Rescaling the CRR formula so that utility and marginal utility at $x = 0$ equal zero and one respectively yields the expression $U(x) \equiv \dfrac{(1 + x)^{1-c} - 1}{1 - c}$, which technically isn't defined at $c = 1$ but converges to $\ln(1 + x)$ there. In most cases of practical interest c exceeds one, in which case we can just consider $U(x) \equiv -(1 + x)^{1-c}$.

In fact, CRR is the only utility function that makes all comparisons in percentage terms. To see this, note that if only relative wealth matters, then for any positive scalar m, $U(m\cdot)$ and $U(\cdot)$ must define the same risk preferences. That means $U(mW) \equiv a(m) + b(m)U(W)$ for some functions a and b that depend on m but not on W. Differentiating both sides with respect to m and W and evaluating at $m = 1$ shows that $\dfrac{WU''(W)}{U'(W)} = b'(1)$ for all W. Hence, relative risk aversion must be constant.

MAXIMUM TOLERABLE RISK WITH CRR UTILITY

Suppose you can take a risk λ of losing a fraction F of your wealth in return for garnering limitless wealth otherwise. For $c > 1$ even limitless wealth offers only finite utility, so you will never take this bet unless $-\lambda(1 - F)^{1-c} > -1$, or equivalently $\lambda > (1 - F)^{c-1}$.

PORTFOLIO OPTIMIZATION WITH CRR UTILITY

Suppose a rational investor with CRR utility allocates her portfolio between a risky index and risk-free bills. Assuming risk parameters and preferences remain stable, and ignoring transaction costs, she will choose a risky asset/ portfolio share ω to maximize her expected utility. If x denotes the percentage excess return on the risky asset, the net excess percentage return on the portfolio will be ωx. Expected utility maximization requires that:

$$\frac{d}{d\omega}\left(E\left[\frac{(1 + \omega x)^{1-c}}{1 - c}\right]\right) = E\left[(1 + \omega x)^{-c}x\right] = 0$$

So if we can observe the long-run portfolio return ωx, we can estimate c as the value that zeroes out the expected marginal utility $E\left[(1 + \omega x)^{-c}x\right]$.

In practice, it's harder to identify an appropriate risky asset share ω than to choose an appropriate time period. Lowering ω raises the estimated risk aversion in roughly inverse proportion. However, lowering ω also dilutes the holdings of a given risky asset, so to some extent the differences offset each other.

SIMPLIFYING EXPECTED CRR UTILITY

Expected CRR utility isn't well-defined for normal and other unbounded densities. The latter imply positive odds of generating negative wealth, whose CRR score is negative infinity, so the expected utility will be negative infinity too.

Even densities confined to positive wealth rarely yield simple analytic expressions for expected CRR utility. However, we can make some headway by taking a binomial expansion:

$$\frac{(1 + x)^{1-c} - 1}{1 - c} = x + \frac{-c}{1 \cdot 2}x^2 + \frac{(-c)(-c - 1)}{1 \cdot 2 \cdot 3}x^3 + \cdots$$

Integrating term by term, and denoting the jth moment by M_j, expected CRR utility works out to:

$$M_1 + \sum_{j=2}^{\infty} \frac{(-c)\cdots(-c-j+2)}{j!} M_j$$

SIMPLIFYING EXPECTED CAR UTILITY

CAR expected utility takes the form $E[-e^{-\kappa W}]$. Treating this as a function of $-\kappa$ and ignoring the first minus sign, it closely resembles three other familiar functions:

- the Laplace transform, except for the need to integrate over negative values as well as positive ones
- the moment-generating function, except that $-\kappa$ is negative rather than positive
- the characteristic function, except that $-\kappa$ is real rather than imaginary.

For most commonly used probability densities, expected CAR utility reduces to a simple expression. In particular, given a normal density with mean μ and standard deviation σ, expected CAR utility equals $-\exp(-\kappa\mu + \frac{1}{2}\kappa^2\sigma^2)$.

A TEMPTING CONFUSION

Occasionally one sees utility scores formulated as $-\exp(-\kappa x)$ where x measures the percentage returns. This looks like a hybrid of CAR and CRR utility. In reality it isn't even a proper utility function, since the only expected utility comparisons that can be reduced to relative changes are CRR. That being said, if you're dealing with high-frequency data, say daily or hourly, where absolute returns are typically less than 2%, an exponential function in returns can reasonably approximate a CRR function. That's because, when x is small,

$$(1+x)^{1-c} = \exp\big((1-c)\cdot\ln(1+x)\big) \cong \exp\big((1-c)x\big).$$

Later chapters will delve more into this issue. For now, I simply call it to readers' attention as a tempting confusion.

17 | Optimal Overlays

Conway didn't tell anyone at work about his Saturday outing. While investment bankers are confirmed workaholics, asset managers consider it bad form to work weekends. *And if they knew I was consorting with crazy people ... Might as well wait to see what Devlin comes up with.* For once Conway was glad to have a big inbox. He devoted himself to whittling it down, and the week sped by.

The next Saturday, when Conway arrived back at Club Mad, Devlin and Regretta were waiting for him. "What took you so long?" asked Devlin.

"I took the first ferry I could. They don't leave until 10 a.m. on weekends."

"Never mind," said Regretta. "That's just Devlin's way of saying he's glad to see you."

"Thanks, Regretta," said Conway. "I knew that. But I'm glad you do too."

Devlin hid a blush. "Hey, cut the small talk. We've got work to do." Flashing a wad of papers, he led them back to the lounge. "Are you ready for the answer, Conway?"

"I'm all ears."

"Partition functions."

"Partition which functions into what?"

"No, no. That's their name. Partition functions. They're weighted sums of exponentials."

"Never heard of them."

"I hadn't either until I read Schrödinger on statistical thermodynamics. All we have to do is reinterpret the variables."

"And what do you do with these partition functions?"

"Compare their values using different portfolio weights. The lowest value maximizes the overall certainty equivalent."

"And that's it?"

"As a first pass, yes." Devlin beamed.

Conway was dazed. Before he could respond, Regretta cut in. "Excuse me, Devlin. Now that you've told Conway the answer, would you mind telling me the question?"

"No problem. The question is: how do you combine CRR utility with conditional multivariate normality to quickly rank portfolios?"

"What makes you so keen on conditional multivariate normality?"

"Regretta, I'm surprised you should ask. I thought I explained that clearly at group therapy last month."

"Gee, Devlin, I must have spaced out. I'm sure it was fascinating," replied Regretta in mock seriousness.

"It was to me. It started back when I was working for Conway at Megabucks and we had to estimate value at risk on three binary options that were uncorrelated but not independent ..."

Oh no, I've got to get us back on track. Conway cut in. "In a nutshell, Regretta, Devlin and I like conditional normality because it's flexible enough to approximate nearly any kind of portfolio distribution without forcing you to estimate a lot of higher-order cross-moments."

"Thanks," said Regretta.

"Conditional multivariate normality," corrected Devlin. "Let me explain the differences ..."

"Later," said Conway. "You and Regretta will have plenty of time after I leave."

"Ooh, I can hardly wait," said Regretta. "So, Devlin, how do partition functions help you get the answer?"

"They don't <u>help</u> you get the answer. They <u>are</u> the answer. Since the expected utility in any given regime is exponential, the overall expected utility is just the weighted average of exponentials, with a minus sign stuck in front. And that's what partition functions are, except for the sign."

"Hold on, Devlin," said Conway. We went through that last time. Expected CAR utility is exponential given normal distributions. Expected CRR utility isn't. It isn't even defined for normal distributions."

"That depends on how you measure the portfolios."

"You've been reading too much physics, Devlin. Whatever currency or time frame you choose, it's still not going to allow you negative wealth."

"We don't need wealth to be negative. Unbounded returns will work nearly as well."

"Fine, but returns have to be bounded too."

"Not if you measure in logarithms."

"What difference does that make?"

"Not much for changes of less than 10%. But the differences can be huge. Here are two charts I prepared to illustrate."

Logarithmic change versus percentage change

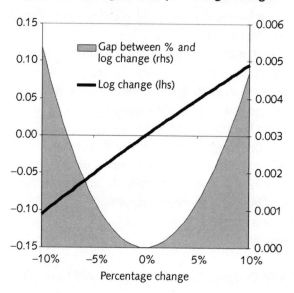

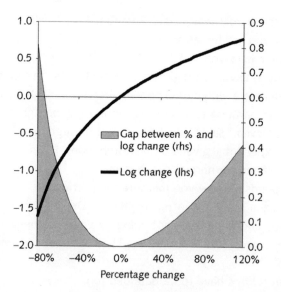

"Very pretty, Devlin, but I am familiar with logarithms. What's your point?"

"Think about it. If we focus on log returns rather than percentage returns, we don't have to worry about infeasible values. Normality is allowed again, which makes it a lot easier to calculate expected utility."

"I don't see how. You still have to integrate over a negative power function times an exponential. I'm not familiar with any reduced form for that."

"Oh, I see," said Regretta. "While CRR utility is a power function of gross percentage returns, it's an exponential function of log returns."

"Bingo. So if we assume log returns are normal, what does the expression for CRR expected utility look like?"

"It looks like the expression for CAR expected utility, except that you're integrating over log returns instead of absolute wealth. So it's essentially a moment-generating function for the distribution of log returns."

"Which works out to what? Here's a pen and paper if you need it."

Regretta took the pen and paper and worked through the integration. "It's an exponential. That makes the overall expected utility a weighted average of these exponentials, with the weights given by the probabilities of the various regimes. There's your partition function."

"You got it, except that the exponentials are typically preceded by a minus sign. Now let me ask you a harder question. What does each exponent in each exponential tell you?"

Regretta went back to her paper and experimented rearranging terms. "It's a multiple of the certainty equivalent in that regime, the guaranteed return that will yield the same expected utility."

"Guaranteed log return," corrected Devlin. "And what multiple of the certainty equivalent is it?"

"The power in the power function, which equals one minus the CRR."

"That's right. What does that make the formula for certainty equivalent in each regime?"

"The conditional mean log return less $\frac{1}{2}(\text{CRR} - 1)$ times the conditional variance."

"So what is the economic interpretation of $\frac{1}{2}(\text{CRR} - 1)$?"

"The price of variance in terms of an equivalent guaranteed log loss. The more risk averse you are, the higher the price."

"Good job, Regretta. Perfect. Do you understand now, Conway?"

"Not completely. When we first tried to calculate expected CRR utility under normality, the answer was negative infinity. How did remeasuring things in log terms get rid of it?"

"I didn't just remeasure. I redefined the probability density so that log returns are normal instead of percentage returns."

"How do you know that's better?"

"With most daily returns you can't tell the difference. For huge crashes, though, lognormality won't let you wind up with less than nothing while normality will."

"I grant you lognormality is better in that respect. But who's to say lognormality doesn't screw up big somewhere else?"

"There's also a theoretical reason for favoring long-term lognormality. It's the difference between multiplication and addition."

I wish Devlin's explanations needed less explanation. "Meaning?"

"The cumulative gross return equals the product of the gross return over each subperiod, so the logs are additive. If the subperiod returns are independent and identically distributed, the long-term log is bound by the Central Limit Theorem to approach normality, making the cumulative gross return lognormal."

"I see. So what are the implications for horizons of a few quarters to a few years?"

"The only noticeable difference is that lognormality adds skewness. Here's an example I charted where log returns are normally distributed with mean 10% and standard deviation 20%. The dark heavy line marks their density. The solid area represents the corresponding lognormal density for percentage returns."

Lognormal versus normal densities for $\mu = 10\%$, $\sigma = 20\%$

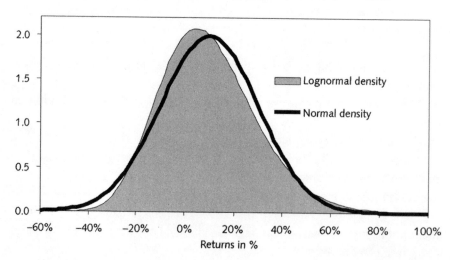

Conway pondered the chart. "You know, it's really not such a big deal. Strange we didn't think of this before."

"That's because we were thinking too much like standard portfolio theorists. If we had been options theorists we would have thought of it right away. They nearly always assume lognormality."

"Why don't portfolio theorists assume it too?"

"Because portfolios of lognormal assets are a lot harder to deal with than portfolios of multivariate normal assets."

"Really? In what way?"

"Portfolios of lognormal assets aren't lognormal. They aren't normal either."

"Not even if they're multivariate lognormal?"

"Not even then. They're sort of part-normal, part-lognormal, and how much they lean toward one or the other depends on how many assets you have and how big the weights are."

"It doesn't sound very tractable."

"It isn't. So when options theorists deal with portfolios – currency baskets, say – they typically just gloss over the differences between logs and percentages. Specifically, they assume the portfolio is lognormal, with a log mean that's the weighted average of the asset log means and a variance that's a quadratic form in the covariance matrix."

"How good an approximation is that?"

"It's a first-order Taylor's approximation: great if the changes are small enough, awful if they're huge. To take an extreme example, suppose an asset comprising 1% of your portfolio completely bites the dust, while the other 99% holds its value. What's the log portfolio return?"

"Minus 1%."

"Of course. But that's not what the standard approximation would tell us. The log return on the failing asset would be minus infinity, so that the average of the logs would have to be minus infinity too, making the whole portfolio look worthless."

"Ahhh, so that's why portfolio theory tries to avoid log returns."

"Even while the other half of finance theory can't live without it. It's schizophrenic, isn't it?"

Conway nodded. *And here I had to come to a madhouse to find out.* "So what do you propose to do?"

"For now I'm simply going to ignore the discrepancy too."

"Did I hear that right? You, Devlin, going with a standard practice you know is wrong?" *It's hard enough getting you to follow standard practice when it's right.*

Devlin smiled. "Give me time. I can't see any way around it yet. Besides, it's not as if I'm confusing something that single-regime models keep straight."

"Speaking of keeping things straight," said Regretta, "I'm having some trouble myself. Do you mind quickly reviewing your multi-regime alternative?"

"No problem. Estimate the conditional mean and variance using the log-linear approximation for portfolios. Subtract a multiple of the variance from the mean to form the certainty equivalent for every regime. Convert to conditional expected utilities and calculate total expected utility as their probability-weighted average. Then pick the portfolio weights to maximize the total expected utility."

"Each step sounds easy. Still ..."

"It is easy. Like baking a layer cake. Here's a recipe I printed up to help you both remember. I put tildes on most of the variables to remind you that we're dealing with log returns rather than the more commonly used percentage returns."

QUICK RECIPE FOR PORTFOLIO OPTIMIZATION

1. Divide world into various conditionally lognormal regimes, assigning probability p_k to each regime k.
2. For each regime, estimate the vector mean $\tilde{M}_k$ and the covariance matrix $\tilde{\Sigma}_k$ of excess log returns.
3. Given portfolio weights ω, estimate the conditional log mean $\tilde{m}_k$ of the portfolio as $\omega'\tilde{M}_k$ and the conditional variance $\tilde{v}_k$ as $\omega'\tilde{\Sigma}_k\omega$.
4. Given constant relative risk aversion $c > 1$, estimate the conditional log certainty equivalent $\widetilde{CE}_k$ as $\tilde{m}_k - \frac{1}{2}(c-1)\tilde{v}_k$.
5. Calculate the conditional expected utility EU_k as $-\exp\big((1-c)\widetilde{CE}_k\big)$.
6. Calculate the aggregate expected utility EU as the probability-weighted average $\Sigma p_k EU_k$.
7. Calculate the aggregate log certainty equivalent $\widetilde{CE}$ as logarithm of $|EU|$ divided by $1 - c$.
8. Choose ω to maximize EU or $\widetilde{CE}$.

Conway read over the recipe. "Thanks, Devlin. But all this talk about cakes and recipes makes me hungry. How about you?"

"Famished," said Devlin. "Let's go to lunch."

"I'm not that hungry but I'll join you," said Regretta. And they headed off to the dining room.

While they're eating, let's chew over these partition functions. Given the tools we've developed already, they won't be hard to digest. The biggest challenge is to keep the distinction between logarithms and percentages only partially straight. Think of it as an exercise in studied carelessness. We'll tidy up later.

TERMINOLOGY

For P_t the price of an asset or portfolio at time t net of the risk-free rate (that is, the nominal price divided by a cumulative risk-free index), let x_t denote the excess percentage return $\dfrac{P_t - P_{t-1}}{P_{t-1}}$ and $\tilde{x}_t$ the logarithmic excess return $\ln\left(\dfrac{P_t}{P_{t-1}}\right) = \ln(1 + x_t)$. I will usually shorten "logarithm" to "log" and drop the time subscript as understood. I will denote the vector counterpart of $\tilde{x}$ by $\tilde{X} = \ln(1 + X)$ and indeed use ~ (tilde) to identify log counterparts more generally. However, do not assume that the log moments equal the logs of one plus the corresponding percentage moments. Due to nonlinearity this will hardly ever be the case.

As a shorthand I will also sometimes describe the percentage mean $\omega'M$ and variance $\omega'\Sigma\omega$ of a portfolio by the letters m and v, without explicitly including the risky asset weights ω on which m and v depend. To be more precise, m, v, and their log counterparts will serve as placeholders for various approximations. Similarly, ω^* will identify an approximately optimal portfolio mix. Most of both this chapter and the next are devoted to working out and refining the approximations.

DIFFERENCES BETWEEN LOG AND PERCENTAGE CHANGE

A Taylor series expansion shows that:

$$\tilde{x} \equiv \ln(1+x) = x - \frac{x^2}{2} + \frac{x^3}{3} - \frac{x^4}{4} \cdots$$

When x is close to zero, the higher-order terms in the Taylor expansion will be small compared with the first, so that $\tilde{x}$ will approximately equal x. The gap $x - \tilde{x}$ is only 0.0002, or 2 basis points (bps) at $x = 2\%$, 12 bps at 5%, and 47 bps at 10%. As x gets larger the gap widens rapidly: 600 bps at $x = 40\%$ and 9000 bps at $x = 200\%$. The widening is even more dramatic when x is negative: 1100 bps at $x = -40\%$ and infinite at $x = -100\%$.

Two Notions of Average Change

If the average log changes have been zero, the ending price will equal the starting price, because $\ln\left(\dfrac{P_t}{P_0}\right) = \ln\left(\dfrac{P_t}{P_{t-1}}\right) + \ln\left(\dfrac{P_{t-1}}{P_{t-2}}\right) + \cdots + \ln\left(\dfrac{P_1}{P_0}\right) = \sum_1^t \tilde{x}_t = 0$. Since percentage changes always exceed log changes except at zero, the average percentage change will be positive even though the price has returned to its original value. In an extreme case, average percentage changes can be positive even when the asset is now worthless. This makes percentage change a misleading measure in finance.

However, log changes can be misleading too. Consider a portfolio composed of many equally weighted assets. The portfolio will be stable if and only if the average percentage change on each asset is zero. Now if the average percentage change is zero, the average log change will be zero unless every price is still. So logarithms will understate the changes in a portfolio. In an extreme case, if one of the assets becomes worthless, the average log change will be $-\infty$ even though the portfolio as a whole might have appreciated.

Average Log Change and Relative Risk Aversion

Average changes can be related to relative risk aversion as follows. An investor is risk neutral with a CRR coefficient c of 0 if she is indifferent to any bet with a zero expected percentage return. Her c equals 1 if she is indifferent to any zero expected return to her log wealth – for example, even odds of halving her wealth or doubling it. Conversely, an investor whose c exceeds 1, as is considered typical, would rather hold cash than expect the average logarithm of her wealth to drift downward. As noted earlier, $c < 1$ would switch the sign of the partition function.

LOGNORMALITY

A normal distribution is unbounded. That is, any value is feasible, including extremely negative ones. That can't be true of prices. So analysts typically assume logarithmic normality. A gross percentage return $1 + x$ is said to be lognormally distributed if its log is normally distributed. That is, the cumulative distribution F is given by:

$$F(1 + x) \equiv \int_{-\infty}^{\ln(1+x)} \frac{1}{\tilde{\sigma}\sqrt{2\pi}} \cdot \exp\left(-\frac{(\tilde{x} - \tilde{\mu})^2}{2\tilde{\sigma}^2}\right) d\tilde{x}$$

where $\tilde{\mu}$ and $\tilde{\sigma}^2$ denote the mean and variance respectively of $\tilde{x} = \ln(1 + x)$. Differentiating both sides shows that

$$f(1 + x) = \frac{1}{\tilde{\sigma}(1+x)\sqrt{2\pi}} \cdot \exp\left(-\frac{(\ln(1+x) - \tilde{\mu})^2}{2\tilde{\sigma}^2}\right)$$

MOMENTS OF A LOGNORMAL DISTRIBUTION

The nth moment of a lognormal distribution can be calculated as:

$$E[(1+x)^n] = \int_0^\infty \frac{(1+x)^n}{\tilde{\sigma}\sqrt{2\pi}} \cdot \exp\left(-\frac{(\ln(1+x) - \tilde{\mu})^2}{2\tilde{\sigma}^2}\right) \frac{dx}{1+x}$$

$$= \int_{-\infty}^\infty \frac{\exp(n\tilde{x})}{\tilde{\sigma}\sqrt{2\pi}} \cdot \exp\left(-\frac{(\tilde{x} - \tilde{\mu})^2}{2\tilde{\sigma}^2}\right) d\tilde{x}$$

$$= \mathcal{M}(n) = \exp(n\tilde{\mu} + \tfrac{1}{2}n^2\tilde{\sigma}^2)$$

where $\mathcal{M}(\cdot)$ denotes the moment-generating function for a normal distribution. It follows that:

- $E[x] = \exp(\tilde{\mu} + \tfrac{1}{2}\tilde{\sigma}^2) - 1$. A Taylor series expansion indicates that the mean percentage change exceeds the mean log change by $\tfrac{1}{2}(\tilde{\mu}^2 + \tilde{\sigma}^2)$ plus higher-order terms.
- $Var[x] = Var[1 + x] = \exp(2\tilde{\mu} + 2\tilde{\sigma}^2) - \exp(2\tilde{\mu} + \tilde{\sigma}^2) =$

$\exp(2\tilde{\mu} + \tilde{\sigma}^2) \cdot \left(\exp(\tilde{\sigma}^2) - 1\right)$, which reduces to $\tilde{\sigma}^2 + 2\tilde{\mu}\tilde{\sigma}^2$ plus higher-order terms.

- Skewness $E\left[\left(\dfrac{x - E[x]}{\sqrt{Var[x]}}\right)^3\right]$ works out to — I will spare readers the gory details — $\left(\exp(\tilde{\sigma}^2) + 2\right)\sqrt{\exp(\tilde{\sigma}^2) - 1}$, which reduces to $3\tilde{\sigma}$ plus higher-order terms. So the lognormal density is indeed positively skewed, but only modestly if $\tilde{\sigma}$ is small.

- Kurtosis $E\left[\left(\dfrac{x - E[x]}{\sqrt{Var[x]}}\right)^4 - 3\right]$ works out to — again I shall be gracious — $\exp(4\tilde{\sigma}^2) + 2\exp(3\tilde{\sigma}^2) + 3\exp(2\tilde{\sigma}^2) - 6$, which reduces to $16\tilde{\sigma}^2$ plus higher-order terms.

DEPENDENCE ON TIME PERIODS

Finance theory generally assumes that the underlying laws of motion are stable and that price movements at different, non-overlapping times are uncorrelated. In that case, mean returns and variances will both scale linearly over time, while standard deviations will scale with the square root of time. To verify this, decompose a given change into the sum of uncorrelated component changes and apply the formulas for moments of sums.

At short time periods σ will dominate μ even though they both are shrinking toward zero. In that case, lognormal and normal densities will essentially match subject to a mean shift of $\frac{1}{2}\sigma^2$. Conversely, over long horizons lognormal densities will be far more upward skewed and fat-tailed than normal. In practice, asset allocation decisions tend to focus on intermediate time periods, where one can reasonably convert from one form to the other but a mean shift of $\frac{1}{2}\sigma^2$ may not suffice.

MULTIVARIATE LOGNORMALITY

A vector $\mathbf{1} + X$ is said to be multivariate lognormal if its log $\tilde{X} \equiv \ln(\mathbf{1} + X)$ is multivariate normal. I denote the latter's mean and variance by $\tilde{M}$ and $\tilde{\Sigma}$ respectively. Multivariate normality of the logs is of course equivalent to saying that every linear combination $\omega'\tilde{X}$ is normal with mean $\omega'\tilde{M}$ and variance $\omega'\tilde{\Sigma}\omega$.

PORTFOLIOS OF LOGNORMAL ASSETS

Let's consider a one-shot portfolio game. An allocation is made among risky assets with percentage weights ω, and the portfolio is held undisturbed for one period. The net excess percentage returns on the portfolio then takes the simple form $\omega'X$. Unfortunately, the corresponding log return is not $\omega'\tilde{X}$. Rather, it equals $\ln(1 + \omega'X) = \ln(1 + \omega'(\exp(\tilde{X}) - 1))$. That makes portfolios of lognormal assets messier to deal with than portfolios of normal assets, at least in one-shot games.

Moreover, portfolios of lognormal assets are hardly ever lognormal, and don't fit any other standard distribution type either. However, this shortcoming is not peculiar to lognormality. Any portfolio that can be neatly characterized by a few summary parameters, regardless of the numbers of assets or their weights, has to be 100% multivariate normal. To make any other approach tractable we have to look for approximations.

FIRST APPROXIMATIONS FOR LOGNORMALITY

To deal with portfolios of lognormal assets, finance typically encourages some selective amnesia. One approach treats X as multivariate normal, ignoring the ludicrous implications for long-term asset prices or likelihoods of negative wealth. The other approach treats log portfolio returns as if they were $\omega'\tilde{X}$ instead of $\ln(1 + \omega'X)$. Using the first approach, the portfolio percentage mean return and variance equal $\omega'M$ and $\omega'\Sigma\omega$ respectively. Using the second approach, the log portfolio mean and variance are estimated as $\omega'\tilde{M}$ and $\omega'\tilde{\Sigma}\omega$ respectively.

We can semi-justify either approach by taking a very short time period and ignoring possible jumps. Applying successive first-order Taylor series approximations reduces the logarithmic return $\ln(1 + \omega'X)$ to the net percentage return $\omega'X = \omega'(\exp(\tilde{X}) - 1)$ and in turn to the average log return $\omega'\tilde{X}$. I say "semi-justify" because the time horizons and risks we're interested in warn us not to ignore second-order terms and jumps. But Devlin's approach already addresses much of that by allowing for multiple regimes. So I will follow Devlin's lead and accept the approximations as a starting point.

EXPECTED CRR UTILITY UNDER LOGNORMALITY

CRR utility can be written as $sign(1-c) \cdot (1+x)^{1-c} = sign(1-c) \cdot \exp((1-c)\tilde{x})$. Given lognormality, expected CRR utility given by:

$$EU = sign(1-c) \cdot \int_{-\infty}^{\infty} \frac{\exp((1-c)\tilde{x})}{\tilde{\sigma}\sqrt{2\pi}} \cdot \exp\left(-\frac{(\tilde{x}-\tilde{\mu})^2}{2\tilde{\sigma}^2}\right) d\tilde{x}$$

$$= sign(1-c) \cdot \exp\left((1-c)\tilde{\mu} + \tfrac{1}{2}(1-c)^2\tilde{\sigma}^2\right)$$

$$\cong sign(1-c) \cdot \exp\left((1-c)\omega'\tilde{M} + \tfrac{1}{2}(1-c)^2\omega'\tilde{\Sigma}\omega\right)$$

The second step is yet another application of moment-generating functions, while the third step follows from the log-linear approximation.

CERTAINTY EQUIVALENCE UNDER LOGNORMALITY

The log certainty equivalent $\widetilde{CE}$ of a risky portfolio is the guaranteed log return that would yield the same expected utility EU. It is readily checked that $\widetilde{CE} = \dfrac{1}{1-c}\ln(|EU|)$. Applying the approximations for lognormality discussed above, it follows that for a portfolio $\omega'X$ with log mean $\tilde{m}$ and variance $\tilde{v}$:

$$\widetilde{CE} \cong \tilde{m} - \tfrac{1}{2}(c-1)\tilde{v} \cong \omega'\tilde{M} - \tfrac{1}{2}(c-1)\omega'\tilde{\Sigma}\omega$$

The factor $\tfrac{1}{2}(c-1)$ measures the cost of variance in terms of equivalent certain loss. At first glance this suggests that someone with $c < 1$ likes risk. For example, when $c = 0$, connoting risk neutrality, $\widetilde{CE}$ equals $\tilde{m} + \tfrac{1}{2}\tilde{v}$, so the investor might willingly accept a bet with negative $\tilde{m}$. However, the apparent mistake vanishes when we recall that $\tilde{m}$ denotes the mean log return rather than the log mean return. The log mean return is indeed $\widetilde{CE}$ itself, as it should be for risk neutrality.

EXPECTED CRR UTILITY UNDER CONDITIONAL LOGNORMALITY

For each possible risk regime k, calculate a conditional certainty equivalent $\widetilde{CE}_k$ and convert to a conditional expected utility EU_k. Then calculate the overall expected utility EU as the expectation of EU_k given perceived probabilities p_k that regime k occurs:

$$EU = \sum_k p_k EU_k = sign(1 - c) \cdot \sum_k p_k \exp\big((1 - c) \cdot \widetilde{CE_k}\big)$$

$$\cong sign(1 - c) \cdot \sum_k p_k \exp\bigg((1 - c)\Big(\omega'\tilde{M}_k - \frac{c - 1}{2}\omega'\tilde{\Sigma}_k\omega\Big)\bigg).$$

Devlin's recipe presents only the formula for the typical case $c > 1$.

ANALOGY TO THERMODYNAMICS

In his lectures on statistical thermodynamics, Schrödinger defined the partition function $Z = \sum_\ell \exp\Big(-\frac{\epsilon_\ell}{\kappa T}\Big)$, where κ is the Boltzman constant, T is the temperature, and ϵ_ℓ is the energy in state ℓ. He noted that $-\kappa T \ln(Z)$ measures free energy. So if we interpret $1 - c$ as $1/\kappa T$, EU as $-Z$, $\widetilde{CE_k}$ as the conditional energy and $\widetilde{CE}$ as the aggregate free energy, the equation is analogous. Higher risk aversion corresponds to lower temperature and more muted energies.

To generate the probability measure p over the various states, simply allow each state to occur multiple times with p_k measuring its relative frequency. Thermodynamics uses this procedure too. In fact, each conditional expected utility EU_k is itself the reduced form of a partition function. Variance represents random collisions that dissipate energy and hence reduce $\widetilde{CE_k}$, with a given collision rate relatively more costly when the risk aversion is high or temperature low.

18 | Adjusted Advice

"That was delicious," said Conway after lunch. "I always wondered what truffles tasted like."

"Not me," said Devlin. "Mom taught me to throw away any food with fungus growing in it. But I did like the double fudge chocolate cake. At least the bit that Regretta left me."

"Don't exaggerate, Devlin. I just took a little nibble," said Regretta, guiltily.

"If you call that a little nibble, you're a capybara." Devlin chuckled. Regretta's face turned red.

Poor Devlin, so artlessly gauche. I better help him out. "Devlin, this may come as a surprise to you, but not every woman likes to be compared to a giant water rodent. Is it possible you meant a hungry sleek mink instead?"

"All I said was . . . ," Devlin began to reply, until he saw Conway motion him to zip it. Devlin turned to Regretta and eyed her slowly up and down. "Yes, I suppose I did. Sorry, Regretta."

"Never mind," said Regretta, "but thank you both. Let's get back to work, shall we?"

"I agree," said Conway. "Come on, Devlin, it's time to show us the solution."

"What do you mean? I already gave you the whole recipe."

"Not quite. It's missing the last line."

"Oh, I get it. You want an explicit formula for the optimal portfolio mix."

"Of course."

"And you figure I gave you the recipe only to whet your appetite for the simpler answer."

"That thought had crossed my mind."

"Then brace yourself. There's no explicit closed-form formula. Not with multiple risky regimes."

"You mean we have to solve it numerically case-by-case?"

"I'm afraid so. But it's not as bad as it sounds. With only a few assets and scenarios, I've found that a spreadsheet solver optimizes in a few seconds at most. And exponential polynomials seem sufficiently well-behaved that I suspect even complicated problems can be solved reasonably quickly, though I haven't tested this with any rigor."

"Can you draw out any qualitative implications of your model without crunching a lot of numbers?" asked Regretta.

"A few. For example, if the CRR exceeds one, rational gamblers won't like downward skews or fat tails. They'll prefer thin-tailed distributions that slant upwards."

"That's reassuring. How did you verify that?"

"By taking a fourth-order Taylor series expansion in the certainty equivalents and examining the signs on skewness and kurtosis."

"Interesting. Do the higher moments make a lot of difference or just a little?"

"That depends. Remember your chart on the maximal CRR tolerance for risk? I could drive up the Sharpe ratios sky-high on some of those boom-or-bust bets without the investor taking them. Conversely, if I dilute the risk enough, any investor will stomach it given a positive expected return."

"So much for ranking portfolios by their Sharpe ratios."

"I wouldn't say that. They do rank most portfolios correctly, provided you can lever or dilute risk as needed. In fact, the optimization itself can be interpreted as a modified Sharpe ratio maximization. The optimal risky portfolio weights equal the inverse of a weighted average covariance matrix times the corresponding weighted average vector of excess returns, divided by the CRR less one. The risk-free asset picks up the slack."

"What are the weights? The probabilities of each regime?"

"No, they're risk-adjusted probabilities. They're proportional to the actual probabilities times the marginal expected utility in that regime. The worse the regime, the higher the expected marginal utility. So the adjustments make you focus more on improving performance in the worst regimes than the pure probabilities alone suggest."

"Doesn't this give you an explicit formula for the portfolio weights? I thought you said there wasn't one."

"There isn't. When you modify the portfolio, you modify the risk adjustments. So you would need to start with an initial guess and iterate. Or rather, have a computer do it quickly."

Conway spoke up. "Alright, Devlin, I think I understand how your model works and its theoretical merits. What are its main practical benefits?"

"Confidence, mostly. In most of the examples I've played with, the portfolio recommendations don't improve much over a single-regime approximation."

"Oh, really? Don't they help you deal with uncertainty?"

"Not if the uncertainty is just white noise around the true means. Then the single-regime method is just as good, provided the unconditional variance incorporates both the risk and the uncertainty the way you suggested."

"So what makes the two approaches noticeably differ?"

"Icebergs. To mitigate disasters my model will emphasize keeping low-earning lifeboats around – T-bills and the like – even at the expense of lower Sharpe ratios. Do you recall the example you gave in your first visit with small odds of a common 30% crash?"

"And uncorrelated otherwise? Yes, I remember."

"Well, I took the same parameters as yours – mean returns of 5% and 3% respectively barring crash, volatility of 10% barring crash – and optimized subject to a crash risk of 4.5% and a CRR of 4. Treating the asset pair as bivariate normal, as standard theory requires, advises investing about five times as much in the first asset than the second, with virtually no T-bill holdings. The partition function method boosts the cash holdings to 30%. Moreover, it takes roughly equal bites out of both assets, resulting in the second asset nearly disappearing from the portfolio." Devlin laid out a chart.

Common disaster risks, different advice

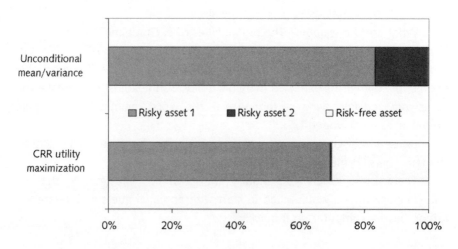

"That's a sharp contrast. Only how am I supposed to persuade someone who doesn't know one model from the other that yours is better?"

Devlin shrugged his shoulders. "Beats me. You know how finance people are. They're so geared to figuring out the consensus view that they have trouble thinking for themselves. The first question you'll be asked when you walk in the door is who else uses the system you're recommending. The second question is why not. You'll have two strikes against you before you sit down."

Regretta chimed in. "On top of that, you're not likely to be judged fairly, comparing the portfolio outcomes with the information you had *ex ante*. Most often a crisis won't occur, in which case your recommendations will appear to have fallen short. And if a crisis does occur, people will be inclined to fault you for not hedging even more."

"I realize that. But isn't there anything I can say to make the new approach more palatable?" asked Conway. Regretta and Devlin gave him a blank look. "Please, help me out."

After a pause Devlin spoke. "I can't identify with the bozos. Maybe that's why I'm cooped up and they're running free. But I can tell you what intuitively appeals to me. First, the allocations don't tend to be as extreme as standard theory recommends. You don't need as many *ad hoc* bounds to generate an interior solution or weight the market consensus as highly. You just need to acknowledge the iceberg risks that most investors and fund managers have in the back of their minds anyway."

"I thought one of the features of iceberg risk is that people don't know exactly what it is. If the captain of the *Titanic* had even thought about icebergs he probably would have taken more precautions."

"I agree. You can never fully expect the unexpected. That limits how much you can forestall. Still, the very exercise of looking for possible disasters tends to expand your awareness. And by tweaking the probability forecasts within the model you can better appreciate what thresholds matter and how. That's the second great appeal of the model. It helps embed risk management into asset allocation, instead of imposing it as an afterthought."

"Can you give us an example?"

"Sure. I have to warn you: it's very stark and stylized. But it does spotlight iceberg risk. Moreover, it's simple enough to calculate without normal or log-normal approximation."

"Good. I'm all for simple."

"Imagine a risky asset has only two possible outcomes: the first outcome falls s standard deviations below the mean . . ."

"Hey, I remember that one. It's the distribution you used to show that an s-standard deviation tail can have probability $\dfrac{1}{s^2 + 1}$. The second outcome falls $1/s$ standard deviations above the mean."

"Exactly. Now suppose an investor's portfolio consists of this asset and risk-free T-bills. Her only choice is what fraction to hold in each. How according to standard theory should s affect her choice?"

"It shouldn't. The mean, the standard deviation, and Regretta's risk aversion will decide everything. Tail risk *per se* won't matter."

"Right. And that's not very intuitively appealing, is it?"

"We've gone over that already. Nearly everyone feels that tail risk matters. Sometimes it matters a lot."

"Then you'll like what the partition functions have to say. I worked through some examples with an excess mean return of 5%, a standard deviation of 10%, and a CRR of 3. When $s = 1$, so that the tails are short and symmetric, the recommended portfolio weight on the risky asset is nearly 2, meaning that you should borrow to double up. At $s = 3$ – that is, a 10% chance of a 25% loss with an 8.3% gain otherwise – you don't lever at all. At $s = 10$, that is a 1% chance of losing 95% and 99% chance of gaining 6%, you shouldn't put more than half of your portfolio at risk."

"Double up or cut in half: that's a huge variation. But we all know that two portfolios can look quite different and still yield comparable risk-adjusted returns. How much difference does strategy choice make here?"

"Well, we know it makes a huge difference to apply advice founded on limited downside to the case of $s = 10$. If you lever up a bet that already risks you losing nearly everything, then your expected utility will be minus infinity."

"In theory, yes. In real life bankruptcy considerations would kick in so that's not such a clean example."

"Fair enough. But even when $s = 2$, wrongly assuming $s = 1$ can cut your risk-adjusted return nearly in half. And if $s = 4$, the error can cost you over 15 percentage points in risk-adjusted return and the gap widens exponentially as s increases. Here's a chart I prepared to illustrate."

Conway admired the chart. "Superb. Even your bozos will be impressed. But if I may offer a friendly editing suggestion, why not say 'standard advice' instead of 'advice using $s = 1$'? It's shorter and clearer."

"It's shorter but not clearer. Standard advice assumes normality, which we know is technically incompatible with CRR utility. I could convert normality to a

Costs of ignoring tail risk for $\mu = 5\%$, $\sigma = 10\%$, CRR $= 3$

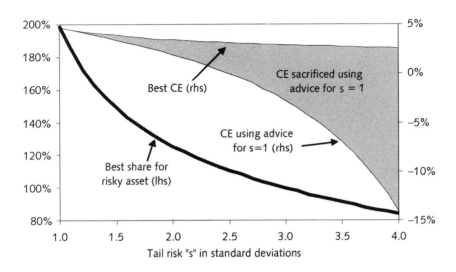

Tail risk "s" in standard deviations

lognormal approximation but that's not standard either, and there's more than one way to do the conversion."

Regretta was intrigued. "Multiple conversion techniques? What do you mean? Don't you just want to match the means and variances?"

"Depends what you mean by match. Suppose I apply the approximation favored in options theory, where the log and percentage returns have identical variances and means that differ by half the variance. Suppose I also apply the approximation of my recipe, which treats log returns just like percentages when it comes to calculating portfolio means and variances. The optimal portfolio share for the risky asset then works out to 225%, which exceeds the 199% recommended for $s = 1$ and will sacrifice even more risk-adjusted return. However, for more accuracy, you might want to drop either approximation or both."

"What difference does it make?"

"If you drop the first approximation but not the second, the optimal share is 245%. If you drop the second approximation but not the first, it's 167%. If you drop both approximations, the answer is 211%. In any case the recommended advice leaves you way over-exposed to iceberg risk for any s over 2.5."

"That's still a big divergence in the recommendations. What do you think causes it?"

"Two things. To begin with, you're approximating risk-adjusted returns rather than the optimal portfolio mix. A second-order change in the returns means a first-order change in their slope, and a first-order change in their slope can easily mean a first-order change in the location of the maximum. On top of that, the top risk-adjusted returns tend to be characterized less by sharp peaks than by ridges, so that two substantially different portfolio mixes may both yield nearly optimal results for a given problem."

"But I take it some near-solutions may be much less robust to misspecification than others."

"Exactly. The near-solution for normality with a 245% risky asset share is much more vulnerable to icebergs than the near-solution with a 167% share. Lack of robustness is one of the main weaknesses of standard mean-variance optimization."

"But you can't prevent misspecification even in your model. 'Garbage in, garbage out' is a fundamental law. You can't repeal it."

"No, I can't. But my model does serve to amplify even modest warnings of risk. For example, suppose you're certain that one of the two-point distributions we've been looking at applies and that s equals either 1 or 4, but you're completely uncertain which. A naïve approach would average the best portfolio for $s = 1$ with the best portfolio for $s = 4$, yielding a risky asset share of 142%. But my approach would tell you to model your uncertainty as two different, equally likely regimes, one in which $s = 1$ and one in which $s = 4$. What do you think it will advise?"

"Less than 142%, I presume."

"A lot less. Expected utility is maximized when the share is just 101%, as if you were certain s were 2.9. Your risk-adjusted return will be 299 basis points, nearly half again as high as the naïve approach would yield."

Regretta nodded in approval. "Neat. Really neat. I think you've won a convert."

"Make that two," said Conway. "How about building me a portfolio optimizer that implements your recipe? I have a budget for consultants I can pay you out of."

"Not so fast. I have to improve the recipe first."

You just hate being agreed with, don't you? "I thought you were happy with the recipe."

"Not happy enough. Those approximations to portfolio moments bother me. I'm worried they're too crude."

"Is that all? Don't make better the enemy of good."

"It's not always good. For example, for a CRR of less than one my recipe goes berserk and tells you to opt for unbounded risk."

"Aahhh, so that's why you restricted it. But according to you and Regretta it's not a very important case anyway."

"It's important that my recipe fails without my knowing why."

Such a perfectionist. "Look, Devlin, why not build the simple version first and tweak it later?"

"Build the simple version yourself if you want. Maybe Regretta will help you. I'd rather think more about the problem."

"Now that's a good idea. How about it, Regretta?"

Regretta glanced at Devlin before replying to Conway. "Well, I wouldn't want to undercut Devlin ..."

"I don't mind," said Devlin. "Really."

"OK, then, I'll do it. But can I ask you one question, Conway?"

"Sure, go ahead."

"How much are you willing to pay?" ...

While Conway and Regretta negotiate terms, let's review Devlin's calculations and try to understand his concerns.

AN APPROXIMATE CERTAINTY EQUIVALENT

While the formula synthesizing the conditional certainty equivalents into the aggregate is straightforward, it doesn't provide much intuition for their interaction. Here's one way to gain some insight. First, using fourth-order Taylor series expansions for the various $\exp\big((1-c)\widetilde{CE}_i\big)$, estimate the partition function as:

$$|EU| \cong 1 + (1-c)E[\widetilde{CE}_i] + \frac{(1-c)^2}{2}E[\widetilde{CE}_i^2] + \frac{(1-c)^3}{6}E[\widetilde{CE}_i^3]$$
$$+ \frac{(1-c)^4}{24}E[\widetilde{CE}_i^4]$$

which we can express by the shorthand $1 + Q$. Next, use a fourth-order Taylor series expansion $\ln(1+Q) \cong Q - \frac{Q^2}{2} + \frac{Q^3}{3} - \frac{Q^4}{4}$ to approximate $\frac{1}{1-c}\ln(|EU|)$. Ignoring terms of fifth order and higher, some tedious algebra yields:

$$\widetilde{CE} \cong Mean - \frac{c-1}{2}Var + \frac{(c-1)^2}{6}Var^{3/2}Skew - \frac{(c-1)^3}{24}Var^2Kurt$$

where *Mean*, *Var*, *Skew*, and *Kurt* denote respectively the mean, variance, skewness, and kurtosis of the $\widetilde{CE}_i$.

Negative skewness (a leftward slant in the distribution) penalizes the aggregate $\widetilde{CE}$ over and above variance, as does positive kurtosis (fat tails). Disaster risk – a small chance of a huge loss – nearly always subtracts from the skewness and adds to the kurtosis. Hence it reduces risk-adjusted returns more than mean-variance analysis suggests. The more risk averse the investor is, the more the higher-order moments matter.

OPTIMIZATION GIVEN A SINGLE REGIME

With only a single regime, maximizing expected utility amounts to maximizing a single $\widetilde{CE}$ expression. For a perfectly lognormal asset, as we recall, this would equal the mean log return less $\frac{1}{2}(c-1)$ times the variance of log returns. For a portfolio of lognormal assets, Devlin's recipe approximates $\widetilde{CE}$ as $\omega'\tilde{M} - \frac{1}{2}(c-1)\omega'\tilde{\Sigma}\omega$. Maximizing with respect to ω yields optimal risky shares ω^* of $\frac{1}{c-1}\tilde{\Sigma}^{-1}\tilde{M}$.

The second derivative matrix, or Hessian, of $\widetilde{CE}$ is just $(1-c)\tilde{\Sigma}$, which is negative or positive definite depending on the sign of $c-1$. Therefore, ω^* does indeed maximize risk-adjusted returns in the typical case $c > 1$. However, when $c < 1$, ω^* yields a minimum rather than a maximum, and investors are advised to seek unbounded risks. We'll be looking for ways to patch that.

RELATION TO STANDARD SHARPE RATIO MAXIMIZATION

Recall that multiples of $\Sigma^{-1}M$ maximize the Sharpe ratio. So Devlin's model appears to incorporate standard Sharpe ratio maximization as a special case. Unfortunately, along the way we shifted the definition of means and covariances to apply to log returns instead of percentage returns. That makes the correspondence only approximate.

Some of the discrepancy reflects errors in Devlin's method. For example, while his method treats log portfolio returns as linear in the portfolio weights, a second-order Taylor's expansion reveals a quadratic element as well:

$$E\left[\ln(1 + w'X)\right] \cong E\left[w'X\right] - \tfrac{1}{2}E\left[(w'X)^2\right] = w'M - \tfrac{1}{2}w'MM'w - \tfrac{1}{2}w'\Sigma w$$

If we substitute this quadratic form for $w'M$ in Devlin's approximation to $\widetilde{CE}$ while assuming that $\tilde{\Sigma} \cong \Sigma$, the optimal mix is revised to

$$w^* \cong (c\Sigma + MM')^{-1}M = \frac{1}{c + M'\Sigma^{-1}M}\Sigma^{-1}M$$

$$= \frac{1}{c + S^{*2}}\Sigma^{-1}M = \frac{1}{c + S^2}\Sigma^{-1}M$$

where S^* denotes the maximal Sharpe ratio and S the actual Sharpe ratio. The first equality can be verified by pre-multiplying both sides by $c\Sigma + MM'$. The second equality follows from the equation for the maximum Sharpe ratio, while the last equality follows from w^* maximizing the Sharpe ratio.

In short, the revised optimal mix maximizes the Sharpe ratio without unbounded risk, even for $c < 1$. That's an important step toward reconciling different measures. Bear in mind, however, that the revision applies a second-order approximation only to the portfolio mean and not the variance.

LOGNORMAL APPROXIMATIONS VIA MOMENT-MATCHING

One way to fit a lognormal approximation to returns is to match the first two moments. Recalling the formulas for lognormal moments from the previous chapter, we must choose $\tilde{\mu}$ and $\tilde{\sigma}^2$ to satisfy:

$$\exp(\tilde{\mu} + \tfrac{1}{2}\tilde{\sigma}^2) - 1 = \mu \quad ; \quad \exp(2\tilde{\mu} + \tilde{\sigma}^2)\left(\exp(\tilde{\sigma}^2) - 1\right) = \sigma^2$$

where m and v denote the target percentage mean and variance. This has solution:

$$\tilde{\sigma}^2 = \ln\left(1 + \frac{\sigma^2}{(1 + \mu)^2}\right) \cong \frac{\sigma^2}{(1 + \mu)^2}$$

$$\tilde{\mu} = \ln(1 + \mu) - \tfrac{1}{2}\tilde{\sigma}^2 \cong \mu - \tfrac{1}{2}(\mu^2 + \sigma^2)$$

The same relation applies between portfolio statistics m, v, $\tilde{m}$ and $\tilde{v}$. We can thus relate the Sharpe ratio $\tilde{S} \equiv \tilde{m}/\sqrt{\tilde{v}}$ based on log returns to the standard Sharpe ratio $S \equiv m/\sqrt{v}$ as:

$$\tilde{S} \cong \frac{m - \frac{1}{2}(m^2 + v)}{\sqrt{v}/(1 + \mu)} \cong (1 + m)(S - \frac{1}{2}mS - \frac{1}{2}\sqrt{v})$$

$$\cong S + \frac{1}{2}mS - \frac{1}{2}\sqrt{v} = S + \frac{1}{2}\sqrt{v}(S^2 - 1)$$

Hence, the two Sharpe ratios give nearly the same readings around the value of one. Above one the log-based Sharpe rewards more for variance than the standard Sharpe. Below one it penalizes more for variance.

A FEW EXAMPLES

To illustrate the impact of the various approximations mentioned above, let us consider Devlin's example in which the risky asset has mean $\mu = 5\%$ and standard deviation $\sigma = 10\%$, for a Sharpe of exactly 0.5. For a lognormal density to match that mean and standard deviation, it must set $\{\tilde{\mu} = 4.428\%, \tilde{\sigma} = 9.502\%\}$ for a log-based Sharpe of 0.466. In comparison, the standard lognormal approximation used in finance would set $\{\tilde{\mu} = 4.5\%, \tilde{\sigma} = 10\%\}$ for a log-based Sharpe of 0.450. The approximations $\sigma(1 - \mu)$ and $\mu - \frac{1}{2}(\mu^2 + \sigma^2)$ given above are much sounder: they set $\{\tilde{\mu} = 4.424\%, \tilde{\sigma} = 9.500\%\}$ for a log-based Sharpe of 0.466.

Now let's consider a portfolio that doubles up on the risky asset. Applying the approximations in Devlin's recipe to fit a lognormal density to the portfolio, we will calculate $\{\tilde{m} = 9\%, \tilde{v} = 20\%\}$ using the standard benchmark estimate versus $\{\tilde{m} = 8.855\%, \tilde{v} = 19.005\%\}$ using the better benchmarks. However, an even better procedure would be to apply the conversion formulas directly to the doubled-up portfolio, that is, to $m = 10\%$ and $v = 20\%$. This generates $\{\tilde{m} = 7.905\%, \tilde{v} = 18.039\%\}$ for a log-based Sharpe of 0.438.

Devlin's approximation fares better when the risky asset is diluted. For example, if the risky asset comprises only half the portfolio, Devlin's recipe would set $\{\tilde{m} = 2.214\%, \tilde{v} = 4.750\%\}$ using the best lognormal approximation, whereas a more direct calculation on the portfolio would set $\{\tilde{m} = 2.350\%, \tilde{v} = 4.875\%\}$. Still, the discrepancies remain a bit too large for comfort and help explain Devlin's dissatisfaction.

OPTIMIZATION WITH MULTIPLE REGIMES

With multiple possible regimes, the first-order conditions for optimizing Devlin's approximate formula $\widetilde{EU}$ for expected utility become:

$$\frac{d\widetilde{EU}}{d\omega} = \sum_k p_k EU_k \big((1-c)\tilde{M}_k - (1-c)^2\tilde{\Sigma}_k\omega\big) = 0$$

This implies

$$(c-1)\omega^* = \left(\sum_k p_k EU_k \Sigma_k\right)^{-1} \sum_k p_k EU_k M_k$$

for the optimal portfolio ω^*. The Hessian is $(c-1)^2 p_k EU_k \tilde{\Sigma}_k$, and since the EU_k all carry the sign of $1-c$, this will be negative semi-definite and thereby guarantee that ω^* maximizes $\widetilde{EU}$ if $c > 1$. If $c < 1$, Devlin's method will fail as miserably as it does in the single-regime case: ω^* will minimize $\widetilde{EU}$ and investors will be advised to take unbounded risks.

DEPENDENCE OF OPTIMAL MIX ON RISK AVERSION

In classic finance theory, the optimal mix is proportional to the inverse of a covariance matrix times a vector of means, while risk aversion has no impact apart from leverage. At first glance, the formula above for ω^* preserves the same properties. On closer examination, risk aversion enters the expressions for EU_i in a way that's impossible to disentangle. There is no general closed-form solution and the risky bundle's composition varies with investor risk aversion. Optimization has to be done iteratively to readjust utility weights.

A SHARPE RATIO INTERPRETATION OF THE OPTIMAL MIX

There is a sense however in which a kind of Sharpe ratio maximization still applies. Form a new vector λ with elements $\lambda_k = \dfrac{p_k EU_k}{\sum\limits_k p_k EU_k}$. Since the λ_k sum to one, they can be interpreted as defining risk-adjusted probabilities for the various regimes. Provided $c > 1$, a "disaster regime" in which expected utility is highly negative will carry more weight than its simple probability of occurrence suggests. The more investors dislike risk, the more they will weight the worst regime relative to the best regime.

Next form a weighted average excess returns vector $\bar{M} \equiv \sum_k \lambda_k \tilde{M}_k$ and an adjusted covariance matrix $\bar{\Sigma} \equiv \sum_k \lambda_k \tilde{\Sigma}_k$ using the λ_k as weights. In economic terms $\bar{M}$ and $\bar{\Sigma}$ represent risk-adjusted means and risk-adjusted covariances respectively. The optimal portfolio then takes a very simple form:

$$\omega^* = \frac{1}{c-1} \bar{\Sigma}^{-1} \bar{M}$$

with an implied risk-free share of $1 - \omega^{*\prime}\mathbf{1}$. The optimal portfolio maximizes a risk-adjusted Sharpe ratio, with the same multiplier as in the single-regime case.

INCORPORATING NORMALLY DISTRIBUTED UNCERTAINTY

Suppose you are confident that log returns are multivariate normal, with true covariance matrix $\tilde{\Sigma}$, and that while you are uncertain about the mean log return, your beliefs about the mean can be described as multivariate normally distributed with mean $\tilde{M}$ and covariance matrix $\tilde{\Xi}$. Operationally, this is identical to saying that your beliefs about log returns are multivariate normal with mean $\tilde{M}$ and covariance matrix $\tilde{\Sigma} + \tilde{\Xi}$.

One way to verify this result is to model expected utility in two steps. First calculate expected utility conditional on mean $\tilde{X}$ and port-folio share ω as $\exp\big((1-c)\big(\omega'\tilde{X} - \frac{1}{2}(1-c)\omega'\tilde{\Sigma}\omega\big)\big)$. Then integrate the latter over your beliefs about $\tilde{X}$:

$$EU = \int_{\Re^n} \exp\big((1-c)\big(\omega'\tilde{X} - \tfrac{1}{2}(1-c)\omega'\tilde{\Sigma}\omega\big)\big) \cdot (2^n \pi^n \tilde{\Xi})^{1/2}$$

$$\cdot \exp\big(-\tfrac{1}{2}(\tilde{X} - \tilde{M})'\tilde{\Xi}^{-1}(\tilde{X} - \tilde{M})\big)d\tilde{X}$$

$$= \exp\big(-\tfrac{1}{2}(1-c)^2\omega'\tilde{\Sigma}\omega\big) \cdot M_n\big((1-c)\omega\big)$$

$$= \exp\big(-\tfrac{1}{2}(1-c)^2\omega'\tilde{\Sigma}\omega\big) \cdot \exp\big((1-c)\omega'\tilde{M} - \tfrac{1}{2}(1-c)^2\omega'\tilde{\Xi}\omega\big)$$

$$= \exp\big((1-c)\big(\omega'M - \tfrac{1}{2}(1-c)\omega'(\tilde{\Xi} + \tilde{\Sigma})\omega\big)\big)$$

This is just the expected utility given a portfolio ω of risky assets having mean M and covariance matrix $\tilde{\Sigma} + \tilde{\Xi}$.

MOMENT-GENERATING FUNCTION FOR MULTIVARIATE NORMAL DENSITY

In the calculations above, $\Re^n$ denotes the n-dimensional space of real numbers, while $\mathcal{M}_n$ is a moment-generating function for an n-variate normal distribution. Let us verify that $\mathcal{M}_n(\omega)$ is indeed $\exp(\omega'\tilde{M} - \frac{1}{2}\omega'\tilde{\Xi}\omega)$. One method is to rearrange the exponents in the integral:

$$\mathcal{M}_n(\omega) = \int_{\Re^n} \exp(\omega'\tilde{X})(2^n\pi^n\tilde{\Xi})^{-1/2}\exp\left(-\tfrac{1}{2}(\tilde{X} - \tilde{M})'\tilde{\Xi}^{-1}(\tilde{X} - \tilde{M})\right)d\tilde{X}$$

$$= \exp\left(\omega'\tilde{M} - \tfrac{1}{2}\omega'\tilde{\Xi}\omega\right)$$

$$\cdot \int_{\Re^n} (2^n\pi^n\tilde{\Xi})^{-1/2}\exp\left(-\tfrac{1}{2}(\tilde{X} - \tilde{M} - \tilde{\Xi}\omega)'\tilde{\Xi}^{-1}(\tilde{X} - \tilde{M} - \tilde{\Xi}\omega)\right)d\tilde{X}$$

$$= \exp(\omega'\tilde{M} - \tfrac{1}{2}\omega'\tilde{\Xi}\omega)$$

The last step follows from the need for probability densities to integrate to one. An even simpler method notes that the integral in question equals the characteristic function value $\mathcal{M}(1)$ for a univariate normal random variable having mean $\omega'\tilde{M}$ and variance $\omega'\tilde{\Xi}\omega$.

MOMENTS OF MULTIVARIATE LOGNORMAL VARIABLES

The preceding formula makes it easy to calculate the mean and covariance matrix of multivariate lognormal variables. To calculate the mean μ_i of $x_i = \exp(\tilde{x}_i) - 1$, set $\omega_i = 1$ and zero out all other components of ω. This verifies that $\mu_i = \exp(\tilde{\mu}_i + \frac{1}{2}\tilde{\sigma}_{ii}) - 1$.

To calculate the expectation of $(1 + x_i)(1 + x_j)$ set $\omega_i = \omega_j = 1$ and keep the rest zero. Subtract off $(1 + \mu_i)(1 + \mu_j)$ to form the covariance:

$$\sigma_{ij} = \exp\left(\tilde{\mu}_i + \tilde{\mu}_j + \tfrac{1}{2}(\tilde{\sigma}_{ii} + 2\tilde{\sigma}_{ij} + \tilde{\sigma}_{jj})\right) - \exp(\tilde{\mu}_i + \tfrac{1}{2}\tilde{\sigma}_{ii})\exp(\tilde{\mu}_j + \tfrac{1}{2}\tilde{\sigma}_{jj})$$

$$= \exp(\tilde{\mu}_i + \tfrac{1}{2}\tilde{\sigma}_{ii})\exp(\tilde{\mu}_j + \tfrac{1}{2}\tilde{\sigma}_{jj})\left(\exp(\tilde{\sigma}_{ij}) - 1\right)$$

$$= (1 + \mu_i)(1 + \mu_j)\left(\exp(\tilde{\sigma}_{ij}) - 1\right)$$

When $i = j$ this reduces to the formula, derived in Chapter 17 (pages 271–2), for the variance of a univariate lognormal variable.

19 | Higher-Order High Jinks

I am not fat, thought Regretta the next morning as she looked at herself in the mirror. She turned sideways to take a better look. *No, definitely not fat.* Just to be sure she skipped breakfast and did a double workout. Afterwards, exhausted and hungry, she ate a chocolate bar and berated herself for letting Devlin get to her.

Realizing she had overreacted, Regretta settled down. She had to admit that she enjoyed Conway's and Devlin's company. *Strange. Who would have imagined that? Devlin used to be such a jerk.*

Suddenly the realization hit Regretta. Devlin must have a crush on her. That's why he had stopped calling her Misery Girl and apologized so quickly about the capybara joke. *Poor Devlin. He must be lonely. But no good can come out of him getting false hopes. I'll have to put a stop to that.*

Monday morning in group therapy Regretta glanced over her shoulder several times to check whether Devlin was looking at her. A few times she caught his eye. He quickly turned away as if it were an accident, but Regretta knew better.

Sure enough, after the session Devlin came up to her. "Hi Regretta, do you have a few minutes? We need to talk."

"Yes, I think we do. Not here, though." She didn't want to embarrass him in front of others.

"Good idea. How about we take a walk in the park?"

Regretta agreed. Outside it was lovely, warm without being hot. They walked across the grounds into a stand of oak trees, sat down on a bench and watched the squirrels play.

Devlin cleared his throat. "Let me get straight to the point, Regretta. I think we need to take things to a higher level."

Regretta squirmed. "Sorry, Devlin, but I don't. I think things are fine just the way they are."

"They are definitely not fine. But we can make them fine. We can do it three ways."

Regretta was aghast. "Now look here, Buster. I don't know what goes on inside your squirrelly brain but I am not that kind of girl. Conway doesn't strike me as that kind of guy either."

Devlin screwed up his lips and nodded. "I think you may be right about Conway. But I'm sure you can handle it. Let's go through it together first and introduce him later."

"How dare you, Devlin? We hardly know each other."

"That's true. There's a lot of stuff you're not familiar with. But I can tell you're a quick learner."

You arrogant sonofa-! "What makes you so sure you have something to teach me?"

"Now don't get offended, Regretta. I've just had more time to work things out on my own."

"That must be fun."

"Most of the time, yes. But maybe others will help come up with some new twists."

"Why don't you and Conway start twisting on your own?"

Devlin shook his head. "Please Regretta. I know Conway. He's a great guy, but that's just not his forte. Maybe we should hide the really kinky stuff from him and just let him focus on results. What do you think?"

"I think you're gross. I don't want anything to do with the kinky stuff, either."

"Oh, Regretta, I am so disappointed in you. Can you not just go through it once? It helps me check that everything works."

"If you need a checkup, go see a doctor."

"You must be kidding, Regretta. What do these doctors know about our problems anyway? They'll just try to switch the conversation to something irrelevant, like my relationship with my mother."

"It may be more connected than you think."

"Ha, ha, ha. Very funny, Regretta. Let's just get down to business, shall we? I have something I want to show you." He reached down in his pocket.

"No, Devlin, definitely not!" She turned away.

"Relax. It's not going to bite you." Devlin pulled out a folded paper from his pocket and unfolded the following chart.

Common disaster risks, refined advice

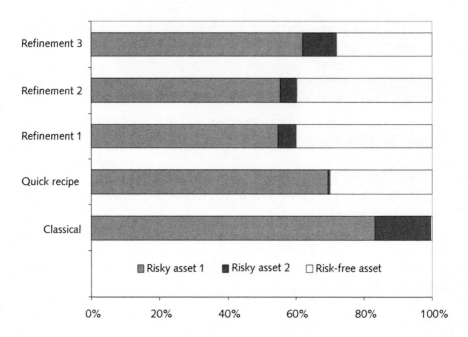

Regretta was stunned. "What the ...!" she exclaimed and then bit her tongue. She jumped up, purple-faced.

"Are you OK?"

Regretta was too ashamed to explain. *Quick, think of something.* "Ouch! I must have sat on a thorn." She brushed the back of her pants, pretending to search. "Ah, there it is." She flicked the imaginary thorn away and then slowly straightened out her clothes, keeping her head turned away from Devlin.

"Do you want to go inside?"

"No, I'm fine now." She sat down. "So tell me, what's this chart supposed to represent?"

"Remember Conway's two-regime scenario in which two assets have uncorrelated 5% and 3% returns respectively except in crisis when they both drop 30%? And the probability of crisis is 4.5%?"

"Oh yes. The first two bars must represent the portfolio mixes advised by classic mean-variance methods and your recipe. What are these refinements?"

"That's just what I was talking to you about. They represent three different ways to refine the estimates."

"Why not just pick one way?"

"Because I'm not sure which is best. They're all better than my original recipe, though, just as my recipe is better than ordinary mean-variance."

"How do you know that?"

"Because they all rest on higher-order Taylor series approximations to valuations in the various regimes."

"Which valuations? The mean and variance of log returns?"

"Partly. I mean, yes. That's what the third approach does. It assumes lognormality."

"And the other two?"

"They focus on percentage returns."

"If the other two focus on the same thing, then what's the difference between them?"

"The first approach takes a fourth-order approximation to conditional expected utility. The second approach takes a second-order approximation to conditional risk-adjusted returns."

"Shouldn't a fourth-order approximation be a lot better than a second-order approximation?"

"Not necessarily. The first approach focuses on outcomes close to the conditional mean of the distribution, while the second approach integrates over a full multivariate normal distribution."

"I thought percentage returns can't be fully multivariate normal."

"They can't. I told you I'm not sure which approximation is best. Fortunately, it rarely seems to make much difference."

"Why do you say that? In your chart, the third refinement gives a noticeably different mix from the others."

"I meant: not a big difference in utility terms. No matter which refinement you think is 'right', the others come close in expected utility terms. Actually my original recipe isn't bad either. But the ordinary mean/variance approach lags well behind, as it takes too much risk."

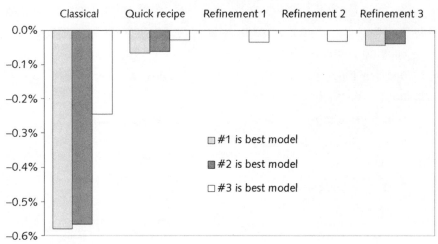

Regretta studied the chart. "Is this all the refinements add relative to the quick recipe?"

"In this example, yes. In general, no. The bigger the tails, the more useful the refinements are."

"So when are you going to show me the new recipes?"

Devlin smiled. "I was beginning to think you wouldn't ask. Here they are." He pulled another paper out of his pocket.

Recipe Refinements

Refinement #1: Let $m_k \equiv \omega' M_k$ denote the mean percentage return in regime k and $\hat{v}_k \equiv \omega' \Sigma_k \omega (1 + m_k)^{-2}$ the variance of the return relative to its gross mean. Calculate EU_k as:

$$sign(1-c) \cdot (1+m_k)^{1-c} \left(1 + \tfrac{1}{2}(c-1)c\hat{v}_k \right.$$
$$\left. + \tfrac{1}{8}(c-1)c(c+1)(c+2)\hat{v}_k \right)$$

Refinement #2: Using the same notation, calculate EU_k as:

$$sign(1-c) \cdot p_k(1+m_k)^{1-c}(1+(1-c)\hat{v}_k)^{-1/2} \exp\left(\tfrac{1}{2}\frac{(1-c)^2\hat{v}_k}{1+(1-c)\hat{v}_k}\right)$$

Refinement #3: Denote by $\tilde{A}_k \equiv \ln\left(1 + \omega'(\exp(\tilde{M}_k) - \mathbf{1})\right)$ the log portfolio return when log asset returns match their means, by $\tilde{B}_k = \mathrm{diag}(\omega)'\exp(\tilde{M}_k - \tilde{A}_k\mathbf{1})$ the portfolio weights adjusted for different relative expected log returns, and by $\Psi_k \equiv I + (c-1)\left(\mathrm{diag}(\tilde{B}_k) - \tilde{B}_k\tilde{B}_k'\right)\tilde{\Sigma}_k$ an adjustment for curvature. Calculate EU_k as:

$$sign(1-c) \cdot |\Psi_k|^{-1/2}\exp\left((1-c)\left(\tilde{A}_k + \tfrac{1}{2}(1-c)\tilde{B}_k'\Psi_k^{-1}\tilde{\Sigma}_k\tilde{B}_k\right)\right)$$

"Oh, my," said Regretta. "That's a lot to swallow."

Devlin nodded. "I agree. Fortunately, you don't need to understand them to use them. Just wire the calculations into a spreadsheet. But are you sure you don't want me to walk you through them once?"

"Well, if you insist ..."

While Devlin is explaining things to Regretta, let me try to do the same here.

A QUICK RECAPITULATION

Devlin's initial recipe approximated percentage portfolio returns $1 + \omega'X$ as $\exp(\omega'X)$, reasoning as follows:

$$1 + \omega'X = \exp\left(\ln(1 + \omega'X)\right) \cong \exp(\omega'X)$$

$$= \exp\left(\omega'(\exp(\tilde{X}) - \mathbf{1})\right) \cong \exp(\omega'\tilde{X})$$

This turned conditional expected utility into a moment-generating function with a simple closed-form expression. The conditional certainty equivalent was linear in both the mean log return and variance, with a penalty per unit variance of $\tfrac{1}{2}(c - 1)$.

This chapter offers three ways to further refine the approximation. All rely on higher-order Taylor series expansions. The first approach creates quartic approximations to conditional expected utilities. The other two approaches create quadratic approximations to the conditional certainty equivalents, with one approach focusing on percentage returns and the other on log returns.

A Few More Terms

I beg readers' indulgence to tolerate a few more terms. While I could get by without them, they will make the derivations below much easier to follow. The most useful is $\hat{\epsilon}$, which remeasures portfolio outcomes as a percentage deviation from their mean value. That is, given a portfolio mix ω, $\hat{\epsilon} \equiv \dfrac{\omega'X - m}{1 + m} = \dfrac{\omega'(X - M)}{1 + \omega'M}$. It is readily checked that $\hat{\epsilon}$ has mean 0 and variance $\dfrac{v}{(1 + m)^2}$, which I will denote by another shorthand $\hat{v}$. Recall from Chapter 18 (page 289) that $\hat{v}$ is close to $\tilde{v}$, the log variance parameter in a lognormal portfolio having log mean $\hat{m}$, percentage mean m, and percentage variance v.

Other new terms are $\tilde{A}$, $\tilde{B}$ and $\tilde{C}$. They represent, respectively, log returns, their first derivative or gradient, and their second matrix derivative or Hessian, evaluated at the mean log return $\tilde{M}$.

Refinement #1

Approximating CRR Utility Using Percentage Returns

The first refinement starts with a Taylor series expansion of percentage portfolio returns $\omega'Y$ around their conditional mean $m_k \equiv \omega'M_k$ in regime k:

$$(1 + \omega'X)^{1-c} = \sum_{j=0}^{\infty} \binom{1-c}{j} (1 + \omega'M_k)^{1-c-j}(\omega'X - \omega'M_k)^j$$

$$= (1 + \omega'M_k)^{1-c} \sum_{j=0}^{\infty} \binom{1-c}{j} \left(\frac{\omega'X - \omega'M_k}{1 + \omega'M_k}\right)^j$$

$$\equiv (1 + m_k)^{1-c} \sum_{j=0}^{\infty} \binom{1-c}{j} (\hat{\epsilon}_k)^j$$

where $\binom{n}{j} \equiv \dfrac{n(n-1)\cdots(n-j+1)}{j!}$ even when n is not a positive integer. Taking expectations over the various possible regimes establishes that:

$$EU = sign(1 - c) \cdot \sum_k p_k (1 + m_k)^{1-c} \sum_{j=0}^{\infty} \binom{1 - c}{j} E_k\left[(\hat{\epsilon}_k)^j\right]$$

CAVEAT ABOUT FEASIBILITY

The preceding summations need not necessarily converge, since EU may not be well-defined for the distribution in question. For example, none of the $\hat{\epsilon}_k$ can be fully normal, even conditionally, since CRR utility can't handle a loss of more than 100%. Let's carry out the Taylor expansion anyway and see what happens. Clearly, the odd moments of $\hat{\epsilon}_k$ will be zero due to symmetry. Each even $2j$th moment works out to $(\hat{v}_k)^j$ times all the positive integers less than $2j$: this can be checked by evaluating the central derivatives of the moment-generating function $\mathcal{M}(n) = \exp(\frac{1}{2}\hat{v}_k n^2)$. Expected utility then reduces to:

$$EU = sign(1 - c)$$

$$\cdot \sum_k p_k (1 + m_k)^{1-c} \sum_{j=0}^{\infty} \frac{(c-1)c \cdots (c+2j-3)(c+2j-2)}{2 \cdot 4 \cdots (2j-2) \cdot 2j} (\hat{v}_k)^j$$

Now look at the ratio of neighboring terms in this expansion. It equals $\dfrac{(c+2j-3)(c+2j-2)}{2j}\hat{v}_k$ or roughly $2j\hat{v}_k$. No matter how small this ratio starts out, it will eventually exceed one, making the summation infinite.

EXPECTED UTILITY OF QUASI-NORMAL PORTFOLIOS

I will call a portfolio quasi-normal if both its skewness and kurtosis are close to zero. In that case $E[\hat{\epsilon}^3] \cong 0$ and $E[\hat{\epsilon}^4] \cong 3\hat{v}^2$. Note that a portfolio can be quasi-normal even if its constituent assets are decidedly non-normal. Indeed, if a portfolio is composed of enough independent, roughly equally weighted assets, the Central Limit Theorem indicates it must be quasi-normal.

Now our model doesn't assume quasi-normality for the portfolio as a whole. Far from it. But we can try to carve up the world into conditionally quasi-normal regimes. Evaluating the Taylor expansion out to the fourth order then indicates that:

$$EU \cong sign(1 - c) \cdot \sum_k p_k (1 + m_k)^{1-c} \left(1 + \left(\frac{1-c}{2}\right) \hat{v}_k + \left(\frac{1-c}{4}\right) 3\hat{v}_k^2\right)$$

$$= sign(1 - c) \cdot \sum_i p_i (1 + m_k)^{1-c} (1 + \tfrac{1}{2}(c - 1)c\hat{v}_k$$

$$+ \tfrac{1}{8}(c - 1)c(c + 1)(c + 2)\hat{v}_k^2)$$

where again $m_k \equiv \omega' M_k$ and $\hat{v}_k \equiv \dfrac{\omega' \Sigma_k \omega}{(1 + \omega' M_k)^2}$.

SHARPE RATIO MAXIMIZATION AS SECOND-ORDER APPROXIMATION

Suppose that all the means and variances are tiny or that we're just too lazy to include any terms higher than second-order; indeed that we even use a second-order approximation to $(1 + m_k)^{1-c}$. Then the expression for EU will dramatically simplify, and we can simplify even further by expressing in terms of $EU^{\#} \equiv \dfrac{|EU| - 1}{1 - c}$, which implies exactly the same preferences:

$$EU^{\#} \cong \sum_k p_k (m_k - \tfrac{1}{2}cm_k^2) - \sum_k p_k (\tfrac{1}{2}c\hat{v}_k)$$

$$= m - \tfrac{1}{2}c(m^2 + Var[m_k] + E[\hat{v}_k])$$

$$= m - \tfrac{1}{2}c(m^2 + \sigma^2) \equiv \omega' M - \tfrac{1}{2}c\left((\omega' M)^2 + \omega' \Sigma \omega\right)$$

$$= \omega' M - \tfrac{1}{2}c\omega'(MM' + \Sigma)\omega$$

where the variables without subscripts are aggregate, unconditional means and variances. The expected utility approximation will be maximized at:

$$\omega^* = \frac{1}{c}(\Sigma + MM')^{-1} M = \frac{1}{c(1 + M'\Sigma^{-1}M)} \Sigma^{-1}M = \frac{1}{c(1 + s^2)} \Sigma^{-1}M$$

where S denotes the Sharpe ratio. This recalls an approximation derived in the previous chapter except for the multiplier of c on the MM' term. To verify the second equality, pre-multiply both sides by $\Sigma + MM'$. The solution, which is valid for all c, always achieves the maximum Sharpe ratio $(M'\Sigma^{-1}M)^{1/2}$, implying the last equality. The only difference from previous Sharpe-based solutions is that this formula recommends less leverage.

CONTRIBUTIONS OF HIGHER ORDERS

The more risk averse the investor is, the more important it is to include higher-order terms. For the plausible case $c = 3$, the fourth-order expression for expected utility reduces to:

$$EU_k \cong -\frac{1 + 3\hat{v}_k + 15\hat{v}_k^2}{(1 + m_k)^2}$$

The higher-order terms in this expression don't matter much for $|m|$ less than 10% or $\hat{v}$ less than 20%. For $\hat{v}$ above 35%, this expression probably isn't high-order enough, but such high downside risk makes quasi-normality suspect anyway.

INCENTIVES TO MITIGATE HIGH RISKS

For the general quasi-normal case, the risk-adjusted return for each regime works out to:

$$CE_k = |EU_k|^{1/(1-c)} - 1 \cong \mu_k + \left(1 + \tfrac{1}{2}(c-1)c\hat{v}_k\right.$$
$$\left. + \tfrac{1}{8}(c-1)c(c+1)(c+1)\hat{v}_k^2\right)^{1/(1-c)}$$
$$\cong m_k - \tfrac{1}{2}c\hat{v}_k - \tfrac{1}{8}c(3c+2)\hat{v}_k^2$$

where the last step follows from a Taylor expansion after dropping all terms in $\hat{v}_k^3$ and higher. The negative sign on $\hat{v}_k^2$ imposes an extra penalty on high variance over and above the standard mean/variance formulation. Moreover, because $\hat{v}_k^2$ itself measures variance relative to the conditionally expected return, variance in bad regimes gets penalized more than variance in good regimes.

REFINEMENT #2

A DIFFERENT APPROXIMATION TO CRR UTILITY

Refinement #2 returns more to Devlin's original recipe. It rewrites $(1 + \omega'X)^{1-c}$ as $\exp((1 - c) \cdot \ln(1 + \omega'X))$, approximates the logarithm with a more tractable expression, and then draws on moment-generating functions to evaluate the expectation. However, the second approach does not approximate $\ln(1 + \omega'X)$ as $\omega'X$. Instead, it takes a second-order Taylor series expansion around the mean:

$$\ln(1 + \omega'X) \cong \ln(1 + \omega'M) + \frac{\omega'X - \omega'M}{1 + \omega'M} - \frac{1}{2}\left(\frac{\omega'X - \omega'M}{1 + \omega'M}\right)^2$$

$$\equiv \ln(1 + m) + \hat{\epsilon} - \tfrac{1}{2}\hat{\epsilon}^2$$

EVALUATING EXPECTED UTILITY

To evaluate the expectation, the second approach assumes conditional normality of percentage returns $\omega'X$ rather than just conditional quasi-normality. It follows that:

$$EU_k \cong sign(1 - c) \cdot \int_{-\infty}^{\infty} \exp\left((1 - c)\left(\ln(1 + m_k) + \hat{\epsilon}_k - \tfrac{1}{2}\hat{\epsilon}_k^2\right)\right)$$

$$\cdot (2\pi\hat{v}_k)^{-1/2}\exp\left(-\frac{1}{2}\frac{\hat{\epsilon}_k^2}{\hat{v}_k}\right)d\hat{\epsilon}_k$$

$$= sign(1 - c) \cdot (1 + m_k)^{1-c} \cdot$$

$$\int_{-\infty}^{\infty} \exp\left((1 - c)\hat{\epsilon}_k\right) \cdot (2\pi v_k)^{-1/2} \exp\left(-\frac{1}{2}\frac{\hat{\epsilon}_k^2}{H}\right)d\hat{\epsilon}_k$$

$$= sign(1 - c) \cdot \frac{H^{1/2}}{v_k^{1/2}}(1 + m_k)^{1-c} \cdot$$

$$\int_{-\infty}^{\infty} \exp\left((1 - c)\hat{\epsilon}_k\right) \cdot (2\pi H)^{-1/2} \exp\left(-\frac{1}{2}\frac{\hat{\epsilon}_k^2}{H}\right)d\hat{\epsilon}_k$$

$$= sign(1 - c) \cdot \frac{H^{1/2}}{v_k^{1/2}}(1 + m_k)^{1-c}\exp\left(\tfrac{1}{2}(1 - c)^2 H\right)$$

The third line is just a rearrangement of terms, while the fourth evaluates a moment-generating function. The second step requires that $\frac{1}{H} = 1 - c + \frac{1}{\hat{v}_k}$ or $H = \frac{\hat{v}_k}{1 + (1 - c)\hat{v}_k}$. Hence:

$$EU \cong sign(1 - c)$$

$$\cdot \sum_k p_k(1 + m_k)^{1-c}(1 + (1 - c)\hat{v}_k)^{-1/2}\exp\left(\frac{1}{2}\frac{(1 - c)^2\hat{v}_k}{1 + (1 - c)\hat{v}_k}\right)$$

A Caveat

The integral is not well-defined if H is negative, as happens when $c > 1$ and $\hat{v}_k > \dfrac{1}{c-1}$. However, unless the investor is extremely risk averse, this limit falls well beyond the bounds where a normal approximation makes sense. For example, for $c = 3$ the standard deviation must exceed 70% of the conditional gross return, implying significant odds of losing more than all your wealth.

Risk-Adjusted Returns

In each regime, the log risk-adjusted return works out to:

$$\widetilde{CE}_k = \ln(1 + m_k) + \frac{1}{2}\frac{(1-c)\hat{v}_k}{1 + (1-c)\hat{v}_k} + \frac{1}{2}\frac{\ln(1 + (1-c)\hat{v}_k)}{c-1}$$

$$\cong \ln(1 + m_k) - \tfrac{1}{2}c\hat{v}_k - \tfrac{1}{4}(c-1)(2c-1)\hat{v}_k^2$$

These results look very familiar. If we approximate $\ln(1 + m_k)$ by $\tilde{m}_k + \frac{1}{2}\tilde{v}_k$ and $\hat{v}_k$ by $\tilde{v}_k$, and drop higher-order terms, we generate Devlin's $\tilde{m}_k + \frac{1}{2}(1-c)\tilde{v}_k$ recipe again. Moreover, both this formula and the CE formula from Refinement #1 include a term that's quadratic in both $\hat{v}_k$ and c. Indeed, when CE is converted into $\widetilde{CE} \equiv \ln(1 + CE)$ terms, it yields the same approximation as above.

Refinement #3

CRR Utility in Terms of Log Returns

Refinement #3 comes closest to Devlin's original recipe. Like Refinement #2, it rewrites $(1 + \omega'X)^{1-c}$ as $\exp\big((1-c) \cdot \ln(1 + \omega'X)\big)$ and takes a second-order Taylor approximation to the logarithm around its mean. However, it carries out the approximation in terms of log returns rather than percentage returns:

$$\ln(1 + \omega'X) \equiv \ln\big(1 + \omega'(\exp(\tilde{X}) - \mathbf{1})\big)$$

$$\cong \tilde{A} + \tilde{B}'(\tilde{X} - \tilde{M}) + \tfrac{1}{2}(\tilde{X} - \tilde{M})'\tilde{C}(\tilde{X} - \tilde{M})$$

CALCULATING $\tilde{A}$

To determine $\tilde{A}$, evaluate log portfolio returns at $\tilde{X} = \tilde{M}$:

$$\tilde{A} = \ln\left(1 + \omega'\left(\exp(\tilde{M}) - \mathbf{1}\right)\right) \neq \ln(1 + \omega'M) = \ln(1 + m)$$

In words, $\tilde{A}$ equals the log portfolio returns evaluated at the mean log return on assets, not at the mean percentage return.

CALCULATING $\tilde{B}$

To determine $\tilde{B}$, differentiate log portfolio returns with respect to log asset returns and then evaluate at $\tilde{X} = \tilde{M}$. Let's be careful and do this one element at a time:

$$\tilde{b}_i = \left. \frac{d}{d\tilde{x}_i} \ln\left(1 + \omega'\left(\exp(\tilde{X}) - \mathbf{1}\right)\right) \right|_{\tilde{X}=\tilde{M}} = \left. \frac{\omega_i \exp(\tilde{x}_i)}{1 + \omega'\left(\exp(\tilde{X}) - \mathbf{1}\right)} \right|_{\tilde{X}=\tilde{M}}$$

$$= \frac{\omega_i \exp(\tilde{\mu}_i)}{1 + \omega'\left(\exp(\tilde{M}) - \mathbf{1}\right)} = \omega_i \exp(\tilde{\mu}_i - \tilde{A})$$

where the subscript i refers to vector components rather than regimes. Hence, $\tilde{b}_i$ represents the asset's portfolio weight if all assets achieve their expected log return over the period. To express the aggregate result in matrix form, I make use of $\mathrm{diag}(\omega)$, the diagonal matrix of ω:

$$\tilde{B} = \mathrm{diag}(\omega)' \exp(\tilde{M} - \tilde{A}\mathbf{1})$$

CALCULATING $\tilde{C}$

To determine $\tilde{C}$, differentiate log portfolio returns twice with respect to log asset returns and then evaluate at $\tilde{X} = \tilde{M}$. Again let's do this an element at a time. Provided $j \neq i$,

$$\tilde{c}_{ij} = \left. \frac{d}{d\tilde{x}_j} \left(\frac{\omega_i \exp(\tilde{x}_i)}{1 + \omega'\left(\exp(\tilde{X}) - \mathbf{1}\right)} \right) \right|_{\tilde{X}=\tilde{M}} = \left. -\frac{\omega_i \exp(\tilde{x}_i) \cdot \omega_j \exp(\tilde{x}_j)}{\left(1 + \omega'\left(\exp(\tilde{X}) - \mathbf{1}\right)\right)^2} \right|_{\tilde{X}=\tilde{M}}$$

$$= -\frac{\omega_i \exp(\tilde{\mu}_i) \cdot \omega_j \exp(\tilde{\mu}_j)}{\left(1 + \omega'\left(\exp(\tilde{M}) - \mathbf{1}\right)\right)^2} = -\omega_i \exp(\tilde{\mu}_i - \tilde{A}) \cdot \omega_j \exp(\tilde{\mu}_j - \tilde{A})$$

In addition,

$$\tilde{c}_{ii} = \frac{d}{d\tilde{x}_i}\left(\frac{\omega_i \exp(\tilde{x}_i)}{1 + \omega'(\exp(\tilde{X}) - 1)}\right)\Bigg|_{\tilde{X}=\tilde{M}}$$

$$= \frac{\omega_i \exp(\tilde{x}_i)}{1 + \omega'(\exp(\tilde{X}) - 1)}\Bigg|_{\tilde{X}=\tilde{M}} - \frac{\omega_i \exp(\tilde{x}_i) \cdot \omega_j \exp(\tilde{x}_i)}{\left(1 + \omega'(\exp(\tilde{X}) - 1)\right)^2}\Bigg|_{\tilde{X}=\tilde{M}}$$

$$= \omega_i \exp(\tilde{\mu}_i - \tilde{A}) - \left(\omega_i \exp(\tilde{\mu}_i - \tilde{A})\right)^2$$

Reconstituting the matrix $\tilde{C}$, it becomes apparent that:

$$\tilde{C} = \mathrm{diag}(\tilde{B}) - \tilde{B}\tilde{B}'$$

$\tilde{C}$ adjusts the curvature to fine-tune the optimization. Basically it says that you should apply the adjusted weights $\tilde{b}_i$ not to the deviations $\tilde{x}_i - \tilde{\mu}_i$ alone but also to half of $\tilde{x}_i - \tilde{\mu}_i$ squared, and then subtract half of the square of the portfolio deviation as a whole.

EXPECTED UTILITY

Once we've done our $\tilde{A}\tilde{B}\tilde{C}$'s, the rest of the EU calculations are exact assuming lognormality. Denoting $\tilde{X} - \tilde{M}$ by the shorthand $\bar{X}$, and recalling that parallel lines around a matrix denote its determinant, calculate:

$$EU_k = sign(1 - c) \cdot \int_{-\infty}^{\infty} \exp\left((1 - c)\left(\tilde{A}_k + \tilde{B}_k'\bar{X} + \tfrac{1}{2}\bar{X}'\tilde{C}_k\bar{X}\right)\right)$$

$$\cdot \frac{1}{\sqrt{2^n \pi^n |\tilde{\Sigma}_k|}} \cdot \exp\left(-\tfrac{1}{2}\bar{X}'\tilde{\Sigma}_k^{-1}\bar{X}\right)d\bar{X}$$

$$= sign(1 - c) \cdot \frac{\exp\left((1 - c)\tilde{A}_k\right)}{\sqrt{|\tilde{\Sigma}_k|\,|\tilde{\Sigma}_k^{-1} + (c - 1)\tilde{C}_k|}}$$

$$\cdot \int_{-\infty}^{\infty} \frac{\exp\left((1 - c)\tilde{B}_k'\bar{X}\right)}{\sqrt{2^n \pi^n |\tilde{\Sigma}_k^{-1} + (c - 1)\tilde{C}_k|^{-1}}}$$

$$\cdot \exp\left(-\tfrac{1}{2}\bar{X}'(\tilde{\Sigma}_k^{-1} + (c - 1)\tilde{C}_k)\bar{X}\right)d\bar{X}$$

$$= sign(1 - c) \cdot \frac{\exp\big((1 - c)\tilde{A}_k\big)}{\sqrt{|I + (c - 1)\tilde{C}_k\tilde{\Sigma}_k|}}$$

$$\cdot \exp\big(\tfrac{1}{2}(1 - c)^2\tilde{B}_k{}'(\tilde{\Sigma}_k^{-1} + (c - 1)\tilde{C}_k)^{-1}\tilde{B}_k\big)$$

$$= sign(1 - c) \cdot |\Psi_k|^{-1/2}\exp\Big((1 - c)\big(\tilde{A}_k + \tfrac{1}{2}(1 - c)\tilde{B}_k{}'\Psi_k^{-1}\tilde{\Sigma}_k\tilde{B}_k\big)\Big)$$

for $\Psi_k \equiv I + (c - 1)\tilde{C}_k\tilde{\Sigma}_k$.

RISK-ADJUSTED RETURNS

The conditional log risk-adjusted returns work out to:

$$\widetilde{CE} = \tilde{A}_k + \tfrac{1}{2}(1 - c)\tilde{B}_k{}'\Psi_k^{-1}\tilde{\Sigma}_k\tilde{B}_k + \tfrac{1}{2}\frac{\ln|\Psi_k|}{c - 1}$$

Here $\tilde{A}_k$ serves as an average log return, $\tilde{B}_k$ as the adjusted portfolio weights (which unlike ω vary by regime), and Ψ_k adjusts for curvature. For a bit more insight we can rewrite Ψ_k^{-1} as a matrix series expansion:

$$\Psi_k^{-1} \equiv \big(I - (1 - c)\tilde{C}_k\tilde{\Sigma}_k\big)^{-1} = I + (1 - c)\tilde{C}_k\tilde{\Sigma}_k + \big((1 - c)\tilde{C}_k\tilde{\Sigma}_k\big)^2 + \cdots$$

This implies that the effective portfolio covariance, dropping the subscript k for convenience, equals:

$$\tilde{B}'\Psi^{-1}\tilde{\Sigma}\tilde{B} = \tilde{B}'\tilde{\Sigma}\tilde{B} + (1 - c)\tilde{B}'\tilde{C}\tilde{\Sigma}^2\tilde{B} + (1 - c)^2\tilde{B}'\tilde{C}^2\tilde{\Sigma}^3\tilde{B} + \cdots$$

The first term in the expansion is just the covariance of a portfolio with weight $\tilde{B}$ and covariances $\tilde{\Sigma}$, but I don't have much intuition for the other terms or for the $\ln|\Psi_k|$ adjustment above. Fortunately, we can use the recipe without totally understanding it.

SWITCHING BETWEEN LOGNORMALITY AND NORMALITY

To avoid $\tilde{C}$ calculations, switch from multivariate lognormal to multivariate normal specifications and apply refinements #1 or #2. To make the switch, apply the previously derived formulas:

$$\mu_i = \exp(\tilde{\mu}_i + \tfrac{1}{2}\tilde{\sigma}_{ii}) - 1$$

$$\sigma_{ij} = (1 + \mu_i)(1 + \mu_j)\big(\exp(\tilde{\sigma}_{ij}) - 1\big)$$

If for some reason you want to convert from normal to lognormal specifications, calculate:

$$\tilde{\sigma}_{ij} = \ln\left(1 + \frac{\sigma_{ij}}{(1 + \mu_i)(1 + \mu_j)}\right)$$
$$\tilde{\mu}_i = \ln(1 + \mu_i) - \tfrac{1}{2}\tilde{\sigma}_{ii}$$

20 | A Question of Rebalance

It took Devlin two hours to shepherd Regretta through the math. He was unusually clear, for Devlin anyway, and had broken down everything into bite-sized nuggets. Regretta for her part listened very carefully, chastened by her earlier misinterpretation. Occasionally she replicated some calculations herself just to make sure she understood.

"Well, what do you think?" asked Devlin when they had finished.

"I think it's very impressive."

"But will Conway think so?"

"I think he'll be impressed too."

"That's a relief. I was worried you two wouldn't like it."

"I didn't say we – I mean he – will like it. Being impressed and liking something are two different things."

"You think there are too many formulas, don't you?"

"Too many, and too messy. Practical finance types just don't get turned on by Taylor series." *Unlike you.*

Devlin avoided Regretta's gaze. "That's what I feared. But what can I do about it, apart from burying the calculations in spreadsheets?"

"Search for ways to simplify."

"I've done what I can."

"Are you sure? How about trying to reformulate the problem in different ways?"

"Like what?"

"I don't know. I'll try to think about it too."

"Thanks, Regretta."

"You're welcome. Now how about your taking a lady to lunch?"

"Is it time for lunch already?" Devlin looked at his watch. "Gee whiz.

Lunch is almost over. I better run or I'll miss it. See you later, Regretta." He ran off, leaving a bewildered Regretta behind.

That night, Devlin slept fitfully. He dreamt he was at one of the church socials his mother would take him to as a child. All the ladies of the church joined in to prepare a feast. Devlin went up with a plate to be served. But the woman wouldn't serve him. It was Regretta, and she was whispering something to his mother. His mother shook her head. "Sometimes I just don't understand that boy," she said. "Aren't you hungry, son?"

When Devlin awoke, the first thing he thought was that he should have asked Regretta to lunch. Too bad she confused him yesterday by mentioning church ladies. Very odd. None of the church ladies he knew could hold a candle to Regretta. She was prettier than the rest of them put together and twice as fiery. Too bad all Regretta and he had in common was math.

Or was it? Devlin had never really tried talking with Regretta about anything else. Math and finance theory. If that's all she saw in him, whose fault was that? He better take some initiative.

It took Devlin the better part of a day to figure out what he should say and how. He spent most of the next day summoning up the courage to say it. He just couldn't bear the thought of rejection.

Thursday they met again at group therapy. Afterwards Devlin asked if she had time to get together again and to his relief she said yes. As they walked back to the oaks they had sat in before, Devlin cleared his throat and began to speak. "Listen, Regretta, I'm sorry about not asking you to lunch on Monday. I didn't think . . ."

"That I'm a lady?" Regretta cut in.

"No. I mean, yes, you're a great lady. Just not a church lady. I got confused."

You and me both. "That's OK, Devlin. I think you just get too caught up sometimes in one way of thinking."

"Yes, you're probably right. All that time focused on complicated Taylor series expansions. I should have aimed for a better balance."

"You see that now, do you? I'm impressed, Devlin. What made you realize that was the problem?"

"Nothing in particular. I just started to put things in perspective, and realized that the best way forward is to make amends."

"And keep making amends."

Devlin nodded sadly. "You're right. I guess I'll never stay completely on track. But what I wanted to ..."

"No one stays completely on track, Devlin. Rebalancing is a continual struggle. It's hard to figure out how much is enough, how much is too much. I ran a little spreadsheet for insight."

"Spreadsheet? On what? On the chances of ..."

"On some simple rebalancing problems. Here, let me show you." Regretta pulled a chart out of her bag and handed it to Devlin. "Suppose your target weight is 5% while the asset falls 80%. Without rebalancing, the portfolio loss is 4%. If you rebalance once in the middle – by which I mean halfway down in log terms rather than a 40% loss – the total loss is 5.45%. With sufficiently frequent rebalancing the portfolio loss exceeds 7.7%."

Rebalancing with one risky asset for $\omega = 5\%$ and $x = 80\%$

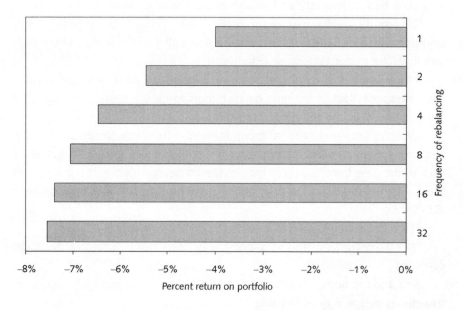

Despite the other things on his mind, Devlin was hooked. "What's your point?"

"My point is that continual costless rebalancing makes the log of portfolio returns linear in both the log returns and the target portfolio weights. That simplifies your recipes a lot. The conditional log risk-adjusted return simplifies to the log portfolio return less $\frac{1}{2}c$ times its variance. And that's exact rather than an approximation. That's amazing, isn't it?"

"It sure is."

"I tell you, I was really looking forward to explaining it to you. I didn't realize that you had figured it out on your own."

"Well, I . . ."

"Then again, maybe there are a few things I figured out that you haven't. For example, I thought I ran into a paradox when I let the reset period vary."

"Reset period?"

"I mean the time interval of observation. To keep things tractable I allow the regimes and portfolio targets to change only at specified resets."

"And what was the paradox?"

"That everything collapsed to a single-regime case as the reset shrank to zero even though you're allowing the maximum switching of regimes. But now it all makes sense."

"Why?"

"Aha! So I did figure out something you didn't. You see, when regime-switching gets sufficiently frequent, a kind of law of large numbers effect kicks in. Assets start behaving as if they spent all their time in an average composite regime. To make quick resets interesting I had to introduce Poisson jumps, where there's a constant instantaneous probability of decay. That yielded another neat recipe, which is generally quite easy to calculate. In fact, as long as the Poisson risks aren't too severe, the optimal mix looks like the solution to a Sharpe ratio maximization problem. Here, let me show them to you." Regretta pulled another sheet out of her bag:

SIMPLIFIED RECIPES

1. With lognormal returns and continual, costless rebalancing, conditional log risk-adjusted returns $\widetilde{CE}_k$ equal

$$\omega'\ln(\mathbf{1} + \mathrm{M}_k) - \tfrac{1}{2}c\omega'\tilde{\Sigma}_k\omega$$

   or equivalently

$$\omega'\tilde{\mathrm{M}}_k + \tfrac{1}{2}\omega'[\tilde{\sigma}_{11k}\ldots\tilde{\sigma}_{nnk}]' - \tfrac{1}{2}c\omega'\tilde{\Sigma}_k\omega$$

2. If resets are frequent, then the aggregate $\widetilde{CE}$ approaches

$$\omega\tilde{\mathrm{M}} + \tfrac{1}{2}\omega'[\tilde{\sigma}_{11}\ldots\tilde{\sigma}_{nn}]' - \tfrac{1}{2}c\omega'\tilde{\Sigma}\omega$$

   where $\tilde{\mathrm{M}} = \sum_k p_k\tilde{\mathrm{M}}_k$ and $\tilde{\Sigma} = \sum_k p_k\tilde{\Sigma}_k$

3. If the base regime 0 is lognormal Brownian and Poisson vector losses of $100L\%$ occur with frequency ℓ, $\widetilde{CE}$ equals

$$\omega'M_0 - \tfrac{1}{2}c\omega'\tilde{\Sigma}_o\omega + \ell\frac{(1 - \omega'L)^{1-c} - 1}{1 - c}$$

4. If Poisson risks are moderate, the optimal portfolio mix ω^* can be estimated as

$$\frac{1}{c}(\tilde{\Sigma} + \ell LL')^{-1}(M_0 - \ell L)$$

Devlin looked over the recipes. "That's neat. But in the last recipe, how do we know whether Poisson risks are moderate?"

"It depends on the risk of a jump, the square of the risk aversion, and the cube of the percent of the fund at risk. The sensitivity is a good reason for trimming concentration risks and betas in your portfolio."

"I have a sense that most fund managers strive for that, over and above what standard portfolio theory suggests."

"Yes, I think so too. Our approach – I mean your approach – seems to accord better with practical intuition. But it allows a more quantitative assessment. Here, for example, are some indications of how much log risk-adjusted

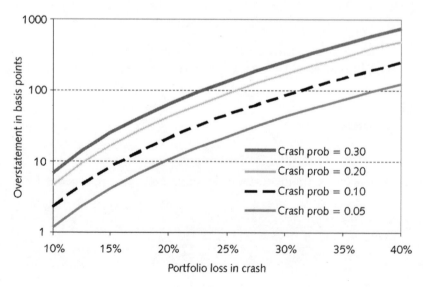

Overstatement of $\widetilde{CE}$ by second-order Poisson approximation

returns get distorted when we ignore third- and higher-order effects in Poisson jumps, assuming a CRR of 3.

"It's our approach now. But this time you need to explain it more to me. How about your taking a fellow to lunch?"

"What fellow?" asked Regretta, and then smiled. "Yes, please. I'd be delighted."

Now it's Devlin's turn to catch up on the math. It serves him right for foisting all those messy calculations on everyone. I'll try to keep this section a bit simpler than the last.

SUBDIVIDING LOGNORMAL RETURNS

Recall that log returns, unlike percentage returns, are additive over time: e.g., the log yearly return equals the sum of the log daily returns over that year. Suppose that we divide an interval into N distinct subintervals and find that the returns on each subinterval are independent and identically distributed. Then if the log returns over the whole interval are multivariate normal with mean $\tilde{M}$ and covariance matrix $\tilde{\Sigma}$, the log returns over each subinterval will be multivariate lognormal with log mean $\tilde{M}/N$ and variance $\tilde{\Sigma}/N$.

INFINITELY DIVISIBLE DISTRIBUTIONS

Suppose no matter how finely we slice a given interval, the returns in each nonoverlapping, equally long subinterval are independent and identically distributed. In that case, the returns distribution is said to be infinitely divisible.

Clearly, lognormal returns can be viewed as infinitely divisible. But other distributions can be infinitely divisible too. For example, if returns occasionally make discrete jumps, their aggregate distribution will still be infinitely divisible provided that the probability of any given jump in the next instant is constant, regardless of what happened earlier. This kind of jump is known as Poisson. Statistical theory has proven, using methods too complex to enter here, that all infinitely divisible distributions are mixtures of Poisson jumps and something called Brownian motion.

BROWNIAN MOTION

A continuously moving random variable is said to follow Brownian motion if it never makes discrete jumps, its variance is finite, and its distribution is infinitely divisible. The Central Limit Theorem tells us that the sum of many small independent, identically distributed, finite-variance motions must be asymptotically normal. So this suggests Brownian motion must be normally distributed. Moreover, the basic formulas for sums of independent variables indicate that the means and variances must scale linearly with time. Indeed, the distribution of Brownian motion must always be multivariate normal with mean Mt and covariance Σt over any time period t, for some vector M and positive semidefinite Σ.

Brownian motion is the simplest way to model risky, continuously moving financial assets. It's especially appealing to model log returns as Brownian, which I will call "lognormal Brownian" for short. Lognormal Brownian motion prohibits negative wealth and simplifies calculations of aggregate returns.

REBALANCING

Portfolio weights are always spontaneously changing, except in the rare case that all assets earn exactly the same percentage returns. Rebalancing aims to maintain a target percentage allocation ω. It does this by purchasing disproportionately more of the assets that fall and/or selling more of the assets that rise.

Rebalancing tends to make log portfolio returns linear in the log returns $\tilde{X} \equiv \ln(1+X)$ of assets. To see this, suppose that rebalancing occurs at the end of each of T equally spaced subintervals. The log return will equal

$$T \cdot \ln\left(1 + \omega\left(\exp\left(\frac{\tilde{X}}{T}\right) - 1\right)\right) \cong T \cdot \ln\left(1 + \omega\frac{\tilde{X}}{T}\right)$$

which approaches $\omega'\tilde{X}$ as T approaches infinity.

TRADEOFFS IN REBALANCING

Some rebalancing is the norm rather than the exception. If you haven't changed your forecasts or beliefs you shouldn't change your targets.

Indeed, if you think a security's move is aberrant and due for a rebound then if anything you should overcompensate the other way. But no one continually rebalances: it's too time-consuming and too costly.

A lot of rebalancing gets smuggled into other transactions. A manager who receives new funds to invest takes the opportunity to top up assets that have fallen below target weights. Conversely, assets that exceed target weights tend to be sold off disproportionately in redemptions. This makes it hard to measure the costs and benefits of rebalancing, much less work out an optimal rebalancing policy.

In most cases, I suspect that most portfolios are reasonably approximated by continuous rebalancing at a transaction cost of a few dozen to a few hundred basis points per year. But I could be wrong. That's why I provide tools to calculate things either way.

EXPECTED UTILITY WITH REBALANCING

Let's rework expected utility calculations assuming that the assets follow lognormal Brownian motion and that the portfolio is costlessly rebalanced along the way. With absolute expected utility $|EU|$ expressed in power function form, the $|EU|$ of the whole will equal the product of the $|EU|$ of its parts. Given T equal subdivisions the log certainty equivalent $\widetilde{CE} = \dfrac{\ln|EU|}{1-c}$ will be T times the $\widetilde{CE}$ on each subinterval.

Now the subinterval $\widetilde{CE}$ can be rewritten in a form $\dfrac{R_1}{T} + \dfrac{R_2}{T^2} + \cdots$, where each R_i is independent of T. The $\widetilde{CE}$ for the whole interval will equal $R_1 + \dfrac{R_2}{T} + \cdots$, which converges to R_1 as T approaches infinity. So let's focus on identifying R_1.

Let $m^{\#}(\omega, T)$ and $v^{\#}(\omega, T)$ denote the percentage mean and variance respectively on each of the T subintervals. Using Refinement #2, it's easy to establish that:

$$\frac{R_1}{T} \cong \ln\left(1 + m^{\#}(\omega, T)\right) - \tfrac{1}{2}cv^{\#}(\omega, T) \cong m^{\#}(\omega, T) - \tfrac{1}{2}cv^{\#}(\omega, T)$$

Next apply the lognormal to normal conversions derived previously. While the portfolio won't be exactly lognormal, the mean/variance conversions based on second-order Taylor expansions will still be approximately valid. Again focusing only on first-order terms, $m^{\#}(\omega, T) \cong$ $\omega'\left(\dfrac{\tilde{M}}{T} + \dfrac{1}{2}\dfrac{[\tilde{\sigma}_{11} \ldots \tilde{\sigma}_{nn}]'}{T}\right)$ while $v^{\#}(\omega, T) \cong \omega'\left(\dfrac{\tilde{\Sigma}}{T}\right)\omega$. Taking limits as T approaches infinity shows that:

$$\widetilde{CE} = A_1 = \omega'\tilde{M} + \tfrac{1}{2}[\tilde{\sigma}_{11} \ldots \tilde{\sigma}_{nn}]\omega - \tfrac{1}{2}c\omega'\tilde{\Sigma}\omega$$

THE TRACE OF A MATRIX

You can easily check that $[\tilde{\sigma}_{11} \ldots \tilde{\sigma}_{nn}]\omega$ equals the sum of diagonal elements of $\mathrm{diag}(\omega)'\tilde{\Sigma}$. The sum of diagonal elements is known as the trace, denoted "tr". It has some handy properties, including commutativity. That is, the order of a matrix product doesn't affect its trace, provided both AB and BA are both well-defined, square matrices. This implies an alternative way to express the preceding result:

$$\widetilde{CE} = \omega'\tilde{M} + \tfrac{1}{2}\mathrm{tr}\big((\mathrm{diag}(\omega) - c\omega\omega')\tilde{\Sigma}\big)$$

which will prove useful below.

CONFIRMATION

Although every intermediate step of the calculation was approximate, the result expresses an exact asymptotic limit. To check, I will recalculate using Refinement #3. First I approximate the Greeks as:

$$\tilde{A} \cong \ln\left(1 + \omega'\left(\exp\left(\frac{\tilde{M}}{T}\right) - 1\right)\right) \cong \ln\left(1 + \omega'\frac{\tilde{M}}{T}\right) \cong \omega'\frac{\tilde{M}}{T}$$

$$\tilde{B} = \mathrm{diag}(\omega)'\exp\left(\frac{\tilde{M}}{T} - \tilde{A}1\right) \cong \omega + o\left(\frac{1}{T}\right)$$

$$\tilde{C} = \mathrm{diag}(\tilde{B}) - \tilde{B}\tilde{B}' \cong \mathrm{diag}(\omega) - \omega\omega' + o\left(\frac{1}{T}\right)$$

where $o(1/T)$ refers to terms that are on the order of $1/T$ and take the appropriate matrix dimension. Substituting into the certainty equivalent formulas and taking limits:

$$\widetilde{CE} = \omega'\tilde{M} + \tfrac{1}{2}(1 - c)\omega'\tilde{\Sigma}\omega$$

$$+ \frac{1}{2(c - 1)}\lim_{T \to \infty}\left(T \cdot \ln\left|I + (c - 1)(\mathrm{diag}(\omega) - \omega\omega')\frac{\tilde{\Sigma}}{T}\right|\right)$$

Recall that a determinant is the sum and difference of the products of elements taken from each row and each column. One product will contain only diagonal elements and will be on the order of 1. Each of the other products will contain at least two off-diagonal elements and be on the order of T^{-2}. Hence a first-order approximation to the determinant has to evaluate the diagonal product only. Now the log of a product equals the sum of the individual logs, and all the elements we're taking logs of are close to one. So the determinant collapses to the trace of the matrix that's being added to I. In other words,

$$\frac{1}{2(c-1)} \lim_{T\to\infty} \left(T \cdot \ln \left| I + (c-1)(\text{diag}(\omega) - \omega\omega') \frac{\tilde{\Sigma}}{T} \right| \right)$$

$$= \tfrac{1}{2} \text{tr}\left((\text{diag}(\omega) - \omega\omega')\tilde{\Sigma} \right)$$

Substitute back into the preceding formula and simplify in order to confirm previous results.

AN APPEALING SIMPLIFICATION

To express the $\widetilde{CE}$ formula more compactly, recall that for a multivariate lognormal distribution, $\tilde{M} + \tfrac{1}{2}[\tilde{\sigma}_{11} \ldots \tilde{\sigma}_{nn}]' = \ln(1 + M)$ where M denotes the corresponding percentage means. It follows that:

$$\widetilde{CE} = \omega' \ln(1 + M) - \tfrac{1}{2} c\omega' \tilde{\Sigma}\omega$$

This formula is simple and intuitively appealing. The log risk-adjusted returns equal the log of the gross expected returns less a markdown for the continuous variance. It makes sense to use the continuous variance because the portfolio is continually being rebalanced. Variance now appears slightly more costly than before, at $\tfrac{1}{2}c$ rather than $\tfrac{1}{2}(c-1)$. However, the "missing" cost is mostly an offset for enhancing expected gross returns.

YET ANOTHER VERIFICATION

The preceding results can be obtained much more neatly by modeling Brownian motion as the limit of a discrete random walk, which in a short time dt moves by either $\mu dt + \sigma\sqrt{dt}$ or $\mu dt - \sigma\sqrt{dt}$ with equal probability. Here μ denotes the mean percentage return; if you're dealing with lognormal motion you must set $\mu = \tilde{\mu} + \frac{1}{2}\sigma^2$. It follows that:

$$|EU| = E\left[\left(1 + \mu dt \pm \sigma\sqrt{dt}\right)^{1-c}\right]$$

$$\cong 1 + (1-c)E\left[\mu dt \pm \sigma\sqrt{dt}\right]$$

$$- \frac{1}{2}(1-c)cE\left[\mu^2(dt)^2 \pm 2\mu dt\sqrt{dt} + \sigma^2 dt\right]$$

$$\cong 1 + (1-c)dt\left[\mu - \frac{1}{2}c\sigma^2\right]$$

so that in the limit $\widetilde{CE} = \mu - \frac{1}{2}c\sigma^2$.

The multivariate analogue allows movements of $Mdt + \Sigma^{1/2}J\sqrt{dt}$ where J is a random vector with independent elements $+1$ or -1 and mean $\mathbf{0}$. With lognormality, M is replaced by $\ln(\mathbf{1} + M)$. Given continual rebalancing, the portfolio continues to follow univariate Brownian motion. Substituting in portfolio moments we get $\widetilde{CE} = \omega'\ln(\mathbf{1} + M) - \frac{1}{2}c\omega'\tilde{\Sigma}\omega$ as before.

Optimal Portfolio Mix Given Brownian Motion

The $\widetilde{CE}$ expression is concave in ω for all c, unlike Devlin's original recipe, and hence always yields an interior maximum. The optimal portfolio mix is:

$$\omega^* = \frac{1}{c}\tilde{\Sigma}^{-1}\ln(\mathbf{1} + M)$$

The maximal log risk-adjusted return is:

$$\widetilde{CE}^* = \frac{1}{2c}\ln(\mathbf{1} + M)'\tilde{\Sigma}^{-1}\ln(\mathbf{1} + M)$$

The expected return at the optimum is twice that high but variance takes away half.

Incorporating Conditional Brownian Motion

Unfortunately, standard Brownian modeling preserves the biggest drawback of its discrete normal counterpart. Both treat the mean and variance as fixed for all time. The simplest fix is to allow for different Brownian regimes and switches between them. But how should we model the switches?

In one-shot models, any regime applies for the whole period or not at all, with a single probability distribution summarizing the uncertainty. Continuous time opens a lot more complications. I will start simply, by allowing regime changes only at predetermined times called "resets". Between resets I will assume costless rebalancing.

If there is no rebalancing between resets, all we have is a sequence of one-shot models. At every reset we would just re-optimize the portfolio based on our current beliefs, using the recipes from the previous two chapters. If at the other extreme rebalancing is continuous and costless, then given probabilities p_k for each regime we should choose ω to maximize:

$$EU = sign(1 - c) \cdot \sum_k p_k \exp\Big((1 - c)\big(\omega' \ln(\mathbf{1} + \mathbf{M}_k) - \tfrac{1}{2} c\omega' \tilde{\Sigma}_k \omega\big)\Big)$$

OPTIMAL MIX WITH CONDITIONAL BROWNIAN MOTION

First-order conditions for optimization require that:

$$\sum_k p_k |EU_k| \big(\ln(\mathbf{1} + \mathbf{M}_k) - c\tilde{\Sigma}_k \omega^*\big) = 0$$

at the optimal ω^*. Second-order conditions require that:

$$(1 - c) \sum_k p_k |EU_k| \big(\ln(\mathbf{1} + \mathbf{M}_k) - c\tilde{\Sigma}_k \omega^*\big)^2 - c \sum_k p_k |EU_k| \tilde{\Sigma}_k < 0$$

The second term is always negative, while the first term is negative for $c > 1$. As c approaches zero the first term will be positive and start to outweigh the second, except in the single-regime case where the first term will vanish. But this isn't a defect of the equation; it just indicates that under some conditions nearly risk-neutral investors might seek unbounded risks. Assuming the second-order conditions are satisfied,

$$\omega^* = \frac{1}{c} \Big(\sum_k p_k EU_k \tilde{\Sigma}_k\Big)^{-1} \sum_k p_k EU_k \ln(\mathbf{1} + \mathbf{M}_k)$$

In the special case of uncorrelated assets, this simplifies to:

$$\omega_i^* = \frac{1}{2c} + \frac{1}{c} \Big(\sum_k p_k EU_k \tilde{\sigma}_{iik}\Big)^{-1} \sum_k p_k EU_k \tilde{\mu}_{ik}$$

Once again ω^* can be interpreted as a modified Sharpe ratio maximization, where worse expected regimes are weighted more heavily than better ones. The divisor of c instead of $c - 1$ seems to advise more cautious behavior than previous approximations did, although differences in other terms make up some of the gap.

QUICK RESETS

Suppose that we make resets more frequent without any other changes in the model. While the equation above remains the same, the relevant moments have to be calculated on a shorter time horizon. To make this dependence explicit, I will rewrite the log means and variances as $\tilde{M}_k dt$ and $\tilde{\Sigma}_k dt$ where dt denotes the interval between resets. Let $M_k = \exp(\tilde{M}_k + \frac{1}{2}[\tilde{\sigma}_{11k} \ldots \tilde{\sigma}_{nnk}]') - \mathbf{1}$ denote the percentage mean return in unit time.

With very quick resets, $|EU_k|$ for each Brownian regime approaches one, implying

$$\omega^* \to \frac{1}{c}\left(\sum_k p_k \tilde{\Sigma}_k\right)^{-1} \sum_k p_k\left(\tilde{M}_k + \tfrac{1}{2}[\tilde{\sigma}_{11k} \ldots \tilde{\sigma}_{nnk}]'\right)$$

$$= \frac{1}{c}\left(\sum_k p_k \tilde{\Sigma}_k\right)^{-1} \sum_k p_k \ln(\mathbf{1} + M_k)$$

In this formulation, risk aversion doesn't seem to matter except thru c. In fact, the optimal mix is exactly what would be advised for a single lognormal regime having $\tilde{\Sigma} = \sum_k p_k \tilde{\Sigma}_k$ and $\tilde{M} = \sum_k p_k \tilde{M}_k$. We don't need multiple regimes after all!

On closer inspection, this result is an artefact of our formulation. Every reset you're taking what amounts to a random draw on regimes. The more frequently you take these draws, the less you care about the outcome of any single draw. In the limit, you might as well treat returns as if they spent all their time in one single average regime. And that's just what the math confirms.

POISSON JUMPS

We can restore excitement even with quick resets by allowing for random discrete jumps. Poisson jumps are characterized by an instantaneous probability rate ℓ of occurrence. By that I mean that the probability of occurring in a short time dt equals ℓdt plus higher-order terms. Think of ℓ as the mean frequency of occurrence.

To make this maximally tractable, I will assume that a jump if it occurs causes an instant vector loss of $100L\%$. It follows that the expected percentage loss in time dt will be approximately $\ell L\,dt$ and its variance approximately $\ell LL'dt$.

EXPECTED UTILITY OF BROWNIAN-POISSON MIXTURES

Suppose that the base regime 0 is lognormal Brownian with log mean $\tilde{M}_0$, covariance matrix $\tilde{\Sigma}_0$ and percentage mean M_0 per unit time. Conditional on that regime, expected utility for a short time period t is approximately:

$$EU_0 \cong sign(1-c)\cdot\left(1+(1-c)\omega'M_0dt - \tfrac{1}{2}(1-c)c\omega'\tilde{\Sigma}_0\omega dt\right)$$

If the Poisson jump occurs, risky asset returns will be $-L$. I could model the jump as an overlay on Brownian motion rather than a substitute for it but no overall results would change. Utility in the jump regime is $sign(1-c)\cdot(1-\omega'L)^{1-c}$. Aggregate expected utility works out to:

$$|EU| \cong (1-\ell dt)|EU_0| + \ell dt(1-\omega'L)^{1-c}$$

$$\cong 1+(1-c)\omega'M_0dt - \tfrac{1}{2}(1-c)c\omega'\tilde{\Sigma}_0\omega dt - \ell dt + (1-\omega'L)^{1-c}\ell dt$$

$$\cong 1+(1-c)\cdot\left(\omega'M_0 - \tfrac{1}{2}c\omega'\tilde{\Sigma}_0\omega + \ell\frac{(1-\omega'L)^{1-c}-1}{1-c}\right)dt$$

Taking limits, the log certainty equivalent per unit time will be exactly:

$$\widetilde{CE} = \omega'M_0 - \tfrac{1}{2}c\omega'\tilde{\Sigma}_0\omega + \ell\frac{(1-\omega'L)^{1-c}-1}{1-c}$$

OPTIMAL PORTFOLIO MIX WITH MODERATE POISSON RISKS

Rewriting the power series as a Taylor expansion yields:

$$\widetilde{CE} = \omega'M_0 - \tfrac{1}{2}c\omega'\tilde{\Sigma}_0\omega - \ell\omega'L - \tfrac{1}{2}c\ell(\omega'L)^2 - \tfrac{1}{6}c(c+1)\ell(\omega'L)^3 - \cdots$$

The term $\tfrac{1}{6}c(c+1)\ell(\omega'L)^3$ will often be tiny. For example, if $c=3$, if the risk of a jump is 10% on a one-year horizon and if the portfolio would lose 10% if the jump occurred, then the term subtracts only 2 bps.

In that case we can get by with a second-order approximation to the power series and estimate the optimal portfolio mix as:

$$\omega^* \cong \frac{1}{c}(\tilde{\Sigma}_0 + \ell LL')^{-1}(M_0 - \ell L)$$

This looks like a Sharpe ratio maximization in which the unconditional variance equals the expected conditional variance plus the variance of the jump, and the unconditional mean equals the mean Brownian movement less the mean Poisson jump. However, there are some subtle differences related to the differences between ordinary moments and log moments. For example, I don't have a good intuitive explanation for why the unconditional variance mixes a log variance with a percentage variance.

CONCENTRATION RISKS

If the portfolio stands to suffer more than about a one-third loss in a Poisson jump, then it is dangerous to rely on mean-variance calculations alone. We can think of $\omega'L$ as the portfolio's exposure to that particular risk multiplied by the maximum likely loss due to that risk. The odds of crash, the likely scale of crash, and the beta or concentration risk with respect to the crash all need to be taken into account. Of these, the easiest to get a handle on is concentration risk. Moreover, doubling the concentration quadruples the vulnerabilities and vice versa. So it makes sense for risk managers to emphasize limits on concentration risks, measured in various ways. The preceding equations help to quantify the tradeoffs.

21 | Weighing the Options

Devlin would have enjoyed lunch with Regretta even if Club Mad hadn't been serving burritos. She was so lively, so sharp, so insightful. And she looked so good in black. But afterwards something about their conversation began to gnaw at him. "Keep things simple," she kept admonishing him. At the time he thought she just wanted him to trim his explanations. But now he realized she might have been hinting at something deeper. *Was she trying to keep her distance? Trying to let me down gently? Did I come on too strong, too intense?*

Devlin sighed. *That's it. Too intense. Everybody thinks that. Everybody but me, that is. Why do they all get so uptight? If a problem waylays you and keeps you hostage until you solve it, that's not your fault. It's the problem's fault. Granted, I do seem to get waylaid more than most people. But that's just bad luck.*

Bad luck? Get real. Everybody has options. Life isn't some linear trajectory. It's full of options, and you can switch from one branch to another. Maybe it's time to think more about options . . .

My options. Regretta's options. Our options. There's so much to sort out. Devlin scribbled down some thoughts, twirled them around, and scribbled down some more. At first they didn't amount to anything. Page after page he wadded up and threw in the waste basket.

Remember what Regretta said. Yes, keep things simple. But how? And then it dawned on him. Not exactly simple. But as simple as it could be. He couldn't wait to share his thoughts with Regretta.

Now hold on a second. Why rush over there straight away? To appear even more intense? That might ruin everything. No, I mustn't do that. Not again. Not so quickly. So Devlin kept his thoughts to himself. He kept his distance from Regretta, and confided only in his notebooks.

Devlin's self-control lasted nearly a week. But not quite. One morning Regretta found an envelope under her door, opened it, and began to read:

Dear Regretta,

I'm sorry. I've been trying not to bug you about this, but I can't hold back any longer. We've come a way long way I agree, and I'm thankful for that. But keeping things the way they are won't give us nearly the satisfaction we can get from advancing to the next higher step. So I'd like you to think about various options while I make some proposals.

No doubt you already realize the problem. Options are too nonlinear to fit into conventional portfolio analysis. The best you can do is model them as a fixed fraction "delta" of regular assets, which kind of misses the point. What straight line best approximates a put or call?

Pricing curves for ordinary options

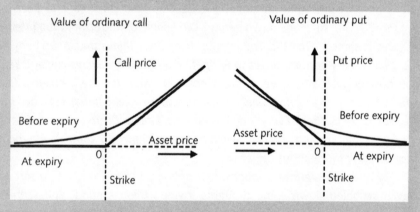

But our framework can handle them. It can handle them in two ways. The first way is by allowing the delta to vary across regimes. A put might have a delta of nearly zero in a boom and nearly one in a bust. The second way is by allowing delta to change even within a regime, assuming a constant rate of change "gamma" that itself might vary by regime.

All you need for calculation, over and above what we already have, are the mean option value and its delta and gamma at the mean of each regime. The general formulas for portfolio risk remain the same; the deltas just change the effective variance. I can't imagine any simpler way to incorporate nonlinearity. And it sure seems to beat the next best alternative because I can't recall seeing one.

Granted, it's not perfect. Gamma's not constant, not even within a regime. Indeed, it can spike very sharply around the strike price close to expiry. To deal with that you should take discrete approximations to delta and gamma, based on average values over a range. This isn't as messy as it sounds: option values at the mean and one standard deviation above and below it will generally suffice for the calculation.

If you can continually and costlessly rebalance, the errors in approximation essentially vanish. One way to see this is to compare our framework's advice with the advice Black-Scholes would give. They're identical, at least in the range where the two approaches overlap. Indeed, you can use our framework to regenerate Black-Scholes. But our approach is theoretically richer, because we allow for multiple regimes and mispricing.

Most likely it's richer in practice too. I won't say "for certain" because even if you can make profits trading options, simple longs and shorts might boost your risk-adjusted portfolio return just as much. Still, I do think it will occasionally help, either by identifying a genuinely great opportunity or by debunking some bogus claim. And it's near essential for a bank or hedge fund that actually uses a lot of options, as opposed to mutual funds that just dabble in them.

Ultimately, what we're really looking for from options is iceberg insurance. To illustrate the difference it can make, imagine your portfolio is perfectly lognormal except for vulnerability to a sudden crash. The crash is Poisson: it occurs at rate ℓ per unit time and causes a $100L\%$ loss when it does. The chart below shows how much risk premium – that is, fees over and above the expected payout – an investor with a CRR of 3 would be willing to pay for perfect insurance from the crash.

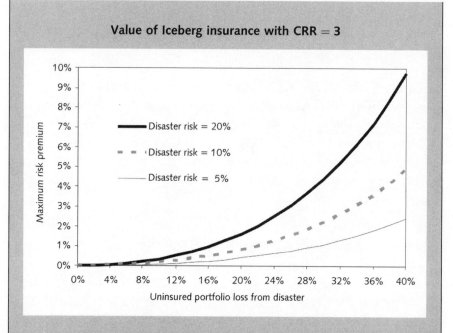

Value of Iceberg insurance with CRR = 3

Incorporating options sure looks appealing, doesn't it? But there's one catch. The recipes get messy. Not so messy you can't work with them. Not so messy you can't figure out what they mean: basically just to adjust the portfolio means and variances for the deltas and gammas. But messy enough that some people will just throw up their hands and walk away.

I know you want me to simplify. I tried. I really did. But once you distinguish between assets and underlying price drivers and allow for nonlinear relations between them, there's no way to avoid extra terms, even when you compress things like I did by summarizing all the deltas and gammas in two matrices. Actually, to store the gammas I needed a three-dimensional matrix. I hope that doesn't bother you.

Anyway, here are the recipes:

INCORPORATING OPTIONS

Let Y denote an N-vector of nonlinear assets tied to conditionally multivariate normal drivers X. Conditional on $X = \mathrm{M}$, denote the value of Y by $\hat{\Pi}$, the partial derivatives of Y with respect to X by the $N \times n$ matrix $\hat{\Delta}$, and the second partial derivatives of Y with respect to X by the 3-D $N \times n \times n$ matrix $\hat{\Gamma}$, where $\omega'\hat{\Gamma} \equiv \sum_{h=1}^{n} \omega_h \hat{\Gamma}_h$. A tilde marks the corresponding values when $\tilde{X} = \tilde{\mathrm{M}}$, while a bar marks the limiting values with continuous rebalancing. Then previous refinements apply subject to the following changes:

Refinements #1 and #2: recalculate portfolio moments as

$$m_k = \omega'\hat{\Pi}_k + \tfrac{1}{2}\mathrm{tr}\big((\omega'\hat{\Gamma}_k)\Sigma_k\big)$$

$$v_k = \omega'\hat{\Delta}'_k\Sigma_k\hat{\Delta}_k\omega + \tfrac{1}{2}\mathrm{tr}\Big(\big((\omega'\hat{\Gamma}_k)\Sigma_k\big)^2\Big)$$

Refinement #3: recalculate $\tilde{A}$, $\tilde{B}$, $\tilde{C}$, and Ψ as:

$$\tilde{A}_k = \ln\Big(1 + \omega'\big(\exp(\tilde{\Pi}_k) - \mathbf{1}\big)\Big)$$

$$\tilde{B}_k = \mathrm{diag}\big(\exp(\tilde{\mathrm{M}}_k - \tilde{A}_k\mathbf{1})\big)\tilde{\Delta}_k'\omega$$

$$\tilde{C}_k = \mathrm{diag}(\tilde{B}_k) - \tilde{B}_k\tilde{B}_k' + \mathrm{diag}\big(\exp(\tilde{\mathrm{M}}_k - \tilde{A}_k\mathbf{1})\big)\big(\tilde{\Gamma}_k\omega\big)\mathrm{diag}\big(\exp(\tilde{\mathrm{M}}_k)\big)$$

$$\Psi_k \equiv I + (c - 1)\tilde{C}_k\tilde{\Sigma}_k$$

Continuous rebalancing: recalculate $\widetilde{CE}$ as:

$$\widetilde{CE} = \omega'\bar{\Pi} + \tfrac{1}{2}\mathrm{tr}\Big(\big(\mathrm{diag}(\bar{\Delta}'\omega) + \omega'\bar{\Gamma}\big)\bar{\Sigma}\Big) - \tfrac{1}{2}c\omega'\bar{\Delta}\bar{\Sigma}\bar{\Delta}'\omega$$

If you want me to show you the calculations, I'll be glad to. Any time.

Your friend,

Devlin

Any time? Too bad Devlin didn't offer the same services to everyone. While Regretta rereads the letter for deeper meaning, let's try to reproduce the recipes.

OPTIONS

An option is a contract that offers the right but not the obligation to trade a security at a specified price. For example, a "call" is an option to buy at a specified price known as the "strike"; a "put" is an option to sell. The specified price is known as the "strike", a decision to trade is known as the "exercise", and the last possible trading date is known as the "expiry". An option is "in the money" if the price currently exceeds the strike; otherwise it is "out of the money". A "European" option can be exercised only at expiry, whereas an "American" option can be exercised any time before.

The crucial mathematical feature of options is their nonlinearity in the underlying asset price. For example, at expiry a call is worthless below the strike, whereas above the strike it's worth the asset price less the strike.

OPTIONS VALUATION

Most options are hard to value. In addition to estimating the distribution of asset prices at expiry, often you need to analyze the likely time path of asset price evolution and/or optimal exercise strategies. To illustrate the difficulties, there is no closed-form solution for an ordinary American put. Also, a single option's value may depend on several assets; say, a call on the best item in a basket.

The favored way to describe options is to estimate numerically their expected values at some particular scenario and their sensitivities to small changes in these scenarios. The most important sensitivities are the partial derivative with respect to the underlying asset's price ("delta"), the second partial derivative with respect to price ("gamma") and the partial derivative with respect to time ("theta").

CONDITIONAL APPROXIMATIONS FOR OPTIONS

Standard portfolio theory cannot handle nonlinearity. It can incorporate options only by approximating them as some constant fraction of the underlying asset. A multiple-regime framework can accommodate them better. For example, a short-term put on Nasdaq struck 25% below the current market price might be modeled as worthless in ordinary times and a full or nearly full Nasdaq short in a crash regime.

Better approximations use the option deltas, gammas, and thetas or their discrete counterparts. Mathematically this amounts to modeling options as quadratic functions, or rather conditionally quadratic functions because their coefficients may vary across regimes.

Incorporating these quadratic functions into portfolio analysis involves two challenges. One challenge is to calculate the various expectations. The other is to keep track of all the terms. The second is in some respects more daunting than the first. Before proceeding further, let's develop some more matrix shorthand.

TERMS FOR OPTION VALUES

Let me begin by distinguishing between the N risky assets that investors can hold or short and the n underlying drivers of the assets' prices. I will denote the percentage returns on the former by Y and reserve X for the percentage returns on the drivers. While X will usually refer to ordinary securities, it doesn't have to. Likewise, Y doesn't have to incorporate all of the securities in X though it usually will. The salient mathematical difference is that X is modeled as conditionally multivariate normal while Y is modeled as conditionally multivariate quadratic in X.

As before, P will denote the n-vector price of X, discounted at the risk-free rate. Think of this discounting as a re-measurement that converts the risk-free rate to zero. For clarity I will sometimes subscript P by the time t it refers to. For example, P_0 denotes the price at the initial time 0. The base interval is assumed to be 1, so $P_1 = \text{diag}(1 + X)P_0$. When looking at returns over other time intervals I will subscript X too.

An N-vector V will denote the option value expected at price P and time t, again discounted at the risk-free rate. Clearly, $V_1 = \text{diag}(1 + Y)V_0$. I will denote by $\hat{\Pi} \equiv Y|_{X=M}$ the excess percentage returns if $X = M$ and by $\tilde{\Pi} \equiv \tilde{Y}|_{\tilde{X}=\tilde{M}} \equiv \ln(1 + Y)|_{\tilde{X}=\tilde{M}}$ the excess log returns if $\tilde{X} = \tilde{M}$. As the time period contracts, so do the relevant returns. $\bar{\Pi}$ will denote the limit

$$\frac{d\ln(1 + Y_t)}{dt}\bigg|_{\tilde{X}=0, t=0} \equiv \frac{1}{V_0} \cdot \frac{dV(\tilde{M}t, t)}{dt}\bigg|_{t=0}.$$

DELTAS

Δ will denote an $N \times n$ matrix with elements $\delta_{hi} \equiv \dfrac{\partial V_h(P,t)}{\partial P_i}$, the partial derivative of the expected price of option h with respect to the price of driver i. Usually Δ will have only one nonzero element per row, because assets typically depend on only one driver.

Actually, I'm less interested in the sensitivities of V to P than in the sensitivities of percentage returns Y to X. However, there is a close relation between the two:

$$\frac{\partial y_h}{\partial x_i} = \frac{\partial \dfrac{V_h}{V_{h0}}}{\partial \dfrac{P_i}{P_{i0}}} = \frac{P_{i0}}{V_{h0}} \cdot \frac{\partial V_h(P,t)}{\partial P_i} = \frac{P_{i0}}{V_{h0}} \delta_{hi}$$

We can express this in matrix form as:

$$\frac{\partial Y}{\partial X} = \operatorname{diag}(P_0)\Delta\big(\operatorname{diag}(V_0)\big)^{-1}$$

$\hat{\Delta} \equiv \left.\dfrac{\partial Y}{\partial X}\right|_{X=\mathrm{M}}$ and $\tilde{\Delta} \equiv \left.\dfrac{\partial Y}{\partial X}\right|_{\tilde{X}=\tilde{\mathrm{M}}}$ will denote the end-period first derivative evaluated respectively at the mean of X and the mean of $\tilde{X}$. $\bar{\Delta} \equiv \operatorname{diag}(P_0)\dfrac{\partial V(P_0,0)}{\partial P}\big(\operatorname{diag}(V_0)\big)^{-1}$ denotes the corresponding initial period values.

3-D MATRICES

I interrupt this discussion of derivatives to introduce a three-dimensional matrix. Just as a rectangular matrix is a vector of vectors, a 3-D matrix Γ is a vector of rectangular matrices Γ_h, whose elements can be denoted γ_{hij}. Multiplication of 3-D matrices is potentially confusing due to the extra choice of directions, but for the $N \times n \times n$ matrices I am interested in, here are four situations where it's (nearly) unambiguous:

- For w a scalar, $w\Gamma \equiv [w\gamma_{hij}]$
- For ω an ordinary N-vector, $\omega'\Gamma \equiv \sum_{h=1}^{N} \omega_h \Gamma_h$

- For W a diagonal $N \times N$ matrix, $W\Gamma$ is a vector of rectangular matrices $w_{hh}\Gamma_h$
- For W a diagonal $n \times n$ matrix, $W\Gamma W$ has elements $w_{ii}w_{jj}\gamma_{hij}$

GAMMAS

The particular Γ I'm interested in is an $N \times n \times n$ matrix with elements $\gamma_{hij} \equiv \dfrac{\partial^2 V_h(P,t)}{\partial P_i \partial P_j}$. Each component Γ_h is just the Hessian (matrix second derivative) of asset h with respect to prices. Again, I'm more interested in sensitivities of Y to X, so I use the relation:

$$\frac{\partial^2 y_h}{\partial x_i \partial x_j} = \frac{P_{j0}}{V_{h0}} \cdot \frac{\partial}{\partial x_i}\left(\frac{\partial V_h}{\partial P_j}\right) = \frac{P_{j0}}{V_{h0}} \cdot \frac{\partial^2 V_h}{\partial P_i \partial P_j} \cdot \frac{\partial P_i}{\partial x_i} = \frac{P_{i0}P_{j0}}{V_{h0}}\gamma_{hij}$$

to populate the $N \times n \times n$ matrix $\dfrac{\partial^2 Y}{\partial X^2}$. Alternatively,

$$\frac{\partial^2 Y}{\partial X^2} \equiv \mathrm{diag}(P_0)\Gamma \mathrm{diag}(P_0)\big(\mathrm{diag}(V_0)\big)^{-1}.$$

Since options typically depend only on a single asset, they will have only one nonzero gamma element. Ordinary "linear" securities won't have any nonzero gamma. So these potentially huge 3-D matrices will typically have less than N nonzero elements. In practice, to simplify tabulations you should try to group the assets according to which security they depend on.

In analogy to the deltas, $\hat{\Gamma} \equiv \dfrac{\partial^2 Y}{\partial X^2}\Big|_{X=M}$ and $\tilde{\Gamma} \equiv \dfrac{\partial^2 Y}{\partial X^2}\Big|_{\tilde{X}=\tilde{M}}$ will denote the end-period second derivatives evaluated respectively at the mean of X and the mean of $\tilde{X}$. The 3-D matrix $\bar{\Gamma}$ with elements $\bar{\gamma}_{hij} = \dfrac{P_{i0}P_{j0}}{V_{h0}} \cdot \dfrac{\partial^2 V_h(P_0,0)}{\partial P_i \partial P_j}$ denotes the corresponding initial values.

SMOOTHING THE KINKS

Consider a simple single-security option that expires exactly at end-period, with a strike very close to the mean. You'll calculate its future δ as 0 or 1 depending on which side of the mean the strike falls, and γ as 0 unless the strike exactly equals the mean, in which case γ will be infinite. Setting $\delta = \frac{1}{2}$ with a positive but finite γ would be much more reasonable.

The general problem stems from a kink or near-kink in the option, causing a sharp spike in γ. That suggests the following practical fix. Calculate for time 1 the option value V_1^+ at $x = \mu + \sigma$, and the value V_1^- for $x = \mu - \sigma$ in addition to V_1 at $x = \mu$. Then fit a quadratic approximation through those three points. While the $\hat{\theta}$ estimate will remain the same, δ will be re-estimated as $\dfrac{V_1^+ - V_1^-}{2\sigma}$ and γ as $\dfrac{V_1^+ - 2V + V_1^-}{\sigma^2}$. If you are more concerned about fitting the tails than the center you can value the option at points that are more than a standard deviation apart.

EXPECTED UTILITY

Once we've identified appropriate asset parameters, we can shift our attention to portfolio calculations. The portfolio weights ω are now an N-vector. Portfolio returns can be approximated as a second-order Taylor expansion:

$$\omega'Y \cong A_k + B_k'(X - M_k) + \tfrac{1}{2}(X - M_k)'C_k(X - M_k)$$

where:

$$A_k = \omega'\hat{\Pi}_k$$

$$B_k = \hat{\Delta}_k'\omega$$

$$C_k = \omega'\hat{\Gamma}_k = \sum_{h=1}^{N} \omega_h \hat{\Gamma}_{hk}$$

As before, A denotes a scalar, B an n-vector, and C a symmetric $n \times n$ matrix. Assuming conditional multivariate normality, this implies portfolio moments of:

$$m_k = A_k + \tfrac{1}{2}\mathrm{tr}(C_k\Sigma_k) = \omega'\hat{\Pi}_k + \tfrac{1}{2}\mathrm{tr}\big((\omega'\hat{\Gamma}_k)\Sigma_k\big)$$

$$v_k = B_k'\Sigma_k B_k + \tfrac{1}{2}\mathrm{tr}\big((C_k\Sigma_k)^2\big) = \omega'\hat{\Delta}_k'\Sigma_k\hat{\Delta}_k\omega + \tfrac{1}{2}\mathrm{tr}\Big(\big((\omega'\hat{\Gamma}_k)\Sigma_k\big)^2\Big)$$

We then calculate $\hat{v}_k = \dfrac{v_k}{(1 + m_k)^2}$ and substitute into either Refinement #1 or #2:

$$EU_{\#1} \cong sign(1-c)\cdot$$

$$\sum_i p_i(1+m_k)^{1-c}\left(1+\tfrac{1}{2}(c-1)c\hat{v}_k+\tfrac{1}{8}(c-1)c(c+1)(c+2)\hat{v}_k^2\right)$$

$$EU_{\#2} \cong sign(1-c)\cdot$$

$$\sum_k p_k(1+m_k)^{1-c}\left(1+(1-c)\hat{v}_k\right)^{-1/2}\exp\left(\tfrac{1}{2}\frac{(1-c)^2\hat{v}_k}{1+(1-c)\hat{v}_k}\right)$$

MEANS AND VARIANCES OF QUADRATIC FORMS

The preceding results apply the following formulas for the moments of quadratic forms when X is multivariate normal and C is any symmetric matrix (not necessarily diagonal):

$$E\left[(X-M)'C(X-M)\right] = \text{tr}(C\Sigma)$$

$$Var\left[(X-M)'C(X-M)\right] = 2\cdot\text{tr}\left((C\Sigma)^2\right)$$

To prove this, first define a new vector $Y \equiv \Sigma^{-1/2}(X-M)$, which is multivariate normal with mean 0 and covariance matrix I, and a new matrix $Q \equiv \Sigma^{1/2}\Gamma\Sigma^{1/2}$. Observe that:

$$(X-M)'C(X-M) = Y'\Sigma^{1/2}C\Sigma^{1/2}Y \equiv Y'QY$$

Evaluate the expectation as:

$$E[Y'QY] = E\left[\sum_{i=1}^n\sum_{j=1}^n q_{ij}y_iy_j\right] = \sum_{i=1}^n q_{ii}E\left[y_i^2\right]$$

$$= \sum_{i=1}^n q_{ii} = \text{tr}(\Sigma^{1/2}C\Sigma^{1/2}) = \text{tr}(C\Sigma^{1/2}\Sigma^{1/2}) = \text{tr}(C\Sigma)$$

Next observe that for any subscripts the expectation of $y_iy_jy_ky_l$ will equal 0 except for the combination $y_i^2y_j^2$ whose expectation equals 3 when $i=j$ and 1 otherwise. It follows that:

$$E\left[(Y'QY)^2\right] = E\left[\left(\sum_{i=1}^n q_{ij}y_iy_j\right)^2\right]$$

$$= \sum_{i=1}^n q_{ii}^2 E\left[y_i^4\right] + \sum_{\substack{i=1\\i\neq j}}^n q_{ii}E\left[y_i^2\right]\left(\sum_{j=1}^n q_{jj}E\left[y_j^2\right]\right)$$

$$+ \sum_{\substack{i=1 \\ j \neq i}}^{n} \sum_{j=1}^{n} q_{ij}q_{ji}E[y_i\,y_j\,y_j\,y_i] + \sum_{\substack{i=1 \\ j \neq i}}^{n} \sum_{j=1}^{n} q_{ij}q_{ji}E[y_i\,y_j\,y_i\,y_j]$$

$$= 3 \sum_{i=1}^{n} q_{ii}^2 + \sum_{\substack{i=1 \\ i \neq j}}^{n} q_{ii}q_{jj} + 2 \sum_{\substack{i=1 \\ j \neq i}}^{n} \sum_{j=1}^{n} q_{ij}q_{ij}$$

$$= \left(\sum_{i=1}^{n} q_{ii} \right)^2 + 2 \sum_{i=1}^{n} \sum_{j=1}^{n} q_{ij}q_{ji} = (\mathrm{tr}(Q))^2 + \mathrm{tr}(Q^2)$$

and hence that:

$$Var[Y'QY] = E[(Y'QY)^2] - (E[Y'QY])^2 = \mathrm{tr}(Q^2) = \mathrm{tr}((C\Sigma)^2)$$

COPING WITH FREE OPTIONS

Options packages can be free. For example, an out-of-the-money put may be financed by selling out-of-the-money calls. When $V_{h0} = 0$ for some asset h, its percentage returns are undefined. In that case, just drop all the V_{h0} terms from the calculation of $\hat{\pi}_h$, $\hat{\delta}_h$ and $\hat{\gamma}_h$ and reinterpret ω_h as the weight needed to achieve gross return V_{h1}. This is equivalent to setting V_{0h} to equal some tiny ϵ, redefining the weight on that option h to equal $\epsilon\omega_h$, and letting ϵ approach zero. In short, all we need to do to keep the problem tractable with free options is to redefine slightly the relevant choice variable.

MODIFICATIONS FOR LOGNORMALITY

Additional modifications are needed to apply Refinement #3. A second-order Taylor expansion establishes that:

$$\ln(1 + \omega'Y) = \ln\left(1 + \omega'(\exp(\tilde{Y}) - 1)\right)$$

$$\cong \tilde{A} + \tilde{B}'(\tilde{X} - \tilde{M}) + \tfrac{1}{2}(\tilde{X} - \tilde{M})'\tilde{C}(\tilde{X} - \tilde{M})$$

where:

$$\tilde{A} = \ln\left(1 + \omega'(\exp(\tilde{\Pi}) - 1)\right)$$

$$\tilde{B} = \mathrm{diag}\left(\exp(\tilde{M} - \tilde{A}\mathbf{1})\right)\tilde{\Delta}'\omega$$

$$\tilde{C} = \mathrm{diag}(\tilde{B}) - \tilde{B}\tilde{B}' + \mathrm{diag}\left(\exp(\tilde{M} - \tilde{A}\mathbf{1})\right)(\tilde{\Gamma}\omega)\mathrm{diag}\left(\exp(\tilde{M})\right)$$

Although I have omitted the subscript k, each of these new variables will generally vary across regimes. So you'll need to do these calculations repeatedly. Also calculate $\Psi_k \equiv I + (c - 1)\tilde{C}_k\tilde{\Sigma}_k$. Then substitute back into Refinement #3:

$$EU_{\#3} = sign(1 - c)$$
$$\cdot \sum_k p_k |\Psi_k|^{-1/2} \exp\left((1 - c)\left(\tilde{A}_k + \tfrac{1}{2}(1 - c)\tilde{B}_k'\Psi_k^{-1}\tilde{\Sigma}_k\tilde{B}_k\right)\right)$$

VERIFYING THE GREEKS

The formula for $\tilde{A}$ is immediately verified by evaluating the formula at $\tilde{X} = \tilde{M}$. Each element $\tilde{b}_i$ of $\tilde{B}$ can be calculated as:

$$\tilde{b}_i = \frac{d}{d\tilde{x}_i}\ln(1 + \omega'Y)\Big|_{\tilde{X}=\tilde{M}} = \left[\frac{1}{1 + \omega'Y}\left(\sum_{h=1}^{N} \omega_h \frac{dy_h}{dx_i}\right)\frac{dx_i}{d\tilde{x}_i}\right]_{\tilde{X}=\tilde{M}}$$

$$= \exp(-\tilde{A})\left(\sum_{h=1}^{N} \omega_h \delta_{hi}\right)\exp(\tilde{\mu}_i) = \exp(\tilde{\mu}_i - \tilde{A})\left(\sum_{h=1}^{N} \omega_h \delta_{hi}\right)$$

where $\tilde{\omega}_i \equiv \omega_i \exp(\tilde{\mu}_i - \tilde{A})$. The off-diagonal elements of $\tilde{C}$ are

$$\tilde{c}_{ij} = \frac{\partial}{\partial\tilde{x}_j}\left(\sum_{h=1}^{N}\left(\frac{\omega_h \exp(\tilde{x}_i)}{1 + \omega'Y}\cdot\frac{\partial y_h}{\partial x_i}\right)\right)\Big|_{\tilde{X}=\tilde{M}}$$

$$= \sum_{h=1}^{N}\left[-\frac{\omega_h \exp(\tilde{x}_i)}{(1 + \omega'Y)^2}\cdot\frac{\partial y_h}{\partial x_i}\left(\sum_{g=1}^{N} \omega_g \frac{\partial y_g}{\partial x_j}\exp(\tilde{x}_j)\right)\right.$$

$$\left.+\frac{\omega_h \exp(\tilde{x}_i)}{1 + \omega'Y}\cdot\frac{\partial^2 y_h}{\partial x_i\partial x_j}\exp(\tilde{x}_j)\right]_{\tilde{X}=\tilde{M}}$$

$$= -\left(\sum_{h=1}^{N} \omega_h \exp(\tilde{\mu}_i - \tilde{A})\tilde{\delta}_{hi}\right)\left(\sum_{h=1}^{N} \omega_h \exp(\tilde{\mu}_j - \tilde{A})\tilde{\delta}_{hj}\right)$$

$$+\sum_{h=1}^{N} \omega_h \exp(\tilde{\mu}_i + \tilde{\mu}_j - \tilde{A})\tilde{\gamma}_{hij}$$

$$= -\tilde{B}_i\tilde{B}_j + \left(\sum_{h=1}^{N} \omega_h \tilde{\gamma}_{hij}\right)\exp(\tilde{\mu}_i + \tilde{\mu}_j - \tilde{A})$$

while the diagonal elements $\tilde{c}_{ii}$ include these terms (obviously with $i = j$) plus an additional term:

$$\frac{1}{1 + \omega'Y} \sum_{h=1}^{N} \omega_h \frac{\partial y_h}{\partial x_i} \cdot \frac{d\exp(\tilde{x}_i)}{dx_i}\bigg|_{\tilde{X}=\tilde{M}} = \exp(-\tilde{A}) \sum_{h=1}^{N} \omega_h \exp(\tilde{\mu}_i)\tilde{\delta}_{hi}$$

$$= \exp(\tilde{\mu}_i - \tilde{A}) \sum_{h=1}^{N} \omega_h \tilde{\delta}_{hi}$$

OPTIONS WITH CONTINUOUS REBALANCING

As options draw closer to expiry their values, deltas, and gammas change even if underlying prices do not. This makes option exposures even more difficult to rebalance than ordinary securities. Nevertheless, for the sake of argument let's assume costless rebalancing is feasible and work out its analytic implications. Retracing the argument of the preceding chapter, if rebalancing occurs at T equally spaced subintervals, the risk-adjusted return can be approximated as:

$$\widetilde{CE} = \bar{A} + \tfrac{1}{2}(1 - c)\bar{B}'\tilde{\Sigma}\bar{B} + \tfrac{1}{2}\text{tr}(\bar{C}\tilde{\Sigma}) + o(\tfrac{1}{T})$$

where:

$$\bar{A} = T \cdot \ln\left(1 + \omega'\left(\exp(\bar{\Pi}/T) - 1\right)\right) = \omega'\bar{\Pi} + o(\tfrac{1}{T})$$

$$\bar{B} = \text{diag}\left(\exp(\tilde{M}/T - \bar{A}\mathbf{1})\right)\bar{\Delta}'\omega = \bar{\Delta}'\omega + o(\tfrac{1}{T})$$

$$\bar{C} = \text{diag}(\bar{B}) - \bar{B}\bar{B}' + \omega'\bar{\Gamma} + o(\tfrac{1}{T}) = \text{diag}(\bar{\Delta}'\omega) - \bar{\Delta}'\omega\omega'\bar{\Delta}' + \omega'\bar{\Gamma} + o(\tfrac{1}{T})$$

Recall that $\bar{\Pi}$, $\bar{\Delta}$ and $\bar{\Gamma}$ reflect limits at the starting values. Letting T approach infinity,

$$\widetilde{CE} = \bar{A} + \tfrac{1}{2}(1 - c)\bar{B}'\tilde{\Sigma}\bar{B} + \tfrac{1}{2}\text{tr}(\bar{C}\tilde{\Sigma})$$

$$= \omega'\bar{\Pi} + \tfrac{1}{2}(1 - c)\omega'\bar{\Delta}\tilde{\Sigma}\bar{\Delta}'\omega + \tfrac{1}{2}\text{tr}\left((\text{diag}(\bar{\Delta}'\omega) + \omega'\bar{\Gamma} - \bar{\Delta}\omega\omega'\bar{\Delta}')\tilde{\Sigma}\right)$$

$$= \omega'\bar{\Pi} + \tfrac{1}{2}\text{tr}\left((\text{diag}(\bar{\Delta}'\omega) + \omega'\bar{\Gamma})\tilde{\Sigma}\right) - \tfrac{1}{2}c\omega'\bar{\Delta}\tilde{\Sigma}\bar{\Delta}'\omega$$

This is a lot simpler than Refinement #3. And the modifications for options are fairly easy to understand. The two delta terms adjust the portfolio mean and variance respectively for the effective weight of the underlying drivers X. The gamma term adjusts the portfolio mean for the convexity of the assets.

As in the preceding chapter, all this can be neatly verified by reformulating the portfolio as a discrete random walk and compressing the interval between steps. However, it doesn't bring out so clearly the connection between the various approaches, and the use of $\sqrt{dt}$ terms may put off some readers. That's why I've taken a more circuitous approach.

SINGLE RISK, SINGLE OPTION, SINGLE REGIME

An interesting special case involves a single underlying risk driver in a single regime. Suppose the investor can purchase asset 1 that directly embodies this risk, asset 2 which is an option on asset 1, or risk-free T-bills. By construction asset 1 has mean μ, variance σ^2, $\delta = 1$ and $\gamma = 0$, with an initial price P_0 of 1. Applying previous formulas we can calculate:

$$A = \omega_1 \mu + \omega_2 \hat{\pi}_2$$
$$B = \omega_1 + \omega_2 \hat{\delta}_2$$
$$C = \omega_2 \hat{\gamma}_2$$
$$m = A + \tfrac{1}{2} C \sigma^2 = \omega_1 \mu + \omega_2 \hat{\pi}_2 + \tfrac{1}{2} \omega_2 \hat{\gamma}_2 \sigma^2$$
$$v = B^2 \sigma^2 + \tfrac{1}{2} C^2 \sigma^4 = \left(\omega_1 + \omega_2 \hat{\delta}_2 \right)^2 \sigma^2 + \tfrac{1}{2} \omega_2^2 \hat{\gamma}_2^2 \sigma^4$$

and substitute m and v into Refinement #1 or #2. I will spare readers the messier formulas for Refinement #3, except for the limiting case with continual rebalancing where:

$$A = \omega_1 \tilde{\mu} + \omega_2 \bar{\pi}_2$$
$$B = \omega_1 + \omega_2 \bar{\delta}_2$$
$$C = \omega_2 \bar{\gamma}_2$$
$$\widetilde{CE} = \omega_1 \tilde{\mu} + \omega_2 \bar{\pi}_2 + \tfrac{1}{2} \omega + \tfrac{1}{2} (\omega_1 + \omega_2 \bar{\delta}_2) \tilde{\sigma}^2$$
$$+ \tfrac{1}{2} \omega_2 \bar{\gamma}_2 \tilde{\sigma}^2 - \tfrac{1}{2} c (\omega_1 + \omega_2 \bar{\delta}_2)^2 \tilde{\sigma}^2$$

MARKET EQUILIBRIUM WITH A SINGLE REGIME

One distinction between derivatives and ordinary securities is that the net market supply of derivatives must be zero. Hence, if investors were all alike, derivatives must be priced in equilibrium so that the optimal long or short position is zero. So let's look at first-order conditions and see what they require at $\omega_2 = 0$ and the optimal ω_1^*. Focusing on the continually rebalanced scenario,

$$\left.\frac{d\widetilde{CE}}{d\omega_1}\right|_{\substack{\omega_1=\omega_1^* \\ \omega_2=0}} = \tilde{\mu} + \tfrac{1}{2}\tilde{\sigma}^2 - c\omega_1^*\tilde{\sigma}^2 = 0$$

The second condition then requires that:

$$\left.\frac{d\widetilde{CE}}{d\omega_2}\right|_{\substack{\omega_1=\omega_1^* \\ \omega_2=0}} = \bar{\pi}_2 + \tfrac{1}{2}\bar{\delta}_2\tilde{\sigma}^2 + \tfrac{1}{2}\bar{\gamma}_2\tilde{\sigma}^2 - c\omega_1^*\bar{\delta}_2\tilde{\sigma}^2$$

$$= \bar{\pi}_2 + \tfrac{1}{2}\bar{\delta}_2\tilde{\sigma}^2 + \tfrac{1}{2}\bar{\gamma}_2\tilde{\sigma}^2 - \bar{\delta}_2(\tilde{\mu} + \tfrac{1}{2}\tilde{\sigma}^2)$$

$$= \bar{\pi}_2 - \bar{\delta}_2\tilde{\mu} + \tfrac{1}{2}\bar{\gamma}_2\tilde{\sigma}^2 = 0$$

We can simplify further by noting that:

$$\bar{\pi} = \frac{1}{V_0}\left.\frac{dV(\tilde{\mu}t,t)}{dt}\right|_{t=0} = \left.\frac{\partial V(\tilde{\mu}t,t)}{\partial P}\right|_{t=0} \cdot \left.\frac{dP(\tilde{\mu}t)}{dt}\right|_{t=0} + \left.\frac{\partial V(\tilde{\mu}t,t)}{\partial t}\right|_{t=0} = \tilde{\mu}\bar{\delta} + \bar{\theta}$$

where theta (θ) denotes the partial derivative of option value with respect to time, also known as "time decay". Again recall that prices are discounted at the risk-free rate r; the standard θ is measured in nominal terms so $\bar{\theta} = \theta - r$. Substitution into the preceding equation yields:

$$\bar{\theta}_2 + \tfrac{1}{2}\bar{\gamma}_2\tilde{\sigma}^2 = 0$$

This must hold in market equilibrium for all times and prices. Multiplying thru by the option value, writing out the partial derivatives, and dropping the subscripts, we obtain:

$$\frac{\partial V}{\partial t} + \tfrac{1}{2}\gamma\tilde{\sigma}^2 P^2 \frac{\partial^2 V}{\partial P^2} = 0$$

BLACK-SCHOLES INTERPRETATION

If a security follows lognormal Brownian motion, any option on that security must satisfy a partial differential equation known as the Black-Scholes equation. The preceding equation is precisely the Black-Scholes equation given a risk-free rate of zero. If we remeasured V and P in nominal terms, we would generate the standard Black-Scholes equation, which contains extra terms of $-rV + rP\dfrac{\partial V}{\partial P}$. Hence, the approach recommended here for incorporating options into portfolio analysis embraces standard options theory as a special case. Note in particular that the relative risk aversion parameter c drops out, just as Black-Scholes says it should. Indeed, we don't even need to assume that c is constant.

USELESS OPTIONS

The consistency with Black-Scholes means that the availability of options *per se* doesn't change optimal portfolio strategy. It's tempting to believe that the very structure of an option – say, that a put is struck well below the mean – makes it a useful addition to a portfolio. That's not true. Absent mispricing there's no need to buy options.

Even when there is mispricing, options may not best exploit it. Returning to the example of a single regime with a single underlying stock, suppose you believe that the true drift of the stock is ϵ higher than the market thinks. Then you should also believe that $\bar{\pi}_2$ on your option is growing $\epsilon\bar{\delta}_2$ faster than the market thinks. Still, your portfolio could be optimized without relying on options:

$$\left.\frac{d\widetilde{CE}}{d\omega_1}\right|_{\substack{\omega_1=\omega_1^* \\ \omega_2=0}} = \tilde{\mu} + \epsilon + \tfrac{1}{2}\tilde{\sigma}^2 - c\omega_1^*\tilde{\sigma}^2 = 0$$

$$\left.\frac{d\widetilde{CE}}{d\omega_2}\right|_{\substack{\omega_1=\omega_1^* \\ \omega_2=0}} = \bar{\theta}_2 + \bar{\delta}_2(\tilde{\mu} + \epsilon) + \tfrac{1}{2}\bar{\delta}_2\tilde{\sigma}^2 + \tfrac{1}{2}\bar{\gamma}_2\tilde{\sigma}^2 - c\omega_1^*\bar{\delta}_2\tilde{\sigma}^2$$

$$= (\bar{\theta}_2 + \tfrac{1}{2}\bar{\gamma}_2\tilde{\sigma}^2) + \bar{\delta}_2(\tilde{\mu} + \epsilon + \tfrac{1}{2}\tilde{\sigma}^2 - c\omega_1^*\tilde{\sigma}^2) = 0$$

ICEBERG INSURANCE

However, options can be very useful if you are bracing for regimes that the options market is ignoring. For example, suppose you think that the default risk on a security completely neutralizes its attractions. If the options market is ignoring default risk then you should buy some of the security and a lot of cheap out-of-the-money puts.

Let's estimate how much iceberg insurance is worth. Suppose a Poisson disaster that occurs with frequency ℓ would knock $100L\%$ off of wealth. Let $\widetilde{CE}_0$ denote the risk-adjusted rate of return absent disaster, whereas $\widetilde{CE}$ takes disaster into account. Retracing the calculations in the last chapter for Poisson jumps:

$$\widetilde{CE} = \widetilde{CE}_0 + \ell \frac{(1-L)^{1-c} - 1}{1-c}$$

Hence investors should be willing to pay up to $\ell \dfrac{1 - (1-L)^{1-c}}{1-c}$ for full disaster insurance. Of this amount, ℓL represents the expected loss. The remainder is the risk premium:

$$\ell \frac{1 - (1-L)^{1-c}}{1-c} - \ell L = \tfrac{1}{2} c\ell L^2 + \tfrac{1}{6} c(c+1)\ell L^3 +$$

$$\tfrac{1}{24} c(c+1)(c+2)\ell L^4 + \cdots$$

$$= \tfrac{1}{2} c\ell L^2 \left(1 + \sum_{j=1}^{\infty} \frac{(c+1)\cdots(c+j)}{3\cdots(2+j)} L^j \right)$$

22 | Fixing the Focus

The next Visitors' Day Conway arrived bright and early. Devlin and Regretta took turns briefing him on the higher-order refinements, on the simplifications that continuous rebalancing can provide, and on the incorporation of options.

"I'm amazed how much you two have accomplished in two weeks," said Conway. *Almost as amazing as how well you two seem to be getting along.* "But I hope you're not expecting me to remember all this."

"Of course not," said Regretta. "Just remember the really important stuff."

"Which is?"

"That the approach is comprehensive," said Devlin.

"But flexible," said Regretta,

"And as detailed as you want," said Devlin.

"Or neat and parsimonious. So you can focus on what you want and pull out the recipe that suits you best."

"Or better yet, have you two pull it out for me" interjected Conway before they both got carried away. "How about I try to bring you two onboard with me at Megabucks?"

"Not me," said Devlin. "I don't want to rejoin a club that wouldn't have me for a member."

"Me neither," said Regretta. "Too many bad memories of life in the fast lane."

"Trust me, the asset management side isn't fast. Half-fast is more like it." Conway smiled, but couldn't elicit one in return. "Look, suit yourself. But I'm going to need some help handling all these assets and regimes. How do you suppose I get it?"

"Simplify," said Devlin and Regretta nearly in unison. They laughed. "Tell him your idea," said Devlin to Regretta.

"You might call it a CAPM-type approach," said Regretta.

"The Capital Asset Pricing Model? What's that have to do with regime-switching?"

"In its original form, nothing. And I'm not talking about market pricing in equilibrium. I just mean the idea of decomposing all assets into common factors and independent residuals."

"What's the point of that?"

"If you can do it, it saves tons on information needs."

"How so? Don't you need even more parameters to track all the alphas and betas?"

"Sure, but then most of the covariances vanish. They're all zero except for the covariances between the market indices themselves. And all the alphas and betas and residual variances are assumed not to vary across regimes. Here's a chart illustrating how much fewer parameters are needed, not counting what you'd need to handle options. The contrast was so great I had to put it in log terms."

Degrees of freedom in portfolio analysis of 100 assets

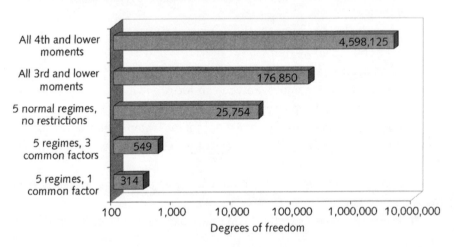

"Those really are huge savings. But doesn't that eliminate iceberg risk?"

"Hardly. What you're really worried about is a huge chunk of your portfolio crashing together. Barring some extraordinary concentration of assets, that won't happen unless one or more core indices crash too. So you may as well focus your iceberg watch on those core indices. Let their means vary a lot across regimes, and covariance matrices too, and most important try to get the regime odds right."

"What happens to all the other assets?"

"Well, the parts of the assets that track core indices get included with the core indices. As for the residuals, they get treated like independent normal variables. You try to maximize their Sharpe ratio using the standard rules, regardless of what happens in the rest of the portfolio. Convenient, isn't it?"

"Definitely. But I've seen convenience cause trouble before. Devlin, what do you think? Don't the errors that are bound to creep into the approximations bother you?"

"Yes, they do bother me. But multiplying the number of estimated parameters fifty-fold won't get rid of them. I'd rather do sensitivity analysis on a few key parameters, or better yet model the uncertainty about them directly."

"You mean like Black-Litterman does?"

"Not exactly. I don't dilute views with the market consensus because when there are multiple regimes it's hard to impute what the consensus is. Instead I model doubts as extra noise-making random variables. Sometimes you can calculate their impact exactly; sometimes you just approximate it."

"And are five regimes enough?"

"Maybe not enough. Maybe more than enough. It depends on your concentration risks."

"You mean clusters in one sector or market?"

"Partly. More generally I mean any common vulnerability. If Korean stocks that you own start moving in tandem with Nasdaq, you've got extra Nasdaq concentration risk regardless of the sector or market listing."

"Isn't that what the multiple regime specs are supposed to capture?"

"Supposed to, yes. But it's easy to miss the iceberg for the ice cubes. I'm beginning to doubt you should model more than a handful: say, BULL and BEAR or WALK, FLY, and DIVE."

"Then how would you capture the multiple vulnerabilities of Korean stocks to Korea-specific shocks, to dollar/yen, to Nasdaq, and to the global market as a whole?"

"Multiple common factors can handle that without necessarily requiring a separate regime for each blow-up risk. If your absolute portfolio beta with respect to Korean risk is less than 0.05, for example, I wouldn't generally bother to model it separately."

Conway shook his head with mock disapproval. "You've let me down, Devlin, old boy. I was expecting higher standards. Next thing I know you'll be advocating absolute concentration caps on everything, just like an old-fashioned risk manager."

"Concentration caps are primitive. And I don't like the word 'absolute'. But a lot of what the new theory advises looks like a combination of Sharpe ratio maximization and concentration caps."

"Which is kind of what happens in practice."

Devlin shrugged his shoulders. "Are you sure?"

Touché, Devlin. "No, I'm not sure. Maybe they're just trying not to fall too far below the benchmark, whatever that happens to be. I guess your theory doesn't cover that."

"Not exactly," said Regretta. "But there's a quick fix that I think will do the trick."

"Really? What is it?"

"Just remeasure returns relative to the benchmark rather than to the risk-free rate."

"Say, that is easy. But how does the new optimum compare to the old?"

"Think about it. You'll be looking for a portfolio that's optimal after you subtract off one unit of excess returns on the benchmark. So that means you just take the previously optimal portfolio and add to it one unit of the benchmark or its proxy funded with borrowed T-bills."

"Thanks, Regretta. But what if the portfolio managers don't agree?"

"Then maybe you should score the portfolio on its performance."

"Don't you want to take risk into account?"

"By performance I mean the utility of returns, not the returns themselves. In the long run this should average out to expected utility if forecasts are correct."

"I'm afraid utility won't be very intuitively appealing. Not everyone will accept the framework."

"Then convert average utility to a certainty equivalent. That's just the risk-adjusted return. Everybody in the business claims to understand that."

"I'm not sure they do."

"They will if you start factoring it into their rewards."

Conway nodded. "Fair point. But these utility measures apply to the portfolio as a whole. How am I supposed to score individual performance in a multi-manager fund?"

"There's no perfect way to do this. But on the whole I favor measuring marginal contributions. Something like the risk-adjusted return of the whole fund less what the risk-adjusted return would have been if the manager hadn't been there."

"If the manager hadn't been there, a lot of things might have changed. There could be more than one measure of what might have been."

"Which will mean more than one measure of managerial performance. So be it. But overall you want to encourage managers to add diversified alpha in normal times without aggravating iceberg risk in crises. That's what measures of marginal contributions try to do. Here's an example I charted for a bivariate normal world in which the rest of the portfolio has a Sharpe ratio of 0.5. If the correlations didn't matter the lines of equal marginal contribution would be horizontal. Instead, for the most part they're very steep."

Marginal contributions to risk-adjusted return (CE)

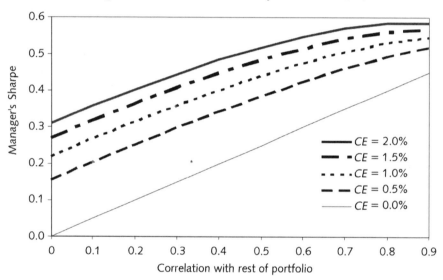

Baseline Sharpe = 0.5, CRR = 3.

"Yes, I understand," said Conway. "I was using Sharpe ratios to make the same point. How do your measures compare with that?"

"In a multivariate normal world the certainty equivalent will be proportional to the aggregate Sharpe ratio squared. But it will penalize more for iceberg risk than the Sharpe squared will."

"Great. This is all very clear, Regretta. Thanks."

Devlin suddenly spoke up. "Well it may all be very clear to you two but it's not to me."

"What's the matter?" asked Regretta. "I thought you agreed with performance scoring. We talked about this earlier."

"I did agree then. And in principle I still do. But while you were explaining things to Conway I got to thinking about reliability."

"Reliability of what?"

"Of the average utility scores. How much are they likely to deviate from the expected utility?"

Regretta reflected a moment. "I suppose it depends on how noisy the portfolio is – volatility and all that – and on how long you evaluate the portfolio."

"So why don't we try to estimate the reliability and factor that into the evaluation?"

"I don't get it," said Conway.

"I do," said Regretta. "The actual performance scores might be thought of as random observations on the true expected performance score. I've been arguing that in the long run the average will converge to the expected value."

"Which it should," said Conway. "Do you disagree with that, Devlin?"

"No I don't disagree. In the long run Regretta's method should work fine. But in the short run we need to be wary. You wouldn't fire a manager or carry out a major portfolio reshuffle solely on account of one bad trading day, would you?"

"Not unless the day were really extreme. Even then I'd be tempted to dismiss it as an outlier."

"Agreed. But the long run is only a chain of daily results. So each result carries some information value and I'd like to know how much."

"Ah, I see. That is a good question. But if you don't mind, let's defer it to another time. My brain is overloaded. It can't handle any more."

"How about I sign you up for a session at the spa?" asked Regretta. "It's one of Club Mad's many comforts."

"That sounds wonderful. You know, I'm starting to get envious of you two."

While Conway takes on some steam, let's probe some more into CAPM-type reductions and performance scoring. But not too deeply: Conway's isn't the only brain getting overloaded.

THE ATTRACTIONS OF SIMPLICITY

As noted before, models of N multivariate normal assets under K regimes can have $\frac{1}{2}K(N+1)(N+2) - 1$ degrees of freedom: KN for the means, $\frac{1}{2}KN(N+1)$ for the variances and covariances and $K-1$ for the regime probabilities. That's typically a lot simpler than trying to specify all third or fourth moments and cross-moments. Still, the sum mounts linearly with K and quadratically with N. Moreover, every option adds at least $3K$ degrees of freedom; indeed $\frac{1}{2}K(J+1)(J+2)$ if it depends on J securities. While computers easily handle the complexity, humans don't. That creates a strong incentive to simplify further.

CAPM-TYPE DECOMPOSITION

The Capital Asset Pricing Model (CAPM) assumes that every asset's risk can be divided into two types. "Market" risk is perfectly correlated with the aggregate market index. "Idiosyncratic" risk is independent of every other risk. In effect, CAPM decomposes each asset h into β_h units of the market index plus an independent residual having mean α_h and variance η_h. The only extras needed to characterize the mean m and variance v of a ω-weighted portfolio are the mean μ and variance σ^2 of the market index. Describing N assets this way requires only $3N+2$ parameters.

The simplest way to incorporate non-normal market risks into CAPM is to allow μ and σ^2 to vary by regime but not the α_h, β_h, or η_h. Defining A, B, and H as the vectors of α_h, β_h, and η_h respectively, we can readily calculate:

$$M_k = A + \mu_k B$$

$$\Sigma_k = \mathrm{diag}(H) + \sigma_k^2 BB'$$

for substitution into Refinements #1 or #2 of the optimization recipe. Alternatively, we can apply the CAPM decomposition to log returns, do the analogous calculations for $\tilde{M}_k$ and $\tilde{\Sigma}_k$ and then substitute into Refinement #3.

WHEN THE MARKET INDEX IS TRADABLE

The CAPM decomposition gets even easier to work with when the market index is freely tradable. Replace each asset h with a hedged bundle consisting of asset h less β_h units of the market index. Then add a new asset consisting of the market index alone. Redefining ω to encompass the weight w on the market index and the weights $\bar{\omega}$ on the various hedged bundles, we then have:

$$m_k = \omega'M = \bar{\omega}'A + w\mu_k = \sum_{h=1}^{N} \bar{\omega}_h \alpha_h + w\mu_k \equiv \bar{m} + w\mu_k$$

$$v_k = \omega'\Sigma\omega = \bar{\omega}'\text{diag}(M)\bar{\omega} + w^2\sigma_k^2 = \sum_{h=1}^{N} \bar{\omega}_h^2 \eta_h + w^2\sigma_k^2 \equiv \bar{v} + w^2\sigma_k^2$$

in Refinements #1 or #2. I have summarized the contributions of hedged asset bundles to the mean and variance as $\bar{m}$ and $\bar{v}$ respectively to emphasize their invariance to the regime or weight on the market index. They do, however, vary with $\bar{\omega}$. Given $\bar{v}$, the investor always prefers the highest possible $\bar{m}$ and should choose $\bar{\omega}$ accordingly. Carrying through that constrained maximization shows that $\bar{\omega}_h = \dfrac{\alpha_h}{\eta_h} w_0$ for some common factor w_0.

In other words, pick the relative weights on the various uncorrelated hedged bundles to maximize their aggregate Sharpe ratio, using the simple Sharpe-squared rules. Denoting the individual Sharpe ratios by $\bar{S}_h \equiv \alpha_h / \sqrt{\eta_k}$, we can rewrite the aggregate moments as:

$$m_k = \omega_0 S^2 + w\mu_k$$
$$v_k = \omega_0^2 S^2 + w^2\sigma_k^2$$

where $S^2 = \bar{S}'\bar{S} = \sum_{h=1}^{N} \bar{S}_h^2$ denotes the Sharpe ratio for the aggregate hedged bundle. Our optimization now depends on two free parameters only: ω_0 and w. This is the most spartan possible way to incorporate non-normal market risk given less-than-continuous rebalancing.

MULTI-INDEX DECOMPOSITION

Standard CAPM assumes that the only common portfolio risk is the market aggregate itself. Sometimes that's too crude. For example, a global fund that largely tracks the popular MSCI World benchmark might still bear a lot of aggregate Nasdaq risk, even after we strip out the risks that Nasdaq and MSCI World bear in common.

Decomposing assets into n core indices plus residuals requires

$n + 2$ parameters per asset or $N(n + 2)$ in total. In addition $\frac{1}{2}K(n + 1)(n + 2) - 1$ parameters are needed to describe the indices' first two moments and the probabilities of the various regimes. If n is much less than N this can slash information needs. When there are 5 possible regimes, decomposing 50 assets into 3 indices plus 50 idiosyncratic risks cuts the number of free parameters by over 95%, down to 299 from 6,629.

To squeeze out more free parameters you can assume that the conditional correlations are identical across regimes. In that case $2nK + \frac{1}{2}n(n - 1) + K - 1$ parameters will suffice to describe the indices' moments and the regime probabilities. If you go even further and constrain the conditional variances to be identical across regimes, only $nK + \frac{1}{2}n(n + 1) + K - 1$ parameters will be needed. However, I will not impose these restrictions here.

MATRIX FORMULATION

Suppose we obtain a linear decomposition, or "alpha/beta reduction", of N assets into n core indices plus N independent normal or quasi-normal residuals. Denoting the assets by Y, the core indices by X, and the residuals by E, we can write:

$$Y = BX + E$$

where $B \equiv [\beta_{hi}]$ is an $N \times n$ matrix of betas, with β_{hi} denoting the sensitivity of asset h with respect to core index i. Let us denote the vector mean of E by A and its diagonal $n \times n$ covariance matrix by $\text{diag}(H)$. The portfolio mean and variance in each regime work out to:

$$m_k = \omega'(A + BM_k)$$
$$v_k = \omega'B\Sigma_k B'\omega + \omega'\text{diag}(H)\omega$$

Hence Refinements #1 and #2 continue to apply provided that we replace M_k with $A + BM_k$ and Σ_k with $B\Sigma_k B' + \text{diag}(H)$.

If we apply the CAPM decomposition to log returns rather than percentage returns, essentially the same equations apply with tildes over the variables. That is, both Refinement #3 and Regretta's recipe with continual rebalancing would replace $\tilde{M}_k$ with $\tilde{A} + \tilde{B}\tilde{M}_k$ and $\tilde{\Sigma}_k$ with $\tilde{B}\tilde{\Sigma}_k \tilde{B}' + \text{diag}(\tilde{H})$.

MATRIX REFORMULATIONS

For more insight into the previous results, form an augmented X vector $X^+ \equiv \begin{bmatrix} X \\ E \end{bmatrix}$, which has mean $M^+ \equiv \begin{bmatrix} M \\ A \end{bmatrix}$ and covariance matrix $\Sigma^+ \equiv \begin{bmatrix} \Sigma & 0 \\ 0 & \text{diag}(H) \end{bmatrix}$. Also form an augmented beta matrix $B^+ \equiv [B\ I]$. Since $Y = B^+ X^+$, Y must be conditionally multivariate normal with conditional mean $B^+ M_k^+ = A + BM_k$ and conditional covariance matrix $B^+ \Sigma_k B^{+\prime} = B\Sigma_k B' + \text{diag}(H)$. The results for Refinements #1 and #2 follow immediately. For Refinement #3, apply the corresponding decomposition $\tilde{Y} = \tilde{B}^+ \tilde{X}^+$ where $\tilde{B}^+ \equiv [\tilde{B}\ I]$ and $\tilde{X}^+ \equiv \begin{bmatrix} \tilde{X} \\ \tilde{E} \end{bmatrix}$.

Alternatively, we can regard the investible assets in Refinements #1 or #2 as X^+ with portfolio weights $B^{+\prime}\omega$. However, this interpretation isn't valid for Refinement #3, since the log portfolio return is $\ln(1 + \omega' \exp(\tilde{B}^+ \tilde{X}^+))$ rather than $\omega' \tilde{B}^+ \tilde{X}^+$.

TRADABLE INDICES ENCORE

If all the core indices are freely tradable we can simplify some more, along the same lines as for a single core index. First, replace the assets Y with the hedged bundles $Y - BX$. Let $\bar{\omega}$ as before denote the portfolio weights on the hedged bundles and w the vector weights on the J indices. Since the hedged bundles replicate E, once again it's clear that:

$$m_k = \bar{\omega}'A + \omega'M_k \equiv \bar{m} + w'M_k$$

$$v_k = \bar{\omega}'\text{diag}(H)\bar{\omega} + w'\Sigma_k w \equiv \bar{v} + w'\Sigma_k w$$

The same logic applies as before. For any $\bar{v}$, the investor prefers the highest possible $\bar{\omega}$ and hence strives to maximize the Sharpe ratio $\bar{S}$ of the aggregate hedged bundle. We thereby obtain:

$$\bar{\omega} = \bar{\omega}_0 \big(\text{diag}(H)\big)^{-1} A$$

$$m_k = \bar{\omega}_0 \bar{S}^2 + w M_k = \bar{\omega}_0 A' \big(\text{diag}(H)\big)^{-1} A + w M_k$$

$$v_k = \bar{\omega}_0^2 \bar{S}^2 + w'\Sigma_k w = \bar{\omega}_0^2 A' \big(\text{diag}(H)\big)^{-1} A + w'\Sigma_k w$$

Again, the m_k and v_k need to be substituted into Refinements #1 or #2.

Results for Continual Rebalancing

Recall that with continual costless rebalancing,

$$\widetilde{CE} = \omega'\ln(\mathbf{1} + \mathrm{M}) - \tfrac{1}{2}c\omega'\tilde{\Sigma}\omega = \omega'\tilde{\mathrm{M}} + \tfrac{1}{2}\mathrm{tr}\Big(\big(\mathrm{diag}(\omega) - c\omega\omega'\big)\tilde{\Sigma}\Big)$$

To apply the alpha/beta reduction, replace $\tilde{\mathrm{M}}$ with $\tilde{\mathrm{A}} + \tilde{\mathrm{B}}\tilde{\mathrm{M}}$ and $\tilde{\Sigma}$ with $\tilde{\mathrm{B}}\tilde{\Sigma}\tilde{\mathrm{B}}' + \mathrm{diag}(\tilde{\mathrm{H}})$:

$$\widetilde{CE} = \omega'(\tilde{\mathrm{A}} + \tilde{\mathrm{B}}\tilde{\mathrm{M}}) + \tfrac{1}{2}\mathrm{tr}\Big(\big(\mathrm{diag}(\omega) - c\omega\omega'\big)\big(\tilde{\mathrm{B}}\tilde{\Sigma}\tilde{\mathrm{B}}' + \mathrm{diag}(\tilde{\mathrm{H}})\big)\Big)$$

$$= \omega'\big(\tilde{\mathrm{A}} + \tilde{\mathrm{B}}\tilde{\mathrm{M}} + \tfrac{1}{2}[\tilde{\mathrm{B}}_1'\tilde{\Sigma}\tilde{\mathrm{B}}_1 \cdots \tilde{\mathrm{B}}_N'\tilde{\Sigma}\tilde{\mathrm{B}}_N]' + \tfrac{1}{2}\mathrm{H}\big)$$

$$- \tfrac{1}{2}c\omega'\big(\tilde{\mathrm{B}}\tilde{\Sigma}\tilde{\mathrm{B}}' + \mathrm{diag}(\tilde{\mathrm{H}})\big)\omega$$

If all the indices $\tilde{X}$ are freely tradable, place weights w on them and weights $\bar{\omega}$ on the hedged bundles $\tilde{Y} - \tilde{\mathrm{B}}\tilde{X}$, obtaining:

$$\widetilde{CE} = \bar{\omega}'\big(\tilde{\mathrm{M}} + \tfrac{1}{2}[\tilde{\sigma}_{11} \cdots \tilde{\sigma}_{nn}]'\big) + \bar{\omega}'(\tilde{\mathrm{A}} + \tfrac{1}{2}\tilde{\mathrm{H}}) - \tfrac{1}{2}cw'\tilde{\Sigma}w - \tfrac{1}{2}c\bar{\omega}'\mathrm{diag}(\tilde{\mathrm{H}})\bar{\omega}$$

If the indices are also subject to Poisson shocks of $-L$ occurring at average rate ℓ, simply subtract the adjustment $\ell\dfrac{1 - (1 - w'L)^{1-c}}{1 - c}$ derived before:

$$\widetilde{CE} = w'\ln(\mathbf{1} + \mathrm{M}) - \tfrac{1}{2}cw'\tilde{\Sigma}w - \ell\frac{1 - (1 - w'L)^{1-c}}{1 - c}$$

$$+ \bar{\omega}'(\tilde{\mathrm{A}} + \tfrac{1}{2}\tilde{\mathrm{H}}) - \tfrac{1}{2}c\bar{\omega}'\mathrm{diag}(\tilde{\mathrm{H}})\bar{\omega}$$

Since w and $\bar{\omega}$ never appear in the same term, they can be solved separately. For $\bar{\omega}$,

$$\bar{\omega}^* = \frac{1}{c}\big(\mathrm{diag}(\tilde{\mathrm{H}})\big)^{-1}(\tilde{\mathrm{A}} + \tfrac{1}{2}\tilde{\mathrm{H}}) = \frac{1}{c}\big(\mathrm{diag}(\tilde{\mathrm{H}})\big)^{-1}\tilde{\mathrm{A}} + \frac{1}{2c}$$

with elements $\bar{\omega}_h^* = \dfrac{\tilde{\alpha}_h}{\tilde{\eta}_h c} + \dfrac{1}{2c}$. In this case, the absolute allocation to each hedged bundle $\tilde{Y}_h - \tilde{\mathrm{B}}\tilde{X}_h$ is determined by its mean and variance and the investor's overall risk aversion, regardless of risk and performance elsewhere. Conversely, w depends only on the means and covariances of the common risks X.

INCORPORATING OPTIONS

Alpha/beta reductions are very similar in spirit to the pi/delta/gamma reductions used for options. With options,

$$\omega'Y \cong \omega'\hat{\Pi}_k + \omega'\hat{\Delta}_k(X - M_k) + \tfrac{1}{2}(X - M_k)'(\omega'\hat{\Gamma}_k)(X - M_k)$$

so we can fold $Y = B^+X^+$ into the options framework by replacing X and M with X^+ and M^+ respectively and by setting $\hat{\Delta}_k = B^+$, $\hat{\Pi}_k = A + BM_k$ and $\hat{\Gamma}_k = 0$. All options tied directly to X can be incorporated "as is".

The only remaining problem is to express options tied to Y or to a mixture of Y and X as a second-order expansion in X^+. Letting Z denote a vector of options tied to Y,

$$\omega'Z \cong \omega'\Pi_k + \omega'\Delta_k(Y - B^+M_k^+) + \tfrac{1}{2}(Y - B^+M_k^+)'(\omega'\Gamma_k)(Y - B^+M_k^+)$$
$$\cong \omega'\Pi_k + \omega'\Delta_kB^+(X^+ - M_k^+)$$
$$+ \tfrac{1}{2}(X^+ - M_k^+)'B^{+'}(\omega'\Gamma_k)B^+(X^+ - M_k^+)$$

Hence, converting a second-order X-based expansion into an X^+-based expansion is straightforward. Just substitute Δ_kB^+ for Δ_k and $B^{+'}(\omega'\Gamma_K)B^+$ for $\omega'\Gamma_k$. A parallel conversion applies for log returns.

"CRASH" BETAS

To gain more flexibility, add a subscript k to A, B, and H everywhere they appear. This allows the decomposition estimates to vary by regime, distinguishing between "regular" betas and "crash" betas. While appealing, I do worry about possible overkill. Most of the effect you're trying to capture is embodied in the regime change itself, so this adds extra variables for what are likely to be small marginal benefits. Moreover, I fear that estimating multiple sets of coefficients will make each set so much less reliable that it saps more confidence than it builds. Financial analysts rarely have enough data they're sure is relevant to current conditions to feel comfortable even with one set of estimates.

PARAMETER UNCERTAINTY

As noted earlier, classic portfolio optimization models don't seem to care about possible measurement error. They just assume the numbers you feed it are right. Black-Litterman's great merit is that it allows you to say "this estimate may be garbage" and fall back on some implied market consensus. Unfortunately, it's hard to estimate a consensus market view when there are multiple possible regimes.

Instead, I suggest incorporating the uncertainty directly by padding the relevant covariance matrices. Chapter 14 already worked through one example. If you're confident that log returns are multivariate normal with covariance matrix $\tilde{\Sigma}$ but uncertain about the mean, and if your beliefs about the mean are multivariate normally distributed with mean $\tilde{M}$ and covariance matrix $\tilde{\Xi}$, you might as well say that log returns are multivariate normal with mean $\tilde{M}$ and covariance matrix $\tilde{\Sigma} + \tilde{\Xi}$.

Although they trim the number of free parameters, alpha/beta reductions don't reduce the associated uncertainty. Rather, they concentrate it into doubts about the estimates of A, B, and H, with effects that vary according to what is doubted and how.

Doubts as Random Variables

Doubts about a set of parameters Φ are most easily modeled as hidden random variables E_Φ that are multivariate normally distributed with mean $\mathbf{0}$ and covariance matrix Ξ_Φ. The E_Φ for different Φ are usually assumed to be independent of all Φ, which simplifies the calculations. However, this assumption is not always justified and should be examined for plausibility.

For example, whereas the alpha/beta reduction performs the decomposition $Y = BX + E$, we can imagine that the true relationship is $Y = (B + E_B)X + E + E_A = BX + (E + E_A + XE_B)$. It makes sense to assume that E_A and E_B are independent of B, X and E. It does not make sense to assume that for a given asset h, $\epsilon_{\alpha h}$ and the various $\epsilon_{\beta h}$ will be independent of each other, since it's difficult to unravel the individual influences of correlated components of X.

What about the relationship between the various $\epsilon_{\alpha h}$ and $\epsilon_{\beta h}$ across assets? Dependence between such doubts is most likely to stem from some hidden common factor that wasn't included in X. If you think this factor is important to the portfolio as a whole, incorporate some proxy for it into X. Otherwise forget it, to retain the convenience of a diagonal covariance matrix across residuals.

The proxy should be a tradable asset if possible. For example, suppose you are managing a huge options book that would be vulnerable to a general liquidity squeeze, such as occurred to Long-Term Capital. Using an index of credit spreads as a proxy for that squeeze might encourage you to short credit spreads as a hedge. If your proxy isn't tradable then it will just encourage diversification or downsizing of the options book. Of course, if you choose a bad proxy or greatly understate the risk, then portfolio analysis won't help you.

PADDING H

Suppose your only doubts concern A. In effect that replaces E with $E + E_A$, which is still independent of X. The only change you need to make in expected utility calculations is to replace the variance diag(H) with diag(H) $+ \Xi_A$. Furthermore, assuming X has captured all common factors, Ξ_A will be diagonal. Just bump each η_h up to $\eta_h + \xi_{\alpha hh}$.

When your doubts involve B too then the residual $E + E_A + X E_B$ is no longer independent of X. However, it is tempting to pretend that it is, because then we can just pad H some more without making any other changes. For example, suppose our doubts concern one particular beta in a one-factor decomposition. Given any particular x the associated variance is $x^2 \xi$. Hence the unconditional variance is $E[x^2 \xi] = (\mu^2 + \sigma^2)\xi$ and we might try to just add this to η_h.

More generally, doubts about each B_h will have an $n \times n$ covariance matrix Ξ_{Bh} as well as an n-vector Ξ_{ABh} of covariance between A and B. For each asset h we can calculate:

$$E_{X|k}\left[Var\left[\epsilon_{\alpha h} + E_{Bh}X|X\right]\right] = \xi_{\alpha hh} + 2\Xi_{ABh}M_k + E_{X|k}\left[X'\Xi_{Bh}X\right]$$

$$= \xi_{\alpha hh} + 2\Xi_{ABh}M_k + M'_k\Xi_{Bh}M_k + vec(\Xi_{Bh})'vec(\Sigma_k)$$

$$= \xi_{\alpha hh} + 2\sum_{i=1}^{n}\xi_{ABhi}\,\mu_{ik} + \sum_{j=1}^{n}\sum_{i=1}^{n}\xi_{Bhij}\left(\mu_{ik}\mu_{jk} + \sigma_{ijk}\right)$$

where vec($\cdot$) converts a rectangular matrix to a vector by stacking columns sequentially. Assuming again that X has captured all common factors, our approximation just adds this to η_h, ignoring all other terms.

Sharpe-Squared Rules Blunted

The previous variance adjustments vary by regime. That's not surprising: errors in betas are bound to matter more when $E[x_i x_j]$ is large. However, they blunt the application of Sharpe-squared rules to the residuals or the hedged bundles that proxy for them, because the residuals' Sharpe ratios will no longer be constant across regimes. With a single regime we can still apply the Sharpe-squared rules to the residuals, at least under this approximation.

Uncertainty with More Precision

A more precise treatment calculates expected utility for every estimate of A and B and then integrates over the perceived probability density of the estimates. This can get quite messy, so I will focus on the relatively neat case of continuous rebalancing with no Poisson jumps. If our supposedly hedged bundles actually have aggregate weights $\tilde{Z} \equiv \tilde{E}'_B \bar{\omega}$ on $\tilde{X}$, the expected utility calculations must replace w with $w + \tilde{Z}$:

$$\widetilde{CE} = (w + \tilde{Z})' \ln(\mathbf{1} + \mathrm{M}) - \tfrac{1}{2} c (w + \tilde{Z})' \tilde{\Sigma} (w + \tilde{Z})$$

$$+ \bar{\omega}'(\tilde{A} + \tfrac{1}{2}\tilde{H}) - \tfrac{1}{2} c \bar{\omega}' \mathrm{diag}(\tilde{H}) \bar{\omega}$$

which can be expressed in the form:

$$\widetilde{CE} = \tilde{A} + \tilde{B}'\tilde{Z} + \tfrac{1}{2}\tilde{Z}'\tilde{C}\tilde{Z}$$

provided:

$$\tilde{A} = \widetilde{CE}\big|_{\tilde{Z}=0}$$

$$\tilde{B} = \ln(\mathbf{1} + \mathrm{M}) - cw'\tilde{\Sigma}$$

$$\tilde{C} = -c\tilde{\Sigma}$$

Then convert $\widetilde{CE}$ to $\widetilde{EU}$ and integrate over the probability density of $\tilde{Z}$. $\tilde{Z}$ is multivariate normal with mean $\mathbf{0}$ and covariance matrix $\tilde{\Upsilon} \equiv E[\tilde{E}'_B \bar{\omega} \bar{\omega}' \tilde{E}_B]$. (Provided X covers all common factors, $\tilde{\Upsilon}$ has elements $\tilde{\upsilon}_{ij} \equiv \sum_{h=1}^{N} \bar{\omega}_h^2 \xi_{hij}$.) It follows that:

$$|EU| = E\left[\exp\left((1 - c)\widetilde{CE}\right)\right]$$
$$= EU|_{\tilde{Z}=0} \cdot |\mathrm{I} + (c - 1)\tilde{C}\tilde{\Upsilon}|^{-1/2}$$
$$\cdot \exp\left(\tfrac{1}{2}(1 - c)^2\tilde{B}'\left(\tilde{\Upsilon}^{-1} + (c - 1)\tilde{C}\right)^{-1}\tilde{B}\right)$$

An even more advanced treatment would incorporate uncertainty about covariances and option gammas. This is much more complicated, not least because errors in covariance estimates tend to follow chi-squared distributions rather than normal distributions. I will not pursue the analysis here.

AGGREGATE PERFORMANCE MEASURES

If your forecasts are correct, the utility of portfolio returns ought to average out to the expected utility. That makes average utility an obvious way to measure portfolio performance. However, the certainty equivalent will provide the same performance ranking and is far easier to grasp intuitively, for it measures risk-adjusted return.

The various measures we have developed offer differing interpretations of optimality. But all agree that, absent big iceberg risks, the certainty equivalent should be in the neighborhood of $\frac{1}{2c}$ times the square of the aggregate Sharpe ratio S. That's because the CE for a single regime resembles $\omega'M - \frac{1}{2}c\omega'\Sigma\omega$, which is maximized at $\omega = \frac{1}{c}\Sigma^{-1}M$ for a maximum value of $\frac{1}{2c}M\Sigma^{-1}M = \frac{S^2}{2c}$. The various deviations from this formula reflect the time until rebalancing and the differences between logs and percentages. It's tempting to say that the (log) Sharpe ratio squared is an even more fundamental measure than risk-adjusted return, since the Sharpe ratio doesn't depend on the risk aversion c. However, the Sharpe ratio can stumble over iceberg risks whereas the certainty equivalent does not.

MARGINAL PERFORMANCE MEASURES

The marginal contribution of an investment to a portfolio is the difference between the expected utilities with and without the investment. Both measures should assume the portfolio is optimized for the instruments available to it. If the investment you're focusing on is a small part of the whole, its presence or absence shouldn't significantly change the optimal structure of the rest of the portfolio, allowing us to estimate "would have been" by looking at actual performance without re-optimization. The calculations below assume that approximation is justified.

The two most important influences on an investment's marginal contribution are its Sharpe ratio S and its correlation ρ with the rest of the portfolio. To quantify this, let's ignore iceberg risks and compare Sharpe squared ratios. Denoting the Sharpe ratio of the rest of the portfolio by S_0, the marginal contribution will be:

$$\frac{S^2 + S_0^2 - 2\rho S S_0}{1 - \rho^2} - S_0^2 = \frac{S^2 - 2\rho S S_0 + \rho^2 S_0^2}{1 - \rho^2} = \frac{(S - \rho S_0)^2}{1 - \rho^2}$$

The contribution rises with the square of the gap between S and ρS_0.

MANAGERIAL CAVEAT

The preceding formula shows that a lower Sharpe might be more valuable than a higher one. However, that presumes we short an investment whose S is less than ρS_0. That may be difficult to do, especially if the marginal investment is a fund manager's favored portfolio. Once the manager realizes that he's prized for his bad calls he's likely to amend them; only what's better for him may be worse for the portfolio that's shorting him. The only stable equilibrium I've ever seen involves some Wall Street analysts with terrible track records but a great client following, and whose salespeople shield them from the connection.

If we can't short either the marginal manager or the rest of the portfolio, then we won't invest in both unless $\rho \leq \dfrac{S_0}{S} \leq \dfrac{1}{\max(\rho, 0)}$. The higher ρ is, the narrower the range will be. The secret to successfully managing a multi-manager fund is ensuring that each $S - \rho S_0$ is positive. This is known in the industry as seeking "diversified alpha".

PERFORMANCE ATTRIBUTION

Performance attribution subdivides performance measures of a whole into performance measures of the parts. Ideally the attribution should both measure the parts' marginal contributions and ensure that the individual contributions sum to the whole. When all components are normally distributed and independent and the portfolio is chosen optimally, multiples of the Sharpe ratio squared will do the trick. Otherwise it's highly unlikely for the marginal contributions to sum exactly to the whole.

Consider again a portfolio with two bivariate normal components, where the two components have Sharpe ratio S and S_0 respectively with nonzero correlation ρ between them. Again assume the portfolio is formed optimally. The marginal contributions of the two components to aggregate performance will be $\dfrac{(S - \rho S_0)^2}{1 - \rho^2}$ and $\dfrac{(S_0 - \rho S)^2}{1 - \rho^2}$ respectively. Their sum will be less than the aggregate $\dfrac{S^2 + S_0^2 - 2\rho S S_0}{1 - \rho^2}$ if $\max\left(\dfrac{S}{S_0}, \dfrac{S_0}{S}\right) < \dfrac{1 + \sqrt{1 - \rho^2}}{\rho}$ and greater than the aggregate if $\max\left(\dfrac{S}{S_0}, \dfrac{S_0}{S}\right) > \dfrac{1 + \sqrt{1 - \rho^2}}{\rho}$.

UNFAIRNESS AND MISMANAGEMENT

One way to deal with this problem is to give each manager credit for his marginal contribution divided by the sum of all marginal contributions. However, this could be unfair if two portfolio managers Tom and Dick are both running very successful but highly correlated portfolios. While these two portfolios may jointly drive fund performance as a whole, neither Tom nor Dick will derive much credit for them.

One possible alternative allows Tom and Dick to divvy up credit for the marginal contribution of their joint portfolio. But this isn't wholly satisfactory either. Why not consider subgroups of three or more managers as well? If you do this it will dilute Tom's and Dick's share.

On reflection, the underlying problem isn't the use of marginal attributions. Possibly the measurement period was too short and picked up what was only a temporary correlation. If the high correlation persists, however, then Tom and Dick are being used redundantly. Their portfolios should be consolidated, and if two heads don't prove better than one then perhaps one should be sent to create diversified alpha somewhere else.

BENCHMARKING

A benchmark is a standard used for judging performance. Usually it's some index of what everyone else does. That's not quite in the spirit of expected utility theory, which says your utility should depend on your own wealth and consumption and not on other people's. Reconciling the two concepts would require a deeper discussion of managerial incentives and their costs than this book can offer. However, there is one simple way to incorporate a benchmark without reworking the theory.

Instead of maximizing the expected utility of excess portfolio returns $\omega'Y$, maximize the expected utility of $\omega'Y - q$, where q denotes the excess returns on the benchmark. If ω^* is the optimal portfolio for the first problem, then the optimal portfolio with a benchmark must be "ω^* plus one unit of the benchmark". In other words, do all your optimizations as if there were no benchmark, and then at the end buy one unit of the benchmark (or its proxy) funded with Treasury bills. Similarly, to evaluate managers' performance you might measure the expected utility not of their excess returns but of their returns relative to the benchmark.

MEASUREMENT IMPRECISION

Over the span of a few months or years, average ex-post utility will often deviate substantially from what was expected. So if you focus too much on short-term performance, you will reward too much for luck. Not only can this drive good managers away, but also it risks turning portfolio strategy into a futile chase after yesterday's best investments.

A sounder approach concedes that all performance estimates are imprecise. That doesn't mean you ignore them. Rather, you update your information Bayesian-style, weighting each estimate by its precision. This warrants more attention but I'm afraid we're running out of attention capacity.

23 | The Rooster Principle

For weeks Conway had kept mum about his outings to Club Mad. He had been far from sure they'd be productive and didn't want to be judged by the company he kept. But now he had something to crow about. Devlin and Regretta had delivered a portfolio analysis scheme far beyond his expectations.

Surely Jim will appreciate this. But when Conway sketched the new approach, Jim was cautious. "It's intriguing. Very creative and possibly useful. But I'm afraid a lot of it is over my head."

"A lot of it is over my head too. Fortunately I had friends to help me with the math. We can program in the calculations so they're done for us."

"I don't feel comfortable using things I don't fully understand."

"You drive a car and use computers. Do you fully understand internal combustion engines and silicon chip semiconductors?"

"No, but I understand what I need to do to use them, because I watched a lot of other people use them first. Here you're asking me to be a pioneer. I don't think I'm up to it."

"Somebody has to start. Why not us?"

Jim leaned back in his chair and grinned. "One thing I've learned in finance is the importance of being second. The pioneer is the guy with the arrow in his back."

Conway laughed. "Well put. Only this is different. It's designed to reduce our risks, not raise them."

"Even if I believe you, others might not. Remember, we have to manage the appearances of risk, and not just risk itself."

"Yes, your brother explained that to me once. I haven't forgotten. I just want a chance to win people over. Some experiment, some forum, some ..." Conway's voice trailed off. "I don't know," he said quietly and lowered his eyes.

"Conway, let me give you some friendly advice," said Jim in a fatherly tone. "Never hold strong convictions in finance. They'll just be a burden to you."

"I never suffered them before. But this one's got hold of me."

"I can see that. OK, Conway, here's what I'll do for you. I'll invite all the portfolio managers to a meeting on 'Iceberg Risk and How to Deal with It'. I won't make them come and I won't make them stay. But I will give you a forum to make your case. Depending on the reception, we can discuss launching an experiment afterwards."

Conway's eyes brightened. "Thanks, Jim. I really appreciate the opportunity. You won't regret this."

"I hope you won't either. Is Friday afternoon too soon for you?"

"No, that will be great."

Conway spent the next few days preparing. The challenge wasn't to cram everything in but to strip everything inessential out. *I have to show them how simple it really is.* Somehow he managed. By Friday morning Conway was quite satisfied with the presentation and confident of success.

Jim opened the meeting with a brief introduction. "Thanks for coming, everybody. It suggests we're all interested in the same question. It also suggests we're still looking for answers. Conway here claims to have some. He shared them with me and I was impressed. Impressed both by the parts I understood and the parts I didn't." Jim smiled and drew a few chuckles. "So I asked him to run thru it again with a smarter audience – namely, you – while I check out whether I understand it better the second time. Now I want you all to lend him your ears, while Conway tries to repay with interest."

Conway walked over to the slide projector. "Thanks. I want to show you all a new way to analyze portfolio risk. It does everything the old way does and more. It's also the simplest possible way to extend the old way without violating theory or common sense. I'll try to be clear, but if I'm not feel free to interrupt with questions."

A hand shot up. "Is this going to involve a lot of math?"

"No. Just a smidgen. The new way is based on a theory that does involve a lot of math. It's more complicated than the standard theory and requires more computation to apply. But I say let's leave the computation to mindless computers, so we can focus on what you need your noggin for. In fact, a good part of what I want to say can be summarized in two pictures. Here's the first."

Normal risk

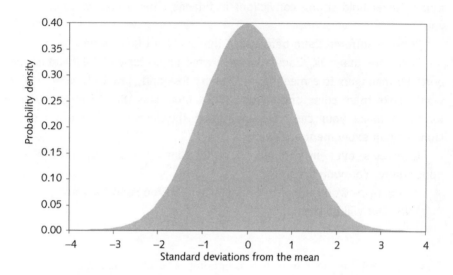

"This is a picture of normal, bell-shaped risk: 95% of the action occurs within 2 standard deviations of the mean; occasionally you go out to 3 standard deviations, and 4 or more standard deviations you can basically forget. Now I know you're all familiar with this. But I'm showing you all again to remind you of something very important: this is the *only* risk that the standard way looks at. Yes. The standard way assumes that every risk in every portfolio looks like this. The only differences are the values for the mean and standard deviation, which you calculate using standard formulas."

"Now, if you have to choose one risk to look at, this is the right one to choose. Why? There are two reasons. The first is that if you average out a lot of independent variables the risks always look normal, except maybe in the extreme tails. That was proved centuries ago in the Central Limit Theorem, the most famous theorem in statistics. The second reason is that a lot of correlated risks can be viewed as independent if you just change the way you measure them, so that you can apply the Central Limit Theorem to them too."

"However, often vast blocs of assets share a common driving factor. For example, most US stocks ultimately depend on the health of the US economy, so if the latter falters they'll falter too. Some will falter more, some less – economic growth may affect some stocks more than others, and in no stock is growth the only influence. Still, that group will share a common vulnerability."

"When asset returns have a common risk factor, they can't be viewed as independent no matter how you try to slice them or dice them. In that case, a portfolio's risks won't be normal unless the common risk is normal."

Another hand went up. "What if the common risk is approximately normal, or if it's small relative to other common risks?" asked a woman.

"Good question. Yes, in that case, the standard approach will be good enough. With regard to US economic growth, for example, I'm inclined to treat it as an approximately normal influence. But some driving factors aren't even approximately normal."

"Like what?"

"Like the influence of the market as a whole. If Nasdaq crashes, then most of the stocks will crash with it."

"Of course. If they didn't, Nasdaq wouldn't crash. Isn't that a circular argument?"

"Yes and no. I suppose it would be more precise to say that Nasdaq crashed because some combination of a common shock and contagion effects made a lot of stocks in Nasdaq fall together. So the true common factor is the shock and/or contagion, which I'm proxying by the Nasdaq index itself. Having said that, I don't see any harm in identifying a common factor with its index proxy. In fact, in some ways it's better, because we can mitigate a risk by shorting its proxy, even we can't trade the risk itself. Does that answer your question?"

"Yes." The woman nodded.

"Good. Now I don't think I need to convince anyone here that Nasdaq risk isn't normal. Not after what we've seen the last two years. Its spectacular rise and fall might be likened to the launch and sinking of the *Titanic*. Iceberg risk. Only it's a lot more prevalent in finance than in shipping. How can we amend standard risk analysis to incorporate iceberg risk?"

"That's a severe challenge. To begin with, what assumptions should we make about the probability distribution of iceberg risk? Does it mean lumpy tails or a general thickening? Is it skewed downward, and if so by how much? And how do we incorporate the likelihood that we're not even sure exactly what the distribution is? For iceberg risks nearly always come shrouded in uncertainty. In fact, the more I think about it, there's only one good way to summarize iceberg risk in a picture. Here it is."

Iceberg risk

Conway waited for the laughter to subside and then continued. "How do you make a useful model out of the notion that anything might happen? A friend of mine wrestled with this for months before he found the only tractable answer. Let the common factor or factors determine the general state of the world, also called the 'regime'. Within each regime assume everything is normal. But the parameters of different regimes and their probabilities of occurrence can vary as you wish. That's called 'conditional normality'. Graphically it amounts to an overlay of different bell curves."

"Any risks you're interested in can be modelled this way. But the important thing is that a handful of regimes typically suffice to capture your main concerns."

Henry spoke up. "Conway, why do you call this the only tractable answer? There's a host of distributions you could choose from. Some of them capture fat tails a lot easier than normal distributions do."

"Fat tails of individual assets, yes. But in portfolio analysis we're not nearly as concerned about fat tails of individual assets as we are fat tails of portfolios. There's not a necessary connection between the two. A portfolio of high-yield bonds, each with huge default risk, might look very normal in aggregate if you diversify enough and hedge out market risk. Conversely, assets with virtually no tails might all be vulnerable to the same common risk, causing a huge fat tail in the portfolio."

"So model the correlation too."

"Correlation alone can't capture the odds that a lot of things tank together. Not unless every asset and combination of assets is normal. With any other distribution you need to specify higher-order moments and cross-moments. The co-skewnesses and co-kurtoses of an average-size portfolio easily number in the millions. So you may as well model the conditional dependence directly, and conditional normality is the easiest way to do this."

"I need to think about that one," said Henry.

"When I first heard it I didn't believe it either. Now it seems obvious. Come by my office afterwards and I'll show you the evidence that turned me around. In the meantime, whether you think I could do this other ways or not, do you understand what I mean by conditional normality?"

"Sure," said Henry. "Each regime is fully normal, but the means, variances, and covariances are liable to change."

"Exactly. A regime is something like 'bull market' or 'bear market' or 'liquidity squeeze'. It's what most people regard as the big market picture. Actually, if you strip away the math, that's the natural way of thinking about big risk. Standard mean-variance analysis focuses more on little risks. Sometimes that's enough. Sometimes it misses the iceberg for the ice cubes."

"No approach can completely avoid icebergs," said Henry. "How do you weigh the risks against the forgone rewards?"

"Another good question. The truth is, conditional normality on its own won't get you anywhere. You need a scoring system: some way to compare normal risks, iceberg risks, and rewards so that you can judge which portfolio is best."

Another hand went up. "Do you mean something like Sharpe ratios?"

"Yes. But Sharpe ratios ignore iceberg risk, since they look only at mean and variance. And since Sharpe ratios are independent of leverage, they can't tell you how much leverage to apply. You need a more sophisticated measure."

"How can you decide something like leverage without knowing the investor's tolerance for risk?"

"You can't. At the same time, we don't want our scoring rules to demand too much information about investors' risk tolerance, because we rarely have much information at hand. For example, it would be nice if, all else being equal, the optimal percentage allocations of a portfolio don't depend on its absolute amount. Let's also assume our investors aren't suckers: that they will never knowingly take bets guaranteed to lose them money. Or at least that they don't want Megabucks to take sucker bets on their behalf. That doesn't sound too restrictive, does it?"

Conway waited for objections but none came, so he continued. "Great. We all seem to be on the same page. And guess what? Under the conditions I laid out, economists have proved that there's basically only one kind of scoring rule to use. It's the expected value of a power function of the investor's wealth, with a sign chosen to ensure that more is better than less. I've written it out for you in this slide."

Given a coefficient of relative risk aversion CRR $\geq$ 0,

$$\text{maximize expected utility } \textbf{\textit{EU}} \equiv \frac{E[\textbf{\textit{Wealth}}^{1-\textbf{CRR}}]}{1 - \textbf{CRR}}$$

"Actually you could add any constant, or multiply by any constant, and get the same implied behavior. And when the CRR equals one you should replace the power function with a logarithm. Apart from that it's unique. 'Expected utility' is just economists' name for a scoring rule that people appear to maximize even if most likely they're not consciously doing so. The $E[\cdot]$ is just the statistical symbol for expectation given the relevant probability distribution on wealth. As for the CRR, underneath its long-winded title it's just an ordinary number: zero if you don't mind risk, positive if you do."

"There are two tricky parts to applying this formula. The first is deciding the definition of wealth. Any economist worth his salt will tell you that wealth includes not just liquid assets but also real estate and human capital; that is, the discounted future stream of earnings from employment. For most people human capital is the biggest part. But we finance types love to simplify so let's just restrict wealth to portfolio wealth. In fact, to keep things tidy we'll often just restrict this to the portfolio wealth we happen to manage."

"The second tricky part is to set a CRR appropriate to the definition of wealth. If you assume that most investors more or less correctly apply this approach, then some calculations I won't try to defend here suggest using a CRR in the range of two to four for the stock market as a whole. Alternatively, you can directly ask investors some loaded questions about their willingness to take big bets. If a bet offers even odds of doubling your total portfolio or halving it and you won't take the bet, then your CRR is at least 1. If you would be willing to risk half of your portfolio for a 94% chance of huge gain, your CRR is less than 5."

"It's an interesting parlor game to ask the same person different loaded questions and check how consistent her answers are. More to the point, it would be useful to ask these questions of each other, with the reference being not our personal wealth but how we think our clients would like us to manage their funds. Let's see whether we share roughly the same opinions and check whether our clients agree."

Several people stirred in their seats and a few hands were raised. "That might be premature," said Jim. "I don't want to confuse our clients or get them thinking we've lost our way." Others murmured their approval and the hands went back down.

Uh-oh, they're awfully touchy. "Yes, perhaps we should just keep it among ourselves. Besides, nothing keeps us from experimenting with different CRR values and seeing what difference it makes. So with your permission I'd like to proceed to the next step, namely how to score conditionally normal portfolios. Are you all still with me?"

"Wait a second," said Henry. "Normal returns are unbounded. But your expected utility is defined only for positive wealth. So you can't legitimately mix the two."

Conway wagged his finger at Henry as if to scold him. "Shame on you, Henry. If it weren't for you I would have made a clean getaway. But you're right. To reconcile the two concepts you have to either shift from normality to lognormality or ignore the negative terms. It makes the math a lot hairier and forces you to accept some approximations. Which approximation to choose partly depends on how frequently you rebalance your portfolio to restore target weights."

"Am I the only one who finds this confusing?" asked Jim. Other voices replied. "No." "Me too." "This is over my head."

I'm losing them. "You're right, Jim, and the rest of you too. It is confusing. That's why I want to leave the details to computers. What I want to present here is just the broad structure, with a formulation that captures the essence and ignores the rest. I think you'll find it illuminating."

"Well, I'd like to see it," said Jim. "But there's no point to keeping people who feel they've had their fill. If any of you want to leave, go ahead."

Nearly half the people left. Conway pretended he didn't mind. "I'm not surprised we've thinned out. Let's face it: expected utility isn't the usual way of thinking about returns. It does have the attraction though that the expected utility of the whole averages out the expected utility of its parts. That is,

If each regime k has probability p_k and conditional expected utility EU_k,

$$EU_k = \sum_k p_k EU_k$$

"Next let's convert expected utility into something a bit more natural, namely the guaranteed return that would yield the same satisfaction. Economists call that the 'certainty equivalent'. In other words:

Define the certainty equivalent **CE** such that $|EU_k| \equiv (1 + CE_k)^{1-CRR}$

"The brackets around the *EU* denote absolute value. I imposed them so as not to worry about the sign. I also divided thru by baseline wealth to convert everything to percentage returns. The reason I did this is that there turns out to be a very simple and intuitive way to estimate *CE*:

$$CE_k \cong \text{ConditionalMean}_k - \frac{CRR}{2} \times \text{ConditionalVariance}_k$$

"In other words, the risk-adjusted return in each regime approximately equals the mean in that regime less a multiple $\frac{1}{2}CRR$ of the variance in that regime. Note that the penalty on variance rises directly with your risk aversion, which makes sense."

Conway paused for feedback. "Is that it?" asked Henry.

"Basically. You need some small adjustments to compensate for the differences between logs and percentages and expected slippage in portfolio weights. Actually it's better to convert everything to logs. Among other things that lets you reinterpret portfolio optimization as a kind of entropy minimization. It makes finance look more like physics. But I'm trying to keep things simple here."

"Where's the formula for the optimal portfolio mix?" asked Henry.

"There is no explicit formula except for the special case of one regime. Then it reduces to standard Sharpe ratio maximization plus a rule that makes the absolute weights on risky assets inverse to the CRR. The optimal portfolio for the general case also represents a kind of Sharpe ratio maximization, provided you replace the regime probabilities with risk-adjusted probabilities."

"What kind of adjustments are you talking about?"

"The adjustments give more weight to the regimes with lower expected utilities and make you more sensitive to iceberg risk."

"How much more sensitive?"

"That depends on your CRR and the specific risk/reward tradeoffs. You wouldn't want it any other way."

"Can your approach handle options?"

"Yes, it can. You just need to feed it estimated option values, deltas, and gammas at the means of different regimes. In contrast, standard mean/variance analysis has to pretend that the option delta is fixed, ignoring all the nonlinearities that distinguish options from ordinary securities."

"Gee, I don't know about this," said Jim. "You said you tried to economize on information. But it looks like overload to me."

"It doesn't have to be. You can reduce each asset CAPM-style to a random deviation around a beta-weighted sum of some core factors plus a constant. Assuming these random deviations are independent, you can focus on the correlations and iceberg risks you think are most important, with minimal information needs and distraction."

"I still doubt most of our managers and analysts would take the information requests seriously. We're practitioners, not a bunch of theorists."

"Then maybe we should keep track of how much everyone contributes to risk-adjusted returns and use that as part of their evaluation. Practical folks tend to understand a performance objective pretty well when it's tied to money."

"What do you mean by that, Conway?" Jim's voice took on a harder edge.

Did I say something wrong? "Nothing, really. I'm just pointing out that by scoring the utility of performance and converting it to risk-adjusted returns, you can measure not only the performance of the whole but also the marginal contributions of its parts."

"Oh really?"

"Yes. For example, you might measure a manager's marginal contribution as the difference between the risk-adjusted return of the whole portfolio and what it would have been without the manager – say, replacing the manager's actual subportfolio with some benchmark index. In principle, we could measure everyone's performance objectively, without regard to rank or seniority."

"I thought this meeting was supposed to be about iceberg risk," said a grey-haired man. "What's that have to do with performance measurement?"

"I would think they ought to have a lot to do with each other," said Conway. "For example ..."

The grey-haired man cut Conway off. "Jim, we seem to be getting highly speculative here. Why bother fixing what isn't broken? Granted, we did go down with Nasdaq over the past 15 months, but so did a lot of other people; we didn't lose that much more than the market average. I resent the insinuation that something is wrong with our incentives."

"Likewise," said someone else. "If you ask me, the very notion of introducing a new system to analyze iceberg risk involves a lot of iceberg risk. Who knows what new problems could arise?"

"Here, here," said another.

Before Conway could defend himself, Henry asked a question. "Conway, have you done any calculations of the errors likely to arise from using ex-post performance as a proxy for expected utility?"

"Well, no," replied Conway, awkwardly, "but I never meant to suggest that one should reward solely on that basis. It would need much more work to ..."

Jim cut in, "Yes, I think we can all agree on that. It's always nice to end a discussion with consensus. Conway, on behalf of everyone here, and I'm sure everyone who left as well, I'd like to thank you for your very stimulating presentation. It's good every few years or so to get this kind of abstract theoretical perspective."

Others nodded in assent and then left quickly, whispering to each other. Conway and Jim were left alone. Conway buried his face in his hands.

"Disappointed?" asked Jim.

"Shattered." Conway looked up. "What went wrong?"

"You violated the most important principle in practical finance: the Rooster Principle."

"What's that?"

"The Rooster makes all the rules."

"Who's the Rooster?"

"You mean you don't know? That's another violation."

"So it's you."

"Me, some of the senior managers, or any finance hotshot. The folks at the top of the heap. We make the rules. Not some math theory."

"Don't you believe in merit?"

"Sure I believe in merit. But there are many kinds of merit. There's merit in managing big egos and getting them to work well with each other. There's merit in attracting new clients. There's even more merit in convincing the clients you already have that your skill accounted for most of their gains and bad luck for most of their losses."

"What's meritworthy about that?"

"It soothes them. Skill and luck are woven together so tightly in finance. Why should clients torture themselves trying to unravel them? Instead I help them feel better both about their investments and themselves." Jim spoke without a trace of sarcasm.

Conway was puzzled. "I don't get it, Jim. If that's how you feel, why bother hearing out my presentation? Why even hire me?"

"Because the Rooster Principle has a qualifier: one day a rooster, the next day a feather duster."

Conway laughed. "Perhaps this principle is deeper than I thought. So I take it you do want to monitor iceberg risk after all."

"It's not a priority right now. We're still reeling from the Nasdaq iceberg we hit. Still, I learned two very important things from your presentation."

"Namely?"

"First, that looking in more sophisticated ways at financial risk can potentially add a lot of value. Second, that this will never be this group's forte."

"You must find that very discouraging."

"Far from it. One of our holdings is a giant financial risk trader. It hires hundreds of PhDs to churn out analytic models of risks and identify arbitrage opportunities. On that basis it makes huge proprietary bets. I never took a big position before because I didn't really understand what they're doing, and you know how I feel about investing in things I don't understand. But your presentation today changed my mind. That combined with the fact that the stock is trading well under half of last year's highs."

"Are you speaking about End Run?"

"Indeed. I'm going to make it our biggest single position: 10% of our total portfolio. I realize that's over our stated limits. But I figured out some creative accounting that will allow it for a while. Long enough to make up some lost ground."

Conway gulped. "There are some rumors going around that End Run can't provide the liquidity to clients it used to, which undercuts many of its proprietary bets, which in turn further constricts the liquidity it can provide."

"I know that. That's partly why the stock has dropped so much. But you've made me confident that smart guys will work things out."

"Long-Term Capital had at least as smart guys and blew up anyway."

"But End Run has Long-Term Capital's experience to draw on. In fact I wouldn't be surprised if they're developing iceberg risk models just like yours. Or better. No offense, Conway, but a hundred heads have got to be better than one."

"Actually it's been three heads. And two of them are quite unusual."

"Conway, stop. One or three, what's the difference compared with hundreds? Don't be jealous; I'll give you full credit for having inspired this idea. Besides, End Run can't possibly lose us more than 10%."

"Well, actually, if you keep rebalancing you can lose far more than 10%."

"You're obviously much too wound up, Conway; 10% is 10%. The weekend's coming; why don't you take off Monday as well to relax? Now, if you'll excuse me . . ."

Conway was left alone.

Later that evening Devlin and Regretta were sitting in the Club Mad lounge. "What are you thinking about, Regretta?" asked Devlin.

"I was just wondering how Conway fared in his presentation today."

"I'm sure it went well. He's got great communication skills. Not like me."

"Don't sell yourself short, Devlin. Without you Conway wouldn't have had anything to communicate."

"Without you neither of us would have had anything to communicate. Thanks for teaching us about utility functions."

"You're welcome. But the key step was how you combined CRR utility with conditional normality. That was ingenious."

"That was primitive. And my higher-order follow-ups were so convoluted. I should have gone right away to continuous rebalancing the way you did. Now that was ingenious. Elegant too."

"And nearly trivial compared with your derivations on options."

Devin blushed. "I have to admit; I kind of surprised myself on that one. But you know the part I liked best? Working with you on the alpha/beta reductions and the scoring rules."

Regretta smiled. "I liked that part best too. And Conway sure seemed to appreciate it."

"Well, I owed him one. The last time I fed him ideas for a presentation, they got him in such hot water he lost his job. I felt terrible about that. That's why I checked into Club Mad. Well, that and general dismay over my ignorance. Whoever said 'ignorance is bliss' didn't know what he was talking about."

"I'm happy for you Devlin. Happy and envious."

"What are you talking about, Regretta?"

"Don't you see? You're cured. You've made amends to Conway and you've overcome your ignorance. There's no longer any reason for you to stay."

"And how about you?"

Regretta sighed and her eyes grew misty. "I can't undo the things that put me here."

"What things? You've never told me. And I've never heard you talk about them in therapy."

"Some things are too personal to talk about in therapy."

"You can talk about them to me," said Devlin, gently.

"Maybe another time. Will you come and visit me sometimes?"

"Who said I was leaving?"

"You're cured. We agreed on that."

"I didn't agree. I just haven't gotten around to explaining why not."

"So why don't you agree?"

"Because I'm still ignorant. All we've done so far is model the iceberg risk that's above the surface. What about the 90% that lies beneath?

"Above the surface? Below the surface? Devlin, what are you talking about?"

"Sorry, I told you I don't communicate very well. What I mean is that the models we've been looking at are superficial. The returns in the various regimes don't depend on our beliefs. On reflection that doesn't make sense. What really happens and what you believe will happen ought to depend on each other."

"I don't get it. A bull market has one distribution of returns. A bear market has another distribution of returns, generally with lower mean and higher volatility. What do your beliefs have to do with it?"

"Plenty. Let's do a thought experiment. Suppose we're currently in a bull market, which we believe will last forever. Suddenly a mysterious but very authoritative stranger informs all us investors that a bear market is likely to start next week. What happens to asset prices today?"

"They spike down because we have to take into account the likely reduction in future returns. Oh, I see now. The odds of various regimes affect the future expected payoffs, which should be discounted into current prices."

"Good. Now for a second thought experiment. Are we in a bull or bear market right now?"

"That's a tough one. I mean, we've been in a bear market for some time but it looks to me like it's drawing to a close. Stocks had a runup a few weeks ago but it kind of faltered. Maybe it will resume soon. Yes, maybe that runup was the beginning of a bull market. Well, then again we've seen so many false bottoms recently, and recent unemployment figures were very discouraging. So perhaps we're still in a bear market after all."

"In other words, you'd feel more comfortable saying that with $X\%$ probability we're in a bull market and with $100 - X\%$ probability we're in a bear market."

"Definitely. Actually, if you will allow the possibility of a sideways market I'll lay odds on that too."

Devlin smiled and wagged his finger. "That's cheating. Stick with the thought experiment. Now suppose new economic statistics are released that surprise on the upside. As a result, you and every other investor decide that the chances we're currently in a bull market are really $X + 1\%$. What should that do to asset prices?"

"Raise them slightly, of course."

"In other words, current prices ought to depend on your beliefs about both the nature of the current regime and the likelihood of various future ones. Yet the regime-switching models we built for Conway don't appear to take that into account."

"Oh my. How do you propose to fix them?"

"I don't know," said Devlin, sadly. "I really don't know."

Regretta looked into his eyes. *Poor Devlin.* "It must be lonely to see things you can't get others to notice." She reached out and put her hand on his.

Devlin smiled back gratefully. "You noticed. Conway noticed."

"There will be others, Devlin. Just be patient. It always takes a while for a new approach to win converts. In the meantime, don't lose sight of what you've already accomplished."

"You mean of finding holes in portfolio theory without filling them?"

"You didn't find just any hole, Devlin. You found an abyss. And then you figured out how to navigate it." Regretta saw Devlin start to object. "OK, not perfectly. But what you've come up with is so much better than the status quo."

Devlin laughed wryly. "Not if you care less about the real risks than in trussing up their appearances. Which seems to be how most people in finance think."

"Appearances will always matter in finance. You know that. But real risks matter too. And more people will come around when they appreciate the difference."

Devlin gazed at Regretta and sat very still. Finally he reached out and touched her arm. Leaning over, he kissed her on the cheek. "Thanks," he said softly.

"I think we're attracting attention," whispered Regretta, looking around. "Perhaps we should continue this conversation elsewhere."

"I'd like that. I'd like that very much. But I would hate for it to cause regrets later."

Regretta smiled at Devlin. "There will be no regrets."

They drifted slowly down the corridor, hand in hand. It was a wonderfully clear evening, and they stopped below a skylight to watch the stars. Then a familiar voice broke the spell. Startled, they turned around.

"Hi, Devlin. Hi, Regretta," said Conway. "It's great to see you again. I'm really looking forward to continuing our discussions."

Devlin instantly let go of Regretta's hand. "Hi, Conway," he said, a bit embarrassed. "I didn't realize they allowed visitors on Friday nights."

"Who said I was visiting?"

(to be continued).

Further Reading

While there's a lot more to Devlin, Conway, and Regretta's story, you won't find it here. Instead I want to tell you about some books and articles that fill in missing pieces or provide a different perspective. I focus on a few I found especially interesting without trying to present a comprehensive list. Still, between the books mentioned and the sources they cite you can find plenty of food for thought. To facilitate your search I have organized the recommendations by topic.

THE MAGIC OF RISK

Primitive peoples, much like personal injury lawyers today, tended to reject the notion of blind chance. That's hardly surprising. It's always tempting to divine an underlying intent, and hard to prove the diviner is wrong. But even scientists find it hard to grapple with risk. How do you pin down the concept of something that can't be pinned down?

Eventually people boxed risk into neat theories, which are widely taught today. Unfortunately, seeing risk only inside boxes is like seeing lions only inside cages. To restore your sense of magic and wonder, I heartily recommend Peter Bernstein's bestseller *Against the Gods: The Remarkable Story of Risk* (New York: John Wiley & Sons, 1998). It conveys excitement about both the centuries of struggles for understanding and the frontiers still left to explore.

One of those frontiers is our own mind. Coping daily with risks for millions of years, our ancestors bequeathed each of us some deep intuition for risks. In the jungles of Africa this intuition helped save our ancestors' skins. Unfortunately in the jungles of Wall Street it often leaves us ripe for skinning. Few people understand those weaknesses better than Nassim Taleb, a successful Wall Street trader with a PhD in statistics. His *Fooled by Randomness* (New York: TEXERE, 2001) is full of entertaining and insightful tales.

PROBABILITY THEORY

If your math is so rusty you can't recall what you forgot, I recommend the Schaum's Outline Series (e.g., *Probability and Statistics*, 2nd edition (New York: McGraw-Hill, 2000) by Murray Spiegel, John Schiller and Alu Srinivasan) for quick refreshers. I especially like the Schaum approach of presenting each new idea in a separate capsule and have tried to emulate it.

Before I could shave I had the good fortune of studying math at Princeton, home of the eminent probability theorist William Feller. Decades later, having squandered my childhood gifts, I dusted off my old copy of his *An Introduction to Probability Theory and Its Applications*, Volume I, 3rd edition (New York: John Wiley & Sons, 1968) and tried to resuscitate old neurons. A few months later, I added Volume II, 2nd edition (1971). If you have the time I highly recommend both. They're not the crispest ticket but they can help teach you how to think . . . or re-teach you.

Granted, if you stop at Feller you'll miss a lot of nifty tricks. For a concise compendium of these tricks and the underlying derivations see Kenneth Lange's *Numerical Analysis for Statisticians* (New York: Springer, 1998).

One topic hardly covered in the above is mixed multivariate normality. If that's what you're thirsting for, drink to your heart's content from *Finite Mixture Models* (New York: John Wiley & Sons, 2000) by Geoffrey McLachlan and David Peel.

FINANCE THEORY

To brush up on basic finance theory I recommend a good business school textbook like *Principles of Corporate Finance*, 6th edition (New York: McGraw-Hill, 2000) by Richard Brealey and Stewart Myers. It provides perspective that deeper treatments often lack.

Jonathan Ingersoll's *Theory of Financial Decision Making* (Savage, MD: Rowman & Littlefield, 1987) provides a more rigorous treatment. It's crisp and well organized, though dry as dust. I use it a lot as a reference.

When you're ready to tackle derivatives pricing, pick up one of Paul Wilmott's books. The latest and greatest is the two-volume *Paul Wilmott on Quantitative Finance* (Chichester, UK: John Wiley & Sons, 2000). It's hard to imagine a clearer treatment and it's good for a few laughs. Also, check out www.wilmott.com, currently the most bubbling site in quantitative finance.

A lot of cutting-edge finance tends to develop everything through martingales (the concept of a fair game made rigorous). I haven't bothered with them here, for the same reason I don't drag out cannons to swat flies. But if you want to master advanced weaponry, Marek Musiela and Market Rutkowski's *Martingale Methods in Financial Modelling* (Berlin: Springer-Verlag, 1998) provides good training. For even better training, gear up first with David Williams' *Probability with Martingales* (Cambridge, UK: Cambridge University Press, 1991).

RISK MANAGEMENT

This book gives short shrift to standard value-at-risk methodology. For a much fuller treatment that is very readable and offers some constructive patches, read Kevin Dowd's *Beyond Value at Risk: The New Science of Risk Management* (Chichester, UK: John Wiley & Sons, 1998).

Portfolio managers wanting detailed practical advice should buy *Active Portfolio Management* (New York: McGraw-Hill, 1999) by Richard Grinold and Ronald Kahn. While it doesn't formally incorporate iceberg risk, it covers a host of things I don't.

Fischer Black and Robert Litterman wrote up their portfolio model in "Asset Allocation: Combining Investor Views with Market Equilibrium", a paper distributed in 1990 by Goldman Sachs. See also the 1999 Goldman Sachs paper "The Intuition Behind Black–Litterman Model Portfolios" by Litterman and Guangliang He.

If all this leaves you hungry for more advanced statistics, check out *Theory of Financial Risks: From Statistical Physics to Risk Management* (Cambridge, UK: Cambridge University Press, 2000) by Jean-Philippe Bouchaud and Marc Potters. By focusing on the characteristic functions of probability distributions it addresses far more advanced topics than I do, like the risks from hedging options in discrete time. On the negative side, its treatment of regime change is very weak. I hope that future developments will integrate their approach with mine.

PHYSICS

You don't need to know any physics to understand finance theory, but it helps. I especially like books that explain how physics came to embrace uncertainty, because they promote hope that someday finance theory will do the same. The Transnational College of LEX provides a delightful mix of history and math in *What is Quantum Mechanics? A Physics Adventure* (Boston: Language Research Foundation, 1996), translated from the original Japanese edition of 1991.

Erwin Schrödinger delivered some brilliant lectures in Dublin in 1944 on partition functions and related topics. I found them in a 1989 Dover reprint of

Statistical Thermodynamics (Cambridge, UK: Cambridge University Press, 1952). But for maximal inspiration read books by or about Richard Feynman; e.g., his three-volume *Lectures on Physics* co-authored with Robert Leighton and Matthew Sands (Reading, MA: Addison-Wesley, 1963–1965) or *Genius* by James Gleick (New York: Random House, 1992). While Feynman couldn't have been Devlin's father, you'll see why I pretended he was.

THE ART OF SEEING

Sometimes a conformist reality envelops us so tightly that we only see it clearly in our dreams. But to find master dream-weavers we must turn from science to art. Want to see Stalin visit Stalinist Moscow and fit right in? Read *The Master and Margerita* by Mikhail Bulgakov. Want to see Latin American history endlessly repeat itself in the lives of a single family? Read *One Hundred Years of Solitude* by Gabriel Garcia Marquez. Want to see the tyranny of well-meaning technocrats? Read *Brave New World* by Aldous Huxley. I've drawn inspiration from all these sources and smuggled a few allusions into this book.

Index

ABOUT TEXERE

TEXERE seeks to become the most progressive and authoritative voice in business publishing by cultivating and enhancing ideas that will illuminate the global business landscape. Our name defines the spirit of our vision: TEXERE is the ancient Latin verb "to weave." In an increasingly global business community, we seek to create an intersection where authors and readers can share the best thinking and the latest ideas. We want to leverage the expertise and insights of leading thinkers by weaving them with TEXERE's capability to deliver them to the marketplace.

To learn more and become a part of our community visit us at:

www.etexere.com

and

www.etexere.co.uk

ABOUT THE TYPEFACE

This book was set in 10/14 Syntax and 11.5/14 Times New Roman. Syntax, a sans serif font, was created by Swiss designer Hans Eduard Meyer in 1968 for the Stempel foundry. Times New Roman was created by British designer Victor Lardent in 1932 as part of a commission from *The Times* in London to create an original typeface for the newspaper.